BELLVILLE, GEORGIA
The First Hundred Years

The Bellville Train Depot as it once looked. (Drawing by Anthony Brown, 1995)

Bellville, Georgia

THE FIRST HUNDRED YEARS

Compiled and Edited by
Colonel Pharris DeLoach Johnson

1997

Southeastern Printech, Inc.
Glennville, Georgia

Copyright © 1997 by Colonel Pharris D. Johnson

All Rights Reserved, no part of this book may be reproduced without permission of the Editor

ISBN: 0-9658544-4-2

Third Printing, 2006.

Library of Congress Cataloging-in-Publication Data

Johnson, Pharris D. 1950-
    Bellville, Georgia: the first hundred years / compiled and edited by Pharris DeLoach Johnson
       p. cm.
    Includes bibliographical references and index.
    ISBN 0-9658544-0-X
1. Bellville, Ga. - History. 2. Bellville, Ga. - Biography. 3. Bellville, Ga. - Genealogy
F294.B45.J65   1996   95-71823
                                                CIP

To my mother

Glenda DeLoach James

The light of my life

Table of Contents

Preface, vii

Acknowledgments, ix

The Story of Bellville, 1

Vintage Photographs of Bellville, 67

Appendix A - Sketches of Early Bellville Families, 83

Appendix B - Interviews, 101

    Herschel Hearn, 102

    Amiel Fountain, 110

    Judge Harry DeLoach, 118

    Delma and Mary Daniel, 125

    Winton Bell, 132

    Jimmie Styles, 144

    Darin McCoy, 148

    David Groover, 153

    Bernie and Hilda Anderson, 161

    Wallace Parker, 166

Appendix C - History of Bellville Methodist Church, 171

Appendix D - History of old Bellville School, 187

Appendix E - History of Pinewood Academy, 211

Appendix F - Bellville Businesses, 221

Appendix G - Historic Houses of Bellville, 239

Appendix H - Tax Lists and Miscellaneous Records, 281

Index, 293

Maps

All maps by Colonel Ed Schwabe, Jr., *Maps for Authors*.

Georgia - 1784 (facing page 4)

Original Land Grants - Bellville Area (facing page 12)

Bellville Town Plat - 1890 (facing page 18)

Bellville Area - 1909 (facing page 24)

Evans County - 1914 (facing page 30)

Illustrations

Numerous residents of Bellville contributed photographs for this book. Their names appear in the photo credits listed in the captions. Any photos that do not have a credit line were taken by the editor during 1995-1996 for this book or were a part of his personal collection.

Preface

This is the story of Bellville, Georgia. Founders established the town, located on the western edge of Evans County, with the coming of the railroad in 1890. Long after the decline of the railroad, Bellville continues to enjoy a zest for life shared by few communities. Its successful endeavors in farming, lumbering, and the naval stores industry link the town's existence and history closely to the land. Although this account focuses on the town in general, it includes the story of what is more commonly described as the Bellville section.

My love affair with Bellville started many years ago, and some of my earliest and fondest memories are comprised of this place and its people. As a child I frequently visited my father's farm, located on the edge of the town's southeastern corner, and learned to appreciate the land and the sacrifices of those responsible for our family's life force. As with other families in the area, my ancestors cleared our farmland, plowed it, timbered it, and hunted on it for a very long time. It is the land of my father's mother and her father's father. From the whistle of the Bob White quail to the beauty of the farm's wild Cherokee roses, I believe there is no place quite like it on earth.

If you say the word out loud, *Bellville* rolls off the tongue with a certain comfortable ring. This town name is not unique to Georgia, for there are Bellvilles in 22 other states.[1] However, despite the popularity of its name, Bellville, Georgia is unique in many ways. The town enjoys an outstanding reputation thanks to the quality of its residents and their maintenance of its homes, buildings, and grounds. According to many older folks in the county, Bellville has always maintained the status of a groomed, well-ordered community. From the charm of its women to the caring and friendliness of all its inhabitants, Bellville holds a special place in the hearts of many.

The idea to compile this book arose from conversations I had with Bellville mayor, Jerry Coleman, at a series of Evans County Historical Society meetings. It seemed that our after-meeting chats always returned to the subject of Bellville, the importance of preserving its history, and, regretfully, the demise of many of the older citizens. This book is the result of my decision to chronicle the Bellville story.

I used many sources in completing my research. Two important ones were Lucile Hodges' *History of Our Locale; Mainly Evans County Georgia* and a Bellville history article written for *The Claxton Enterprise* by my great-uncle, Theodore Brewton. Of tremendous assistance were my interviews with current and former Bellville area residents, Harry DeLoach,

---

[1] According to the U.S. Board of Geographic Names there ia a Bellvill or Belleville in Arkansas, Florida, Kentucky, Missouri, New York, Ohio, Texas, Alabama, Illinois, Indiana, Kansas, Louisiana, Michigan, Mississippi, Nevada, Oklahoma, Pennsylvania, Rhode Island, Tennessee, Virginia, West Virginia, and Wisconsin. National Geographic Names Data Base, May 3, 1995.

Amiel Fountain, David Groover, Jimmie Styles, Wallace Parker, Delma and Mary Daniel, Bernie and Hilda Anderson, Winton Bell, and Darin McCoy. Also employed was a 1990 interview of Herschel Hearn conducted by Emily Groover. Appendix B contains complete texts of these interviews.

Within these pages the reader will learn about many of the people and events that represent Bellville's history. Over the years, the town has been home to many interesting people. For example, Jim B. Smith, son of Daniel H. Smith, was a very successful Hollywood screenwriter in the 1920s and 30s who wrote scripts for such famous actors as John Wayne and Roy Rogers. In the 1930s, Colquitt Sykes was Bellville's first bonafide millionaire and practiced the unusual habit of herding his cattle in his Rolls-Royce automobile. Today, former resident Jack Hearn is a world renowned plant geneticist made famous by his research in development of new citrus fruits. The stories of these individuals and many more make up the rich fabric of this Georgia town's heritage.

Although I have tried diligently to present the Bellville story with accuracy, as with any work of this magnitude, there may be errors. I hope they are few. I do not represent this account to be a complete history of the town, for I could highlight only where my personal research and sources took me. Hopefully, one day, someone will fill in any gaps in this book and continue the story where this work ends. After all, we must preserve the heritage of one of the finest communities in the USA.

Acknowledgments

This book is not the work of one person. Many folks helped me by providing reference material, photographs, and encouragement. Among the contributors are David and Emily Groover, Eloise Hodges, Darin McCoy, Alvin Blalock, Jerry and Ona Coleman, Mary Tippins Conner, Bernie and Hilda Anderson, Walter Emmett Daniel, Winton and Lucy Bell, Bill Pryor, Mona Lee Allen, Dorothy Simmons, Devane Parker Lewis, Wallace Parker, Jessie Tippins, Loulie Perkins, Jimmie Styles, Judge Harry DeLoach, Darin McCoy, Tab Smith, Edra Smith Riggs, Tim Eason, and Shirley Smith.

I especially thank the people who granted me lengthy interviews that are included in this volume. They were Amiel "Cornbread" Fountain, Judge Harry DeLoach, Darin McCoy, Delma and Mary Daniel, Jimmie Styles, Winton Bell, David Groover, Bernie and Hilda Anderson, and Wallace Parker. Also included in this work is a wonderful interview that Emily Hearn Groover conducted with her uncle, Herschel Hearn, in 1990.

The photographs included in this book come from several sources. Emily Groover provided many of them. Delma Daniel, Jerry and Ona Coleman, Loulie Perkins, Eloise Hodges, Mary Tippins Conner, Devane Lewis, Lois Parker Turner, Ruby Brown, Aubrey Strickland, Tab Smith, Edith Smith, Carie Beasley and others were also helpful in providing photos. Many of these pictures came from "sharing sessions" at recent old Bellville School reunions.

Several people helped by reading parts of the manuscript and offering helpful edits and suggestions for further research. Robin Nail, historic preservation planning coordinator for the Heart of Georgia Altamaha Regional Development Center, provided many helpful additions to the narrative history and the appendix on historic homes of Bellville. A Tattnall County native, John Rabun, Jr., of Atlanta, helped enormously with many suggestions for improving the text. Others included Emily Groover, Edra Smith Riggs, and my mother, Glenda James of Savannah. My sister, Linda Hester, of Thomasville, provided great assistance by helping with the page layout. David and Emily Groover also graciously helped me with many research questions about the town. Even though these individuals kindly agreed to assist me, the responsibility for any errors is solely mine.

Bill Werkheiser and his staff at Southeastern Printech, Inc., of Glennville, were very accomodating and very patient in working with me on the many small details necessary to produce this volume. Stephanie Durrence offered many helpful suggestions to improve the appearance of the book.

Colonel Ed Schwabe, of Blacksburg, Virginia, provided the exceptional maps for this book. Colonel Schwabe, a native of Swainsboro, Georgia, is an expert cartographer and a most personable gentleman. He was very helpful in taking my rough sketches and vague ideas and turning them into fine maps. I was very fortunate to find someone of his caliber to produce these maps.

Anthony A. Brown, an artist of great reputation in the middle Georgia area, produced two drawings for this book. The Hearn store in his drawing comes alive thanks to his enormous talent. He also provided the fine frontispiece drawing of the Bellville Depot. Brown's work can be found in the collections of the Carter Presidential Library, Macon's Museum of Arts and Sciences, the Savannah College of Art and Design, and now, in Bellville, Georgia.

The fine folks at both the Tattnall County and Evans County courthouses were helpful in facilitating my research. Thanks to Debbie Crews, Clerk of Superior Court, and Sharon McCall, Probate Judge, in Tattnall County and Gail McCooey, Clerk of Superior Court, and Darin McCoy, Probate Judge, in Evans County.

A special thanks goes to the Rommie Thompson family for their many years of friendship and support. They have been very helpful in taking care of my Bellville farm during my long periods of absence due to an Air Force career.

I thank my wife, Ann, for being patient with me while I worked on this book. Absorbing myself in the history of Bellville meant many days away from home doing weekend research and, then, many nights sitting in front of my computer typing the manuscript.

Finally, I also wish to acknowledge the residents of the Bellville area, both present and past, that make it such a great location to live. Bellville is a place where being a neighbor means a lot. Decency and a strong sense of community pride make it a truly special place.

The Story of Bellville

The Hearn Store and Bellville Post Office. (Drawing by Anthony Brown, 1995)

Bellville's Origin

The town of Bellville, located in the western part of Evans County, Georgia, originated as a railroad community during the last decade of the nineteenth century. Deed records indicate that land owners began selling town lots as early as 1890.

The 1890s must have been an exciting time to live in the new town of Bellville. Life across this rural area was still relatively simple, but the arrival of the railroad would change that forever. From its modest beginnings as a railroad depot town, to the community's outstanding reputation today, Bellville provides an interesting case study in rural progress and development.

Evans County Background

To appreciate Bellville's history, it is helpful to first examine the history of Evans County. One of the later-formed counties in Georgia, Evans did not materialize as a county until 1914. Carved from the much older counties of Tattnall and Bulloch, Evans can further trace its Tattnall roots to Montgomery and Liberty counties, and its Liberty lineage to colonial St. John's Parish. The Bulloch pedigree extends to Effingham County and St. Phillip's Parish. From the early 1800s through the nineteenth century, the Evans County area history is thus synonymous with that of its parent counties.[1]

The site in original Washington County, which would become Bellville, was part of Indian territory prior to 1773. That year marks the date the state acquired the land in an agreement with the Creek Nation.[2] The state formed Washington County in 1784 from this land.

Cut from Washington County in 1793, Montgomery County included the future Bellville site until the Georgia Legislature created Tattnall in 1801. The Bellville location was west of the original Tattnall-Liberty County border and, therefore, became part of Tattnall.[3] Hence, the line of descent for the Bellville area is Indian territory, Washington County, Montgomery County, Tattnall County, and finally, in 1914, Evans County.

Although isolated hunters and traders were in the general area before the Revolutionary War, this part of the country did not gain many residents until after that conflict. Bounty land grants to soldiers and land grants to "heads of households" provided the necessary inducement to populate this land of piney woods and wiregrass. Most of the early settlers hailed from the Carolinas and migrated through northern and central Georgia. Some came west from Liberty County.

Known geographically as the Pine Barren area, this remote country was wild territory during its early years. Criminals, Indians, and adventure seekers roamed the area, making the place suitable for only the most hardy of pioneers to make it their home.

Perhaps one of the first white men to pass through what would later become the Bellville area was Andrew Way. He and his party of surveyors, chain-carriers, markers, guides, and hunters ran a 72-mile survey line in 1773 through the giant pine and black gum bottomland between the Ogeechee and Altamaha rivers.[4]

As a deputy surveyor for Georgia, Way conducted the survey of the southern line of the Creek Indian land granted in the 1773 Treaty of Augusta.[5] The line of the survey, completed in November 1773, ran just west of Bellville, from "the old Indian corner" in what is now Wheeler County to the mouth of Beards Creek. Thus, the state formed the original western boundary of Effingham and Liberty counties.[6]

Small clearings located in well-drained areas created the first opportunity for pioneers to grow corn, wheat, and vegetables for home use. Cattle, sheep, and hogs were the first sources of income. As the population increased, however, cultivated crops began to dominate as a source of income. Later, markets for the products developed in Savannah, and settlers cleared more land for increased crop production.

The state land grant system proved a successful method for populating the area that would become Bellville, as well as the rest of the county. Settlers who met the minimum qualifications as soldiers or "heads of households" applied to the state of Georgia for land. In turn, the headright system provided each head of a family a tract of unoccupied land selected by the settler. The head of household received 200 acres outright. The state allotted fifty additional acres for each family member and each slave owned, with a ceiling set at 1,000 acres.[7] County courts issued a warrant for the land, and the head of the family paid for the land survey. This system continued in the Bellville area until 1890, when vacant land ceased to exist. The state abolished this system in 1909. In the immediate Bellville section, original land grants, issued prior to 1825 and noted as being on the waters of Cedar or Bull creek, included the following individuals, many of whom had multiple grants:[8]

Aaron Baxly	William Hodges[11]	Phillip Tippins[14]
Nathan Brewton[9]	Jeremiah McDaniel[12]	George U. Tippins[15]
Aaron Daniel[10]	Charles B. Mulford	Lewis Williams
David Hennesy	James A. Tippins[13]	Simon Smith

Several of the above pioneer settlers attended church at Cedar Creek Baptist Church in Tattnall County as early as 1812.[16] Among the membership were David and Rebecca Hennesy, Jeremiah McDaniel, Aaron Daniel, and Aaron Baxly. David Hennesy, a pastor of the church from 1813-1815, obtained a land grant of 830 acres in 1815 that includes most of the immediate land on either side of present-day Highway 280 from Bellville to Hagan.[17]

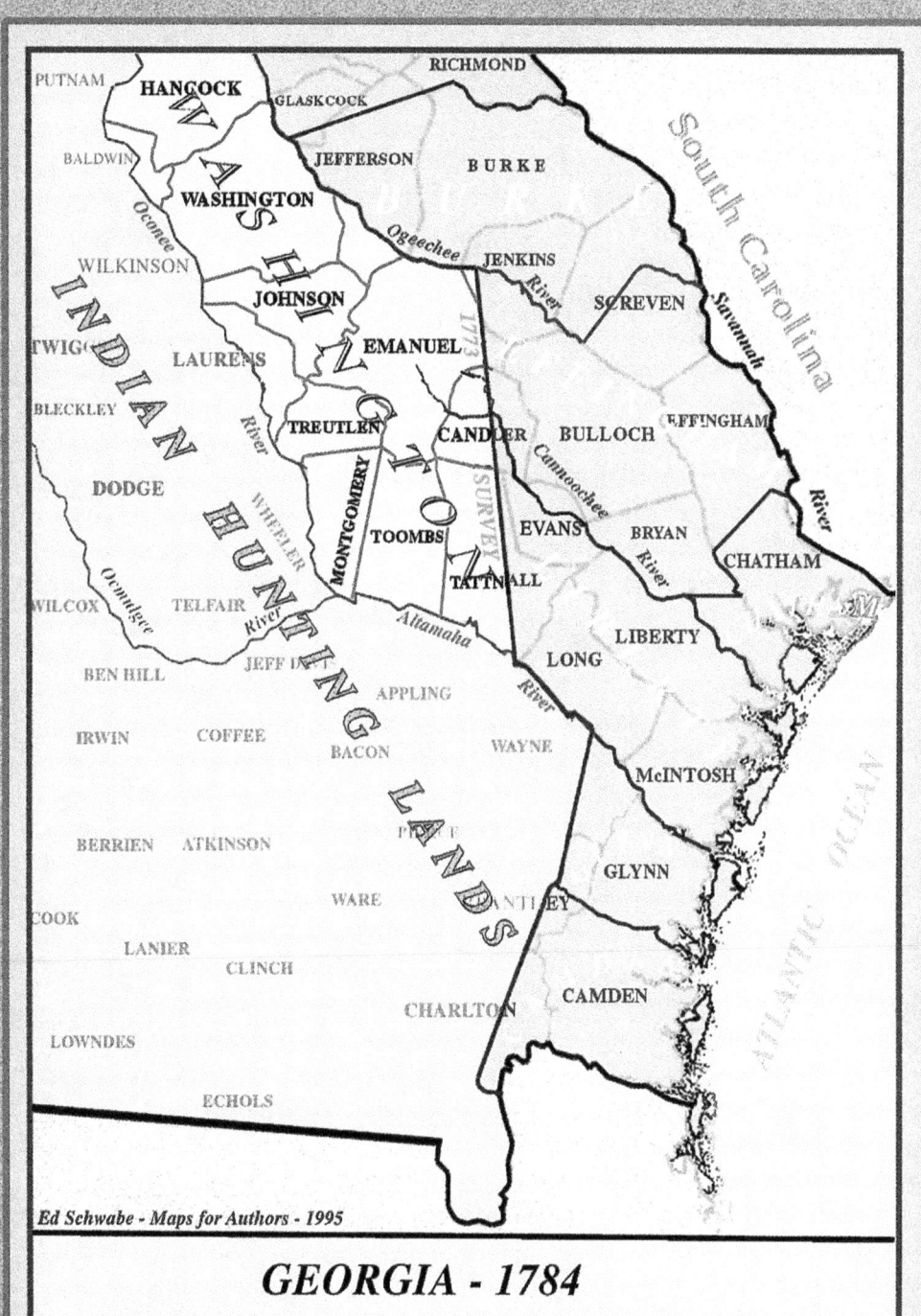

GEORGIA - 1784

with the 1773 survey shown as the boundary between the new county of Washington, and Liberty and Effingham to the east.

Benjamin Brewton established another church in the area when he built Brewton's Church around 1835. Built at the request of his mother, Nancy Fontaine Brewton, the small log chapel served "the religious welfare of the community." The site of this church was at the present-day tabernacle at Brewton's Cemetery in Hagan. Benjamin and his brother Samuel donated the land for this church.[18]

The first settlers in the area dealt with hardship and adversity. Before the railroad, there were no real towns, except the village of Reidsville. People lived on their farms, mostly in log homes, and were self-sufficient. The women turned out thread and cloth from spinning wheels and looms, and they made clothing by hand. Shoes were coarse brogans made locally or bought in Savannah. Residents grew most of their food, and the women cooked it in big kitchen fireplaces. Cook stoves were a luxury.

Transportation was difficult in every way. In the winter time, rains made the roads almost impassable by wagon and the swollen streams unfordable. There were very few bridges, and they frequently washed away. As Joe Grice put it in his 1958 book, *Sketches of By-Gone Days*:

> People would carry their cotton, wool and other products to Savannah and trade them for the things they needed, these trips being made in covered wagons, which means an ordinary wagon with reasonably high sides, with a stiff canvas stretched over hoops connecting one side with the other. This made a safe place for people to store their goods and travel in bad weather. It usually took a wagon two days to go to Savannah and two to return, as the roads were poor and wagons, were, of course, pulled by mules and horses. Small streams were waded, but the rivers were crossed by flat boat ferries, in which horses and wagons were carried across the streams or toll bridges operated by private citizens. This plan and method of trading continued to some extent until the Sea Board Railroad was built through the county in 1890, though after the railroad now known as the Atlantic Coast Line was built through Liberty County in 1845, many people had their freight shipped, and hauled from one of the railroad stations.[19]

In the early days, education was very limited. For those fortunate enough to go to school, the annual term was three months, and parents of the students paid the teacher's salary directly. The curriculum centered mostly on the three R's. Parents wishing a better education for their children boarded them at Hinesville or Savannah to attend schools there.[20]

As the late 1800s approached, however, progress was underway. As one observer put it for Tattnall County:

> Gone forever are the log houses, clay chimneys, rail fences, horse carts, muzzle loading shotguns, coffee mills, long blade turpentine axes, foot logs,

along with such activities as working the roads, sheep shearing and going to the city in covered wagons, but the recollections of these things linger with us.[21]

The Civil War

The residents of the area in the early 1860s prepared for war. Economic, legal, and social issues resulted in the nation's bloodiest conflict. This war, for both the men who served and their families left behind, would change the shape of the county, the state, and the South for decades to come.

Among those serving in the conflict from the general area that would later become the Bellville District were Berry Brewton, Jonathan Brewton, Simon W. Brewton, Issac Daniel, W.W. Daniel, Joshua Collins, M.N.C. Colson, Amos Hearn, Jesse Jernigan, Chadburn Parker, Sheppard Riggs, Daniel N. Sikes, James B. Smith, Glenn Tippins, L.A.H. Tippins, and James Tootle.[22]

Two of the large landowners in the area at the eve of the war were William W. Tippins and Benjamin Brewton. Brewton lived about two miles east from present-day Bellville at Brewton Mill, and Tippins lived south of what is now Manassas.[23] In December 1860 the residents of the county selected Tippins as Vice President of the Tattnall Secession meeting and Brewton to represent the county at the Georgia Secession Convention in Milledgeville. The following article comes from the *Savannah Republican* newspaper, December 13, 1861, and details the Tattnall nomination convention in which Tippins and Brewton participated.

Public Meeting in Tattnall

Reidsville, Tattnall Co., Dec. 8th, 1860.

In conformity with previous notice, the citizens of Tattnall County, irrespective of past party differences, met in Reidsville on Saturday, 8th inst. for the purpose of nominating candidates to represent the County in the Convention to assemble on the 16th January next. The meeting was organized by appointing Henry Strickland President, Wm. W. Tippins Vice President, and requesting A.P. McRae to act as Secretary. The object of the meeting having been explained by the Chairman, the following preamble and resolutions were unanimously adopted:

Whereas, in consequence of the political conditions of the country, there are, in the minds of the people, great apprehensions on the disruptions of that sacred bond which has so long united us as a free, happy, prosperous and mighty people, and in view of the vital interest we feel for the perpetuation of that union, and the veneration we have for our constitutional obligations,

> Resolved, That while we deprecate the election of a President and Vice-president on a sectional issue, by a party whose expressed principles and actions are hostile to our institutions, yet we do not consider the constitutional elections of Lincoln a just cause for dissolution.
>
> Resolved, That we do condemn the actions of those States which have so unconstitutionally annulled the Fugitive Slave Law; that (in the language of the Georgia Platform) "upon the faithful execution of the Fugitive Slave bill by the proper authorities, depends the preservation of our much loved Union."
>
> Resolved, That when the constitutional means have failed to bring about an adjustment of our present difficulties, then, and not until then, are we in favor of a dissolution.
>
> Resolved, That we condemn all hasty and inconsiderate action upon a matter of such vital importance, and that we earnestly entreat the conservative men of all sections to use all honorable means to bring about a peaceable termination of the present difficulties.
>
> On a motion, a committee of three from each militia district were appointed by the Chair to propose the names of two suitable persons as candidates for the Convention. After a short absence, the committee reported the names of Benjamin Brewton and Henry Strickland, which was unanimously ratified by the meeting. Mr. S.D. Bradwell, being called for, addressed the meeting in a short but eloquent and forceful speech, advocating the sentiments embodied in the above resolution.
>
> On motion, the proceedings were ordered to be published in the Savannah and Milledgeville papers. The meeting then adjourned.
>
> A.P. McRae, Secretary   H. Strickland and Wm. W. Tippins
>   Chairmen

The first Confederate company raised in the county was the "Tattnall Rangers." August 31, 1861, marked the date the company formed outside the courthouse in Reidsville. It was here that the men took the oath of allegiance to serve the Confederacy for three years or the duration of the war. After the Rangers, other units started in Tattnall were the "Tattnall Volunteers" and the "Tattnall Invincibles."[24] Some Tattnall men joined units from nearby counties such as the 5th Georgia Cavalry in Liberty.

The war resulted in terrible loss for the South. Georgia alone lost three-fourths of its wealth. Approximately half of the men from the area died in battle, from disease, or were captured. However, one way the soldiers coped with the war was to write letters home. From Virginia, Berry Brewton, who was later one of Bellville's founders, wrote the following letter to his wife, Candacy Tippins Brewton, in 1864.[25]

Blue Ridge
Ineagles Gap   July the 18, 1864

    Dear wife, I take the opportunity of dropping you a few lines which will inform you that I am in tolerable good health hoping it may find you & Flora enjoying the same blessings & am very anxious to hear from you all for I have not heard in some time. The last letter I received was written the 2nd of June. I haven't had the chance to send off a letter since I left Staunton which was the 27 of June. I am going to write one to you & one to Jonathan, perhaps you may get one or the other. The mail is very uncertain that goes from here for the enemy is raiding all through this country. We have just got back from Maryland. We had one very hard fight at Frederick City on the 9th of this inst. Our loss was very heavy. Our brigade was badly cut up as we were in the hottest of the fight, but we routed the enemy & drove them into the city of Washington. We went in about five miles of the city. We went near enough to see the flag on the old capital, but didn't attack it more than to skirmish with them. Colonel Lamar & Lieutenant Col Van Valkinburg (third or bird-there is some question about this) were both killed dead on the field & several others out of our regiment. Four men was shot down under our flag & two of them killed. Gen. Evans was wounded & Lieutenant Gordon both pretty bad & Gen. Gordons horse shot from under him. Lieutenant Mincy is badly wounded through the breast. James Hendrix is wounded in the leg but not very bad & Jesse Jernigan slightly wounded. All left in the hands of the enemy. We brought away a great many horses & cattle & wagons. The Yankees has been following us & very often the cavalry fighting. We have crossed the Blue Ridge with all of our forces & the Yankees is right after us & we are taking a stand for them. There is some skirmishing now on the Blue Ridge but I do not think they will advance. Tell James Hendrixs people that Jimmy is wounded in the leg below the knee, but not very bad & was left in Maryland at Frederick City & was fairing very well when we left. The citizens was paying very good attention to our wounded. We did not have ambulances enough to move our wounded & a great many were left. I want to see you very bad, but I do not know when that will be if ever. You must do the best you can. You must try to get someone to stay with you until you get up again. I feel very thankful that I have been spared whilst so many has fell, but it may be my lot to fall yet, for it seems as though the war will continue. Our regiment has but fifty four men in it for duty. I must close. Give my love & respects to all of my people & friends. I remain your loving husband until death.

                                                          B.B. Brewton

    Although General Sherman's main army did not come through the immediate area on its famous "March to the Sea," an extension of his right wing elements did. This destructive

General Clement A. Evans commanded a brigade in which several area soldiers served. Residents later named the county after Gen. Evans. (Early 1900s photo courtesy *The Confederate Veteran*)

march did unparalleled damage. Judge Simon B. Brewton, of Liberty County, told the story that as a young child he remembered Yankee raiders coming to his homestead just east of present-day Hagan. According to Brewton the Yankees also raided Brewton Mill, just one mile north of current-day Hagan. The Yankees in the area "destroyed fences, cut down the fruit trees, and everything else that came in their way."[26]

In the months following the surrender, the soldiers made it back to their beloved homes the best way they could, often walking most of the way. Residents of the area felt the effects of the Civil War for many years afterward, and the economic ruin required a half century to overcome. This period of loss and hardship ended with people eager to get their lives back in order.

Tattnall County Campground

The year 1867, the time when local citizens founded the Tattnall County Campground, was significant for the families living in what would later become the Bellville community. William E. Tippins contributed 20 acres of land for the campground to trustees A.D. Eason, W.J. Jordan, L.A.H. Tippins, J.J. Grooms, D.H. Smith, Martin G. Tootle and William Harden. The deed granted by Tippins listed the reason for the donation as "for and in consideration of the love I bear for the cause of Christ, and from an earnest desire to promote His heritage on Earth."[27]

Located approximately four miles southwest of Bellville, the campground became an institution attended by residents of the town as well as from throughout the area. One observer noted that the town of Bellville always seemed deserted around campmeeting time. It became quite popular to "tent" at the campground, and worshipers eventually built cabins to replace the tents. They built these small buildings on all four sides of the cleared quadrangle. In 1925, James B. Alexander depicted past life at campmeeting as follows:

> Then (campmeeting of the 1870s and 80s) the neighing of horses, the braying of mules, and the lowing of cows and the barking of dogs were to be heard on every side. In those good old days the two-mule wagon or horse cart, mostly the latter, was loaded with sufficient provisions for the people

and enough provender for the animals and the good wife and children climbed in, and in many instances an entire day was consumed in making the trip to the campground, but when you arrived everybody knew each other and many friends met who had not seen each other since the last camp meeting, and a week was spent delightfully in worship and neighborly discussion of matters of religious and personal interest.[28]

The twelve tenters at the first campmeeting in 1867 were familiar Bellville area family names: Abraham Eason, Berry Brewton, Mrs. Parthenia Brewton (widow of Simon Brewton), Rachel Tippins (widow of Glenn Tippins), Rev. William Harden, Rev. William J. Jordon, Buckie Edwards, William Southwell, John Hammock, L.A.H. Tippins, J.C. (Shad) Parker, and James B. Smith.

There is little surprise that the campground became a landmark in the hearts and minds of the local populace. The following 1935 description gives a sense of the many attributes of the site.

The present site is ideally located, it is only a short distance from Manassas on the Seaboard Air Line Railway, is near State Route 30, and a county highway skirts it on the east side. A splendid spring of water is just under the hill and the grounds are surrounded by a number of tall long leaf yellow pines interspersed with oak, some of both varieties being within the grounds around which the tents all front toward the large tabernacle. The tabernacle has a seating capacity of approximately 1,000 and many are unable to be seated.[29]

The campmeeting served not only as a religious observance, but also as a gathering of social importance. It was a time to worship, renew old friendships, and catch up on the latest news. Parents built bonfires at night, and the youngsters played games in the light of the fire. These week-long observances were also a great time to enjoy the superb food served by the ladies.

Nollie Parker built the current tabernacle in 1920. This building is a masterpiece of carpentry, and the craftsmanship is superb. As he started the structure he brushed the ground clean with a limb of a tree, and drew the tabernacle building plans in the sand. When asked if he needed the plans put to paper, he pointed to his head and said, "No, it is all up here." Nollie's son, Chadburn, carved the pews with a hand plane and foot adz. Chadburn also helped with other parts of the construction, and when he finished outlined his initials with nails in the loft over the altar. He later remarked, "If pap had known I wasted so many nails, he would have tanned my hide."[30]

Local historian Lucile Hodges summed up the benefits of the campground accurately in her book:

> It has through the years been of immeasurable value in spiritual uplift and joy to many in the immediate area and in surrounding counties who "camp" in the houses which outline the tabernacle quadrangle, and to countless others who make the pilgrimage back there as often as possible to renew old friendships and worship there. [31]

Clockwise from top left: Handcarved tabernacle benches, tabernacle structural posts, and Tattnall Campground as it appears in 1996.

Nearby Communities at Bellville's Founding

Prior to Bellville's establishment as a town, there were several nearby communities already in the area. Reidsville, located approximately ten miles west of present-day Bellville, was the Tattnall County seat. Founded in 1829, it was the only full-fledged town in the county until the railroad came through and, until the establishment of Evans County in 1914, the place in which area residents could conduct their court business.

Another nearby community in this sparsely settled area was Brewton Mill, located one mile north of present-day Brewton Cemetery in Hagan. The postmaster at Brewton Mill in 1854 was Benjamin Brewton, who operated a water mill on the Cedar Creek site. Glenn and Nancy Hendricks later bought the land and operated the mill and a store at the same location.[32] The Brewton Mill/Hendricks store was one of only three immediately available to area settlers. The other two were the J.B. Brewton store, located three miles northwest of what is now Claxton, and the William Daniel store in the community of Bull Creek.

In addition to Brewton Mill, several other community post offices served the area. These were in Bull Creek, Danton, and Hawpond. From the residents using these post offices came most of the residents who later populated the town of Bellville.

Bull Creek, located a distance of approximately five miles south of modern Bellville, was later called Bay Branch. William Morgan (1828-1890) was postmaster in 1857. Post Office records indicate the following: "William T. Morgan re-appointed postmaster in 1866; Daniel Barnard, 1866, Morgan again in 1867, discontinued in 1868; re-established June 18, 1874 with Wm. W. Daniel, P.M.; discontinued 1880s. Mail to be sent to Danton."[33] In 1881 the state gazetteer described Bull Creek as follows:

> Bull Creek, Tattnall County. Located near the creek from which it derives its name, and which furnishes power to run a grist and saw mill; 10 miles northeast of Reidsville, the county seat. Timber cutting is the chief industry. Has a Primitive Baptist Church, a common school, and receives a semi-weekly mail by carrier.[34]

Located close to present-day Manassas, the Danton post office served a population of 200 in 1888. In 1884, the post office was first located two miles southeast of the current Manassas post office at the residence of Asbury Tippins. When residents established the town of Manassas, Tippins moved the post office to the railroad station. Founders named the town for Manassas Foy, a large turpentine operator in the area. The government later relocated the Danton post office to a site north of Collins, Georgia.[35] Subscribers at the original Danton were as follows:

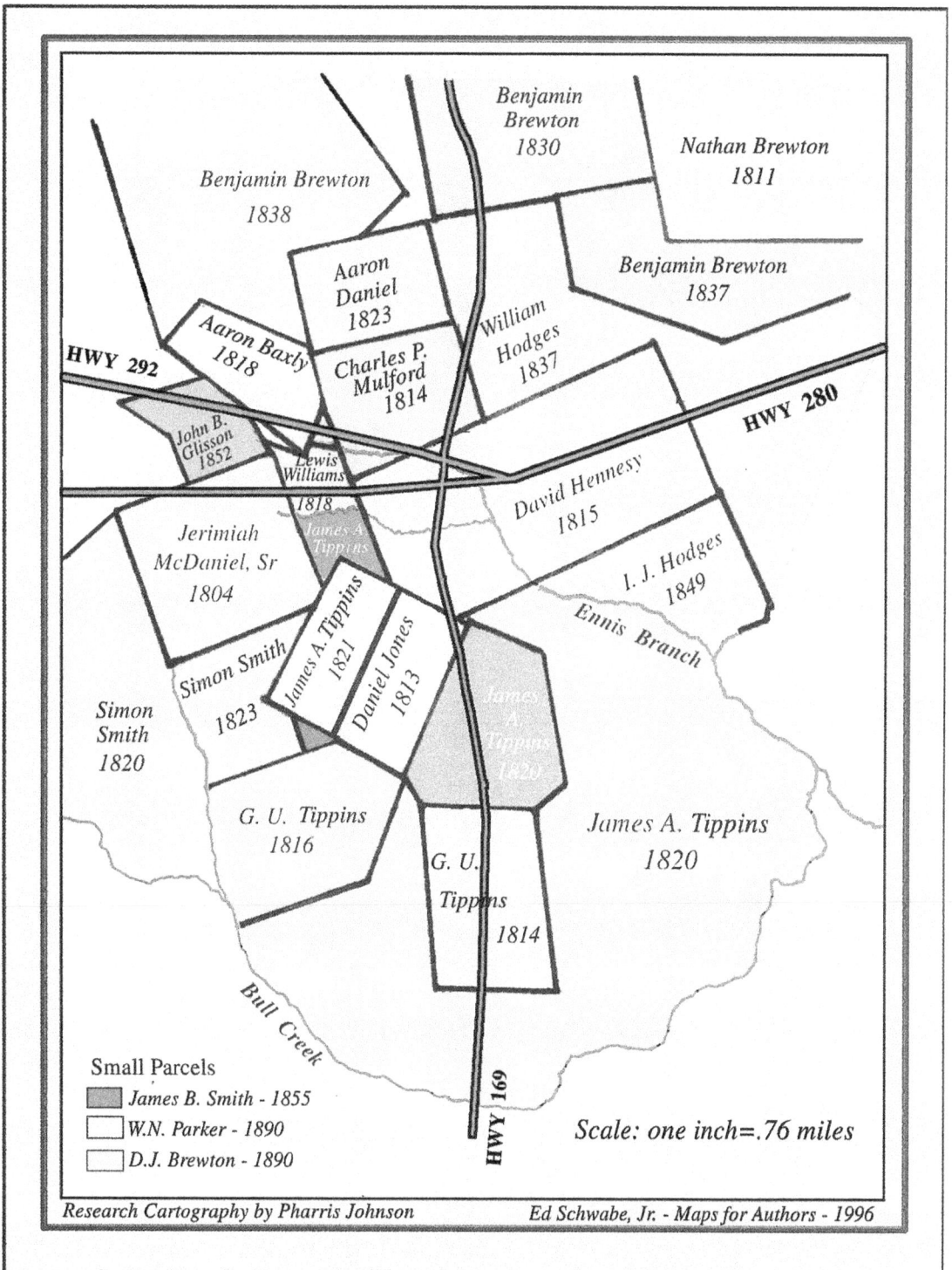

Original Land Grants in the Bellville Area
-- with present-day highway network superimposed --

The Story of Bellville

> W.H. Bazemore, D.J. Brewton, W.B. Brewton, J.A. DeLoach, J.A. Hammond, J.W. Brazell, J.S. Brewton, W.W. Daniel, A.J. Hammond, I.J. Hodges, S.L. Hodges, J.H. Jenkins, H. Kennedy, J.A. Mattox, M.E. Rogers, D.H. Smith, G.W. Tippins, J.S. Howard, A. Kennedy, M. Kennedy, E.F. Morgan, J.B. Sikes, M.W. Smith, and H.W. Tippins.[36]

The J.B. Brewton place, on what is now Route 129, was the site of the Hawpond post office.[37] Hawpond had a population of 50 in 1888-1889, including the following:

> C.D. Anderson, B.B. Brewton, J.B. Brewton, E. Callaway, J.A. Callaway, W.I. Daniel, A.D. Eason, J.T. Eason, M.W. Eason, Nancy and W.R. Hendrix, J.H. Hendricks, T.J. Hodges, J. Holland, J. Jernigan, J.W. Jones, J.C. Parker, J.J. Rogers, J. Sikes, M.A. Smith, P.S. Smith, J.M. Surrency, C.T. Strickland, L.A.H. Tippins, and W.H. Wood.

Jonathan Brewton was postmaster in 1883, and James T. Eason from 1887 to 1889. The government discontinued the post office in February 1889 and sent the mail to Danton.[38]

An area courthouse was available to Bellville residents at Hogwallow. Located in the Bay Branch area close to the home of Alfred Kennedy, the facility was used primarily for voting.[39]

The Arrival of the Iron Horse

The late nineteenth century represented a period of rapid growth for the railroad industry. Given the numerous lumber and naval stores, cotton and other farm products produced in the Tattnall area, the construction of a railroad was a necessity if these products were to be efficiently transported to market.

The roads of the area were "few and poor" and more aptly described as pioneer trails.[40] Construction of a railroad through the county was a logical move and would prove to be extremely important. These routes represented the rise and fall of towns and the growth or decline of entire sections. The railroad accounts for the almost doubling of the Tattnall County 1890 population of 10,253 to 20,419 by 1900.[41]

Tattnall County deed records indicate that the Savannah and Western (S & W) Railroad began acquiring rights of way through the future site of Bellville in 1887. According to the deeds, these 100 foot strips of right of way were to "construct and equip" a railroad, and owners provided the land for nominal amounts and the "advantages accruing."[42]

It is not difficult to imagine the anticipation generated by the coming of the railroad. Lucile Hodges, in *A History of Our Locale*, credited the railroad in this area for bringing about "employment, excitement, optimism and a direct line with the outside world that had never been known before."[43] With its completion most residents hailed the railroad as a symbol of mobility and an avenue that made the world a "smaller" place.

Bellville's early railroad history, a story of competing railroad companies, is quite involved. Of the two railroads planning service through the Bellville area, one company planned an eastward route across Georgia and the other planned a line in a westward direction.

The Savannah and Western line, a subsidiary of the Central of Georgia, started construction in Meldrim (17 miles west of Savannah) in July 1889 and crossed 58 miles west to Lyons, Georgia. Builders planned the route through the towns of Eden, Maldan, Kennedy, Fido (Groveland), Danton (Manassas), Ohoopee, and Stirling (Lyons). At Lyons, the S & W planned to hook up with trackage of the Savannah, Americus, and Montgomery (S.A.M.) which terminated in Lyons, to establish a line from Savannah to Columbus, Americus, and Birmingham, Alabama.[44] The S.A.M. line was building a route eastward to connect Montgomery, Alabama, with Savannah. The S.A.M. laid tracks from Abbeville as far east as Lyons by June 1890. The S.A.M. planned to lay tracks from Lyons to Savannah to compete with the S & W.[45] However, after determining that the two lines would be virtually side by side, builders concluded "the roads were to be built so closely parallel to each other both must suffer, without corresponding benefits to the country."[46]

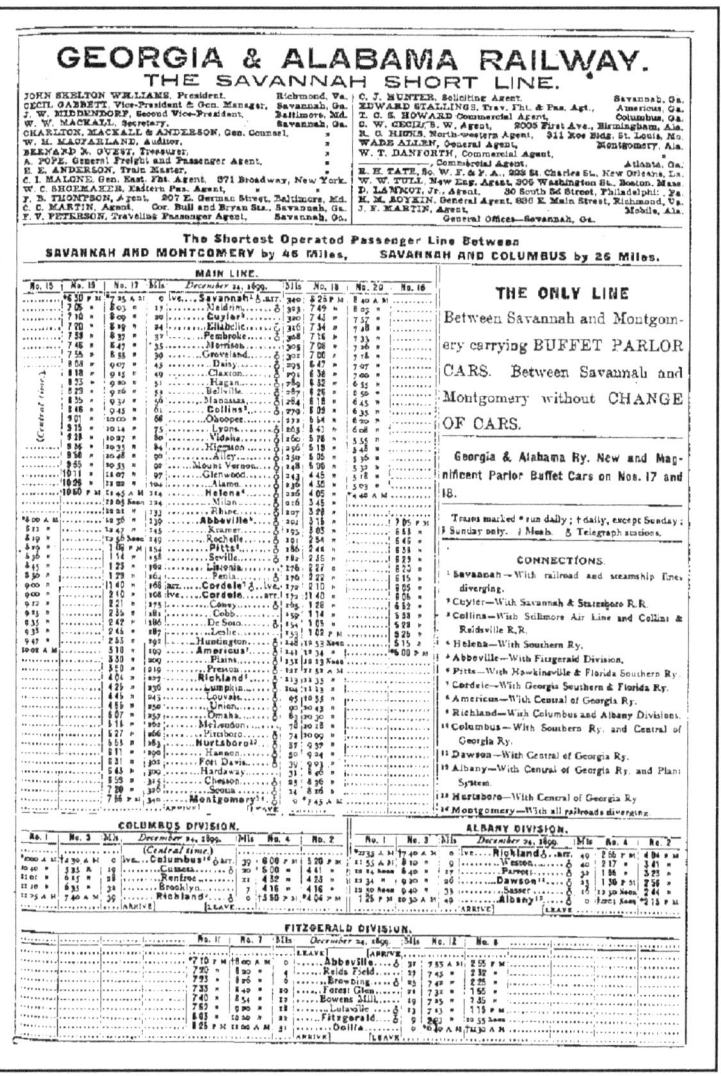

1890s railroad schedule of trains passing through Bellville.

After S & W officials obtained appropriate rights of way in Tattnall, the railroaders began laying track through the county in March 1890. By the 22nd of that month the railroad reached the spot that would become Bellville.[47] Builders completed the S & W line to Lyons three months later in May and met the S.A.M. line. The *Savannah Morning News* hailed the event with the following account:

> It is expected....the S&W and S.A.M. will meet, thus forming a continuous line, giving Savannah a shorter route to the west, and opening a section of country between the city and the Oconee River, that is yet comparatively undeveloped. The completion of this line will give Savannah a large amount of trade that has been going elsewhere. It will also increase her lumber and naval stores exports.[48]

Originally, the two railroads had traffic arrangements to operate trains on one another's track. However, beginning in November 1891, disputes between these rivals resulted in passengers having to change trains in Lyons.[49]

The S & W eventually had second thoughts about the plan to extend the line to Birmingham and abandoned the idea. Since the S & W had no further need for the Meldrim to Lyons route, in 1896 it leased the track for 101 years to the Georgia and Alabama (G & A) Railroad.

The Georgia and Alabama Railway operated through Bellville in the late 1890s.

With its leased trackage, the G & A, successor to the S.A.M., was then capable of offering service between Montgomery and Savannah. Also known as the "Savannah Short Line" during this period, the company boasted that its route was 46 miles shorter than the competing railroad line between the two cities.[50] The Central of Georgia still owned the trackage from Meldrim to Savannah, and it was not until 1899 that the G & A began construction of its own line to connect these two locations. The Seaboard Air Line bought the Georgia and Alabama in 1900 and gained the Savannah-Columbus-Montgomery route.[51] A Georgia industry publication of 1901 described this railroad as follows:

> The Georgia and Alabama road, running almost a bee line from the Alabama line eastward to Savannah with its many branch roads, 376 miles in all, is now part of the Seaboard Air Line system. It transports products of a large section of Georgia and Alabama to swell the exports of Savannah.[52]

1933s railway ticket from Bellville to Savannah.

After putting the track down through Tattnall in 1890, the Savannah and Western approved stations at sites deemed favorable to the railroad. Station locations were important, since towns would invariably spring up around the depots. In general, full stations were to be about 10 miles apart, with half stations mid-way between the full stations. The railroad intended quarter stations at two and one-half mile intervals.[53]

In Evans County, the towns of Daisy, Claxton, Hagan, and Bellville grew up from station requirements. Bellville's designation was station No. 5 1/4, with its depot 53 miles from Savannah and 287 miles from Montgomery.[54] In the late 1890s, one could leave Bellville at 6:26 a.m. and arrive in Savannah at 8:25 a.m. The return train left Savannah at 6:30 p.m. and arrived in Bellville at 9:26 p.m. In 1908, the fare from Bellville to Savannah was $1.50. An extra 25 cents gave the traveler access to Tybee Island, a favorite destination for recreation.[55]

Some of the railroad station agents at Bellville through the years were as follows: Eugene Rackley, Mr. Arnold, Colin Smith, Daisy Sikes, Homer LeGrand, Bascom Tippins, and Paul LeGrand (beginning about 1912). In the early days the agents issued passenger tickets, checked freight, and operated the telegraph.[56] According to a 1918 Rand McNally catalog, services available at Bellville included a money order postal service station and Southern Express shipping.

The Seaboard Air Line Railroad began operation through Bellville in 1900 after the Georgia and Alabama.

Railroads continued to expand until the 1920s when automobiles and trucks presented increased competition. The Seaboard Air Line Railroad changed ownership and names several times over the succeeding years, as the railroads gradually scaled back, merged, or quit operation. While some towns died out when the railroad declined, Bellville adapted to the new, paved highways that ensured the town's continued existence.[57]

The Bellville Site

The site of Bellville was a logical location for a town. Railroaders chose the route through the area because the line was between the Canoochee River and Cedar Creek on the

The Story of Bellville

north and Bull Creek on the south. This siting made building the railroad easier because no major waterways required crossing.

Ennis Branch, a tributary of Bull Creek, passes through Bellville just south of the railroad. This stream provided water for the area's earliest settlers as well as later businesses in the town. Early deed records indicate the original name of the branch was *Hennesy*, not Ennis. The Hennesy Branch was no doubt named for David Hennesy, an original settler in the area in 1811.[58]

Soil-wise, the area is among the richest on the Coastal Plain. Tifton, Fuquay, Irvington, and Dothan soils are present in the Bellville District. The Bellville climate is quite temperate with an approximate average January temperature of 51 degrees, while July's average is 81.[59]

The New Town

According to former Evans County historian Theodore Brewton, Bellville was built upon the lands of Pulaski Sikes Smith (1856-1894), John M. Wood (1861-1953), and Berry Brewton (1842-1911).[60] An original land plat for Bellville shows these three individuals as adjoining landowners at the Bellville location. Their belief in the benefits of the new town is indicated by their comprehensive support of the project. D.J. Brewton owned another small tract of original Bellville land, a vacant tract obtained as a grant in February of 1890. Under the guidance of these visionary men the town began with the intent of developing commerce and creating a better quality of life for the rural area.[61]

Historian Lucile Hodges explained the activity that took place with the creation of the area's new towns as follows:

> As soon as the coming of the railroad was known to be a sure thing (about 1887) and its exact course was surveyed, property owners along its proposed course began to plan for the locations and development of trade centers thereon. There was a shifting of business centers and main highways from the water courses to the railway, which drew many enterprising citizens from adjacent rural areas and other towns. Some came to take advantage of investment possibilities; to be near better schools and churches; to have a part in the excitement of building and developing a new town; or to enjoy a livelier social life than remote areas provided. Others came as part of the labor force needed at the time.[62]

Bellville's name is in honor of Pulaski Sikes Smith's grandmother, Frances Bell Smith. Not only was Sikes Smith one of the landowners at the time of Bellville's founding, he was also the first postmaster and an instrumental figure in the town's early development. Frances

Bell Smith's son, James Bell Smith, owned the old Smith home place still standing just south of the intersection of Highways 169 and 280. The structure, constructed in 1853 or 1854, is one of the oldest in Evans County. Presently covered with weatherboard siding, the house is of original hewn log construction. At one time the structure stood high off the ground, allowing for cotton bale storage underneath.[63]

A romantic explanation of the origin of the town's name is that the railroad builders named the town after its belles, or young ladies. In fact, early documents and photos of the depot show the name spelled as "Belleville." A veteran railroad man once explained that during the time the railroad was built, the local Academy was also getting under way. The boarding students swelled the number of pretty girls who frequented the railway depot for something to do. The railroaders, in turn, were so pleased with their lovely welcomers, they supposedly called the town "Belleville" in the ladies' honor. After many generations, this legend of the belles continues in Bellville, even though there is no doubt that the town, in reality, was named for Fannie Bell Smith.[64]

When the railroad laid the tracks in 1890, there were about a half dozen families in the immediate Bellville area. The Smith family, noted above, lived south of the old Dublin-Savannah Road (now Highway 280). Berry Brewton lived on the eastern edge of Bellville and sold many of the house lots north of the railroad and east of Main Street. The land he lived on was originally owned by his father, Tattnall County farmer and politician Benjamin Brewton. Now located on Warren Wilbank's farm, Berry Brewton's old home place has survived the passing of the years.[65] The John M. Wood family lived on the northwestern edge of Bellville on the old Bellville-Manassas Road; George W. Tippins (1855-1908) lived about a mile southwest of the town, near the Tattnall County Campground; and John C. "Shad" Parker (1836-1917) lived just west of Bellville on what is now known as Highway 280. The J.B. Benton family also lived in the area just west of town.[66]

Another early resident of the Bellville area was Enoch B. "Knuck" Daniel (1840-1919). After moving from Liberty County in approximately 1889, he started a sawmill. The first known business endeavor other than farming in the immediate Bellville area, the sawmill processed much of the lumber used to build the new town's houses.[67] The Daniel family's association with Bellville remains strong to the present day. Mr. Long and Mr. Watkins also operated sawmills in the area.[68]

With the onset of construction, houses and businesses sprang up quickly around the new depot. Both Sikes Smith and George Tippins were instrumental in the layout of the new town, and on August 25, 1890, surveyor A.D. Eason drew up a plan for town lots. The plan shows 38 lots, in addition to two lots previously surveyed for D.C. Newton and H.C. Long. Laid out north of the railroad, most of these lots are 105 feet wide and 220 feet deep.[69] At the same time, Sikes Smith constructed the town's first post office on the west side of Main Street. In this building, he served as the first postmaster of Bellville, from 1890 until his death from an apparent heart attack in 1894.[70]

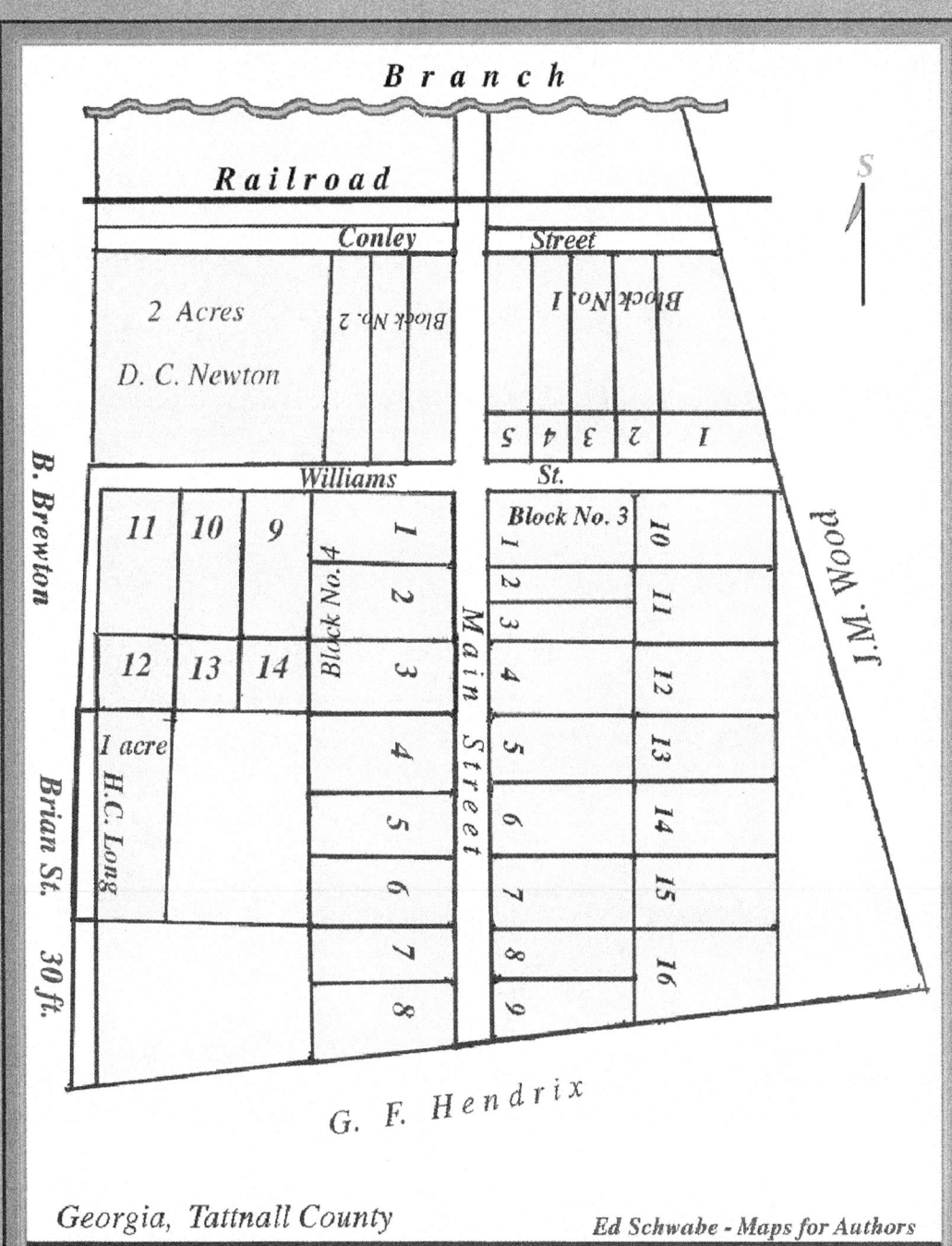

Georgia, Tattnall County

Ed Schwabe - Maps for Authors

The above plat is a true representation of the town lots on the north side of Savannah and Western Railroad at Bellville, executed by A. D. Eason, August 25th, 1890.

On the north side of the railroad, on the east side of Main Street, Berry Brewton sold house lots to Dr. Loving Nichols, P.W. Leak, Tom Leak, and Dr. Moore. He also gave a lot to his son-in-law, Wiley Rowe.[71] Rowe, a builder, constructed several houses in the new town. On other northside lots bought from Brewton, merchants built their stores in close proximity to the Savannah and Western depot (built north of the railroad and west of Main Street). Section hands lived in housing located east of the depot.[72]

D.M. Bradley and Mrs. S.W. LeGrand also purchased lots from Brewton. Just west of Main Street and north of the old Bellville-Manassas Road, Enoch B. Daniel bought his home lot from Nancy Hendricks, a large landowner in the Bellville area.[73] Southwest of Daniel's home, he located his sawmill on land purchased from J.M. Wood. Wood also sold lots to George P. Bird and Mettle Durrence on the north side of the railroad, and to Wearing Durrence, Charles Braswell, Charles Mikel, and D.F. McQuaig on the south side of the railroad.[74]

It was in 1892 that Sikes Smith donated to the school's trustees the land on which the Bellville Academy was built.[75] This school building was a two-story wooden structure. The consideration for the gift of the land was Smith's "interest for the cause of education."

Early 1900s photo of what is today the intersection of Highways 280 and 169. The James B. Smith house can barely be seen in the right center of photo. (Photo courtesy of Walter Emmett Daniel)

In addition to Sikes Smith, early supporters of the school were George Tippins, Berry Brewton, J.T. Grice, John M. Wood, E.B. Daniel, and later, C.W. Hearn.[76] The founding of the academy represented the beginning of Bellville's long association with top-notch educational institutions. During the first decade of the school's existence, the facility was the largest in Tattnall County. It boasted over 200 pupils, a large number of whom were boarding students from as far away as Savannah.[77]

The residents of the town razed the first Bellville school and built a wooden, single story building. Used until 1921, the trustees replaced this structure with a brick building in 1922. The brick school was in use until 1954, when the school board consolidated the Bellville facility with Claxton schools. Many area residents attended Bellville School over the years and fondly recall the school as an excellent one.[78]

Trustees built a house for Bellville schoolteachers east of Main Street and south of the railroad. Tom Grice, an early store owner in Bellville, chose a corner lot south of the teacher's house to build his home. Grice also served as the Bellville postmaster from 1898-1900.[79] His niece Eulalia Hearn and her husband, C.W. Hearn, later bought his home, the current location of The Anderson House restaurant.

The first Sunday School organization in Bellville goes back to the year 1890. Participants, with E.B. Daniel as superintendent and Jesse Brewton as secretary, first met in the old, two-story schoolhouse.[80]

In 1892, on lands belonging to Sikes Smith, Bellville's citizens erected their first church (Methodist Episcopal). At a cost of $1,000, George Bird and O.H. Daniel built the new wooden building. The original structure stood about 200 yards west of the current church located at the intersection of Highways 169 and 280. Its trustees were George W. Tippins, E.B. Daniel, B.G. Tippins, E.B. Daniel, J.A. Fulcher, and D.W. McQuaig.[81] Bellville Church played a very important part in the spiritual development of the town. From an original membership of 17, the church grew to over 60 by 1908. The wooden structure served the congregation until 1946, when the membership built a new brick building. The steeple was added in 1961. The social hall, erected in 1949, has been the site for community meetings since its construction.[82]

In the town's early history, Bellville also had a Baptist church for a short time. References to the Bellville Baptist Church first appeared in the Baptist Union Association minutes in 1896. The minutes list the clerk of the church as A.H. Prince, and total membership was 19.[83] The 1897 Association minutes list the annual session attendee from Bellville as A. Window. The clerk was C.D. Hyman, and the total church membership was 30. According to the minutes, Bellville Baptist Church Sunday School maintained an enrollment of 64, and the condition of the organization was listed as "good." George V. Tillman was the Sunday School superintendent, and another leader of this church was D.C. Newton.[84] The

The Story of Bellville

founders built the church in east Bellville in approximately 1896 on a lot provided by Berry Brewton. However, a severe storm blew down the building around 1897, and the members did not rebuild it.[85]

There was also a black school and Methodist Episcopal church located south of the railroad across from what is now Gold Kist, Inc. on Highway 292. Known as Wright's Chapel, Richard Wright founded the church in the early 1890s. The trustees of this church were Wesley R. Wright and John E. Burch. These leaders operated the facilities for the benefit of black residents from the nearby houses and surrounding area. Members discontinued the church after a storm demolished the building. The school operated into the 1920s.[86]

Early merchants in Bellville included D.M. Bradley, Mr. Burkensteiner, W.A. Savage, P.W. Leak, and Tootsie Alderman. Alderman, who later married Pelam Ward and moved to Brunswick, operated a millinery shop, as did Mrs. D.W. Sikes. Other merchants were J.A. Fulcher, Bert Long, G.M. Cohen, and George Tillman.[87]

In the 1890s, Bellville also had its own resident photographer, Arthur H. Prince. His business moniker was "traveling artist," and many of his early images survive today. His photographs were mostly albumen prints that he mounted on cardboard backing.[88]

```
A. H. PRINCE,
Made this Picture.
BELLEVILLE, GA.
```
Imprint from Prince Photo.

By the late 1890s many of the original merchants had sold out, moved, or died. Among the second wave of merchants was C.W. Hearn who moved from Manassas. Scott Bird had a two-department store in which he sold buggies, wagons and hardware on one side and groceries on the other. J.B. Collins owned another of Bellville's general stores.[89]

In 1898, the *Georgia Gazetteer* listed the Bellville officials and businessmen as follows:[90]

Notaries Public Ex-Officia JP's:
G.M. District 1366--M.J. Stubbs, Bellville

Justices of the Peace:
G.M. District 1366--J.T. Eason, Bellville

Post Offices:
A.S. McMillan, postmaster

Druggists:
J.J. Watkins & Co., Bellville

Grocers:
LeGrand & Son

General Merchandise:
S. Bird
Durrence & Bazemore
G.V. Tillman
J.C. McQuaig & Co.
J.J. Watkins & Co.

Sawmills:
Frank Bowers

Naval Stores Manufactures:
Carter & Co.
A.S. McMillan & Co.

As the nineteenth century came to a close Bellville's population showed significant growth. The state gazetteer lists the residents of the town and the immediate surrounding area.

Georgia State Farmer Gazetteer and Directory, 1898
Bellville, Georgia (Tattnall County)

Anderson, C.W.	DeLoach, Sarah E.	Mikell, C.
Bacon, M. (c)	DeLoach, W.H.	Moore, A.C.
Bacon, W. (c)	Foy, W.M.	Moore, M.R.
Ball, T. S. (c)	Grice, J.T.	Newton, D.C.
Barnard, Sarah L.	Hagans, T. (c)	Parker, Mrs. N.E.
Bazemore, J.S.	Hammock, J.A.	Riggs, E.T.
Bazemore, W.H. Jr.	Hammock, J.M.	Riggs, W.S.
Blocker, J.J.	Hammock, S.P.	Rogers, M.E.
Brady, Manda	Hodges, D.A.	Rogers, M.J.
Brazell, G.	Hodges, N.B.	Rogers, J.H.
Brazell, W.M.	Jenkins, J.H. & wife	Rogers, J.H., agt
Brewton, A.J.	Kennedy, B. (c)	Sikes, J.B.
Brewton, B.B.	Kennedy, D. (c)	Smith, H.G.
Brewton, J. (c)	Kennedy, J.L.	Smith, J.W., agt
Brewton, J.B. Jr.	Kennedy, J.H.	Smith, Mary S.
Brewton, W.B.	Kennedy, M.	Smith, S. (c)
Brewton, W.H.	Kennedy, S. (c)	Strickland, W.A.P.
Callaway, J.A., rec	Kennedy, W. A.	Tippins, G.W.
Crosby, J., agt	Kennedy, W. (c)	Tippins, J. (c)
Cummings, Mrs. M.E.	Lynn, R.A.	Todd, J.M.
Daniel, H.H.	McLeod, D.	Tootle, J.S.
Daniel, W.W.	Madox, C. (c)	Wells, L.T., agt
DeLoach, Eliza	Martin, J.J.	Williams, J.H.
DeLoach, J.	Mattox, E.P.	Wood, W.H.

A note following the list in the gazetteer explains that symbol (c) means "colored."

The Great Bellville Fire

The events of the night of May 6, 1901 significantly changed Bellville's history forever. This date marked the evening in which every store in town, as well as the turpentine still, burned. Although blamed on arson by blacks at the time, no definitive cause of the fire is known.[91] The *Savannah Morning News* reported the fire as "supposed to have been of incendiary origins." The account further said that the town is "now without any place to purchase any supplies whatever." The newspaper went on to say:

> About a week ago a Negro was caught in the house of Mr. Long, and was shot and killed by someone while under guard. Since that time the Negroes have been badly upset in that vicinity, and it is thought through revenge some of them sought to burn up the town. Several parties have been suspected, but as yet have not been charged.[92]

The *Statesboro News* of May 10, 1901 covered the event with details as follows:

> The fire was discovered in the store occupied by J.B. Collins & Bro. of Bellville. It spread rapidly, destroying the store houses of Bert Long, C.W. Hearn, and S. Bird, the turpentine plant operated by Carter & Co., and four vacant houses. The loss is heavy and only partly covered by insurance.

The total estimated loss from the fire was $16,000 and insurance coverage amounted to only $6,300. The *Savannah Morning News* listed the insurance proceeds as divided among Scott Bird, $2,000; Jonathan B. Collins, $2,000; C.W. Hearn, $2,300; and Carter and Co. with no insurance.[93]

Even though owners rebuilt several of the businesses, the town never regained its previous momentum for commerce. D.C. Newton and Frank McQuinn rebuilt the turpentine still in order to process the gum production from their considerable timber leases, and operated the rebuilt still until McQuinn's death in late 1901. For a period thereafter, S.A. Smith operated the still. C.W. Hearn continued to operate his gin, located south of the railroad and spared from the fire. Scott Bird rebuilt his establishment, but soon sold out to his brother, Adam Bird, and Bascom Tippins. C.W. Hearn also rebuilt his store, which would become a Bellville landmark operated by the Hearn family until 1970.[94]

J.R. Rogers was the first to build a new retail outlet after the fire. He operated the business until 1905 when he sold it to Will and George Brewton. In 1908, the two Brewton brothers sold the business to C.W. Hearn, but retained the store building. Will Brewton later reopened the store, but then moved the business to Claxton.[95]

Bert Long also reopened a small store after the fire, but operated it only for a year before selling out and moving. Another merchant, J.A. Fulcher had closed down his store before the fire and moved to Florida.[96]

Five years after the fire the town had partially rebounded. The *Cyclopedia of Georgia*, published in 1906, described Bellville as follows:

> Bellville, a town in the eastern part of Tattnall County, with a population of 300 in 1900, is about nine miles east of Collins, on the Seaboard Air Line Railroad. It has a money order post office, express and telegraph service, some good stores, and is a shipping point of some importance.[97]

A description of Bellville businesses in 1906 provided this information:

> Bellville's banking town was Hagan, and its shops and shopkeepers were: W.H. Brewton, general store; J.C. DeLoach, turpentine and general store; Z.P. Hall, general store; C.W. Hearn, general store and gin; M.Y. Overstreet (five miles from), turpentine and general store; J.A. and J.M. Sikes, sawmill.[98]

Bellville businessmen and residents pose for photo at the railroad depot around 1909. First row, *left to right:* Adam Byrd, Sam Jack Lester, Little Byrd Smith, Rags Nunnally, Stokes Bickley, Clyde Tippins. Second row, Paul LeGrand, Jim Benton, Tom Wood, Shad Parker, unidentified traveling salesman, Jimps Collins, Caughey Hearn. (Photo courtesy of Devane Parker Lewis)

Bellville Militia District

When the State Legislature cut Evans County from Tattnall and Bulloch counties in 1914, Bellville was in the 1607th Georgia Military District of Tattnall, previously part of Tattnall's 1366th.[99]

The militia district system had its origin in the Colonial Acts of 1755 and 1773, whereby the colony authorized a community or section, populated by 125 to 150 men between the

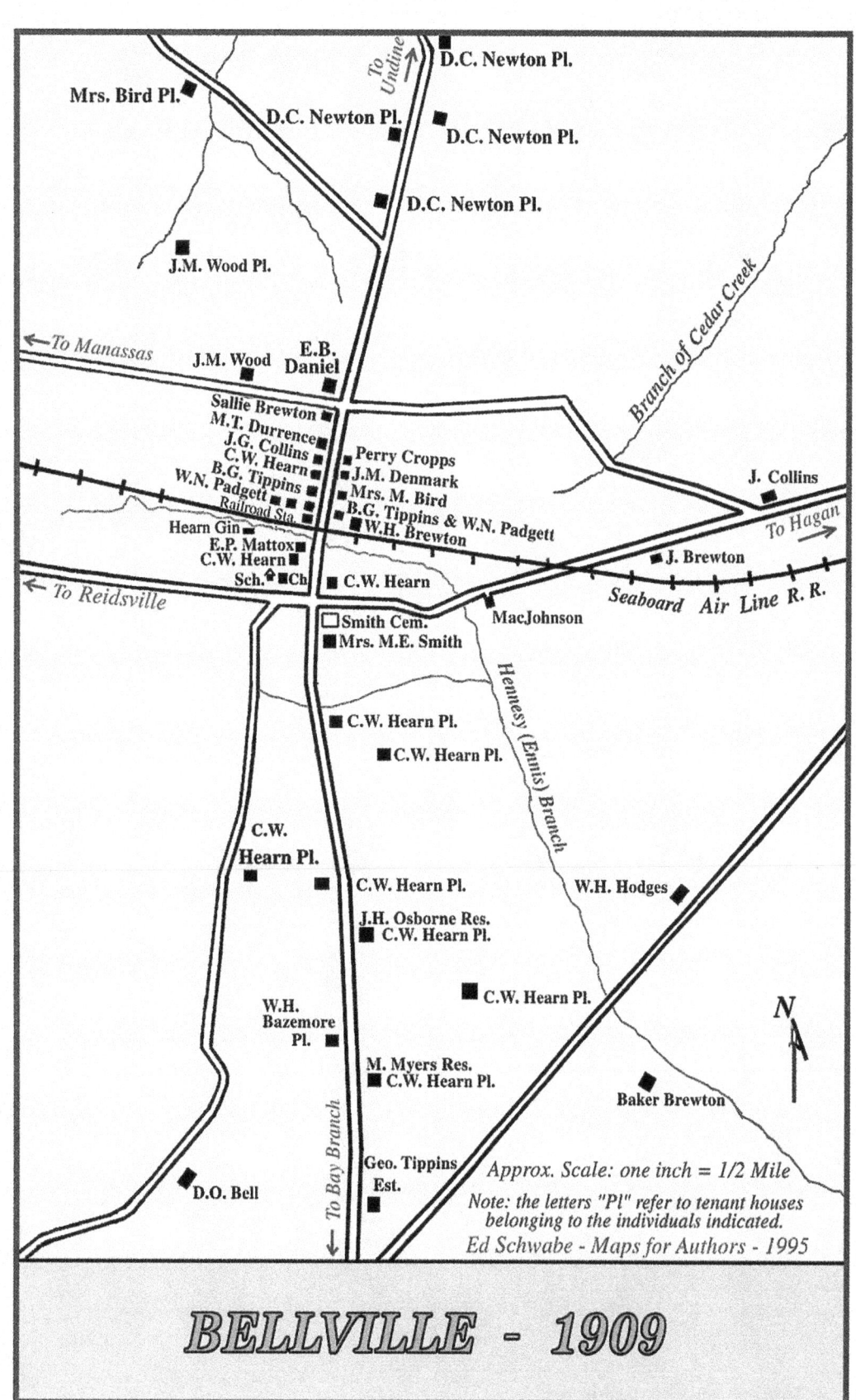

ages of 16 and 50, to have a militia under a captain.[100] These militia units originally served as protection against the Indians and civil disturbances, but they also organized as political units for holding court, collecting taxes, and voting.

The name of the 1366th District was Hawpond. Residents located the Hawpond court house at the J.B. Brewton place, about three miles north of Bellville's present location, on what is now the Metter Highway.[101]

Several of the militia district boundaries required redrawing after the creation of Evans County. One of the resultant districts was Bellville, or the 1739th. *The Claxton Enterprise* carried the following notice in February 1915.

> Notice for formation of the Bellville District, 1739: A new militia district will be established in said county on the first day of March, 1915, if no good cause is shown to the contrary, as follows: A part of the 1376th District cut from the said County of Tattnall and part of the 1607th District cut into said County from the County of Tattnall, lines to run as follows: Starting at the northwest corner of the incorporate limits of the town of Hagan, running the incorporate line south to the southwest corner of said incorporation, thence in a line running twelve degrees east of south to the Tattnall and Evans line, thence west along said County line to Rogers Crossing running north along County line to Cedar Creek, turning east and following Cedar Creek to a point on a line south of the DeLoach watermill, thence in a straight line to original starting point.
> This Feb. 15, 1915
> W.H. Brewton,
> Ordinary.

Known Bellville notaries and Justices of the Peace for District 1739 are the following: J.H. Osborn, J.P., 1915-1923; H. L. Brewton, J.P., 1924, 1937, 1942; T.J. Wood, 1925-c.1950; J.P. Rogers, 1957-1961; and Roger Wood, N.P. and J.P., 1958.[102]

Postmasters of the Bellville post office over the years include the following individuals: Pulaski Sikes Smith, 1890-1892, and 1893-1894; George W. Tippins, 1892 and 1895-1897; Joseph Grice, 1898-1899; Horace E. Leibbett, 1899;[103] Bascom Tippins, 1899-1913; Charles W. Hearn, 1913-1919; C.T. Bickley, 1919-192; H.C. Hearn 1922-1966; Ona Coleman 1966-1971; and Mildred Rogers 1971-present.[104]

County Commissioners from the Bellville District include: H.L. Brewton, 1915-1919; H.H. Daniel, 1927-1930; T.J. Wood, 1943-1950; E. Wright Daniel, 1951-1954; Winton Bell, 1955-1970, 1987-1990, 1995- present; Lex W. Strickland, 1971-1978; W.H. (Bill) DeLoach, 1979-1984; and W.V. Moore, 1985-1986, 1991-1994.[105]

1890 request to establish Bellville Post Office submitted by Pulaski S. Smith. (Courtesy National Archives)

Cotton was King

At the turn of the century, many cotton gins existed across the landscape of rural Georgia. Cotton had been an important crop in the area since before the Civil War. Bellville, boasting one of the most modern gins in southeast Georgia, was the site of considerable cotton commerce. For more than a half century after Bellville's founding, the town's economic fate was almost solely tied to the annual cotton crop, and the crop's importance would remain for many years. However, Georgia cotton production begin to fall in the 1920s, and Bellville's all-cotton economy would not flourish indefinitely.

For a significant number of years, cotton truly was king. During the 1880s, inventors had developed a much improved cotton ginning process. Those early systems ran on steam power, and the plants combined the ginning with the baling and automated cotton movement through the facility.

The Hearn cotton gin operation began in Bellville about 1899 when C.W. Hearn moved his gin and store from Manassas and set the facility up south of the railroad (behind modern-day Bellville's town hall). C.W. Hearn was the son of Amos J. Hearn, who had moved to the area prior to the Civil War.[106] Hearn's arrival in Bellville was not without incident. Shortly after moving his business to the town, he narrowly missed death when lightning struck him. He later recovered, but Buck Guy, who was standing next to him died in the accident.[107]

Early on, the cotton of choice was "Sea Island," also known as black-seed. Hearn's Davis Single Roller gin was designed to process this cotton. Manufactured in Statesboro by Dan Davis, the gin enjoyed a great reputation for efficiency.[108]

Around 1901 Hearn also installed a Munger System gin, which processed short-staple cotton. The Munger gin, equipped with two 70-saw gins, sucked the cotton by vacuum from out of a wagon. A turning brush removed the cotton from the gin saws and, via air vacuum, carried the cotton to the press. This capability established the Munger gin as one of the most modern of its kind in the Southeast.

The Hearns eventually replaced the Davis black-seed gins with Foss gins. C.W. Hearn's sons, Inman and Herschel, operated the air-suction pipe to transport the cotton into the gin. Anything in the way of the pipe, including hats and handkerchiefs, went into the gin and came out in shreds. Employees at the facility often worked extended hours of up to 16 hours a day.[109]

In the early days, the average yield for the short-staple cotton was a half bale an acre. Sea Island would average a bale per every three to four acres. The ginning time for the short-staple was 30 to 40 minutes per bale, while the Sea Island product took about an hour a bale.[110] At least one local boy, Thurmon Smith, could pick over 300 pounds of cotton on good days.[111]

The farmers first used the extracted cotton seeds for planting, cattle feeding, and fertilizer. However, after cotton-seed oil became a valuable commodity, farmers traded the seeds' value to offset the cost of ginning.

In 1917, Hearn re-located from the south side of the railroad and installed the new 4-70 saw gin across the railroad in the location where the Claxton Bank branch sits today. This gin continued to operate with steam power. Hearn also operated a grist and rice mill on the premises of the gin. Local farmers, for private use, often grew brown rice in the low, wet areas of their land.[112]

By 1919, due to boll weevil infestation in their fields, local farmers reduced production of Sea Island cotton. The boll weevil made its trek from Mexico. Therefore, counties to the south and west felt the ravages before Evans County became infested. In 1917, one area farmer complained, "The boll weevils have eaten up one-half of my cotton crop this year and are now scattering out all over the country."[113] Since short-staple cotton was more resistant to the weevil, it made a rapid rise in acres planted.

Still, boll weevil infestation and depletion of the over-used soil caused devastating economic times in the early 1920s. In addition to the destruction caused by arrival of the insect, declining prices, depression, war, government farm programs, and alternative employment opportunities all contributed to the decline in cotton's popularity.[114]

When Mr. Hearn died in 1921, his sons, "Cap," Herschel, and Inman took over the operation as the hard economic times of the early 1920s brought the problems of the traditional cotton cash-crop system to the forefront. Yet, by 1924, a *Savannah Morning News* article of October 23 reported:

> After three years of crop failure and boll weevil destruction, the farmers of Evans County "came back" this year with one of the largest crops in the history of the county. From a little above 2,000 bales of cotton ginned in the county last year, farmers harvested about 4,000 this year, or about the same size crop that had been made before the advent of the boll weevil.[115]

As the late 1930s arrived the county found itself on the road to recovery, with more crop diversification, better roads, demise of the sharecropping system, and an improved quality of life for many people.[116]

After World War II, the ginning process changed considerably. Not only were electric motors in widespread use at the gins, but mechanical harvesters automated the process of picking cotton. The hand-picked cotton season often ran from late summer until December, whereas the mechanical picking season required only about six weeks.

Cotton continued as the area's primary cash crop until the 1960s. By then, several factors combined to contribute to its demise. A loss of foreign markets to overseas competition, trade imbalance problems with traditional foreign cotton buyers, and domestic social and economic conditions drove rural workers from the farms into the cities. By 1950, Georgia's cotton production was 80 per cent lower than in the peak crop year of 1916.[117] By the mid-1950s, with a severe shortage of laborers to pick the crop, cotton had an unpredictable future.

When the gin burned in 1943, the Hearns replaced it with a more modern one. However, in 1963, they finally sold out to Stanley and Pughsley of Lyons, Georgia. The new owners changed the name of the operation to the Bellville Gin Company, but it continued under the management of Inman Hearn until 1970 when the owners closed the establishment. According to Hearn the gin operated until "farmers just quit growing cotton."[118]

Cotton made no significant return to prominence until the 1990s, when it regained its status as "king" in Evans County. Bellville farmers also returned to the staple. For example, Winton Bell and his sons grew over 650 acres of cotton in 1995.[119]

Advertisements for Hearn's Store and Cotton Gin.

Area Farmers Diversify

With cotton's demise, diversification of crops was essential. A dilemma arose in determining which crops could compete with the dominance once claimed by cotton. Bellville farmers found the answer primarily in tobacco and peanuts.

It was the boll weevil which first caused farmers to give tobacco a try, and by 1924, Evans County growers farmed 1,000 acres.[120] Mac Johnson, a North Carolina native, was one of the first to grow the leaf in the Bellville area. By the late 1920s tobacco had become Georgia's second most important cash crop, and Bellville farmers continued to increase acreage. To ensure continued freight revenue, the railroad promoted this diversification.

In the early days, tobacco was a very labor-intensive crop. Some local farmers joked that it took 13 months a year to grow including cultivation, harvesting, curing, and marketing. Farmers picked the ripe leaves over a period of five or six weeks. They put the leaves on narrow sleds pulled by mules to a location where women and children strung the leaves on sticks. They then hung the leaves in a heated barn to cure. After curing, workers put the tobacco in small bundles to form big round sheets to take to market. Tobacco growing, however, had its perils. The tobacco barns were vulnerable to fire, crops sometimes got too much or too little rain, and insect pests were often a problem. Nonetheless, flue-cured tobacco was an important cash crop for many Bellville area farmers.[121]

A *Claxton Enterprise* article of 1939 summed up tobacco cultivation with the following observation:

> From the middle of December, when the seed beds are planted, until late July, the lot of the tobacco grower and his family is one of hard work, early and late; but no one seems to mind the work for the returns in August are usually large enough to make everyone feel well paid for their time.[122]

The boll weevil, as well as high World War I prices for vegetable oil, prompted Bellville area farmers to further diversify by growing peanuts. Originally most farmers who produced peanuts used them to feed their hogs. However, improved machinery for harvesting and increased knowledge of the peanut's food value provided increased incentives for production of this crop.

Another commodity shipped in large quantities from Bellville was watermelons, up to 100 cars per year in the 1920s. However, increased railroad freight rates greatly reduced profits and production of melons plummeted. These rates, which were more expensive shipping south to north than in the reverse direction, were the source of much irritation to local farmers.[123]

Mechanization started in the area in the second decade of the twentieth century. In 1919 Jot Collins was one of the first farmers to use tractors. Tractors were more widely accepted in the mid-1920s and use of mules gradually began to phase out. Collins also had a two-row cultivator in operation by 1925. Large irrigation systems came into existence in the late 1940s.[124]

Tomatoes also played importantly in the history of Bellville area agriculture. Residents planted tomatoes in their gardens for many years. However, there was no market because this vegetable was highly perishable. Then someone discovered that if the tomatoes were picked while green and carefully packed in shipping boxes, the tomatoes would ripen about the time they reached market via truck or rail. By the late 1930s, however, high freight rates and earlier ripening tomatoes in the West began to reduce profitability of tomato farming significantly.

Beginning in 1935, local farmers H.C. and Inman Hearn also grew tomato plants on their Bellville farm for transshipment, often shipping the plants as far away as Virginia and Maryland. The plants were state inspected and certified to insure they were disease and insect free. The Hearn tomato plants enjoyed a fine reputation throughout the area in which farmers planted them.[125]

Tomato plant cultivation on the Hearn farm in the 1950s. *From left:* Marcus Strickland and Elbert Aron. (Photo courtesy Emily Hearn Groover)

This tomato plant growing operation employed up to 200 part-time workers a day. Many old-time residents of Bellville today remember the process of "pulling" the young tomato plants. Laborers put the plants in bundles of 50. The plants reached the Bellville packing shed by truck where damp moss was applied to the roots. Workers then tied the bundles with a pre-cut piece of paper and rubber band. Packers placed the bundles in wooden "pony" baskets with about 400-500 plants per basket. The Hearns then shipped the plants north by rail or refrigerated trucks. Over the years, the Hearns shipped millions of plants in this manner. However, in 1961 tomato plant farming came to an end due to competition from Japanese and other overseas tomato exports.[126]

A 1940 *Savannah Morning News* article had this to say about Bellville's agricultural success:

> Bellville, on the western edge of the county, is a center for producing fine cotton, tobacco, naval stores and lumber, together with many other crops. It was in the Bellville section that the growing of tomatoes for shipment was first developed into commercial proportions.[127]

Soybeans were another important diversification crop. Research revealed that farmers could double their crop land by planting both soy beans and oats or winter wheat in a single year. New varieties of soybeans, less susceptible to weather and insect damage appeared, and Bellville area farmers were on their way to an important substitute for the once all-important cotton. According to local accounts, Inman Hearn was the first farmer in this area to experiment with soybean production.[128]

Pecans also became an important supplemental crop for some area farmers. Beecher Smith provided pecan tree seedlings from his nursery in the 1920s.[129] In addition, he cultivated grapes of superior quality.

Livestock became an important income supplement to row crops. By the mid-1950s, 40 per cent of Georgia's farm production, and one-third of cash income, came from livestock. Bellville farmers also diversified into livestock to reduce the risk associated with their traditional farming methods. English Smith and his sons were notable cattle producers in the Bellville area.[130]

Bellville area farmers followed the trend of the state as cattle, soybeans, peanuts, and other crops replaced cotton as the staple that dominated the area since the town's founding.

Bellville's Naval Stores

The naval stores industry was an important element in Bellville's development. D.C. Newton and D.O. Carter began a turpentine still soon after the founding of the town. Originally located in the proximity of where the Claxton Bank branch now sits, Newton surrounded his still with five or six small houses which he built for his turpentine workers, both black and white.[131]

The "chipper" stood to the side of the tree when using the bark hack. He used a pulling or peeling motion and did not hack or chop into the wood. (Photo courtesy Georgia Agricultural Extension Service)

The main naval stores products are rosin and turpentine. The term "naval" comes from the fact that shipbuilders used these materials to waterproof and seal vessels. Workers performed as "chippers" by periodically reopening the slashes in the pine bark, and as "dippers" when they emptied the collection boxes every week and a half or so. Nearby stills, such as the one in Bellville, cooked the product and produced turpentine spirits and rosin. After transferring the product to barrels, the turpentiners sent their product by rail and later trucks to Savannah, the leading U.S. naval stores transshipment point from 1880 to 1920.[132] Prior to the railroad, turpentine producers hauled their product to Savannah by wagon.

Turpentine stills were a part of the Bellville landscape for many years, since "turpentining" was one of the first and most important industries in the area. In addition to the first still operated by Newton (later owned by S.A. Smith), a second still was located west of Main Street and just south of the railroad.[133] Glenn DeLoach, father of Judge Harry DeLoach, operated this still and then sold it to T. J. "Tom" Wood in 1932. The still remained in operation until about 1944 when Wood moved it to a location south of the railroad and east of Main Street where he operated it until the mid-1960s when the business closed.[134] Remnants of the turpentine operation are still visible today.

Although the turpentine business eventually collapsed, as late as 1939 Tom Wood was optimistic that the industry would make a comeback. A *Claxton Enterprise* interview with Wood concluded:

> Despite the disastrous drop in price of turpentine and rosin, he [Tom Wood] feels that rightly handled, this great industry will come into its own again within a few years, and that people will eventually learn that there is no substitute for turpentine in paint that is quite so satisfactory and serviceable as the product of the pine tree. He believes also that new uses will eventually be found for spirits and gum and that in the years to come that demand will be as much as the industry has capacity to produce. You cannot forsake an industry that has contributed so much wealth back to the citizens of the county just because it is backward at present. Through faith in turpentine and lumber, many have been enabled to secure a livelihood, and a continuance of this faith will bring about stability in the future.[135]

Unfortunately, Tom Wood's predictions did not materialize. The industry's decline continued as a result of diminishing pine forests, and more importantly, new chemical processes which produced turpentine as a by-product of paper production.

The sights and sounds of turpentine stills were long familiar around Bellville. Workers made a booming sound with almost a chant-like cadence as they pounded slats together making the wooden barrels. These sounds often greeted residents with the early morning sunrise. Local folks used a residue from the still called "dross" to start their wood stove fires in winter, and use of this substance was known to be the best way to get a quick, hot fire. Turpentine stills operated in Bellville for most of this century, forming an important part of the town's history.[136]

Continued Development

Many former, old-time residents of Bellville remember the town in terms of its once-present country stores. Much nostalgia surrounds these "institutions." Although many of the original stores burned in the great Bellville fire, country stores prevailed as an integral part of the town's history. Among the later store owners of prominence were C.W. Hearn, Adam Bird, Bascom Tippins, and Tom Wood. Their establishments provided services such as farmers' markets; credit, medicine, and small luxury sources; advice sources; gossip and tale-telling locations, and newscenters. The stores' front porches in the summer and their pot-bellied stoves in the winter were among the favorite gathering spots in the community, and, since banks were scarce, the credit provided by store owners was life-sustaining to many residents.

Hearn Store advertisement from 1902.

In 1922, Tom Wood opened his store located just north of where the Bellville City Hall is today. He later bought the Adam Bird store building and moved north of the railroad.[137] Wood's mercantile business carried groceries, hardware, work clothing, and family supplies. He also operated a freight truck from Savannah that served the entire area. Wood later entered politics and represented Evans County in the Georgia State Senate in 1955/56.[138]

Located north of the train depot, "Cap" Hearn's store (H.C. Hearn and Co.) carried hardware and farm equipment. The store also stocked clothing and groceries. Charlie W. Hearn, "Cap's" father, originally moved his business here from Manassas about 1899. The west side of the store building served as the Bellville Post Office. Grace Flanigan, who came to Bellville to teach, soon caught the eye of the local merchant, and she and Cap were married in 1924. Miss Grace recalls, "He was just waiting for the right girl to come along, but in the meantime, he was busy with his store which sold everything from harnesses to calico." She continued to teach a few years until she gave it up to work full time at the store and post office.[139]

The *Claxton Enterprise* described the Hearn store as follows:

> A modern general store is operated where a most complete stock of groceries, hardware and other merchandise is handled. On your next visit to

Bellville, drop into Hearn's store and look over their stock. It will surprise you to find such a large variety. Housewives are invited to drop in, if buying or only just looking around.[140]

Bellville was also the site of a car dealership for several years. A local merchant, Bascom G. Tippins, Sr., was a dealer in Overland and Brush automobiles, and set up his store north of the railroad on the site later occupied by the T.J. Wood building.[141] Bascom Tippins became one of Bellville's most famous sons. He represented Evans County in the Georgia General Assembly for 12 years, from 1922 to 1934, and served as president of the First National Bank of Claxton for about 10 years.[142] During Tippins' era, candidates visited every part of the county shaking hands, kissing babies, and giving roadside speeches to anyone who would listen. Known as "Tip" to everyone, Tippins was an adept politician, and helped in the development of Bellville as well as the entire county and state.[143]

Bascom Tippins represented Evans County in the Georgia Legislature for 12 years. Tippins did much to improve the roads and conditions in the county. (1932 photo courtesy of Mary Tippins Conner)

The town's earliest doctors were a Dr. Moore and Dr. Loving Nichols. Dr. Moore died soon after arriving in Bellville. When Dr. Nichols arrived in the area, he first boarded in the Bay Branch section at the home of William W. Daniel.[144] He eventually married one of Daniel's daughters, Mattie, and maintained his office and a drug store in the Bay Branch area for a number of years. He then moved to Bellville in the early 1890s to practice medicine in the new town. Other doctors in Bellville included Dr. Watkins and later, A.I. Hendry, from Liberty County.[145]

For many years, the town's life continued to revolve around the railroad, with the depot as the center of activity. The town's people regularly greeted the train and monitored arrivals, departures, and cargo activities. As Lucile Hodges described in her county history:

> Large steam engines pulling loads of crossties, lumber, cotton and naval stores wound their way through this woodsy country and stirred the adventurous ones to get on board when they could and see something of the outside world--a jaunt to a nearby town or a day trip to Savannah was high adventure. And for those who were not going anywhere, the passing of the

train was time to give pause, to admire the daring workmen walking atop the cars, to listen to the signal sound of the great locomotives and to share in the excitement of the rumbling cars. And when the great monsters took on water in the towns....it was something to see.[146]

The World War I period brought prosperity to local farmers as they benefited from the higher prices paid for their products. For example, cotton sold for up to the unheard of price of $1 a pound.[147] Georgia sent over 93,000 men to the war, and Bellville provided its fair share. Among those serving from the area were Thomas Beal, Jesse J. Boyette, Wade H. Brewton, Henry C. Brewton, Henry C. Hearn, Alex D. Mikell, E. Watson Newman, Alphus B. Nunally, and Thomas J. Wood.[148]

The year 1918 ushered in what seemed to be improved conditions for the Bellville area as well as the remainder of the county. The local paper carried the following pronouncement.

> Go where you will and you see improvements being made to farms, homes, and land, and every other evidence for industry, progress, and advancement. Some one-half million dollars of cotton is yet held by growers and better still are the overflowing corn cribs, smoke houses, and all else for man and beast.[149]

Improvements continued in 1919. Even though several of the Bellville boys were off to war, things at home were prosperous. As the "Bellville News" portion of *The Claxton Enterprise* proclaimed on April 18th:

> We are sure having fine weather. The farmers here are very busy these days.
> C.W. Hearn made a business trip to Savannah Saturday.
> Lee Daniel, Misses Dame and Williams motored to Statesboro Saturday, also to Reidsville, and Glennville on Sunday.
> C.L. Daniel and family spent Sunday with Mr. and Mrs. Herschel Durrence.
> W.H. Bazemore, of the Bay Branch neighborhood had a misfortune with his little boy, while trying to climb over a gate, he fell, crashing him to the ground, though no broken bones.
> Our post master's mother has been real feeble for 2 or 3 weeks in Talbot Co. She has passed her 93rd milepost along the journey of life.
> Paul LeGrand caught two extra large rats Monday night in a trap.
> An interesting event of the past week was a program rendered by the Pythian Society of the Bellville High School on Friday afternoon, April 11th.
> The following are the names of pupils deserving places on the honor roll of Bellville High School for the week ending 4-11: Nina Lee Osborne, Roger

Wood, Cora Bell Brewton, Lonnie Brewton, Harold Parker, and Willie Todd.[150]

In January of 1919, Bellville residents had their first occasion to view an airplane at close range. The planes were apparently using the nearby railroad track as a navigation aid. Due to maintenance problems, an airplane force-landed in a vacant field, approximately where Pinewood School stands today. The first plane damaged its propeller when it touched ground. A second plane, flying with the one in distress, also landed. Arrival of a replacement propeller took three or four days, a period in which quite an air of excitement grew in not only Bellville, but the whole county.[151]

With the new propeller finally in place, a great crowd of spectators assembled to watch the planes depart. Unfortunately, during the takeoff the first plane hit an automobile and then a fence at the end of the field. A local teacher from Claxton, Janie Beasley, was injured when she fell from the fence during the commotion. A January 17, 1919 article in *The Claxton Enterprise* described the incident as follows:

> "Airplane Wrecked - Young Lady Hurt, Miss Janie Beasley Narrowly Escapes Death" Miss Janie Beasley, teacher in Claxton School, while out viewing airplanes which were forced to land near Bellville was painfully, if not seriously injured Saturday, when one of the planes, in attempting to rise in flight struck an auto and demolishing it, hit the fence where Miss Beasley had been sitting, her having fallen off, wrecking the plane so it was forced to be taken down and shipped to Americus to be repaired.
>
> Miss Beasley was reported at first to be dangerously wounded, but physicians have hopes of her recovery.[152]

In the 1920s and early 1930s, Bellville was the site of considerable mule trading. William Davis, from North Georgia, purchased the mules in Atlanta and other North Georgia stockyards and brought the animals down on the train.[153] Residents formed a human "fence row" on both sides of the path leading from the railroad cars to the mule lot owned by C.W. Hearn and located behind Mrs. King's house. The mules were then off-loaded from the cars across the road and into the lot, which is behind the present Bernie Anderson house. Davis also served as a layman veterinarian and freely gave advice on mule welfare.[154] In comparison to a horse, a mule could work in hotter weather, thrive with less care, and prove less skittish. Accordingly, Bellville farmers placed great stock in their mules and trading became as much art as science.

The decade of the 1930s marks the time when the United House of Prayer located a church on the western edge of Bellville. Bishop "Sweet Daddy" Grace founded this church for blacks. He purchased the land for the church from Inman Hearn. Bishop Grace's periodic appearances at the church created quite a stir in the community. Wherever he went, gifts of cash awaited him. He traveled in a Cadillac, and was often surrounded by followers in long, bright gowns. Bishop Grace was easily recognized because of his flowing robes, gray curly hair, long fingernails, and unique mustache. White folks were welcome to attend the services, and many of today's older Bellville residents recall doing so. The Bellville United House of Prayer thrives to this day.[155]

In the old days roads were poor and what little maintenance they received came from neighborhood men working one or two days twice a year on "road duty." The first road paved in the county, constructed in 1933, passed through Bellville. The state began acquiring right of way for this road in 1931. It constructed this highway under the State Aid Road System of Georgia as provided by Acts of the General Assembly in 1919 and 1921. The road, part of the old Dublin-Savannah Road passing through Mt. Vernon, Reidsville, and coming through Bellville and Claxton on to Savannah, later became known as Highway 280. Some local maps also denote this road as the Jeff Davis Highway. Its trace is evident on original land grants of the area dating to 1811. At one time residents referred to the highway as the Reidsville to Savannah Public Road and before that as old stage route 30.[156]

The county began paving Highway 169 in the late 1930s. The state obtained most of the rights of way in 1938. The State Highway Department managed construction of this road as a State Aid Road System project. The portion from Bellville south to the county line was known as the Bellville-Mendes Road and the part north of the town as the Bellville-Undine Road. Even though the project began in 1938, it was not completed until 1954. The state then repaved the road in 1959 and brought it in compliance with federal standards.[157]

The state built Highway 292, the last of the three highways that go through Bellville, in 1953. The Highway Department obtained the rights of way in 1952.

Tom Wood and Wright Daniel were instrumental in the development of these roads. Winton Bell succeeded these men as county commissioner and continued improvement of the Bellville area highways. The roads provided better access for the area's residents as well as greater opportunity for economic development.

Theodore Brewton provided the following account of those who helped build the roads in the Bellville section:

> We have been fortunate in having a number of capable and efficient men elected County Commissioners from our district [Bellville], who have helped wonderfully in locating and securing rights of way, and building our highways, and maintaining them. Among them were and are: H.H. Daniel, Wright Daniel, T.J. Wood, and Winton Bell. All these have worked in harmony with the other good men of the area who served from other parts of the county.[158]

The Second World War

The World War II economy brought higher prices for agricultural products and returned prosperity to the area after the depression of the 1930s. Bellville men, as well as those throughout the nation, responded to the emergency by joining our country's armed forces. According to a plaque in Bellville Church, those serving from the area were the following:[159]

Ambrose, Eugene	Crumpton, William D.	Richey, Billy
Bell, Dan	Daniel, Cecil K.	Riggs, Joe H.
Bell, Ernie W.	Daniel, Jr., O. Hines	Riggs, Matha M.
Bell, Jack W.	Daniel, Sid	Riggs, Lamar
Benton, Bob	Denton, Wallace	Rogers, Edwin
Brewton, E.R.	Duncan, Leonard	Rogers, Lawton H.
Brewton, M. Dan	Evans, Nolan	Rogers, Sue Nell
Brewton, W. Ralph	Evans, Thurmond	Shepard, Charles W.
Clark, Johnny	Hearn, Charles W.	Smith, Clarence L.
Coley, Jr., Lee	Hearn, H. Coy, Jr.	Smith, Dewit C.
Colson, Harry D.	Jenkins, Walter	Smith, Dorsey
Cooper, Charles	Johnson, Charles, Jr.	Smith, J. Wallace
Cooper, Herschel	Johnson, Sidney	Smith, Joseph W.
Crumpton, K. Pruit	Morris, James H.	Styles, Roy R. (Bobby)
Crumpton, Samuel F.	Morris, Paul	Tippins, Bascom, Jr.
Crumpton, Wamond A.	Morris, Prather	

The folks back home during WW II were very concerned for the welfare of the area's soldiers. For example, in 1943 the Reverend Roy Styles, principal at Bellville School, wrote the following letter to the Bellville area servicemen and women:[160]

> I hope that you liked the other letter, even though I have not heard from very many of you as yet. I am trying to get another on the way to be sure that you get a letter from some person other than your homefolks; not that it will be so interesting, but will let you know that people are thinking of you.
>
> One of the first things that we heard over the radio that helped us all to be thankful, was the news that Tokyo had felt the weight of our new B-29s; this gave us all in America a thrill. We had been expecting it, but to come on Thanksgiving Day was real cheerful to us here; it all adds up to one thing, that is, it won't be as long as it used to be.
>
> Since we wrote you the last letter we have had our campaign for the enrollment of the Junior Red Cross in the schools, and I had several rooms that went 100% and all the rooms went over the top. This is just another case to show you fellows that the kid brother or the kid sister is doing all they can to help you out there to win as fast as you can for they want you back with them.

Now as we enter the Christmas Season, many of you will be able to get home for the holidays, while many others will not. It is to the ones who will not be able to be home, that I am especially sending these last few lines.

The following prayer is one that Brother Crumpton wrote for me to send you. "To thee, O God, do we pray for the members of our armed forces today. We beseech thee, our Father, to remember and bless our boys and girls wherever they are--whether on the land, in the air, on the water or beneath the water--that thou wouldst watch over them and care for them. We pray for our leaders and for those in authority, and for our Generals who lead our armies on the far-flung battle front. We thank thee for the successes which thou has given them, and pray thee, that thou will lead them on to VICTORY."

Roy T. Styles

One young man from the Bellville area, First Lieutenant John Daniel, lost his life in the service of his country. He was flying a P-51 Mustang aircraft over the North Sea on July 26, 1944, one mile off the shore of Holmpton, England, when another American plane collided with his. Daniel, a graduate of the University of Georgia in 1939, was by all accounts an outstanding young man. His tragic death is an example of a local boy's giving the ultimate sacrifice for his homeland.[161]

First Lieutenant John Daniel. (1944 photo courtesy of Loulie Perkins)

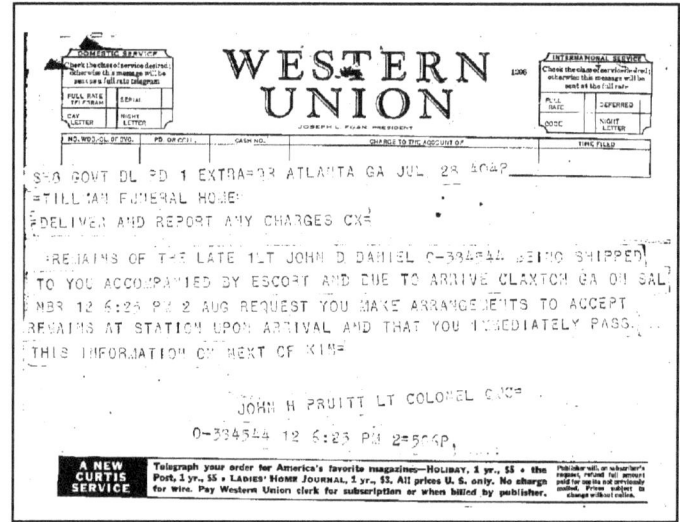
War Department telegram sent to the Daniel family.

Members of the Bellville Methodist Church showed their patriotism by buying a defense bond during the war. A document in the records of Bellville Church reveals the following annotation:

> We the undersigned of Bellville Methodist Sunday School Class number five have given to the Secretary of our class, Miss Mae Hearn, the amount

opposite our names toward buying a defense bond that will mature in 12 years. At the date of maturity the money from this bond is to be used for a building fund or a repair fund for the Bellville Methodist Church. The teacher of the class at the time this bond was sponsored was Roy Styles. Signed: Louise Thompson, Louise Powell, Emily Goff, Sallie Riggs, Margaret Daniel, Pearl Burch, Mae Hearn, C.B. Smith, Martha Hearn, Roy Styles, Roger Wood, Emily Wood, Cecil Daniel, I.C. Hearn, Marie Smith, Mary Thrift, W.E. Daniel, Mrs. W.E. Daniel, H.K. Nease, and Mrs. D.D. Daniel.[162]

The government created nearby Ft. Stewart as a training area in 1940. Although the social and economic costs were great from the displacement of families from that region, the post provided new employment opportunities and several Bellville area residents obtained work there.[163] Some families, forced to leave their homes moved from the Ft. Stewart area to Bellville.

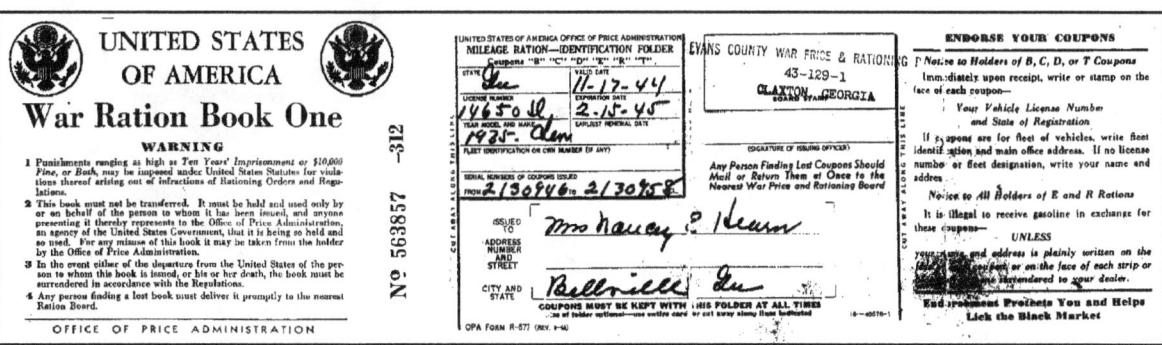

War Ration Book for Bellville resident Nancy Eulalia Hearn.

Social Development

History is more than a record of names and dates. It includes a study of the social and cultural development of our society. The Bellville area provides a rich heritage in the ways and institutions of southern folks, and in this section, we examine some of Bellville's traditions and community development.

Area residents worked hard on their farms during the week. On Saturday afternoons, however, it was time to head to town. By mid-afternoon, Bellville was crowded with those who had come to buy supplies and socialize. For many, these activities continued into the evening. The Hearn store, for example, often stayed open as late as midnight. Supper typically consisted of sardines, "rat" cheese, and soda crackers, washed down with Coca-Colas or other carbonated drinks.[164] Socializing took the form of visiting with one another, discussing the current crop outlook, or exchanging the latest gossip. There was always, of course, the opportunity to meet the train and see who arrived and departed as one was learning the news of the day.

Entertainment was informal. The young boys often played ball on the big stretch of sand in Bellville. Egg and watermelon snitching was a high art for the boys, and the ultimate fun was to boil the eggs in a tin can down by the Ennis Branch.[165]

One form of entertainment was to observe the periodic marches of soldiers through Bellville. In the 1930s, Army troops would march through the town on their way from Ft. Screven, on Tybee Island, to Ft. Benning, near Columbus, Georgia. Their route took them along what is now Highway 280, and Bellville was a convenient stopping point. They camped between the school and Nollie Parker's home, and the hustle and bustle of the Army campsite fascinated the youth of Bellville.[166]

Bellville residents Carolus Daniel and Eloise Mercer during their "sparking" days of the late 1930s. They pose next to a vehicle belonging to a member of the Piney Woods Rooters, a local band. (Photo courtesy of Elouise Hodges)

Women had quilting bees, and young and old gathered for Halloween festivals, cane grindings, peanut boilings, and watermelon cuttings. These events offered the opportunity for conversation, fellowship, and courtship among the young. The John M. Wood home was the site of many of these social functions. Folks held a banjo or fiddle player in high regard, since most country people have always enjoyed music. A local band, called the Piney Woods Rooters, was much in demand to play at local events in the late 1930s and 1940s. The band even played on WTOC radio in Savannah. Among the members of this group over the years were Hearn Lumpkin, Samps Cooper, Charles and Herschel Cooper, Gordon Baggs, Ashton Lanier, and H.M. Tippins. Winton Bell and his brother Dan also played with the group on several occasions.[167]

Country people take care of each other. In times of sickness neighbors usually helped by tending the crops of those who were ill. Other family emergencies were generally met with the help and support of neighbors. For example, even though Bellville never had a formal fire department, residents responded to fires with all sorts of impromptu measures including bucket and wash pan brigades. When local store break-ins occurred, it was not unusual for nearby residents to show up with weapons in hand ready to apprehend the culprits.[168]

The Bellville Church was a mainstay of religious and social life in the town. Sunday School, held in the afternoons, was often taught by Bellville's schoolteachers. Special Sundays called for dinner on the grounds. Fried chicken, ham, biscuits, cornbread, vegetables, pies and cakes were the fare of the day. Church song fests were also very popular. However, according to some long-time residents, the social highlight of the year was the Bellville Church Christmas program and party.[169] Held at the church on Christmas Eve, this program was always an elaborate affair. The centerpiece of the church became a big holly tree chosen and cut especially for the event. Children received gifts, and Bellville area residents welcomed the opportunity to share the holiday with their family, friends, and neighbors.

Basketball was a prominent sport in the 1920s, and even later. It did not seem possible for the Bellville boys to ever tire of it. In fact, several championship basketball teams originated from the town. In 1923 the Bellville High School basketball team made it to the Savannah YMCA tournament after winning 17 straight games. The Bellville team beat Sylvania in the tournament, but later fell at the hands of much larger Savannah High. Herschel Hearn and Bobby Benton were the stars of the team that included C.C. Daniel, Hogan Brewton, and Wallace Smith. The *Savannah Morning News* characterized the boys' play as "splendid" and included the following observation: "The uncanny ability of Benton at looping the ball through the basket with overhand shots, many from difficult angles, was one of the features of the day's play." The accomplishments of the Bellville boys were even greater because they had no substitutes and were unaccustomed to playing on a gym floor.[170]

Two Bellville teachers, Evelyn Williams and Mary Buxton Daniel pose for a snapshot in 1941. The C.W. Hearn home is in the background on the left. (Photo courtesy Eliose Hodges)

Beginning around 1904, free rural delivery of mail greatly helped the residents living around Bellville.[171] Although the Bellville post office had been in place since 1890 and was easily accessible to town residents, individuals on the surrounding area farms had to come to town to pick up their mail. Rural delivery meant Savannah newspapers, advertising flyers, and mail were now available on a daily basis. This service also opened up mail order opportunities for sales from such sources as the Sears and Roebuck catalog, a familiar sight on local farmsteads.

In the early twentieth century, new-fangled, energy-saving devices became more prevalent in Bellville. At first, there were only two telephones. One was at the railroad depot and the other at the Hearn store. Telephones soon became a way to summon doctors in times of sickness or handle other matters of importance. Residents located on the farms south of town had their own local phone system to connect them with the Hearn store.[172]

Electric lights were first powered by small Delco generator plants fueled by kerosene. Electricity from Georgia Power came to Bellville beginning in 1927/1928. However, rural electrification by the Canoochee Electric Membership Corporation (CEMC) of the area surrounding Bellville did not occur until the late 1930s. English G. Smith, from the Bellville area, served as the first president of the board of CEMC from 1938-1940.

Electricity revolutionized daily life with the benefits of incandescent lights, radios, running water and indoor toilets, and refrigeration. Although most initial house wiring called only for naked light bulbs on a wires hung down from high ceilings, electricity eventually became a tremendous convenience to all. Rural electrification improved quality of life for Bellville residents as well as other communities across the state. The first known Bellville house with indoor plumbing was built by Delma Daniel in 1930, and the first electric water pumps were at the homes of O.H. Daniel and Bascom Tippins, Sr.[173]

As the 1950s approached, rural life changed. Churches played a less dominant role, and membership declined. Cars and improved roads made it more convenient for rural folks to travel, and many of Bellville's residents began to commute to work in locations more distant from the town. When the last traditional country store closed in Bellville in 1970, many citizens felt the event marked a giving way to a more urban age.[174]

One of the most active current-day organizations in Bellville is the Lions Club. Organized in 1984, this club is service oriented and promotes civic and community interests. Fund raising events help blind and hearing impaired individuals worldwide. The Bellville Lions Club was one of the first to admit female members, with Emily Groover serving as a past president.[175] The charter members of this club are as follows:

John Hamner	David Groover	Alan Groover
Howard Scarbrough	Jimmy Rogers	James Duron Sapp
Bill Pryor	Bernie Anderson	John Daniel
Rommie Thompson	Lamar Hendrix	Ostelle Smith
Paul Riggs	David DeLoach	Joe Riggs
John Paul Riggs, Jr.	Billy Stewart	Bobby McCoy
Gary Bell	Rev. Bob Norwood	L.W. Bush

Pinewood Academy

The town of Bellville has been known for its educational institutions since its inception. From the old Bellville Academy to today's Pinewood Christian Academy, education has always been a priority.[176] Indeed, Pinewood Academy has become one of Bellville's strongest anchors.

Credit for Pinewood's concept goes to Dr. Charles H. Drake, a Glennville physician.[177] From the turmoil of the late 1960s, Drake had a vision to found a school based on academic excellence, American values, morals and ethics, and Christianity. Dr. Drake conferred with the influential Rev. Sterling Bargeron of Reidsville, and the two men began their efforts to organize the school. The primary counties of proposed enrollment were Tattnall, Evans, and Toombs. The men gained support through several organizational meetings with concerned citizens, and the project was soon on its way.

In January of 1970, Rev. Bargeron and James H. Rogers, a Tattnall County farmer, visited O.H. "Tab" Smith to propose that Smith head the proposed academy. Smith, with a background in education, public relations, and broadcasting, was a well-qualified choice for the task. Because of his hard work, heart-felt devotion, and vision, it is no wonder that O.H. Smith became known as the "Father of Pinewood."[178]

Smith and the other organizers first considered the old Manassas school building as the site for the new school. A series of rallies generated enough support to assure the opening of the school at the Manassas location. Tab Smith suggested the name Pinewood in deference to the large number of pines on the Manassas property and in keeping with the typical South Georgia setting. Legal proceedings to establish the school then began.

However, despite the Manassas plans, in April of 1970, a group of Bellville men came forward to offer a Bellville location for Pinewood Christian Academy. H.C. Hearn, Sr. owned a ten-acre parcel in Bellville and was willing to donate the property for the school. Bernie Anderson, Inman Hearn, Hines Daniel, Alvin Blalock, and Walter Emmett Daniel organized support for the proposed donation. When Albert Parker, Ralph Dixon, C.E. DeLoach, Jr., and H.C. Hearn offered to secure the building loans, the building committee accepted their offer. Albert Parker then served as chairman of the building committee effort.

The original steering committee consisted of Calvin Brewton, Thomas Scott, Charles Strickland, Bill Hearn, Jimmy Rogers, Dr. Charles Drake, Jimmy Kennedy, Harold Kemp, Tab Smith, Don Cobb, and Grady Rogers. The groundbreaking ceremony took place on May 25, 1970, with a large crowd in attendance. Workers soon completed the building, and Smith began hiring teachers, establishing curriculum, and organizing for enrollment.

Headmasters at the school include the following men: O.H. Tab Smith, 1970-1981; L.W. Bush, 1981-1983; Ron Marshall, 1983-1986; J.H. Wells, 1986-1992; Joseph M. Murray, 1992-1994; Charles O. Spann, 1994-1996; and Dewey Hulsey, 1996-present.

The school had several fund-raising concerts in its early life. One of the performers was the country song writer Tom T. Hall. While sitting on the old Bellville Depot landing before the concert, Hall penned a song, "When God Came Through Bellville, Georgia." The song received much air play from local stations. The lyrics are as follows:

> I'll tell you all a story that I think you'll understand, traveling through Georgia, rambling across the land.
>
> I passed the Bellville depot and something said to me, stop here son, there's something you should see.
>
> I stopped awhile and rested on the depot steps, the tall pine tree waiving in the breeze, the air was clear and fresh.
>
> That Georgia winter sunshine was a warming up my back, and I saw a train a coming down the track.
>
> God came through Bellville, Georgia. He was riding on the noonday train. All the power to him and praise his holy name. He never got off of the train, he never got off of the train.
>
>
> I've never had a day like that since I had been alive, my body full of feeling, there was vision in my eyes.
>
> I've traveled this world over just to meet that certain train, and I know my life will never be the same.
>
> Well I don't know where he's going, but I know he likes to ride, across the hills and valleys through the prairies, through the skies.
>
> And I know the time is coming if the world don't ever change. Everybody's got to move that train.
>
> God came through Bellville, Georgia. He was riding on the noonday train. All the power to him and praise his holy name. He never got off of the train. He never got off the train, he never got off that train....[179]

From about 240 students in 1970, Pinewood expanded its rolls to approximately 640 by the 1990s. The school enjoys a fine reputation for education, and places emphasis on modernizing its classrooms and improving its technology. It is an institution which continues to place Bellville on the map of fine educational institutions on a region-wide basis.

The City of Bellville

In 1959, Bellville residents decided to incorporate the town. The primary reason was to establish water service and street lighting.[180] *The Claxton Enterprise* published this notice concerning the proposal to incorporate the city:

> Notice of Intention to Introduce a Bill for Local Legislation. Notice is hereby given that a Bill will be introduced at the January, 1959, Session of the General Assembly of Georgia, for the incorporation of the town of Bellville, in Evans County, Georgia, with the rights and powers of such incorporations. This the 21st day of January 1959.[181]
>
> H.C. Hearn, Sr.

Ernest Strickland, Representative from Evans County, introduced House Bill 297 to incorporate the city. Governor Ernest Vandiver approved the legistation titled, "An Act to create a charter for the city of Bellville, and for other purposes" on March 10, 1959.[182]

Bellville's first mayor was O.H. Daniel, Jr. and the three councilmen were I.C. Hearn, H.K. Nease, and Roger Wood. The charter sets the term of office as two years. Others who have served on the city council over the years are David Groover, Darin McCoy, Alvin Blalock, Frank Benton, O.H. Daniel III, and Durwood Tootle.

According to the act, the corporate limits of the city "shall extend and embrace the following:"

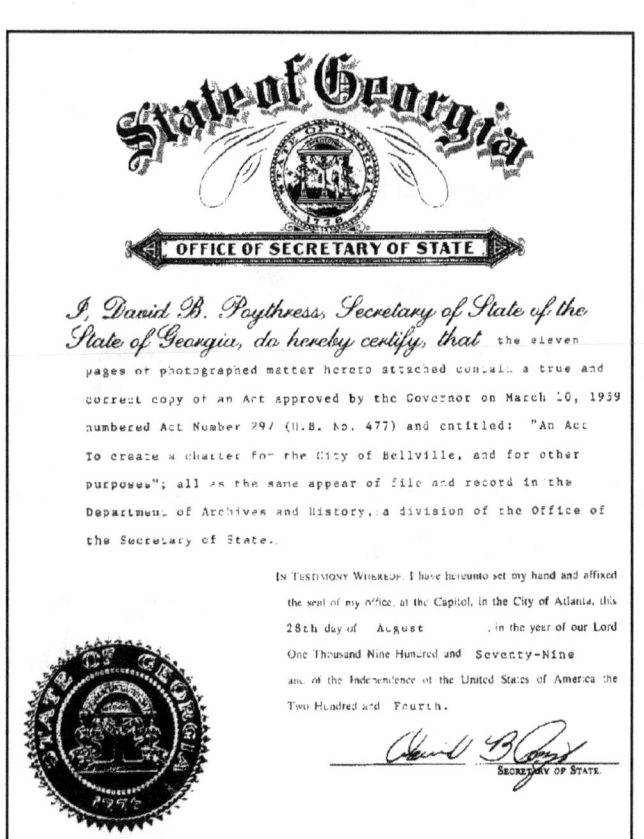

Bellville Town Charter

All that area situated, lying, and being within the area one mile square, the center of said area being at the intersection of State Route 169 and State Route 292 in Evans County with the boundaries thereof as follows: Beginning at the center point northward along the center of State Route 169 for a distance of one-half mile, thence due east a distance of one-half mile, thence due south one mile, thence due west one mile, thence due north one mile, thence east for one-half mile to the center of State Route 169, that is one-half mile north of the center of said area. It being the intent and purpose of this Act to establish the corporate limits as all that area embraced in the above described area.[183]

Bellville Today

The development of Bellville is similar to that of other Georgia railroad towns founded in the late nineteenth century. From a rather isolated area, the town prospered with the coming of the railroad. However, just as it prospered with the advent of rail transportation, it declined with the introduction of another form of transportation: the automobile. Numerous other communities died from this dynamic change. Bellville did not. It adapted.

Although railroad officials closed Bellville's train depot many years ago, the building remains as a memorial to the town's history. Moreover, the strong spirit of the town continues as a tribute to those both past and present who have made it what it is today.

History is full of defining moments. Perhaps the great Bellville fire of 1901 was Bellville's. Without the fire perhaps the town would have retained its considerable commercial momentum and grown commensurately. However, as many residents of the town will tell you today, perhaps the fire was not so bad after all. For if Bellville were any larger, it might not be the same quality place to live. Many residents believe that, contrary to the words of Tom T. Hall's song, "God Came Through Bellville, Georgia" and stayed.

The Bellville Town Hall was once the lunchroom at the old Bellville School.

Notes

[1] Lucile Hodges, *A History of Our Locale: Mainly Evans County, Georgia*, (Macon: Southern Press, Inc., 1965), pp. 3-7. Ms. Hodges' book, cited extensively in this work, contains much information relating to the people and settlements of early Evans County; F. Edward Schwabe, Jr., *The Boundaries of Original Montgomery County*, privately printed, 1989, pp. 1-5.

[2] The western boundary of St. John's Parish was very close to present-day Bellville. In 1773 Andrew Way made his famous survey that formed the western boundaries of old Effingham and Liberty counties. Schwabe, *Montgomery County*, pp. 1-5; Hodges, *Locale*, p. 8.

[3] Georgia Legislature Act No. 29, December 5, 1801. The western Tattnall-Liberty County border ran from the mouth of Cedar Creek on the Canoochee River to the mouth of Beard's Creek on the Altamaha.

[4] Schwabe, *Montgomery County*, pp. 2-3.

[5] Farris E. Cadle, *Georgia Land Surveying History and Law*, (Athens: University of Georgia Press, 1991), p. 53.

[6] Schwabe, *Montgomery County*, p. 2.

[7] The limit was 1,000 acres per warrant, but the grants could exceed this amount. Warrants could be purchased and several warrants could be consolidated on a single grant. Before 1785 and after 1831 a fee had to be paid for the warrant. Between these dates no such fee accrued. Grants were available to any U.S. citizen who was a Georgia resident. The rules required the individual to settle on the land and improve three out of every one hundred acres within eighteen months of receiving the grant, or be liable for a treble tax. Cadle, *Georgia Land Surveying*, p. 68; Several settlers received thousands of acres in what is now Evans County through the land grant system. For example, Nathan Brewton obtained at least 9,573 acres in Tattnall County and 960 acres in Bulloch County; Multiple Tattnall and Bulloch County Deed Books, 1802-1855.

[8] There were, of course, many land grants after 1825. A land grant went to D.J. Brewton as late as March 1890. Ga. Surveyor General Headrights, Book A-J, 1882-1909, Ga. State Archives; also see Tattnall County Land Grant Book, 1802-1837. Further information on many of these men is included in Appendix A.

[9] Nathan Brewton (originally spelled Bruton) settled at the mouth of Cedar Creek on the Canoochee River about 1794. He came to Tattnall County (then part of Liberty County) from North Carolina by way of Warren County, Georgia. He married Nancy Fontaine in 1794. He later moved to the Bulloch County side of the Canoochee River where he died in 1855. His mother, Isabella (Bruton) Askew, moved to Georgia and obtained a land grant in 1824. The name of Nathan Brewton's father is not documented, although there is circumstantial evidence that he was Benjamin Brewton from Dobbs County, N.C. Nathan and Nancy Brewton had a large family, and many of today's Evans County residents trace their lineage to these two pioneers.

[10] Mona Lee Allen, *Isaac Chadburn Daniel and His Descendants*, privately printed, 1992. Aaron Daniel lived approximately two and one-half miles north of present-day Bellville.

[11] Charles Wildes, *Once Upon a Time in Tattnall County, Georgia*, (Glennville: Glennville Printing, 1990), p. 349. "William Henry Hodges, son of John Robert and Tabitha Little Hodges was born June 19, 1770 in North Carolina. He came to Georgia with his parents and married Ann Blitch. Their children were Willis Alexander, James M. and William Riley Hodges. William Henry Hodges married second Hannah Colson (1787-1870). Their children were Seaborn, Samantha, Irvin Jackson, Phillip P., Cynthia, Elizabeth, and Samuel."

[12] Spelling on the original land grant in the possession of Bellville resident Emily Groover appears to be "McDaniel," although later deeds indicate "McDonald."

[13] James A. Tippins was a large landowner in the area, and was also the Tattnall County surveyor from 1814-1818 and 1826-1834. His farm was northwest of where Manassas, Georgia, is today. He and his family later moved to Ft. Crawford (now Brewton), Alabama. Hodges, *Locale*, p. 178.

[14] Zelma Barrow, *Tippins Ancestry*, privately published, 1982; Located on Cedar Creek, Phillip Tippins' land was two or three miles north of present-day Bellville; According to research notes prepared by Robert Brewton in 1955, "He [Phillip Tippins] was buried in the J.B. Brewton Cemetery about two or three miles from Claxton near the Metter Road. The location of his grave was completely lost by 1881 when my mother [his granddaughter and Robert Brewton's mother] undertook to locate it."

[15] George U. Tippins married Penelope Durrence. He left Tattnall County and moved to Florida. This information from typescript prepared by Robert Brewton in 1955.

[16] Charlie Wildes, *Cedar Creek - Mt. Horeb Primitive Baptist Church*, 1982, p. 52.

[17] Tattnall County Land Grant Book 1802-1837, p. 40.

[18] George F. Austin, *One Hundred Years of Methodism in Tattnall County Georgia*, (Reidsville: *Tattnall Journal*, 1908), p. 18. According to Austin, "Brewton's Church was a nondenominational church called 'The Free Church.' The Free Church was maintained here for about nineteen years, when in 1853 the Methodist organized with Rev. John E. Sentell as pastor. There is no record as to the number of members. A new building was now needed. Benjamin Brewton promptly donated the lumber. The record shows the names of the trustees as Nathan J. Brewton, T.A. Durrence, and J.B. Smith. Out of Brewton's Church have grown Bellville, Hagan, Claxton, Eason's Chapel, and other churches." According to a June 23, 1923 *Claxton Enterprise* article, the following men were former members of Brewton's Church: Abraham Eason, Benjamin Brewton, Samuel Brewton, Simon J. Brewton, Jesse DeLoach, Jesse Durrence, T.A. Durrence, William H. Edwards, Dr. Morgan, Uriah Rogers, J.B. Smith, S.P. Smith, Glenn Tippins, Asbury Tippins, William Tippins, Henry Wilkerson, Roger Wood, and others. Members discontinued Brewton's Church in 1899.

[19] Joseph T. Grice, *Sketches of By-Gone Days*, Glennville, Ga., privately printed, 1958, p. 3.

[20] There was a poor school in the 41st District as early as 1843. Students included William Brewton, James F. Brewton, Jane Brewton, James Waters, Berrian Brewton, Martha Brewton, Nancy Waters, Ezekiel Brewton, James W. Brewton, Martin Brewton, John Sikes, Mary Brewton, and Eliza Brewton. J.A.J. Lanes was the teacher and his pay was five cents per day per student. The trustees of this school were Nathan Brewton, Jr., Benjamin Brewton, and Samuel Brewton. Brewton Family Folder, Georgia Department of Archives, Atlanta, Georgia.

[21] Grice, *Sketches*, p. 55

[22] The editor obtained these names by comparing the 1860 census records with the *Roster of Confederate Veterans* by Lillian Henderson.

[23] Benjamin Brewton's land extended into present-day Bellville town limits. Benjamin Brewton also represented Tattnall County in the Georgia legislature in 1841-42, and was sheriff of the county from 1830 to 1832. He donated part of the land and the lumber to build Brewton Church at the site of Brewton Cemetery in Hagan. Hodges, *Locale*, p. 125.

The Story of Bellville 51

[24] The Tattnall County Rangers were Company B, 61st Georgia Volunteer Regiment; the Tattnall Volunteers were Company H, 61st Georgia Volunteer Regiment; and the Tattnall Invincibles were Company G, 47th Georgia Volunteer Regiment. Many Tattnall men joined the 5th Georgia Cavalry in nearby Liberty County.

[25] The editor has a typescript copy of B.B. Brewton's letters. Further editor's notes on the letter: "Flora" was Brewton's daughter, and "Jonathan" was his brother. Brewton describes the July 9, 1864 Battle of Monocacy, Maryland and General Early's raid on Washington in this letter. The "third or bird" comment about Van Valkenburg refers to Brewton's uncertainty about this officer's rank. According to his service record James Hendrix was in Company D of the 61st Georgia Volunteer Infantry, a unit raised in nearby Bulloch County. Yankees captured Hendrix at Monocacy, Maryland in July 1864. He was an exchanged prisoner in Richmond at war's end. Jesse Jernigan, Company B, 61st Georgia was also captured at Monocacy, Maryland. He was at home on wounded furlough at the end of the war. Lt. James Mincey, Company D, 61st Georgia, sustained severe wounds in the lungs, left shoulder, and thigh at Monocacy. The Federals captured him, but returned Hendrix as an exchanged soldier in September 1864. Brewton reports his regiment has only 54 men for duty. The regiment started the war with approximately 1,000 men; Some spelling and punctuation corrections were made to make this letter more readable.

[26] Transcript of Simon B. Brewton speech to Liberty County Chapter of Daughters of the Confederacy, late 1920s or early 1930s.

[27] *Tattnall County Campground--100th Anniversary*, privately published by Tattnall Campground Trustees, 1967, p. 6.

[28] *Savannah Morning News*, August 18, 1935; "Tattnall County Camp Ground Past and Present Are Compared as Diamond Jubilee Year Approaches," *Wesleyan Christian Advocate*, Macon, Georgia, July 30, 1943.

[29] *Savannah Morning News*, August 18, 1935.

[30] The nails forming the initials are still visible today; Wallace Parker, interview with editor, July 6, 1995; Devane Parker Lewis, *Parker and Allied Families*, privately printed, p. 51; *Savannah Morning News*, August 18, 1935.

[31] Hodges, *Locale*, pp. 98-99.

[32] Nathan Brewton, Benjamin's father and an original settler of the area in 1794, operated a mill north of Benjamin's at the spot were Cedar Creek joins the Canoochee River. The Nathan Brewton water mill was known as the Upper Brewton Mill on Cedar Creek; Post Office records, National Archives, MC 841, reel 25; 1963 interviews with Theodore Brewton revealed the following: "Benjamin Brewton and family lived at the mill. Benjamin's son, Berry Brewton, told stories of operating the mill as a boy. There was an up-and-down saw there as well as a grist mill. The Berry Brewton home was built with lumber sawed there. Benjamin Brewton lived at the mill until his death. Nancy and Glenn Hendricks bought the mill from the Benjamin Brewton estate about 1877. They were the first to build a store at the site." Theodore Brewton, interview with Charles P. Johnson, Jr., 1963. The manuscript records of these interviews, in the possession of the editor, provided much valuable information for writing this Bellville history; Hodges, *Locale*, pp. 55, 91.

[33] National Archives, Microfilm MC 841: reel 25; In 1881, subscribers included the following: J.C. Daniel, blacksmith; Wm. T. Morgan, physician; G.F. Hendricks, general store, cotton and wool mills; M.C. Jenkins, blacksmith; Virgil Johnson, blacksmith; J.P.R. Sikes, grist mill; J.M. Smith, grist mill; Marshall Smith, guano agent; L.M. Strickland, teacher; J.M. Surrency, grist mill, saw mill; L.A.H. Tippins, justice; W.H. Tippins, constable. Hodges, *Locale*, p. 78.

[34]*Georgia State Gazetteer and Business Directory, 1881-1882*, (Atlanta: Standard Directory Company, 1881), p. 192.

[35]"Manassas, U.S. Post Office,"Oka Eason, Postmaster, unpublished manuscript, March 10, 1949; Oka Eason was appointed postmaster of Manassas in 1930; Post Office records, MC 841, at the National Archives indicate the year of Danton's establishment as 1884. After Asbury Tippins' death, his widow, Ella, was appointed postmaster in 1894; According to Dot Simmons, local historian, Manassas Foy received his unusual first name in honor of the Civil War Battle of Manassas; Theodore Brewton, interview with Charles P. Johnson, Jr., May 26, 1968; Devane Parker Lewis provides a further sketch on Asbury Tippins in her book, *Parker and Allied Families*, privately printed: "Asbury Tippins was instrumental in the establishment of the Tattnall Camp Ground in Tattnall County, Georgia. He served a year and a half in Company G, 47th Georgia Regiment, Army of Tennessee. He received two land grants totaling 745 acres in Tattnall County. He served as the County Tax Commissioner, and on their way through Georgia, General Sherman's men robbed him of county funds. Afterwards Mr. Tippins was Justice of the Peace for several terms and postmaster at Manassas, Georgia. He and his two wives are buried in the Tippins Cemetery, located on Highway 280 west of Bellville.

[36]Post Office Records, microfilm MC 1120, National Archives; Hodges, *Locale*, p. 84.

[37]The Hawpond Court House building still stands today a few yards southwest of the J.B. Brewton house on Highway 129, the Metter Highway.

[38]Jonathan Bacon Brewton (1827-1897), son of Benjamin and Charlotte Brewton, was a well known leader in the community. After serving 14 months in the 5th Georgia Cavalry of the Confederate Army, citizens elected him Tattnall County Clerk of the Superior Court in 1863. He also represented Tattnall County in the Georgia General Assembly in 1871-1872 and 1888-1889. His son, Jonathan B. Brewton, Jr., operated a store in the new town of Bellville. Hodges, *Locale*, p. 181; *Manual and Biographical Register of the State of Georgia for 1871-2*, (Atlanta: Plantation Publishing Co. Press, 1872), pp. 39-40; Post Office Records, National Archives, MC 841.

[39]Theodore Brewton, interview with Charles P. Johnson, Jr., February 27, 1966.

[40]"Late Theodore Brewton Chronicled Evans County's History in 1964 Enterprise," Theodore Brewton, *The Claxton Enterprise*, August 3, 1989.

[41]*Soil Survey of Candler, Evans, and Tattnall Counties, Ga.*, U.S. Department of Agriculture, 1980.

[42]Tattnall County Deed Book M. The railroad purchased several of the rights of way for nominal sums.

[43]Hodges, *Locale*, p. 167.

[44]*Savannah Morning News*, June 24 and July 13, 1889. "It looks as though the Savannah and Western Railroad will be built without further delay. Gen. Alexander returned June 23, 1889, from New York and said that the $5,000,000 5% bonds have been placed in New York and the money is in the treasury of the railroad company."; *Savannah Morning News*, July 13, 1889; Railroad builder Sam Hawkins named Lyons after the city of Lyons in Europe. Hawkins named many of the stops along his railroads after European cities. Jack F. Cox, *History of Sumter County, Ga.*, (Roswell, Ga: WHW Pub., 1983), p. 406; Fido's name was changed to Uphaupee in 1889, to Belknap in 1890, and Groveland in 1897. Hodges, *Locale*, p. 88; According to the Post Office Route Register, the distances (in miles) from Meldrim to Ellabell, 6.82; to Pembroke, 8.12; to Fido, 7.12; to Danton, 16.97; to Ohoopee 12.5; and to Lyons, 6.6. Georgia Route Register, RG 28, 1888-1892, National Archives; The S.A.M. was originally incorporated as the Savannah, Preston, and Lumpkin Railroad in 1884. Les R. Winn, *Ghost Trains and Depots of Georgia*, (Chamblee, Georgia: Big Shanty Publishing Co., 1995), p. 250.

The Story of Bellville 53

⁴⁵William Williford, *Americus Through the Years*, (Atlanta: Cherokee Publishing, 1975), p. 205; The head of the S.A.M., Col. Sam Hawkins, solicited a $50,000 contribution from Savannah citizens to build the railroad from Lyons to the city. It appears no more than $35,000 was subscribed. Savannahians were reluctant to give the higher sum because they believed the S.A.M. would be the beneficiary of having Savannah, with its considerable commerce, as a terminus point for the railroad. *Savannah Morning News*, July 16, 1889.

⁴⁶*Savannah Morning News*, August 9, 1889.

⁴⁷Brewton, *County History*; Theodore Brewton, interview with Charles P. Johnson, Jr., July 21, 1963. There was originally a wooden trestle about the spot where the railroad now crosses Highway 280 on the eastern edge of Bellville. The trestle was used for about 12 or 13 years, and then railroaders filled in the area with dirt.

⁴⁸*Savannah Morning News*, December 28, 1889.

⁴⁹Williford, *Americus*, p. 205. "Railroad officials in Macon are in receipt of information concerning a change of traffic arrangement of the Savannah, Americus and Montgomery Railroad that is somewhat startling in its nature. The railroads are notified of ...a split between the above road and the Richmond and Danville, controlling the Savannah and Western among its other leased lines. Heretofore, the S. A. & M. road has had traffic arrangements with the S & W, and run trains throughout from its western terminus to Savannah, the eastern terminus of the S & W. The two roads connect at Lyons, and without a proper traffic arrangement, both would seem to be bottled up ...the S. A. & M. can only run its trains to Lyons and there stop. According to prominent authority, Georgia is to experience the fiercest railroad war within the next sixty days that has ever taken place in the country...." *The Macon Telegraph*, November 12, 1891.

⁵⁰Williford, *Americus,* p. 236: "On 17 May 1895 the property and franchises of the Savannah Americus and Montgomery Railways were sold at public auction.... They, in turn, conveyed the property and franchises to the Georgia and Alabama Railway on 27 July. The principal office of the road remained at Americus until 1 January 1899, after which it was located at Savannah. On 20 February 1902 the property and franchises were sold to the Seaboard Air Line Railway."; Richard E. Prince, *Seaboard Air Line Railway*, (Salt Lake City: Wheewright Lth. Co., 1969) p. 81.

⁵¹Ibid., p. 82.

⁵²*Georgia Historical and Industrial, 1900-1901*, (Atlanta: Dept. of Agriculture, Franklin Printing), p. 184.

⁵³Brewton, *County History*.

⁵⁴Tattnall County Deed Book O.

⁵⁵*Tattnall Journal,* advertisement, May 28, 1908.

⁵⁶Theodore Brewton, interview with Charles P. Johnson, Jr., May 26, 1968.

⁵⁷The Seaboard Air Line Railroad merged with the Atlantic Coastline in 1967 forming a new company, the Seaboard Coastline Railroad. *History of Webster County*, (Roswell Ga.: WHW Associates, 1980), p. 11.

⁵⁸Tattnall County Land Grants, 1802-1837, p. 40.

⁵⁹*Soil Survey of Candler, Evans, and Tattnall Counties, Georgia*, U.S. Department of Agriculture, 1980; The town's elevation is 185 feet above sea level.

[60] "Bellville Once A Major Business Center," Theodore Brewton, *The Claxton Enterprise*, August 3, 1989. This article also appeared in the 1964 historical edition of the *Enterprise*. The original paper title was "Early History of Bellville, Ga. 1890 thru 1914." Local historian Dot Simmons provided the editor an original typed manuscript of this account of Bellville's history. This article, written by Theodore Brewton, was a source of much information in this book.

[61] For D.J. Brewton land plat see Georgia Surveyor General Headrights, Book A-J, 1882-1909, Georgia State Archives, Atlanta, Ga., microfilm, Drw. 51, Box 34; Harry DeLoach, interview with editor, September 2, 1994.

[62] Hodges, *Locale*, p. 186.

[63] "Home Brings Back Fond Memories," Edra Smith Riggs, *The Claxton Enterprise*, November 2, 1989. The article states, "The old house, situated at the corner of Highways 169 South and 280 in Bellville, has attracted the attention of many passers-by. It is probably one of the oldest houses in Evans County and is owned by Walter Emmett Daniel....The house has been in the Daniel family for many years. While talking with Walter, I asked him if he would tell me some of the history. He said the house is over 150 years old. Originally it was a hewed log house and was built high off the ground. He remembers when bales of cotton and a wagon or buggy were kept under the house. Other members of the family remember when they, as children, played under the house. In more recent years the house has been lowered and the logs were covered with siding. Walter remembers when his grandparents, Pulaski Sikes Smith and his wife, Mary, lived there. During those years, daughters would return home to birth their babies as opposed to going to hospitals as we do now. My Harry's father, English Smith, was born in that house as were some of his siblings. English Smith remembered eating a fish dinner with the Pulaski Smiths and then walking toward the Bellville Post Office with Pulaski who was then postmaster. Near the railroad track Pulaski fell dead. Four men carried his body back home while his three-year old daughter walked along and held his head in her hands. Pulaski was in his forties."

O.H. Daniel told a humorous story relating to the Smith house in a 1939 *Claxton Enterprise* article, "Fond Memories Part of Bellville's Past." "Mr. O.H. Daniel recalls some very fond memories of his 'courting' days at the old Smith homestead. In fact, they were all pleasant except one. On that particular night, after spending a very satisfactory evening with Miss Helen, he took his leave on foot (as traveling conveyances were not so plentiful in those days). He had to walk all the way across town as the Daniel residence was a good half mile north of the railroad track. Just before he reached the railroad, he heard a weird sound. In fact, it sounded for the world like a wild-cat. Mr. Olin 'took off' so fast he dug holes in the middle of the road and was completely exhausted when he reached home. He 'plum' forgot everything he said to Miss Helen that evening, and forgot what her answer was, so he had to start all over again on his next trip."; Herschel Hearn, interview with Emily Groover, November 10, 1990.

[64] Hodges, *Locale*, pp. 159-161.

[65] Built in the 1850s, the Berry Brewton House is one of the three ante-bellum homes still standing in the immediate Bellville area. The other ones are the James B. Smith House and Jonathan B. Brewton House.

[66] Family sketches of these men can be found in Appendix A.

[67] Delma Daniel, interview with editor, July 7, 1995.

[68] Hodges, *Locale*, p. 160.

[69] Bellville town plan, August 25, 1890, by A.D. Eason, surveyor; Tattnall County Deed Book N.

[70] Mary Daniel, interview with editor, July 7, 1995.

The Story of Bellville

[71] Rowe built a home on one lot and later sold it to W.F. Durrence. Rowe then built another house on the other lot and resided there until he moved to Appling County about 1908. Brewton, *Bellville History*, p. 2.

[72] Ibid.

[73] Site of current Mallard home in Bellville.

[74] This was one of several sites at which Daniel operated a sawmill. See Delma Daniel interview; Brewton, *Bellville History*, p. 2.

[75] Tattnall County Deed Book Q, pp. 452-453.

[76] Brewton, *Bellville History*, p. 3.

[77] Appendix D includes a history of the school.

[78] Brewton, *Bellville History*, p. 2.

[79] *The Claxton Enterprise*, Historical Edition, August 3, 1989. "The Hearn House in Bellville was built in the early 1890s. Tom Grice, who served as Bellville's postmaster from 1898 to 1900, was the first owner of the house. Mr. Grice later sold the house to his niece Eulalia Hearn, and her husband, Charlie W. Hearn, in the late 1890s. C.W. Hearn served as Bellville postmaster from 1913 to 1919. The house was at one time a boarding house for schoolteachers. It was later occupied by Mae and Martha Hearn. The present occupants are Charlie Hearn's great-grandson, Alan Groover, and his wife, Dawn."; The house is the current site of the Anderson House Restaurant.

[80] *Bellville United Methodist Church: 100th Anniversary*, privately printed, February 10, 1991, p. 10.

[81] Tattnall County Deed Book Q, pp. 452-453.

[82] *Bellville United Methodist Church: 100th Anniversary*, p.3. Charlie Johnson retrieved the original church bell from Pembroke and donated it for placement in the new steeple; Appendix C contains further information about Bellville Methodist Church.

[83] Arthur H. Prince was a photographer of great reputation. Prince produced many of the Bellville area photos of the late nineteenth and early twentieth century. His photos often had "A.H. Prince, Traveling Artist, Bellville, Ga." annotated in red ink on the margin of the photo. Editor.

[84] 44th Annual Session, Baptist Union Association Minutes, Liberty Co., Georgia, October 20, 1897.

[85] Hodges, *Locale*, p. 109.

[86] Tattnall County Deed Book T, page 143. Kate Wright conveyed the title to the land to the church members in 1898, "bounded north by the Georgia and Alabama Railroad, east by B.B. Brewton, and south and west by Kate Wright."; Herschel Hearn, interview with Emily Groover, November 10, 1990; "The church lot herein mentioned is a lot on the south side of the S.A.L. railway fronting 50 feet on S.A.L. right-of-way and running back 75 feet. Said church lot being the property of the colored Methodist Episcopal Church." Evans County Deed Book 4, p. 182; Theodore Brewton, interview with Charles P. Johnson, Jr., April 21, 1964.

[87] Tillman was in business in the mid-1890s, but sold out in 1897 or 1898 and moved to Florida to pursue the turpentine business. Brewton, *Bellville History*, p. 1.

[88] Thanks to Prince, many wonderful vintage photos of the Bellville area exist. The quality of these photos, even after a hundred years, points to his outstanding capability with a camera. Editor.

[89] Brewton, *Bellville History*, p. 3.

[90] *Georgia State Gazetteer and Directory*, (Atlanta: Pease Printing Co., 1898), p. 614.

[91] "Bellville Burned Up," *Statesboro News*, May 10, 1901. "News reached here Tuesday that very nearly all of the little town of Bellville, Ga. on the Seaboard Air Line Railway, in Tattnall County, about 54 miles from Savannah, was burned on Monday. The fire is supposed to have been the work of enraged Negroes. The Negroes have been giving the white people a great deal of trouble in that section recently. Only a few days since a Negro was shot and killed in Bellville for entering Mr. Long's house and attempting an assault on a white lady, and since the killing the Negroes have been greatly enraged, and it is supposed it is their work that has laid Bellville in ashes."

[92] *Savannah Morning News*, May 9, 1901; Also, the May 2, 1901 edition carried the following article: "A Killing in Tattnall - Warrants Issued for Two Negroes for Death of Kallop McCade," Tattnall Co., Ga. "May 1. Warrants were secured this evening by Jane McCade charging Bert and Major Long with the killing of Kallop McCade at Bellville this morning." Note: The headline was incorrect, because Bert and Major Long were white residents. A thorough search of the Tattnall County Court records and contemporaneous newspapers revealed no further information on this case. Apparently the case did not come to court and its disposition is unknown. According to a 1966 interview with Theodore Brewton, there was, however, a coroner's inquest of the death and the finding was that the killing was committed by "parties unknown." This information adds to the mystery surrounding the incident. The interview also mentions that there was animosity between the Longs and local blacks because the latter were potential witnesses against Bert Long, who had been indicted for moonshining. Editor.

[93] *Savannah Morning News*, May 9, 1901.

[94] Bernie Anderson, interview with editor, October 6, 1995.

[95] Brewton, *Bellville History*, p. 2.

[96] Ibid.

[97] Allen D. Chandler and Clement Evans, *Cyclopedia of Georgia*, Vol. 1, A-E, (Atlanta: State Historical Association, 1906). The Co-editor of this book, Clement Evans, is the person for whom Evans County is named.

[98] Hodges, *Locale*, pp. 160-161.

[99] Known as Hagan District, the county formed the 1607th in 1904 from parts of the 401st, 1366th, and 1376th. The 1366th was called Hawpond. *U. S. Statistical Census*, 1910, Vol. II, U. S. Printing Office.

[100] Hitz Pamphlet, p. 1.

[101] Hodges, *Locale*, p. 84.

[102] Ibid., p. 193.

[103] Although according to Post Office records Laibbett was appointed in 1899, he apparently never served. Record group MC 841, National Archives.

[104] Post Office Records, MC 841, National Archives, Washington, D.C.

[105] This information provided to the editor by Darin McCoy, Probate Judge of Evans County, April 18, 1996.

[106] Amos Hearn's grandson, the Reverend Anthony Hearn, wrote an interesting account about his grandfather. Emily Hearn Groover provided the editor a copy of the article, "We Moved Our Grandfather's Grave." An excerpt follows. "On April 3, 1956, I had the most unusual experience of helping in the removal of the grave of my grandfather who had been buried ninety-two years. This was on Tuesday after Easter, and on the preceding Sunday the Easter theme of Hope, Faith, and Immortality had been preached and again emphasized, and the experience of opening the grave that had been made nearly a century ago was quite meaningful to me. For my grandfather it was his third burial.

Amos J. Hearn rode away from his home in Tattnall County, Georgia near Bellville, October, 1862, and enlisted in Company H, 5th Regiment, Georgia Cavalry, of the Confederate States Army, at South New Port, in McIntosh County. The official records show that he carried his own gun with him into the service. His regiment was stationed in McIntosh County until May, 1863, when it was transferred to Isle of Hope, near Savannah. In October, 1863, it was ordered to Charleston, but stopped at Green Pond until February, 1864, when it was ordered to Jacksonville, Florida. It passed through Savannah, where the sick were left behind, and our grandfather was included in that group. He died in Mercy Hospital April 7, 1864, and was buried in the Confederate burying ground in Laurel Grove Cemetery in Savannah on April 8, 1864. The original records in the office of the Laurel Grove Cemetery show he died of "erysipelas," and the doctor was named Bulloch. Had he lived until August 7th, he would have been forty years old.

I have a letter written to my father March 24, 1917, by a Mr. J.D. Barnard in which he says that he was in the service with A.J. Hearn and, "He was my tent mate, he was my mess mater, he was my brother soldier, he was a brother F. & A. M. and a Christian brother in the Church."

Amos J. Hearn left behind him his wife, Nancy Emily Brewton Hearn, and three small children: Melvina E., who became the wife of John Rogers, Simon Amos, my father; and Charles William. At the time of their father's death, Melvina was three years old; Simon Amos was two; and Charles William was born April 4, just three days before his father died. The record is that after a short time, Asbury Tippins, an uncle of Nancy Emily, took a Negro slave, Jim Beale, who belonged to Simon Brewton, our great-grandfather, and went in a cart to Savannah and brought the body back home. One story in the family says that the young widow went with them. He was buried this second time in the field near his home, and here he rested for these past ninety-two years.

With the passing of years, and considering the ease with which lonely graves can eventually become totally abandoned, the grandchildren came to desire the grave moved from that sacred spot in the field to the Brewton Cemetery near Hagan and Claxton. In this place are buried many of those dear to him: his wife, who became the wife of John Chadbourne Parker, his two sons, and other relatives of the family. And, it was done.

The legal requirements were properly met, and with Mr. R. D. Tillman, who is both the county coroner and a funeral director, in charge, the workmen opened the grave which was filled ninety-two years before. In that early morning a quietness and reverence prevailed as grandchildren and others stood and watched the soil being tossed out of the grave. He whose grave was being opened had left three children and they were now represented by some of their children.

When the workman had progressed down to the place of the casket, Inman Hearn took the shovel and carefully completed the task. Except for a few square rusty nails no evidence was found of the casket. Two large brass buttons were recovered, with one of them showing evidence of its gray cloth covering, indicating that he had been buried with his Confederate jacket. There were several white pearl buttons, that could have been on his shirt, or undershirt, perhaps sewed on by his young girl-wife. The soil was generally blacker than the other, which could have been top soil put on the casket, or could have been caused in the process of decay. The remains of the skeleton of our grandfather were carefully brought out from their long resting place by the grandson, Inman Hearn. There were the three large bones of each leg and the three large bones of each arm and the skull. In the hush and reverence of the occasion I took them from the hands of my cousin, and tried in imagination to visualize our grandparent. We wondered how he looked, and speculated on his appearance. Mr. Tillman had provided a new box, about five feet long, lined with new white cloth, and into this were placed the soil and contents of the grave, except the buttons, which deferent individuals wished to keep.

Before we left, at my request, we had prayer, and mine was an unusual emotional experience as I prayed at this opened grave of a grandfather who belonged to an era long passed, and who was unknown to his own children."

[107] Harry DeLoach, interview with editor, September 2, 1994; Tattnall County Deed Book T, page 322, shows the date of the deed of conveyance as January 5, 1900. C.W. Hearn bought the land from Julia C. McQuaig, who defaulted on a loan from Moses Dryfus, of Savannah; Theodore Brewton, interview with Charles P. Johnson, Jr., April 3, 1966. Buck Guy was killed by lightning in May 1901. Buck Guy, Grover Cleveland "Coon" Tippins, Charlie Hearn, and Theodore Brewton were walking from town toward the Smith house. A little storm cloud came up. Coon and Theodore went to the house and were on the porch. Lightning struck three trees at once close to where the men were walking and the same bolt also struck Guy, Hearn, and a bulldog walking between the two men. The shock knocked Hearn out, but he finally revived. Buck and the dog did not survive.

[108] *The Bulloch Times*, carried the following article in September of 1897: "One of the busiest places to be found around town (Statesboro) during the past few months has been the establishment of Mr. W. D. Davis. He has been more successful than usual in placing his long staple cotton gins, having sold and shipped eighteen with orders for nine more. This gin has a great reputation, and the steady growth of Mr. Davis' business is evidence sufficient as to their popularity with the ginners. During this season Mr. Davis has kept from three to five extra workmen, and even with this help he had not been able to keep even with his work." A description of the Sea Island and upland cotton gins is as follows: "Dan Davis made single roller gins for sea island cotton. The gin consisted of a wooden roller eight feet long and six inches in diameter. The cast frames that held up the rollers were made in Augusta. The roller was covered by walrus hide nearly an inch thick in long strips about an inch wide. It was put on in a spiral shape, glued to the wood and had oak pegs set in at intervals. The roller was completely covered and put in a lathe and turned perfectly round. The roller turned against a blade about four inches wide that brushed up against it. The lint would stick to the roller and when it got to the underside it would drop off from its own weight. The black seed dropped into a trough and a long auger in a box pulled and twisted the seed as the auger turned and they were discharged from the trough. This type of gin was used because of the delicate way the cotton was removed from the seed. The long fibers could not be cut or torn because they were prized for their length. The cotton was placed in the gin by hand and the lint was removed by hand.

The green seed cotton or short staple cotton was called "upland." The green seed gin was a saw gin. There were 70 saws in a row and they were set about an inch apart from each other. Little claw-like teeth would pick up the cotton and pull the lint from the seed. The cotton went through the gin, which had little slits a little wider than the saw. The lint would go through and the seeds dropped down. Then a brush running faster than the saw knocked the lint off. The cotton was then sucked up and carried to the press without a man to handle it. This process cut and picked the lint, but the short staple cotton was short anyway." Dorothy Brannen, *Life in Old Bulloch, The Story of a Wiregrass County in Georgia*, (Gainesville, Ga: Magnolia Press, 1987), pp. 176-177.

[109] L.L. Foss came out with a double roller gin. This was a Sea Island gin and had to be hand-fed. Each roller was a gin in itself, and one person could feed both gins at the same time. Two double rollers would take about three hours to gin a bale of cotton. Brannen, *Bulloch*, pp. 176-177; "C.W. Hearn Operated Early Cotton Gin at Bellville To Process Important Crop," *The Claxton Enterprise*, November 26, 1964.

[110] David Roller and Robert Twyman, Eds., *The Encyclopedia of Southern History*, (Baton Rouge: Louisiana State University Press, 1979), p. 303. "As in the 1700s innovators sought to save labor by perfecting a cotton gin, so after the Civil War they sought to save labor by automating the movement of cotton from the wagon to the gin stand and from the gin stand to the press. Robert S. Munger (1854-1923) of Mexia, Texas, made the most important contribution. Between 1883 and 1885 he developed a 'ginning system' whereby cotton was moved automatically from the time it left the wagon until a bale was removed from the press. A Munger gin

The Story of Bellville

plant with four gin stands easily processed 24 to 30 bales of cotton in the time it took a pre-Civil War gin to process four. Many improvements were later made, but the basic movement of fiber through a gin plant is still that of the Munger ginning system."

[111] Thurmon Smith, interview with editor, February 17, 1996. An excerpt of the interview follows. Editor: Could you tell me about your exploits at picking cotton? Thurmon: Well, I picked my share of cotton, I reckon. I was only 14 years old when I picked 400 pounds on several days. I once picked over 300 pounds three days in a row. You had to keep your hands moving quickly. My brother, Hoke, worked just as hard as I did, but he could only pick half as much as me. He couldn't move his hands as fast. You had the burlap cotton bags around your shoulder and you emptied the bags onto sheets at the end of the rows. Right out here in these fields I picked 10,000 pounds in one year.

That was short-staple cotton we picked. I wasn't very good with long-staple. It had long spurs that would stick your hands. They were sharp as a needle. Daddy never did plant any black-seed cotton, but my mother's daddy who lived in Reidsville did. He tended a farm there. He was also in the hotel business. When we got finished picking here he wanted me to go up there and pick his black-seed cotton.

The boll weevil hit here one year just like a wave of grasshoppers. They came from Texas to here. They hit this country, and I mean they cleaned up the crop. We didn't make anything, we didn't know what to do with them. We didn't have any equipment to fight them with. In a year or two they did get something to fight them with, but that first year to two was a disaster. Now they've been eradicated.

We were in the field when the sun came up. It didn't matter how cold or how much dew was there. You would be soaking wet with dew by sun up. The sun would rise and the rays would dry you off and you'd feel bad as I don't know what.

We'd work until sundown when we weighed up and hauled in. We would come in and eat. Then we'd haul the cotton to the Hearn gin.

During the Depression cotton prices got to all time lows. I planted five acres of cotton and I made five, 500 weight bales. I got six cents a pound. Now, that's 30 dollars a bale for a year's work. It took the seed to pay for the ginning. Hogs went down to two and one-half cents a pound, and cows too. It was several years before things picked up. The bottom fell out of everything. They called it "Hoover Days." But, you know President Hoover inherited the problem even though people blamed it all on him.

Everything was done with mules. I'm not sure if it were still done with mules people would be better off [laughter]. Everything is so mechanized and computerized now I don't see how they keep up. The country was full of tenant houses for sharecroppers and hired help. There wasn't anyone expecting handouts from the government. Now, things are altogether different.

[112] David Groover, interview with editor, July 9, 1995.

[113] Brannan, *Bulloch*, p. 241.

[114] Willard Range, *A Century of Georgia Agriculture 1850-1950*, (Athens: U. of Georgia Press, 1954), p. 169.

[115] "'Evans County 'Comes Back' with Old-Time Crop," *Savannah Morning News*, October 23, 1924.

[116] "Bellville News," *The Claxton Enterprise*, April 18, 1919.

[117] Range, *Georgia Agriculture*, p. 187.

[118] "Branch Bank's First Depositor--Once Ginned Cotton on Same Site," *The Claxton Enterprise*, June 6, 1974. *The Claxton Enterprise* carried the following article on August 16, 1943. "H.C. Hearn & Co., announce that their new gin will begin operation on Tuesday, August 17th. These ginners have had a lifetime of experience in ginning all kinds of cotton grown in this section, and the new gin that will go into operation in Bellville next Tuesday replaces the gin burned down early last fall."

H.C. Hearn stated that the new outfit is the most modern electrically operated outfit in this section. The huge motor turns four, eighty saw gins fast enough to turn cut seven bales of cotton per hour, when the cotton is in acceptable condition. Included in the outfit are hullers and cleaners that have added so much to the cotton samples in recent years.

The new ginnery adds much to the capacity of the cotton ginneries located in this section and assures that this year's crop will be ginned as soon as brought in.

For many years H.C. Hearn & Co., have furnished one of the highest cash markets for cotton and cottonseed in this section and they will continue this year to buy both products at Bellville."

[119] "King Cotton makes return to throne in Evans County," *The Claxton Enterprise*, August 3, 1995; Winton Bell, interview with editor, September 2, 1995.

[120] "Evans County 'Comes Back' with Old-Time Crop," *Savannah Morning News*, October 23, 1924

[121] Charles Wilson and William Ferris, co-editors, *Encyclopedia of Southern Culture*, "Tobacco Culture, Flue-Cured," (University of North Carolina Press: Chapel Hill, 1989), p. 48.

[122] "Tobacco: Crop Has Grown to Second Rank as Cash Producer," *The Claxton Enterprise*, March 11, 1954.

[123] David Groover, interview with editor, July 9, 1995; Winton Bell, interview with editor, September 2, 1995.

[124] Jot Collins, interview with editor, 1987.

[125] Cleve Freeman, interview with editor, November 29, 1995.

[126] David and Emily Groover, interview with editor, November 29, 1995; Also, Cleve Freeman, interview with editor, November 29, 1995. Cleve Freeman: I was a Georgia state plant inspector for 38 years. I started inspecting the tomato plants about 1947, and Evans was in my 30-county area. I inspected the plants from the time they were planted until they were pulled and processed. I would inspect the plants for disease and insects. Some of the more common diseases were root nematodes and leaf fungus. If you found disease on the plants, they would have to be destroyed. Although this didn't occur very often, it did happen enough to keep you on your toes.

Of course, the worst type disaster could be a late freeze. They started planting about February 22, George Washington's birthday, and planted up to March. The plants were pulled starting between the 1st and 15th of April and the end of May.

As for insects, one of the more common ones for tomato plants was the Colorado potato beetle. I would also look at the general condition of the plant to detect if the stem was firm, etc. If the plants passed all the inspections, a "Georgia Certified" certificate was glued to the shipping basket. The plants were shipped to Virginia, Maryland, and Delaware.

The height of the plants at the time they were pulled was from 6 to 10 inches, with the stalk being one-fourth inch or greater. The workers pulling the plants were normally paid by the thousand. At first the growers planted about 100,000 plants per acre, and this increased later to about 200,000 plants per acre. As you can imagine there were millions of plants shipped from Bellville over the years. The brokers furnished the seed. The Hearn's broker was Sherman T. Griffith from Preston, Maryland. The primary varieties grown were Marglobe and Rutgers. However, later hybrid varieties planted had numbers like F-1, F-2, etc.

Mr. Inman Hearn grew good plants. He covered the fields very thoroughly as a supervisor. I could see his shirttail flying out across the field many days. He would be all over the place.

I visited Maryland a few times to see the tomatoes growing. One day I stood on a hill there and could see seven different canning plants. Tomato farming was big business to those areas. It was also an interesting business.

The Story of Bellville 61

[127]"Most Diversified County Title Claimed by Evans," *Savannah Morning News*, October 31, 1940.

[128]David Groover, interview with editor, July 9, 1995.

[129]Thurmon Smith, interview with editor, February 19, 1996.

[130]English G. Smith, "Life and Experiences of E.G. Smith," manuscript, 1958. This information provided to the editor by Shirley Smith.

[131]Brewton, *Bellville History*, p. 3.

[132]Charles Wilson and William Ferris, co-editors, *Encyclopedia of Southern Culture*, "Naval Stores," (University of North Carolina Press: Chapel Hill, 1989), p. 39; Lucile Hodges gives a good account of naval stores operations in her book, previously cited, p. 233: "In spring and summer, a workman, using a hand tool called a 'hack,' cut one side of the pine tree about an inch wide and deep in a V shape, beginning near the base of the trees eight inches or more in diameter. Just below the first score, a trough-like cup was made in the tree large enough to hold about a pint of gum which oozed down from the gashed face. The scored face and the trough below was called a 'box,' and workmen spoke of this work as 'chipping boxes.' Every week or so during the warm months another score was added above the last (for six, or more feet from the base) and the gum was dipped from the boxes (about once a month) into heavy wooden buckets from which it was poured into conveniently-placed barrels in the woods. Almost every community had a processing plant called a 'still' where some refinement was done before the 'spirits' were shipped away and used in paints, varnishes, drugs and other things. For long years the hard 'rosin' residue from local distilling made excellent kindling, and the liquid turpentine was used as an antiseptic and (diluted) as a gargle. Several years ago all raw gum began to be shipped away to city markets where more thorough refining is done. Several decades ago metal cups began to be nailed to the tree to take the place of the deep tree-cut at the base, and the acid method used in scoring the face. That work, once done by individual workers, whose 'chatter' and maul could be heard for miles, is now done by crews of three or four--one smoothing the bark ahead of the tin tacker, another hanging the cups, leaving one to keep the tins, nails, and cups available."

[133]Harry DeLoach, interview with editor, September 2, 1994.

[134]"Branch Bank's First Depositor--Once Ginned Cotton on Same Site," *The Claxton Enterprise*, June 6, 1974; Harry DeLoach, interview with editor, September 2, 1994.

[135]"Enthusiastic Support Given by Loyal Son of Evans County," *The Claxton Enterprise*, Historical Edition, July 13, 1939.

[136]Harry DeLoach, interview with editor, September 2, 1994; There were several coopers, or barrel makers, in the Bellville area. According to a 1898 voting list from the 1376 District they included J.B. Guy, G.S. Guy, and B. Guy.

[137]Ibid.

[138]Tom Wood represented Evans County in 1955. *The Claxton Enterprise* of June 10, 1954 carried the following political statement: To the people of Evans County. Having lived all my life in what is now Evans County and having seen the rapid growth, development and progress made in this section, in agriculture, forestry, industry, health, welfare and schools, my greatest desire is to see our section continue to progress in every way that will make it a better and more prosperous community in which to reside. Trusting that I might be of some service and assistance to this community, and the people with whom I have always lived, I am announcing as a candidate for senator for the 49th senatorial district, in the primary to be held September 8th, 1954.

[139]Pat Boney, *The Claxton Enterprise*, "Southern Charm And Compassion Have Made Mrs. Grace Hearn a Friend to All," October 8, 1992. An excerpt follows: "Brighten The Corner Where You Are," a song that I sang as a child, came to my mind as I left my interesting interview with Mrs. Grace Hearn and thought of the incidents of her life that she had shared with me. The song just seemed to fit Mrs. Grace, whose life exemplifies the true virtues of outstanding women of the South. Her many years of unselfish service to others and her ability to temper her life with a natural humor has indeed brightened many corners and made people happy that Grace Hearn was a friend or even an acquaintance.

Grace Flanigan Hearn's life began in 1902, February 24. She was the first of six children and spent her childhood in Lincoln County, the place of her birth. One of her earliest recollections was of the cotton fields on her father's farm near the town of Lincolnton which is close to Sparta and Augusta.

It was in the 1920s that she came to Bellville to teach, little knowing that she had found the place that would soon be home. In that special place called Bellville, there was an enterprising young man whom everyone knew as "Cap" Hearn.

He was just waiting for the right girl to come along, but in the meantime, he was busy with his store which Mrs. Grace said, 'Sold everything from harnesses to calico,' and he was also the postmaster. She explained that the post office was in the same building as the store, although they had separate entrances.

Cap Hearn and Miss Grace soon were "courting." By the time she left to teach in Atlanta, they had both been smitten by Cupid's arrows, and after Mrs. Grace had been in Atlanta for a year, they were married in 1924, the day after she completed the school term.

After a short period of living with Cap Hearn's family, the newlyweds moved into a spacious house that was to be their home for their entire married life. Mrs. Grace was soon busy with a family. Two little boys, Charles William and Henry Caughey, were born a year apart.

'Those were wonderful days,' Mrs. Grace thoughtfully continued. 'I kept teaching for a few years and enjoyed it. I taught lower and upper grades as well, until finally one day Cap teased me and said, 'If you don't stop teaching and help me in the store, I'm just going to have to find a young, pretty girl that will.'

Mrs. Grace hastily added that she knew that he really wouldn't, but she made up her mind to stop teaching and help Caughey because she knew that was what he wanted. Thus it was that she began her twenty-year job of working in the post office and helping out in the store.

Besides her family responsibilities and work, Mrs. Grace had other interests that centered around a better community. The church was dear to her heart and a priority in her life. She began working to establish the first choir in the Bellville Methodist Church, and directed the choir for 20 years. All of those years, she was also teaching a Sunday School class and continued to do so for a period of 50 years. Her faithfulness to her church and her constant faith have been outstanding attributes of Mrs. Grace's life.

After Cap's death, Mrs. Grace continued to wield a good influence on those about her while sharing her charm, her love of people and her ability to look on the bright side of life. She was often engaged to speak at church meetings and other places as well because she had such a special way of brightening the dark corners of people's lives by sharing experiences of living in such a delightful way. Mrs. Grace has endeared herself to countless folks of all ages because of her sincerity and interest in other people. There is a strength in her presence that comes from her wisdom and a gleam in her eyes that makes one know she has never dwelt on the gloomy side of life too long. She chose instead to dispel the darkness with her quick wit whenever possible. Consequently, Mrs. Grace has friends from many walks of life who love her and remember her influence on them. She feels fortunate to have her two sons and their families, which include most of her grandchildren, close by.

Mrs. Grace Hearn's life has always been about doing what really matters, 'making the most of her life.' Even now at the age of 90, Mrs. Grace is doing just that."

[140]"H.C. Hearn & Co. Offers a Fine Variety of Real Services," *The Claxton Enterprise*, July 13, 1939.

[141]"You've Come a Long Way Baby," *The Claxton Enterprise*, August 13, 1994.

[142]"Bascom Tippins Dies in Claxton," *The Savannah Morning News*, January 4, 1939.

The Story of Bellville

[143] Mary Tippins Conner, interview with editor, August 3, 1995.

[144] Judge Harry R. DeLoach, *History and Genealogy of One Rogers Family, 1775-1983*, (Reidsville: *The Tattnall Journal*, 1984), p. 365. This book gives the following account: "W.W. Daniel was known far and wide for his hospitality to those needing help. A young doctor is said to have gotten off the train in Bellville, Tattnall County, Georgia, seeking a place to begin his practice of medicine. He was directed to the home of W.W. Daniel, who operated a general community store, a cotton gin, a sawmill and was postmaster of Bull Creek Post Office. The young doctor, L.M. Nichols, set up the practice of medicine at the home of W. W. Daniel and Sarah Frances Rogers Daniel. He was provided an office in the general store, and a place for his drugs to be dispensed. Before the turn of the century, Dr. Nichols had married Mattie Elizabeth Daniel, daughter of W. W Daniel."

[145] Hodges, *Locale*, p. 248; Hendry's daughter Winifred married Henry C. Smith of Claxton.

[146] Ibid., p. 168; The railroad's presence was not, however, without its dangers. The editor's grandmother, "Dolly" Brewton Johnson was killed by a locomotive while walking down the Bellville tracks in July 1941. The accident probably occurred because she was hard of hearing and did not hear the approaching train. She was also wearing a bonnet which further impeded her hearing at the time of the accident.

[147] Herschel Hearn, interview with Emily Groover, November 10, 1990.

[148] WW I Evans County Soldiers, Registration Records, Vol. 1, Evans County Court House.

[149] "A Prosperous County," *The Claxton Enterprise*, April 19, 1918.

[150] *The Claxton Enterprise* "Bellville News" articles carried much "personal" news of Bellville's residents.

[151] Delma and Mary Daniel, interview with editor, July 7, 1995.

[152] "Airplane Wrecked--Young Lady Hurt," *The Claxton Enterprise*, January 17, 1919. Several Bellville residents still recall this incident. See Delma and Mary Daniel interview.

[153] William Solomon Davis, from Dahlonega, became the father-in-law of a local Bellville boy, Sidney Johnson, when Johnson married Davis' daughter, Myrtle. Sidney left Bellville for Dahlonega where he attended North Georgia College. Jim Johnson, interview with editor, July 31, 1995.

[154] Amiel Fountain, interview with editor, February 21, 1995; Jim Johnson, interview with editor, July 31, 1995.

[155] "Sweet Daddy Grace Dies: Followers 'Roll Out' As Usual," *The Savannah Morning News*, January 13, 1960. Also, see Herschel Hearn interview. Bishop Grace died in Los Angeles in 1960. He established more than 350 Houses of Prayer over a 33 year period. Reports estimated his following at more than three million, and his elegant, flamboyant style was extremely popular; Inman Hearn deeded the land to Bishop C.M. Grace, Trustee for the United House of Prayer, on April 25, 1930. Bishop Grace paid $40 for the one acre parcel. The legal description of the property is as follows: "Bounded north by lands of J.M. Wood and the right of way of the Seaboard Air Line Railway; east by land of J.M. Wood and lands of the estate of Nancy E. Parker; south by lands of the estate of Nancy E. Parker; and on the west by lands of Inman C. Hearn." Evans County Deed Book 15, p. 288; The United House of Prayer for all People dedicated a beautiful new church in Bellville, September 23, 1995.

[156] Brewton, *County History*; State land grant to David Hennesy, 830 acres, Tattnall Co. warrant dated March

4, 1811. Tattnall County Land Grant Book 1802-1837, p. 40; For right of way deeds relating to this road see Evans County Deed Book 11, p. 533.

[157] Winton Bell, interview with editor, September 2, 1995; See Evans County Deed Books 17, 25, and 34. A full listing of right of way owners is provided in these deed books; Tom Wood was a county commissioner from 1942 until 1950 and Wright Daniel, from 1950 to 1954. Hodges, *Locale*, p. 192.

[158] Brewton, *County History*.

[159] Church members dedicated the Service Plaque on Sunday, May 28, 1944. The plaque is in the social hall of Bellville Methodist Church.

[160] Letter provided by Jimmie Styles, Ft. Worth, Texas, October 20, 1995.

[161] War Department Letter, Adjutant General's Office, Washington, D.C., August 26, 1944. Letter in possession of Loulie Perkins, Daniel's sister.

[162] This document is in Bellville Church records. It bears the words, "To Whom It May Concern," and "This paper is to be attached to the defense bond."

[163] For a full coverage of the tragic story of displacement of families from the Ft. Stewart area see the book, *Evans County and the Creation of Fort Stewart, Georgia*, by the editor.

[164] David Groover, interview with editor, July 8, 1995.

[165] Ibid.

[166] Amiel Fountain, interview with editor, February 21, 1995.

[167] Eloise Hodges, interview with editor, September 2, 1995; Winton Bell, interview with editor, September 2, 1995.

[168] *The Claxton Enterprise*, January 7, 1954.

[169] Herschel Hearn, interview with Emily Groover, November 10, 1990.

[170] "1st District Tourney Gets Off to Successful Start," *Savannah Morning News*, February 23, 1923.

[171] "Manassas, U.S. Post Office," manuscript, Oka Eason, Postmaster, March 10, 1949.

[172] Winton Bell, interview with editor, September 2, 1995.

[173] Delma Daniel, interview with editor, July 7, 1995; The first member of the Canoochee Electric Corporation Board of Directors from the Bellville area was English G. Smith; Hodges, *Locale*, p. 203.

[174] Amiel Fountain, interview with editor, February 21, 1995.

[175] "Women in Membership Makes Bellville Lions Club Unique," *The Claxton Enterprise*, April 1, 1993.

[176] Harry DeLoach, interview with editor, September 2, 1994.

[177]Information on Pinewood obtained from "Pinewood Christian celebrates silver anniversary," *The Claxton Enterprise*, May 25, 1995, and "The Beginning--Pinewood Concept Credited to Dr. Charles H. Drake," by O.H. "Tab" Smith, special tabloid, 1982.

[178]Tab Smith, interview with editor, July 2, 1996.

[179]Darin McCoy, interview with editor, May 8, 1995; Tom T. Hall's song, "When God Came Through Bellville, Georgia," was the flip side of the 1974 "Country Is" single. Copyright on the Mercury label.

[180]Jerry Coleman, Bellville Mayor, interview with editor, July 6, 1995.

[181]An article from the January 22, 1959 *Claxton Enterprise* is attached to the incorporation request submitted to the state.

[182]The act further states, "To create a charter for the City of Bellville in the County of Evans; to provide for powers and authority of said city; to provide for corporate limits; to provide for a mayor and council; to provide for elections; to provide for voters; to provide for terms of office; to provide for qualifications; to provide for permanent registration; to provide for vacancies; to provide for duties; to provide for employees; to provide for compensation; to provide for police and firemen; to provide a police court and procedures connected therewith; to provide for taxation to provide for licenses; to provide for revenue-producing projects and systems; to grant the power of eminent domain; to authorize the making of ordinances; to provide for an effective date; to repeal conflicting laws; and for other purposes."

[183]House Bill 297, March 10, 1959.

The extremely rare photo above depicts construction of the S&W Railroad through Bellville in 1890. (Photo courtesy of Ray DeLoach)

*Vintage Photographs
of Bellville*

Bellville Railroad Depot. Note spelling (Belleville) of the town's name. *Left to right:* Daisy Sikes (depot agent), Glenn Tippins, Clyde Tippins, and Maggie Tippins. (Circa 1908 photo courtesy Delma Daniel)

Bellville, with a thriving business district, was once the largest town in the area. A disastrous fire in May 1901 burned the business district to the ground. One of the stores was operated by J. B. Collins. The building included a Masonic hall and Dr. Nichol's office. Circa 1900 photo by A.H. Prince. (Photo courtesy of Delma Daniel)

Rosa King and her Bellville Sunday School class. Note Bellville's buildings in the background (looking east, north of the railroad). (Early 1900s photo by A.H. Prince courtesy of Delma Daniel)

Up for a Bellville buggy trip? Helen Smith and her brother-in-law Rufus (Dick) Daniel go for a ride. (Circa 1910 photo courtesy of Delma Daniel)

Bessie *(left)* and Mae Hearn in front of their father's Bellville store in 1918. (Photo courtesy of Emily Hearn Groover)

C.C. Daniel and Herschel Hearn *(right)* in front of Bellville School. (Photo courtesy of Jim Hearn)

The Bellville culvert pipe in front of Tom Wood's store was a favorite gathering spot for the town's youth. (1920s photo courtesy of Emily Hearn Groover)

Three of Bellville's girls cross the "foot bridge" into town circa 1918. (Photo courtesy of Emily Hearn Groover)

Tattnall Campground girls stroll the quadrangle surrounding the tabernacle. Photo from 1920s. (All photos on this page courtesy Emily Hearn Groover)

The Tattnall Campground spring was a popular gathering spot for youngsters. This 1920s photo captures the blurred image of a girl jumping down from the well curb.

The Tabernacle at Tattnall Campground in the early 1930s. Nollie Parker, of Bellville, was the chief builder of the tabernacle. Architectural experts consider the tabernacle to be one of the best examples of this type building in the state.

Bellville street scene. *Left to right:* Adam Bird, Inman Hearn, Clarence Parker, Herschel Hearn, Clyde Tippins. Circa 1913. (All photos on this page courtesy of Emily Hearn Groover)

Bascom Tippins' Store was a popular place for youngsters to congregate. Photo circa 1925.

C.W. Hearn Store and Post Office in 1920. Note railroad wagon on left side of photo.

Vintage Photographs of Bellville

Paul LeGrand, depot agent, at the Hearn Gin in Bellville. The building on the left sits where the Claxton Bank branch is today, and the buildings on the right are still present. (1930s photo courtesy of Lois Parker Turner)

Above: Bellville Depot. Lumber from the Daniel sawmill awaits loading. (1930s photo courtesy of Lois Parker Turner)

Right: Depot as it appeared in 1962. Pictured is a visiting railroad agent. Note snow on the ground.

Bascom Tippins, Sr. Dealership. *Left to right:* Bascom Tippins, Glenn Tippins, Clyde Hammock, B.C. Vaughn, Caughey Hearn, Clyde Tippins, Alvis Nunnaly, Jimps Collins, Lee Kennedy, Adam Byrd, Theodore Brewton. The automobiles are Overland (left) and Brush models. Photo circa 1915. (Circa photo courtesy Delma Daniel)

Bascom Tippins Country Store, complete with a dog and a gas pump. Stores such as this provided important sources of credit, medicines, groceries, and news. (1920s photo courtesy of Mary Tippins Conner)

Mamie Tippins, pictured in 1924 on her first date with her future husband Bascom Tippins, Sr. (Photo courtesy of Mary Tippins Conner)

A vintage auto on the streets of Bellville in the early 1900s. (Photo courtesy of Emily Hearn Groover)

C.C. Daniel and his future wife, Winnie, in 1922. (Photo courtesy of Jim Hearn)

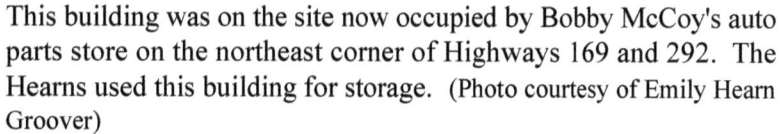

This building was on the site now occupied by Bobby McCoy's auto parts store on the northeast corner of Highways 169 and 292. The Hearns used this building for storage. (Photo courtesy of Emily Hearn Groover)

Bellville was the shopping town for many of the residents of Bay Branch community south of the town. Above is a photo of Bay Branch School, which consilidated with Bellville school in 1921. (Early 1900s photo courtesy Delma Daniel)

The Bellville culvert "pipe" was a gathering place for the town's youth. The spot was located in front of what is now the Bellville City Hall. (Early 1920s photo courtesy of Jim Hearn)

Vintage Photographs of Bellville

Early Bellville merchant and cotton gin owner, Charlie Hearn. (Photo courtesy of Emily Hearn Groover)

The Hearn Store was a landmark in Bellville for many years. The post office was in the left section of the building. Photo from the 1940s.

Interior view of the Hearn Store, circa 1950. *Left to right:* "Cap," Grace, and Charles Hearn. (Photo courtesy of Emily Hearn Groover)

Hearn Store Coke thermometer.

The big moving day in 1971 for the Hearn Store. Observing are Nancy Groover, *left,* and Alan Groover. The building, bought by Bernie Anderson, was in turn sold to Herbert Daniel. Daniel moved it to his farm south of town. (Photo courtesy of Emily Hearn Groover)

Tom Wood's Store. Wood's first store stood just south of the railroad and adjacent to the Bellville Depot. Pictured *(left to right)* are Tom Wood, Johnny Clark, unknown, Johnny Wood, and Roger Wood. (Early 1940's photo courtesy of Jerry Coleman)

The boys of Bellville took advantage of the sandlot to play ball. Looking north, Hearn store is on left and Bascom Tippins House, on right. (1920s photo courtesy Emily Hearn Groover)

Ella Lee, Tom, and Elizabeth Wood *(right)* with Homer Wilson on platform of Wood's turpentine still located south of the railroad and east of Highway 169. The still replaced a former one located west of Highway 169 and just south of the railroad. (1950s photo courtesy of Jerry Coleman)

Tom Wood *(right)* pictured with Frank E. Fulmer, area forester. (1950s photo courtesy of Jerry Coleman)

Troop 57. *From left*: Scout master Roy Styles and troop members Charles Johnson, Charles Hearn, Jimmy Collins *(kneeling)*, B.G. Tippins, Jr., "C" Hearn, and Bobby Styles. (1941 photo courtesy of Jimmy Styles)

Charlie Johnson sports a new Model T in Bellville. Photo circa 1925.

Carolus Daniel pictured by the Bellville depot. Note the cart for offloading from train cars. (1940s photo courtesy of Eloise Hodges)

Vintage Photographs of Bellville 81

1961 Tobacco Farming Scenes. Tobacco has been an important cash crop in the Bellville area since the late 1920s.

Above: Grady Blocker *(left)* and his crew in a 1961 photo at the Charlie Johnson farm.

Right: The editor holds a stick of tobacco at his father's farm in 1962.

Bishop C.M. Grace ("Daddy Grace"), founder of the United House of Prayer for all People. Grace held services in Bellville from the 1930s through the 1950s. (Photo from 1995 church dedication album)

Bellville United House of Prayer dedication of its new building in 1995.

APPENDIX A

Sketches of Early Bellville Families

Bellville Area Families at the Time of the Town's Creation

This appendix provides brief sketches of families living in the Bellville area at the time of the town's founding in 1890.

Benton. James Benton and wife Maria Marinda Seran Guy Benton, daughter of J.B. and Marinda (Best) Guy of Warsaw, N.C., came to Bellville in the 1890s. Their son, Willie J. Benton, was a Seaboard Railroad agent in the area for years, and daughter Hellon married Roy Styles.[1]

Brewton, Benjamin Berrian (1834-1912). "Berry" Brewton was one of the founders of Bellville. His house and farm were on what is now the eastern boundary of the town. Berry Brewton sold many of the original house lots in Bellville in the 1890s. In 1863, he married Candacy Tippins (1835-1914), daughter of William Wayne (1796-1871) and Mary Eason Tippins (1800-1878). Berry was the son of Benjamin (1796-1875) and Charlotte Bacon Brewton (1808-1876) and grandson of Nathan (1762-1855) and Nancy Fontaine Brewton (1777-1864). Berry made his living in the farming and timber trades. In addition to being one of the original tent holders at Tattnall County Campground in 1867, he contributed much to the support of the Methodist Church and the Bellville Academy. He was a Confederate veteran (61st Georgia, Company B) who fought in the thick of many important battles in the Army of Northern Virginia. He was wounded in the Battle of Gettysburg, and later captured in 1864 at the Battle of Winchester. After spending six months at Pt. Lookout Prison in Maryland, he returned to Tattnall County as an exchanged prisoner just before the end of the war in 1865. He was Tattnall County Tax Collector from 1887 to 1889. Berry and Candacy had the following children: Florence (m. Wiley Rowe); Andrew Jackson (m. Frances Eugenia Sikes); William Henry (m. Sheldona Matilda Hodges); Mary (m. Jonathan Collins); Martha P. (m. McCoy "Mac" Johnson); Nancy C.; David Giles; Charley M.; Robert B. (m. Eva Gordon Goss); George Asbury (m. Nancy Elizabeth Callaway); and F. Theodore (see below)[2].

Brewton, Theodore (1882-1973). Theodore's parents were Berry and Candacy Brewton. Educated at Peabody College for Teachers in Nashville, Tennessee, Theodore was a school teacher for many years. He taught at Bellville School and was the Evans County School Superintendent from 1920-29. He married Sarah Galbreth of Glennwood, Georgia in 1914, and they had one child, Eleanor. He was a trustee for Georgia Teachers College for many years.[3]

Brewton, David Jessie (1858-1928). Jessie Brewton was a real estate dealer who lived in Bellville during its early years. His parents were Nathan Brewton, son of Benjamin, and Jane Elizabeth Durrence. Jessie married Euzebia E. Hendrix in 1879. Their children were Allen Jackson, Nettie Iola, Benjamin Lester, Rosa May, Minnie Neta, Maudie Durean, Robert Clanton, Cleo, and Edith Rebecca. He settled in Bellville in 1890 and helped start the Bellville School. Jesse was the first secretary of the Sunday school that later became Bellville Methodist Church.[4]

Brewton, Benjamin B. (1851-1881). Ben B. Brewton was the son of Jonathan B. and Margaret Everett Brewton. Ben married Sallie Calhoun (1852-1923) in 1875 and they settled on a farm two and one-half miles south of Bellville. According to a family sketch, "Ben and Sallie Brewton settled in a log house on the Bellville-Mendes road, now known as State Highway 169, to live and raise a family. They split rails to make fences, and their cattle grazed in the open woodlands on wiregrass. They had a hollowed out log with a partition in it for a washtrough. On this two foot partition in the washtrough, the clothes were beaten with a battling stick as part of the process of cleaning. Also, a black washpot was used to boil their clothes and a well from which to pull their water." Ben died at the age of 30 and is buried in the J.B. Brewton Cemetery behind the old home place on the Claxton-Metter road. Their children were Henry Leonard (1876-1964, m. Laura Julia Jenkins); Margaret Addie (1877-1958, m. William Arthur Butts); and Susan Katherine (died at age 18). Leonard Brewton was one of the first County Commissioners of Evans County from 1915-1919.[5]

Daniel, Enoch B. "Knuck" (1840-1919). From Taylors Creek, Liberty County, Enoch B. moved to Bellville in the Fall of 1889 and started a sawmill in the Bellville area. He was instrumental in establishing the Bellville Academy and was a strong supporter of the Bellville Methodist Church. Enoch B. was the third child of Enoch (1799-1863) and Annaliza Bird Daniel (1807-1869). Enoch (Enoch B.'s father) organized the Liberty Guards, a cavalry troop from Liberty County, and until his death in 1863, served as the troop's captain. Enoch B. married first, Leah Hodges, and second, Margaret Elvina Laing (1835-1921). Their children were James Hardee (m. Jeanette Folsom); Walford Lee (m. Mary Holder); Enoch Angus; Olin Hines (m. Helen Smith); Henry Ross (m. Thessille Williams); and Rufus Lester (m. Ora Rogers).[6]

Enoch B. Daniel's son, Olin Hines Daniel, Sr., was born in Liberty County in 1878. He was a sawmill operator. In 1910 he married Helen Smith, the daughter of Pulaski S. and Mary Eliza Tippins Smith. They are buried in the Daniel-Smith-Tippins cemetery in Bellville. Their children were Walter Emmett (m. Nita Powell); Mary Helen (m. Delma Daniel); Stella Wilson (m. John William Powell); and Olin Hines, Jr. (m. Martha Louise Cumbie).[7]

Grice, Joseph Tom (1836-1916). Tom Grice was a merchant in early Bellville, and was the first owner of the house (later known as the Hearn House) located at the northeast corner of the Highway 169 and Highway 280 intersection. Tom was the son of William and Eveline Smart Grice. He married Nancy Elmira Darsey in 1867 and lived in Liberty County until about 1882 when he moved to Tattnall County. Tom Grice served in the Civil War as a sergeant in Troop D of the 5th Georgia Cavalry. He served as Bellville postmaster from 1898-1900 and Tattnall County Tax Collector in 1904. Nancy and Tom had the following children: Agnes (m. J.P. Smith); Lillie (m. Fred Conley); William (m. first Flora Wilson, m. second Lucille Whitten); Joseph (Joe) T. (m. Lena Kennedy); James B.; and Edwin R. (m. first Stella Sutton, m. second Bertha Peeples). Joe Grice was a lawyer, judge, and Georgia State representative.[8]

Hearn, Amos (1824-1864). Amos J. Hearn, son of Jesse Hearn of Twiggs County, and Amos' wife Emily Brewton Hearn moved to what would become the Bellville area, prior to 1860. He died as a Confederate soldier at Mercy Hospital in Savannah. He was in the 5th Georgia Cavalry Regiment, Company H. Before the war Amos was a widely respected builder. He constructed the A.D. Eason House in the Undine section, and reportedly, the J.B. Brewton home on Highway 129.[9] Amos and Emily Hearn had three children: Melvina (1861-1927), m. John "Duffy" Rogers (1847-1941); Simon A. (1862-1928), Methodist minister, m. Della Anthony; and, Charles W. (1864-1921), m. Nancy

Eulalia Durrence. Emily Brewton Hearn married Chadburn Parker second. Emily was the mother of 18 children. The Hearn family is noted for producing numerous members of the ministry.[10]

C.W. Hearn, son of Amos and Emily Hearn, operated a store and cotton gin in Bellville for many years. His sons, H.C. "Cap" (m. Grace Flanigan) and Inman (m. Elma Riggs) operated these businesses after C.W. died.[11]

Lynn, Redden Asbury. Born in Tattnall County on May 8, 1844, R.A. Lynn was the son of Matilda Yeomans Lynn and Josiah Lynn. He was a private in Company H, Tattnall County Volunteers, 61st Georgia Volunteer Infantry. He was among the survivors who surrendered at Appomattox, Virginia, April 9, 1865. He married Charlotte Jane Daniel (1838-1886) on September 26, 1865. She was the daughter of James P. Daniel and Elizabeth Glisson. Redden died in 1921. Redden and Charlotte are buried at Old Anderson Primitive Baptist Church in Tattnall County. Their farm was about one mile west of Bellville.[12]

Parker, John Chadburn. Born March 13, 1836, in Liberty County, "Shad" Parker became an orphan early in life. He moved to Tattnall County, and settled in the area that later became Bellville. His first wife was Queen Smith, daughter of James B. and Georgia Ann Sikes Smith. She died a short time after their marriage. His second wife, Nancy Emily (Brewton) Hearn, was the daughter of Simon J. (1819-1865) and Matilda U. Brewton. Nancy's first husband was Amos J. Hearn (see Amos Hearn sketch above). Shad and Nancy had fifteen children, with the last two dying young and unnamed. Their children were Alice, (m. William H. Wood); Lila (m. Walter Cox); Matilda Jane (m. Will Smith); Lavenia; Joe E.; Julian H.; Ophelia (m. W.T. Harvey); Georgia; Mary (m. first Se Glisson, m. second J.A. Sconyers); Clarence O.; Walter Nollie; Odessa; and Clara E. Shad Parker, a Confederate veteran, served in Company G, 47th Georgia Regiment, and attained the rank of first lieutenant. A Yankee sharpshooter shot him in the back at the Battle of Kennesaw Mountain, Georgia in 1864. The bullet remained in his body the rest of his life. He was a Mason and also one of the first tent holders at the Tattnall County Campground. He died at the age of 82 in 1917.[13]

Parker, Nollie. Nollie Parker lived in Bellville and was a builder. He married Emma Johnson. His "masterpiece" of construction is the tabernacle at Tattnall County Campground. He built many other homes in the area. He normally built from plans not on paper, but in his head.

Riggs, William Shepherd (1839-1901), born in Tattnall County, married Mary Frances Hammock (1845-1920). His farm was just south of the Tattnall County Campground. He was a Confederate Soldier and served in Company B, Tattnall Rangers, of the 61st Georgia Volunteer Infantry. He was wounded at Gettysburg July 1, 1863. Captured at Winchester, Virginia, September 19, 1864, he obtained a parole in 1865 at Point Lookout Prison in Maryland. He was at home as an exchanged prisoner at the end of the war. Shepherd and Mary Riggs' children were Lalah (m. English Smith); Hattie (m. Charlie Rogers); Lola (m. Walton Rogers); Tim (m. Alma Jones); Shelton (m. Sue McBride); Elliot (Dutchess Morgan); Marvin (m. Rachel McCord); Mode (m. Donnie Jenkins); and Loren (m. Beulah Evans).[14]

Smith, Simon (1754-1827). Simon Smith, his wife Mary, and family came to Georgia from Nash County, N.C., about the time of the Revolution. He performed Revolutionary War service in Georgia. The family first lived in Screven County, and came to Tattnall about 1818. They settled south of present-day Bellville and had very large land holdings. Their children were: James (m. Fannie Bell); Elender (m. Henry Magee); Mary (m. Wilson Conner); and Rebecca (m. Aaron B. Strickland).[15]

Smith, James Bell (1823-1891). Son of James and Frances Bell Smith (for whom Bellville is named), and grandson of Simon and Mary Smith, James B. built the oldest house still standing in the Bellville area and one of the oldest in the county. The house dates to 1854 or 1855, long before the town started. The home, located just south of the intersection of Highways 280 and 169, is of hand-hewn log construction. James B. Smith represented Tattnall County in the Georgia General Assembly from 1855 to 1858 and again in 1877. He entered the Civil War as a captain of Company H, 61st Georgia Volunteer Infantry. He died in 1891 from war related injuries. He married Georgia Ann Sikes (1825-1870), daughter of Dr. Daniel and Elizabeth Julian Eason Sikes. He married Rachel Brazell Tippins (1834-1900) second. She was the widow of Captain Phillip Glenn Tippins, who commanded Company G, 47th Georgia Volunteer Infantry. The children from his first marriage were the following: Daniel Harrison, (m. first Nancy Brewton, m. second Julia C. Rogers); Alexander A. (m. Ann Jane Archer); Queen Ann Mozell (m. John C. "Shad" Parker); Godiva (m. Duncan Wilkes); Euzeby (m. Joe Alexander); Helena Augusta Victoria (m. George W. Tippins); James B. II (m. Martha A. Alexander); Pulaski Sikes (m. Mary Elizabeth Tippins); Oscar M. (m. Clara Graves); Alvarader Beauregard (m. Mary Thompson); Michael (Mike) McKenzie (m. Kate Fry); Ulala, and Georgia Ann (m. Silas Hardee). James B. Smith and his second wife, Rachel Brazell Tippins, had two daughters, Mildred Estela (m. Samuel Mann); and Ursula (m. Stephen M. Tillman).[16]

Smith, Daniel H. (1841-1892), son of James B. and Georgia Ann Sikes Smith, was prominent in the affairs of his community and a leader in church activity. He was one of the first trustees of Tattnall Campground and helped in the building of the first tabernacle. He was a soldier in the Confederate Army and a member of Company B, 61st Georgia Volunteer Regiment. Discharged in 1863 because of disability, he became a mail carrier. He married first, Nancy Brewton (1843-1885), daughter of Benjamin and Charlotte Bacon Brewton, and second, Julia C. Rogers. The children from the first marriage were Claudius Clarence, Ezzie, Queen Ann, Lovick Pierce, Commodore Beecher, Stuart Plunkett, English Gartrell, Labella Maude, and Roscoe Thurman. His second marriage produced two sons, one who died as an infant and a second one, James B. Smith III, who became a Hollywood screenwriter[17]

Smith, Pulaski Sikes (1856-1894), son of James B. Smith, was instrumental in the early development of Bellville. His wife was Mary Eliza Tippins Smith (1859-1939). He sold many of the town lots, and was Bellville's first postmaster. He also helped in the establishment of the church and school. Sikes and Mary Eliza Smith had the following children: Pulaski Sikes II, Dewitt Clinton, J. Colon, Helen, and Carl.[18]

Tippins, William Wayne (1796-1871), son of Phillip Tippins, married Mary Eason, daughter of William and Mary Eason in 1816. They had a large family and large land holdings in the Bellville area. His plantation was in the Tattnall Campground area. He served as Justice of the Tattnall County Inferior Court in 1843-44. He also served as vice-president of the 1860 Tattnall County secession meeting. The children of William and Mary Tippins were as follows: Mary Elizabeth (m. Benjamin Alexander); Sarah Miriam (m. Gabe S. Miller); Nancy Pinkin (m. Roger Wood); Matilda Underwood (m. Simon J. Brewton); George Eason; Phillip Glenn (m. Rachel Brazell); Lucius Asbury Hill (m. first Martha Parker, second Ella Lanier); William Eason (m. Martha E. Brewton); Candacy Ann (m. Berrian Brewton); Parthenia Ann (m. Simon J. Brewton); Cornelia Ann; and John Underwood (m. Eliza Holland).[19]

Tippins, Phillip Glenn (1827-1866), son of William Wayne and Mary Tippins, was a prominent resident from what later became the Bellville area. Elected as Tattnall County Ordinary in 1860, he planned to serve a four-year term. However, when Georgia joined the Confederacy in 1861, he organized a company of men called the "Tattnall Invincibles." He was captain of this unit that later became Company G, 47th Regiment of Georgia Volunteers. He left the Ordinary's office in the care of his father and went off to war. He resigned in 1863 and returned to the county. He died in 1866, and his widow, Rachel (Brazell), married James B. Smith. Phillip and Rachel Tippins' children were: George William (m. Helena Smith); Parthenia Emily (m. first Henry Clay Smith, m. second William Blackstone); Mary Elizabeth (m. Pulaski Sikes Smith); Phillip Glenn, Jr. (m. Rebecca Clark); John Underwood (m. Minnie McArthur); and Henrietta Matilda (m. Abraham D. Eason).[20]

Tippins, George William (1855-1908). George Tippins, oldest son of Captain Philip Glenn and Rachel Brazell Tippins (1831-1900), was one of the early supporters of the Bellville Methodist Church and Bellville Academy. In 1872, he married Helena Victoria Smith (1852-1893), daughter of James Bell Smith and Georgia Ann Sikes Smith. He was a Tattnall County commissioner for one term and was Bellville postmaster from 1895 to 1897. He also had a business to provide crossties to the railroad. George Tippins was killed in an accident in 1908 when his barn collapsed on him. George and Helena Tippins had the following children: James Otto; Bascom Glenn (m. first Maggie May Bird, m. second Mamie Mathews); Anna Cannady (m. Henry H. Strickland); Lala (m. Scott Bird); Grover; Genie; and Stella.[21]

Tippins, Sr., Bascom, son of George W. and Helena, was an Evans County politician and a merchant in Bellville. The following account of his life was included in "Georgia Lawmakers" by John Hammond (*Macon Telegraph*, December 1, 1932). "Born January 4, 1875, in Bellville. Educated in local high school. Engaged as a telegraph operator 12 years. Methodist. Democrat. Mason: Shriner. Postmaster at Bellville several years, office formally held by his father. Son of George William and Helen (Smith) Tippins of Tattnall County. Married first April 7, 1901 (Maggie Mae Bird), and second January 15, 1925 (Mamie Mathews). Merchant and banker. Member of the House of Representatives from Evans County 1923-27 and 1929-34. In the Legislature ranks as an ultra conservative. Has heretofore opposed large appropriations, stood for creation of a budget system and was for state departmental reorganization. Has participated more largely in agricultural legislation and advocated property tax reduction."

Wood, John M. (1861-1953). Son of Roger Wood (1817-1905), an expert craftsman from Blackburn, Lancashire, England, came to Savannah via New York where Roger met and married Nancy Tippins, daughter of William W. (1796-1871) and Mary Evelyn (Eason) Tippins (1800-1878). Nancy Tippins' sister, Sarah Miller, ran a boarding house in Savannah. Nancy was visiting her sister when she met Roger Wood. After their marriage, they moved to Tattnall County where Roger engaged in his trade as a tinner and farmer. John Wood owned some of the original town lots in the city of Bellville and lived just northwest of the town. John's siblings were Willie, George, Charlie, and Carrie (Rogers). John married Evelyn Durrence (1865-1945) daughter of Thomas A. (1831-1893) and Elizabeth Grice Durrence (1838-1922) in 1888. John and Evelyn Wood's children were Carrie Ola (m. Cleburn Daniel); Maggie Elizabeth (m. John Shuptrine); Nina Nancy (m. Felder Jordan); Thomas Jefferson (m. Ella Lee Rogers); Mattie Eulala (m. Stokes Bickley); Jessie Mae (m. Cleve Durrence); John Hartridge (m. Joyce Roberson); and Roger William (m. Emily Guest).[22]

Notes

[1] Lucile Hodges, *History of Our Locale*, (Macon: Southern Press, 1965), p. 233.

[2] *Memoirs of Georgia; Historical and Biographical*, Vol. II, Georgia Historical Association, Atlanta, 1895, p. 851; Hodges, *Locale*, p. 15.

[3] Biographical Questionnaire (Theodore Brewton, Historian of Evans County), June 3, 1931, Georgia State Archives, Atlanta.

[4] *Memoirs of Georgia*, p. 851.

[5] *Family Sketches* in Evans County Courthouse. "Benjamin B. Brewton Family," Grace Brewton Daniel, Claxton, Ga., 1976.

[6] *Taylors Creek, 1760-1986*, Bird and Paul Yarbrough, Editors, (Greenville: A Press, 1986), pp. 211-212.

[7] Ibid., pp. 212-215.

[8] Ibid., p. 247; *Family Sketches* in Evans County Courthouse, "J. Thomas Grice."

[9] Amos Hearn signed his name in chalk in the attic of the Eason house, and his inscription is still visible today, more than 140 years after he built the house; Hearn's involvement with the Brewton house comes from traditional sources. Editor.

[10] Mrs. J.C. Parker, Obituary, *The Claxton Enterprise*, May 3, 1927; Hodges, *Locale*, p. 19.

[11] The business was known as H.C. Hearn & Co. Inman Hearn always joked that his part was the "& Co."; A third son, Herschel, moved to North Carolina.

[12] Information furnished by Bellville resident Ruby Brown; Lillian Henderson, *Roster of the Confederate Soldiers of Georgia*, Vol. 6, (Hapevile, Ga.: Longino and Porter, 1959), p. 262.

[13] J.C. Parker Obituary, *The Claxton Enterprise*, March 2, 1917; Devane Lewis, *Parker and Allied Families*, 1992.

[14] Henderson, *Roster of the Confederate Soldiers of Georgia*, Vol. 6, p. 214; Hodges, *Locale*, 1965, p. 317.

[15] Lawrence M. Edwards, *Simon Smith Family*, typescript, unpublished, 1967; Joseph E. Spann, Jr., *Some Revolutionary Soldiers of Evans County, Georgia*, typescript, date unknown.; Folks Huxford, *Pioneers of Wiregrass Georgia*, Vol. IV, (Waycross: Herrin's Print Shop, 1967), pp. 271-272.

[16] Lawrence M. Edwards, *Simon Smith Family*, typescript, unpublished, 1967; Biographical Questionnaire (Bascom G. Tippins, State Representative), June 15, 1931, Georgia State Archives Atlanta, Ga.; Typescript in Family History volume in Evans County Library, "James Bell Smith (1823-1891)."

[17] Typescript in Family History volume in Evans County Library, "Daniel Harrison Smith (1841-1892)"; Henderson, *Roster of the Confederate Soldiers of Georgia*, Vol. 6, p. 215; A typescript, written by English G. Smith in 1958, and provided to the editor by Gene Smith provides the following information about Daniel H. Smith. "Life and Experiences of E.G. Smith--I was born September 21, 1877 at the old home of my grandfather, James B. Smith. My father was named Daniel Harrison Smith. My father's first livelihood was cutting timber and floating it to Savannah. He was a great hunter. He kept good dogs and was considered the best shot in his day. He shot deer and wild turkey with an old muzzle loading rifle. He was very ambitious and a

hard worker. When I was two years old my grandfather gave him a tract of land. It consisted of 1,000 acres on Bull Creek, two and one-half miles south of Bellville, Georgia. It was well timbered with no buildings or clearing. In 1879 he built a small log house and in 1880 moved in it. He cleared 50 acres of land and went to farming. Later, he built a big frame house and in a few years he was one of the biggest and most outstanding farmers of his day. He was a good provider and good to his children. He belonged to the Methodist Church and managed his house well. He was a good Christian. My mother was one of the most devout Christians I ever saw. The best mother one ever had. She was also a hard worker. She developed T.B. and died in 1885 at the age of 40. She was the mother of nine children, six boys and three girls. The oldest was named Essey which got killed at 9 years old when a well sweep broke. The rest of the children lived until after our Mother died in 1885 leaving my father and eight children."

Tab Smith provided the following account of James B. Smith's life in a letter of August 16, 1996:
"A rough sketch of James B. Smith ("Jim B.") and of his unusual adventures goes like this: Daniel H. Smith married his second wife Julia C. Rogers (who was, interestingly enough, a sister to his son Claude's first wife, Shelldonna Rogers) and Jim B. was their son. (Thus, Jim B. became my dad's uncle and also his first cousin!) Jim B. and Tab Smith, Sr. went to Jacksonville, Fla. to attend Massey Business College, holding down part-time jobs to make their way through. Daddy said that Jim B. could compose a letter and write brief narratives amazingly well even then. After the experience at the bank in Claxton, Jim B. and family were in Atlanta. He secured a job with the YMCA with the help of Bishop Warren A. Candler and saved up sufficient funds to get to California. This would have been in the 19-teens when Hollywood was establishing itself as the movie capital. I often think of how beautiful it must have been when the Smiths from Bellville, Georgia arrived!

Uncle Jim B. somehow obtained a job as business manager for Richard Talmadge, a famous actor during the silent movie days. Near the end of a certain week, Talmadge and his film company met to begin a new feature, only to discover that the script writer had produced nothing for them (they say that the business was pretty much off-the-cuff in those days). Never shy about his own abilities, Jim B. allowed as how he could write a script if Talmadge would give him the weekend to do so. On Monday, he presented a finished script, and his career as a Hollywood writer was underway.

Our information is somewhat sketchy for a decade or so but I have learned that Uncle Jim B., writing under the nom de plume Stuart Anthony (a combination of his brother Stuart Smith's name and that of Bascom Anthony, a famous Methodist preacher), spent much of the 1930s writing scripts for the then-popular western movies. Some of the titles and actors are: *Desert Vengeance* (1931) with Buck Jones, *Whistlin' Dan* (1932) with Ken Maynard, *The Vanishing Frontier* (1932) with Johnny Mack Brown, *End of the Trail* (1932) with Tim McCoy, *Smoky* (1933) with Victor Jory, *Frontier Marshal* (1934) with George O'Brien, *Hell Town* (1937) with John Wayne and Johnny Mack Brown, *Saga of Death Valley* (1939) with Roy Rogers, and *The Ranger and the Lady* (1940) with Roy Rogers. John Tuska, film critic and author, in his comprehensive work, *The Filming of the West*, mentions *End of the Trail* which is listed above, and relates, "In autumn 1932 Tim made his masterpiece of the sound era for Columbia. McCoy persuaded Irving Briskin, who was head of Western production, to appropriate nearly three times the money and take the entire company to Lander, Wyoming, to film a Western using the Arapaho tribes which resided there on the Wind River Reservation. The screenplay was by Stuart Anthony. Anthony was free-lance scenarist.... His plots, while commercial, were nothing extraordinary. But Tim talked with him, and together they worked out Tim's impassioned monologues in which Tim set down in the strongest possible terms the staggering injustices the red man had suffered.... *End of the Trail* was in every way exceptional.... It stands out among not only McCoy's Westerns of the thirties but among any series Western Columbia was ever to make."

At some point, Jim B. was placed under contract to Paramount Pictures Corporation and, at this time, became quite wealthy. My cousin Harry Smith (now deceased) was on a business trip at this time and decided to "drop in" on Jim B. He and his wife were met at the door of Anthony's Beverly Hills mansion by a butler who was not about to admit two uninvited Georgians. Fortunately, Jim B. was home, heard their voices, and warmly received Harry and Dorothy, and insisted that they spend the night. Harry told me of having Jim B. read part of an unfinished script to them following dinner that evening. When Stuart Anthony died in 1942, he was planning his biggest project yet. He intended to come back to Evans County, Georgia, to construct a shack on the Canoochee River, and to write a great script based upon the story of Job in the Bible. Like so many of the Smith clan, he suffered a fatal heart attack. He is buried in Hollywood. Part of this plan was to reestablish ties with his family members. I believe that my father suffered most of all among our clan since he and Jim B. were like close brothers in their youth (and married sisters). To compound the tragedy, Aunt Anne, Jim B.'s widow wrote to my dad about one month after his death in 1960 to ask if she could come and visit! Of course, my mother (Dad's second wife) invited her, and she did visit with Mom, Betty, and me. But it was somewhat bittersweet!

As I mentioned during our conversation here, Pharris, it is shocking to realize that the son of a Confederate soldier became a Hollywood screenwriter. Time is moving on, my friend. Well, I've told you more than you asked for, but I have enjoyed the exercise!"

[18] Typescript in Family History volume in Evans County Library, "James Bell Smith (1823-1891)."

[19] Huxford, *Wiregrass Georgia*, Vol. IV, pp. 307-308.

[20] Huxford, *Wiregrass Georgia*, Vol. VI, p. 265.

[21] Lawrence M. Edwards, *Simon Smith Family*, typescript, unpublished, 1967; Biographical Questionnaire (Bascom G. Tippins, State Representative), June 15, 1931, Georgia State Archives Atlanta, Ga.; The reference to Tippins' crosstie business comes from *Advantages of Georgia*, by Joseph T. Derry, 1904-1905.

[22] Zelma Berry Barrow, *Tippins Ancestry*, privately printed, 1984; Hodges, *Locale*, p. 23; May Boyan, *Georgia Official Records, 1955-1956*, (Atlanta: Longino and Porter, Inc.).

Benjamin Brewton lived about one mile north of the Brewton Cemetery in Hagan. He represented Tatttnall County in the 1861 Georgia Secession Convention. (1870s photo courtesy Mark Baxter)

Emily and Amos Hearn. Amos was a builder of great reputation in ante-bellum times. Among the houses he built is the A.D. Eason house in Undine. (1850s photo courtesy Emily Hearn Groover)

Son of James B. and Georgia Ann Smith, Daniel H. Smith was a community leader. He was a Confederate soldier and shortly after the war helped found Tattnall County Campground. (Photo courtesy Tab Smith)

Redden Asbury Lynn is pictured in a 1800s photo printed on tin and colorized, giving it the appearance of a painting. (Photo courtesy Ruby Brown)

Early Families of Bellville

Berry Brewton, one of the founders of Bellville. He was a Confederate soldier in the 61st Vol. Regiment, Company B. He sold many of the town lots north of the railroad. Photo circa 1861.

Pulaski Sikes Smith was instrumental in the early development of Bellville. He is pictured here as a member of the Liberty Guards. (Circa 1886 photo courtesy of Walter Emmett Daniel)

Enoch B. Daniel moved to Bellville in 1889 to build a sawmill close to the new railroad. He helped establish the local Academy and Methodist Church. (Photo courtesy of Walter Emmett Daniel)

Tom Grice, former Civil War soldier, and early resident and postmaster of Bellville. (Photo courtesy of the late George Durrence)

The Chadburn Parker family lived just west of Bellville on what is now Highway 280. *Left to right, front row:* Mary Parker Sconyers, Clara Parker Martin. Second row: Charlie Hearn, Eulalia Durrence Hearn, Clarence Parker, John Chadburn Parker, Nancy Emily Brewton Parker, Clara Parker Martin, Mellie Hearn Rogers, Alice Parker Wood. Third row: Joe Parker, Tillie Parker Smith, Julian Parker, John Rogers, Willie Wood. Fourth row: Lila Parker Cox, Simon Hearn, Ophelia Parker Harvey, and Walter Nollie Parker. (1890s photo courtesy of Devane Parker Lewis)

Candace Ann Tippins, who married Berry Brewton, is pictured here in an ante-bellum photograph. The man in the photo is thought to be her brother, Phillip Glenn Tippins. (Photo courtesy Dolly Kitchens)

Sallie M. Brewton, long-time resident of Bellville. (Photo courtesy of Emily Hearn Groover)

Tom Wood in his World War I uniform. (Photo courtesy of Jerry Coleman)

Rev. J.C. Brewton, born just northeast of Bellville, was a founder of Brewton-Parker College. (Photo courtesy of John Rabun, Jr.)

Jim B. Smith *(left)* and Tab Smith, Sr., in 1910 when they attended business college in Jacksonville. Jim became a famous Hollywood screenwriter; Tab the Seaboard Railroad depot agent in Daisy. (Photo courtesy of Tab Smith)

George W. Tippins *(top left)* with his brothers. These were the sons of Phillip and Rachel Tippins. (Circa 1875 photo courtesy of Joy Tippins)

Left to right: Dr. Loving Nichols, Mattie Daniel, Miss Harkins (teacher at Bay Branch School), and Harley Daniel. (Circa 1892 photo courtesy of Loulie Perkins)

Dr. Loving Nichols operated this small office in Bay Branch before moving to Bellville in the early 1890s. *Left to right:* Jim Daniel, Dr. Nichols, Mattie Daniel Nichols, and Harley Daniel. (1890s photo courtesy Loulie Perkins)

Henry Leonard Brewton family. Emma Kate, Coy, Hogan, and Edith *(front)*. Their farm was about 2 miles south of Bellville. (1911 photo courtesy of Edith Smith)

C.W. Hearn children. *Left to right:* Bessie, Caughey (Cap), Iman and Mae *(front)*. (Photo courtesy Jim Hearn)

Dan O. Bell and his wife Agnes Valerie Burkhalter Bell had a farm south of Bellville. (Photo courtesy of Winton Bell)

Nancy Eulalia Durrence Hearn, affectionately known as Grandma Hearn. (1940s photo courtesy Emily Hearn Groover)

Jackie Brewton at his 90th birthday dinner in 1954. Brewton possessed a remarkable memory and was a leading local historian. Often referred to as the "sage" of Bellville, he lived on the eastern edge of town. (Photo courtesy of Carrie Beasley)

Four generations of the Joshua Collins family. Jonathan Collins built his home about 1894 on the eastern side of Bellville. *Left to right:* James Daniel Collins, Joshua Berry (Jot) Collins, Jonathan B. Collins, and Joshua Collins. (Circa 1929 photo courtesy of Jimmy Collins)

J.B. Brewton Family: *First row, left to right:* Mrs. J.C. (Sarah Jane) Brewton, Mrs. J.B. (Margaret Everett) Brewton (seated), Elizabeth Brewton, Joshua Collins. Second row, Rev. J.C. Brewton, Margaret Brewton Olliff, Sallie (Calhoun) Brewton, Nancy Brewton Collins. Third row, Henry Jackson Brewton, Lafayette Hodges, Mrs. Henry (Nannie K.) Brewton, Mrs. J.B. (Ida Clanton) Brewton, Steve Collins, and J.B. Brewton, Jr. (Circa 1910 photo courtesy of John Rabun, Jr.)

Four of the sons of Daniel H. and Georgia Ann Smith. *Left to right:* Lovick P., C. Beecher, English, and Roscoe. The Smith family has been present in the Bellville area for many generations. (Photo courtesy Tab Smith)

APPENDIX B

Interviews

Interview with Herschel Hearn
Conducted by Emily Hearn Groover
Bellville, Georgia - November 10, 1990

Question [Q]: Who were some of the early leaders of Bellville Church?

A: Well, Uncle "Knucky" Daniel was the superintendent for years and years. Later on, Mr. Beecher Smith was the superintendent. After that I left home, and I don't know who you've had since.

Q: Can you tell me about old time Christmases in Bellville?

A: Christmas was a big deal. I mean we really celebrated Christmas. We had singing and special programs at church. Santa Claus would be there to top off the program. Our Christmas tree was always brought from out there across the creek. We'd go every year and get a Christmas tree out of the woods. We'd try to get the biggest one we could and still get it in the church. Sometimes it would be too large to get in the door, and we would have to get another tree. Several of us had to turn it, and pull and push it to get it in place in the church. We'd no doubt skin up some paint in the process. People would let us cut the trees every year. They would normally be so large that it would go up to the ceiling of the church. It was usually a cedar tree. No, it was a holly tree. Of course, after Christmas, you'd cut the tree in pieces to make it easier to take out.

The Bells [Winton Bell family] would always come to our house on Christmas before the Christmas program at the church. The kids would get together and play. We'd have a good time.

Q: Were there rooms in the old church?

A: No, there weren't any rooms, just the sanctuary. The Sunday school classes would meet in separate corners of the sanctuary. They didn't interfere with each other much. We had a big Sunday School. We held it in the afternoon. We boys would invariably get in the most trouble before or after Sunday School. For example, one Sunday somebody gave us a cigar to smoke. It made us sick. We went to Sunday school sick and we really messed up things. Of course, then we got a whipping, and felt even worse.

Q: Do you remember any of the Sunday School teachers?

A: Let me see now. All the school teachers usually doubled as Sunday School teachers back in those days. Teaching Sunday School was part of their duty. The teachers boarded in people's homes. Some of the teachers were Grace, Betty, and Gertrude Eves. Miss Mary [Lee] Daniel and Grace [Flanigan] Hearn came about the same time. Later on, Betty Fowler and Mrs. Eves came.

Q: Did the preachers move every three or four years back then?

A: Yes. Our first parsonage was in Hagan. Remember the preacher we had that bought an automobile? Somehow or another he couldn't keep up the payments on it. They were going to repossess it. I think it was Brother Cooper. He got a pitch fork after them and ran them off [laughter].

Q: What did you boys do for entertainment in Bellville?

A: Some afternoons after Sunday school we boys would be up to some mischief. Mr. Howell Mattox had a big watermelon patch there where the old Smith house is, where Mr. Landis Bacon lives now. We used to sneak in the watermelon field just beside the house. Mr. Howell Mattox, we called him "Cob," had the prettiest watermelon patch you've ever seen. Back in those days they shipped as much as 150 to 200 railroad cars of watermelons to market each year. We'd go out around the back of the field after church. There was a lot of watermelon stealing going on around here. He had boasted, one year downtown, that it would be hard to get his melons because of the way his field was situated. He said he could catch anyone in his field. So we decided to find out whether he could catch us or not. We went around back and climbed over the fence in the field. We crawled out there and rolled several of the watermelons in the woods. All we did was eat the heart out of the melons. Then we took the rinds and stuck them on the fence posts so he would be sure to see them. The next morning he looked out there and saw those rinds on the post, and he was the maddest man you've ever seen in your life. He wanted to know who did it so he could prosecute them. Of course, we didn't say a word. He didn't know who did it until a year later. Somebody finally told him. Boy, did he get mad with us about that thing. I thought he was going to beat us up [laughter].

Q: What did they call Mr. Mattox?

A: Cob. Cob Mattox. He was something. He lived in the old Smith house. That house used to be way up off the ground. Well, you could walk right under it without even having to bend over. They cut it lower. There were great wide steps in front. There was a walkway from their house right straight to our house. There was a gate about where the cemetery is. One Sunday afternoon after a big rain and electric storm, the fellow that was living in the house before Mr. Mattox--one of the Smiths, Mrs. Helen Daniel's grandmother's people--had come down to the store to see Papa. They were walking back up the path to their house, and Papa was with them. They had a dog walking between them. Lightning struck and killed the other man and the dog. Papa [Charlie W. Hearn] was knocked out for several days--I don't exactly know how long.

Q: Did you tell me the back of one of Bellville's buildings was a millinery shop?

A: Yes, the millinery shop was right across from the Hearn store. It was operated by Miss America Sikes. She was Mr. Colquit's mother.

They had a farm up the road about halfway to Reidsville. They finally moved downtown. They lived across from the store and post office. Mrs. Rosa Sikes, do you remember Mrs. Rosa? She operated the millinery store. At one time Bellville had a lot of stores. Bellville had many of its stores burn at one time. There used to be a boarding school here too. Bellville was a fairly big, booming town. It was the biggest business town in this area.

I remember an interesting story about Miss America. Back in 1919 cotton got real high. Papa was buying the cotton at 35 or 40 cents a pound. We had long-staple cotton [black-seed] and short-staple cotton. We ginned both kinds. Miss America came up to talk to Papa about five bales of that long-staple cotton. They grew it out on their farm. The long-staple cotton brought more. She said, "Charlie, I'm ready to sell my cotton. How much is it bringing today?" He said, "Well, let me check on it." Then he replied, "Miss America, I can give you a dollar a pound for it today." She said, "Well, go over there and load it up!" So I went over there to the back of the millinery shop and loaded all five bales. I remember that just as good as it was yesterday. She had a store in the back of where the millinery shop had been. She quit running the millinery shop a year before that. She ran it for a long time, and it was quite popular.

Q: What was that building in the picture back of the post office?

A: There used to be a great big barn back there. Mr. Davis, from up in Dahlonega, Georgia, used to bring mules down to sell. He was a mule man. Papa rented that barn to him.

Q: Elma:[1] Didn't Dr. Nichols have an office back there?

A: Yes, I think he did.

Q: Where were the stores that burned in the great Bellville fire?

A: Down toward where the bank is now. Later on they built a turpentine still down there. Gene Ambrose was the stiller back in those days. There were two or three fellows working at the still. You'd hear them early in the morning. They would go around tightening those bands on the barrels. They would play a tune, "Boom, boom." You could hear them all over town. Right down below Mrs. Sikes was where Paul LeGrand lived. He was the depot agent. There was a little street there across the branch before the highway was built. The Kicklighters lived up there on the right hand side and farmed the little field up there. Just the other side of their house, Uncle "Parch" Mattox lived. That field belonged to Uncle John Wood. If you went down that lane there [north] you would go to Uncle John's house. On the other side [east of Main Street] furtherr on, the section hands lived down there. Mr. Gignilliat fixed a road so he could drive down to the section houses south of the railroad.

Q: Who owned the section houses?

A: The railroad. If you went down the road east and crossed the railroad south, there used to be a colored school in there. They also had church there.

Q: What were the other buildings in Bellville?

A: You know, up on this end, the Daniels used to have a big sawmill on the south side of the railroad. There was a big sawmill about where the House of Prayer is today. Uncle Nollie Parker lived there then. Old man Fate Hodges lived in there where the sycamore trees are now.

Then Mr. Daniel moved the sawmill north of the railroad later on. The sawmill had tokens they paid the hands to use for money. The merchants would take the tokens for money. There would be tokens for nickels, dimes, and quarters. Then after the mill moved, the colored people had their community or section there. They had the House of Prayer. When the House of Prayer first started, "Daddy" Grace came down to dedicate it. When "Daddy" Grace came to town, the black people would pin their hard earned dollars on his clothes. It was a big deal. He had a big automobile and

---

[1]Questions or comments by Elma Hearn during the interview are so noted.

a big crowd attended there. When he would arrive in that big automobile and before he got out, they placed a red carpet on the ground for him to walk on so his feet never touched the dirt. There was a pharmacist who lived in Bellville, a Dr. Sheppard, whose family had sterling silver. Mrs. Sheppard gradually missed her big spoons and found that her maid was taking them to play their drums with in the church service. When she got the spoons back they were bent and bruised. There used to be more houses there where the House of Prayer is now. That little settlement developed around the sawmill. Old man Martin, a colored fellow, lived close by there. He had a big family.

Q: What year was the house built that Martha Hearn lived in, the home place?

A: Papa bought that house from the Durrences. He also bought that farm too. That was the Bill Durrence crowd. Some of those Durrences went to Mendes later on.

Q: So you don't know when the house was built?

A: No, it was before I was born.

See, Papa started the business in Manassas in the 1890's. I've got his books there at the house. He worked for Mr. Fate Hodges, who owned a store. Then Papa came to Bellville to work for himself.

When Grandpa Amos died after being wounded in the war, there were three children left. Papa, Uncle Simon and Aunt Mellie [Rogers]. Grandma married again after Grandpa Amos died. It wasn't too long before she married John Parker. See, Uncle Nollie and Papa were half brothers. All the children grew up together. In the will, or something, Papa and those two children got the old Cox place. Evidently it was in his [Amos'] will that the children would get it. They had some land over there where the barn is now. So, Papa got to working for Mr. Hodges. Uncle Simon wanted to be a preacher. Papa worked to send him to school for his [Simon's] part of the Cox place. That's the way it was told to me. Then he went down and worked two or three years for Uncle John Rogers. They used to have a water mill. I think he even had a gin there. He worked down there to earn that part of the farm. That's how he ended up with the place.

Grandma needed a farm to keep that crowd fed [laughter]. So, Papa traded them the farm for woodland. This old colored fellow, Elden Miles, worked with him. I think Papa paid him 75 cents a day. They went out and cleared the land up. Then they started farming it. Later on Papa went in the store business. This was right about the turn of the century. Maybe in '98 or '99. I think Caughey was born in Manassas, maybe Bessie too. But the rest of us were born down here.

Q: When was Mae Hearn born?

A: Mae was born in 1900. She's was older than I was.

Q: Herschel, you'll be 88 in January?

A: Yes.

Q: Who were some of your other acquaintances?

A: Well, I had several cousins. Grace Smith married Ralph Sandiford. Willie Hogan was the oldest boy of that crowd. Then the there were the twins, Sidney and Sankey. There was one younger than that. There was also Benona. Their daddy was Uncle Will Smith and their mother was Aunt Tillie Parker Smith. There must have been six of them. They lived in the next block just beyond the Claxton High School. Sidney and Sankey were my and Inman's age. We'd go fishing at the sewer pipe in front of Theodore Brewton's place. I've got some pictures of that. That was way back. We boys would go down on Sunday and get a burlap bag and put a hoop in it to make a seine and go through that pipe. We'd try to catch fish. You know the little short ones. One day we were supposed to go to Sunday School, but instead we went fishing. Sidney and Sankey were up here that day too. Mama found out we had been fishing, and we all got in trouble [laughter]. You know, we couldn't go fishing on Sunday.

Q: Daddy used to tell about the time you all were supposed to have his surprise birthday party. But you all found out about it and slipped off before the people got there. Was that the story?

A: Yes, we used to pull some things [laughter]. No wonder they beat up on us once and a while. We were always into something. But if we messed up anyone's stuff we were in trouble. Papa got upset. He had to pay the damages. I remember one Sunday afternoon, we had this old Overland automobile that was kept in the old gin building. We moved to the new gin in 1917. The old ginhouse was there south of the railroad in the old days [behind the present site of Bellville Town Hall]. We used to drive wagons in there to unload cotton. Most of the mules were scared to go up there. Yep, after they moved the gin, Papa kept that old automobile in the gin building. We slipped the car out and took some driving lessons. We were about courting age. C.C. Daniel was courting Winnie, and I was courting Edith Elders. Well, we had about a half hour off, and we figured we wouldn't be long in taking the car for a ride. We'd drive right by Mr. Harley's [Daniel] house. His barn was on one side and his house on the other side. Well, he would always be feeding some hogs out there right in the middle of the road. We got the old car cranked up, and we didn't have but a few minutes. So we took off in a hurry. He wanted to see Winnie, and I wanted to see Edith. We turned around that corner down there in the car, and we almost ran completely over those hogs. I mean, those hogs scattered! We turned the corner to try and dodge the hogs and tore a little bit of the fence down. We didn't even slow down or stop. We didn't come back that way, we came back through Hagan. The next morning Mr. Harley came into town and said to me, "Do you want me to tell your daddy about you and C.C.?" "No Sir!" was my reply. He said if we ever did it again he was going to tell our Papa.

Elma: Herbert Daniel's wife was telling me the other day that Edith Elders had been staying with her sister in Cochran. Her sister is way on up there about 100 now. Edith is about your age. Mrs. Gussie has gotten in bad shape. She's not able to stay by herself. Edith is looking after both of them.

Edith was a nurse. Well, we got to courting pretty good. I can't remember if it was Easter or Christmas, but I gave her an umbrella. They were real popular with the girls back then. It was a pretty umbrella too. She and I broke up, and I never got to walk under the umbrella [laughter]. I have seen Edith only one time since then. But back then I went to Cochran to see her several times.

Q: Is that who you were dating when y'all went to Athens and the door fell off?

A: No, that was Betty Fowler. I was courting Betty then [she later became Herschel's wife]. We were in Athens, and I mean right in the middle of town. Martha pulled that on me. I was in there trying to take a bath in the pump shed one day. Well, she had to go to town for something. I had the car, an old Chevrolet Roadster, parked out front. So she just took the car to go to town and come right back. Somehow or another she pulled the door off while downtown. I don't know what she ran into. I don't think she ever told me what she hit. She backed into something with the door open. Well, whatever she hit pulled the hinge off the door. It pulled the whole door off. She found that she could put the door back up there and latch it, and it would stay in place. This was on the driver's side, you see. When she came back she parked the drivers side close to the fence so you'd have to get in the passenger side. So we came out to go and I said, "Martha, I've got to use the car." I asked her why it was so close to the fence. Mae was going with us. She was going to visit Anthony Hearn while I was courting. Anthony lived there in Athens too. We didn't stop till we got up there. We stopped at a traffic light in Athens that Saturday afternoon, and I mean everybody was in town. Well, the car would stall down. The starter wouldn't catch. There was a cog knocked off the flywheel. You had to move the motor just a little bit and it would catch and start. So I was going to have to get out and get it cranked. Well, anyway, as I said I was stopped at the traffic light. When I pushed the door latch back, the door fell completely off. Mae knew all about it. However, she hadn't said a word. She said, "Son, you having any trouble?" [laughter] I said, "A little bit." Mae was just dying laughing. I thought she was going to fall out of the car. Everybody else got to laughing too, even people walking on the sidewalk [laughter].

When I first went up there to see Betty she was teaching school with Mr. Burke. They boarded over with Mr. Little, who was a big farmer over there. They met me at the train station. He had an old Ford with a rumble seat. They put us back there in that seat. I remember that very well. Mr. Burke was a good old fellow. He and Marguerite [Betty's sister] hadn't been married very long. They all boarded there with Mr. Little.

Then later during the Depression, Mr. Little lost everything they had. He was a big farmer and owned a lot of cotton land. His wife was some fancy lady. They had a big automobile and were in high society. They lost everything, and they then moved to Perry. Betty and I visited them one time. We used to go through Perry right much.

Then they built a new school in Athens. After that they made teachers' quarters out of the old school. So, Mr. Burke moved in over there. I came up visiting one time when I was on the way to Kentucky to work in the tobacco market. They met me at the train station. It turned cold as the dickens that night. When I left, I was going by Atlanta. There was no heat on the train, and I mean that train was cold. I took a terrible cold. When I got to Kentucky, I was about out.

Later on, we went up there [Athens] courting. We did the craziest things. We went on a treasure hunt. They would hide a prize somewhere way out in the woods. You go to a place and get a clue. Then that clue would tell you where the next one was. They would describe the place and you had to find it. We'd go all over that county. Dust, you couldn't see a thing. We would drive 50 or 60 mph on dirt roads. We could have been killed. It's a wonder we didn't all go to jail. We finally found the treasure, and it was a hundred pennies [laughter]. It was a lot of fun, but we sure got dirty.

Q: What year was the Bellville brick school building built?

A: It was built in 1921/22. Betty taught part of the time in the old wooden building. They moved it around facing the highway while they were building the new building. She taught part of the year over there in the old building. I think they went into the new building about the middle of the year.

Q: How many grades did they have in the school?

A: Ten. I graduated the tenth at Bellville and then went to Claxton for the eleventh. You see, the war came along in 1918. Caughey went into the Army. You couldn't find anyone to work hardly. They weren't having any school then either. Papa kept us out of school one year at home working. We worked on the farm, the gin, and everywhere else. After the war, I went back to school, but Inman didn't go back. I had finished eighth grade, and he had finished the ninth. When I decided to go back to school, I didn't study much [laughter]. I just sorta passed. Of course, everyone had to pass back then, and there wasn't any summer school. If you didn't pass you repeated the grade. They didn't monkey with you. Since I was out a whole year, I decided to go back over the eighth grade. That made me two years behind. In the meantime, Betty came in to teach. She had finished college at 19. So I was older than she was. When she came in and was taking names for the roll she said, "Are you a student here?" I told her, "Yes." I guess I looked older since I had my hair parted right down the middle [laughter]. She was a good teacher. She taught English and history.

We had a championship basketball team. We won the whole district. We beat Sylvania, Glennville, Pembroke, Reidsville, and all of the rest. We were just up to the tenth and they had an eleventh grade. Claxton wouldn't play us. We didn't lose a game, and we won 17 straight. There was Wallace Smith, Bob Benton, Buck Shannon, Hogan Brewton and myself. Cecil Kennedy was a substitute. We had such a good record that they invited us to the high school tournament in Savannah at the YMCA. Our courts were always on the dirt. We got on that floor, and I mean we were something. We won the championship cup. I wonder what ever happened to that cup?

Elma: There was something about not having a substitute. They called back for Harold Parker. His mother said he didn't have clothes to wear. She had a time trying to get him some clothes ready.

What happened was, I was over the age limit in high school. We got in the tournament in Savannah and played up to the last game. They all thought we were going to win it. The day we played Pembroke someone made a remark about my birthday. Coach Smith, from Pembroke, overheard the remark. So he then told them how old I was. They called me in the office. The tournament official said, "You may be disqualified, you can't play." He said, "Slick, you go outside and wait a few minutes." They talked it over and they voted to let me play, except Hucklebee, the coach at Statesboro. So they wouldn't let me play. That's when they called up and said send somebody else as a substitute. We won the game anyway. We had a good team back then. In those days every time you made a goal, you had to jump from center again. Every play was made from center. Everybody knew where to be on the court. We could turn a play. You'd throw the ball according to the play, and it was your teammates' job to get here. We had some special plays. We started out and Bob Benton would face away from the goal and throw over his head with one arm and hit the goal. He could hit from way out. He'd practice all the time. One time down at Sylvania he put in three or four in a row. Those Sylvania boys had to call time out in the game and said, "We got to stop that thing!" Wallace Smith was a good player too. Hogan was a stationary guard. We had a good time.

One year we beat Reidsville. They were supposed to be tops and our big rival. After we telephoned and told the folks in Bellville we won, somebody here from home put a big sign on a tree beside the highway. They tied a ribbon around a chamber pot and hung it on the tree. The sign said "Reidsville Cup" [laughter]. We'd practice every afternoon. We'd have so many people watching you could hardly find a place to stand.

Q: Why wouldn't Claxton play y'all?

A: We would beat Claxton. They didn't want to get insulted by playing little old Bellville. We weren't big enough to play football, so we played basketball year round. We'd play basketball before Sunday School, then we'd go to Sunday School and start playing again afterwards. We were nuts about the game.

Interview with Amiel Fountain
This and subsequent interviews conducted by the editor.
Bellville, Georgia - February 21, 1995

Question [Q]: Amiel, before we start talking about Bellville, could I ask you a few questions about yourself? When and where were you born?

A. I was born October 1, 1920 in Florence County, S.C. In 1923, my family moved to the Bellville area. In 1925 we moved to Savannah, where I began school, only to move back to Bellville in 1928. I began the third grade at Bellville School in the fall of 1928 and completed the ninth grade there before going to Claxton High School for the tenth grade. We moved from Bellville in June, 1936.

Q: Who were your parents?

A: My father was David T. Fountain. He was born in Florence County, South Carolina, and raised around Scranton and Lake City, S.C. He served an apprenticeship as a carpenter and was thus able to follow the construction trade as a journeyman.

His mother was a Carter from Cartersville, S.C. My great-grandfather on my grandmother Fountain's side was an officer in the Confederate Army. He was killed at Cowpen, S. C. My mother was born Laura B. Phillips in Jenkins County, Georgia. The area was close to Elam Baptist Church. After finishing school in Jenkins County, she went to Savannah to further her education at Richard's Business School. While in Savannah she met my father who was working there at the time. After serving in WWI, he returned to Savannah in late 1918. They were married in July 1919.

Q: How did your family end up in the Bellville area?

A: As a disabled veteran my father was allowed to select a vocation to be trained in as a rehabilitation program. He selected cabinet making. After completing this program he asked for training in farming. The V.A. sent him to the University of Georgia for the purpose of experimenting with and scientifically raising chickens. While at the University he received several courses in the feeding and care of the young chicks. Upon completion of this program my father rented a farm known as the Mulligan place which was about three or four miles south of Bellville. This was from 1923 to 1925. My father farmed and experimented with raising several breeds of chickens, including Barred Rocks, Rhode Island Reds, and White Leghorns. There were several other varieties, the names of which slip my mind at the present. The Department of Agriculture, under the auspices of the University of Georgia, would send the young biddies to our place and my father would place each kind in separate pens so that he was able to give them different types of feed. This enabled him to keep a record of their growth. Sometimes the University would send eggs to be hatched in the incubator which they had furnished. He kept detailed records as to which kind grew the fastest and which began to lay the earliest. He also recorded their food intake. You could say he was doing poultry research when the field was still in its infancy.

He was also a journeyman carpenter and went back to Savannah during 1926 and 1927. However, he decided he'd rather be on the farm, so we moved back to Bellville in 1928. Daddy resumed farming. He grew up on a farm, and he just liked living in a rural environment. However, my mother was an invalid and she couldn't carry water. So, as the oldest boy in the family, I became the water boy, the laundry man, and the doer of all other chores too [laughter]. We then moved up to what was called the Bickley place here in town. It was located where the Roger Wood place is now. We moved into the Bickley place and daddy quit farming. He started doing a little carpentry work with Mr. Nollie Parker who lived here in Bellville. We all called him Uncle Nollie. They built several houses around the Bellville area. Then, in 1932, we finally built our house right up the road [two houses west from present site of Bernie's store].

Q: Was your father a pretty fair farmer?

A. Yes. One time your grandfather Johnson asked my dad for help in starting to grow tobacco. Mr. Mac said, "Mr. Fountain, do you know anything about tobacco growing?" Daddy replied, "I was raised in tobacco." We used to come over and work in that small barn stringing tobacco. He showed your grandfather how to pack it, put it on the sheets, and tie it. That was about 1930/31.

Q: Can you tell me more about old-time Bellville?

A: As you know there were no paved roads here back then. This area in front of Cap Hearn's store was all sand. It was the biggest sand bed you've ever seen in your life [laughter]. In front of Cap Hearn's store you turn west and there was a little dirt road that followed the railroad. It then passed Mrs. King's and Mr. Paul LeGrand's homes, crossed the branch, and then passed our house and Tom Wood's place. The road then crossed the railroad and went by Mr. Flower's place. The road continued down the south side of the railroad to the black church called the House of Prayer.

Now as we return to the center of Bellville you will find that the present building which contains Bernie's and the post office are sitting a little farther back than the previous buildings that were there. At the west end of the original post office, which was part of Cap Hearn's store, there was a large vacant space between the post office and Mrs. King's house. Slightly north, a part of this space, was a large mule barn and lot which Mrs. King owned. They used to bring the mules in rail cars to the siding where there was an unloading ramp. The mules were unloaded and were run across the road to the lot. This was an every year occurrence and the farmers would come to the mule barn to see the mules and at such time they might trade mules or purchase one. Mrs. King's and Mr. LeGrand's houses along with the mule barn and lot are no longer here. These have been replaced by other homes and buildings and that has changed the whole landscape greatly. It doesn't look the same now.

Q: Do you remember when Highways 280 and 292 were paved?

A: Highway 280 was paved sometime around the year 1932 or 1933. It had been designated as a military Highway from Ft. Screven to Fort Benning, Georgia. The paving of Highway 292 in all probability was done after World War II.

Q: When your family came back from Savannah, how long did you live here?

A: From 1928 to 1936. In 1936 a tornado went through the little town of Cordele, Georgia. A man that lived there owned the Crisp County Lumber Company, and he knew my dad did carpentry work. He called down here and said they needed every man they could get to rebuild the town. The town was blown down, flat down. So Daddy went up there and bought a house. Then he came back down here and sold this one in Bellville. We moved to Cordele. I wasn't there but a year. I graduated from Cordele High School in May of 1937.

Q: Can you tell me about some of Bellville's businesses?

A: Cap Hearn had a cotton gin over about where the bank is located. Also, close by, there was a house for the ginner who, with his family, came from out-of-town. The ginner was of the Seventh Day Adventist faith. He and his family would go to church on Saturday because that was their Sabbath. He told Mr. Cap, "I'm not going to gin on Saturday, but I'll gin on Sunday." Mr. Cap told him that if he didn't gin on Saturday around Bellville then he wouldn't gin on Sunday either [laughter]. Usually Cap's brothers, Herschel and Inman, would go over on Saturday and run the gin. Also, Tom Flanigan, Mrs. Grace Hearn's brother, would work at the gin in addition to doing mechanical work on the tractors. As a kid I'd go over to the gin, and Mr. Tom Flanigan would let me do some of the bagging. After the bale of cotton was pressed, he would show me how to put the metal ties around the bale. I was then allowed to paint the weight on the bale before it was pushed to the platform for the farmer to pick up. This was a method of learning and of course, my having an inquisitive mind, I found myself quite often in the way. However, it was interesting to learn how things worked first hand.

Mr. Adam Bird had a store on the east of the main street through town.[2] Mr. Bird carried a large inventory of groceries along with clothing, some hardware items, and of course there was the usual gas pump. Mr. Cap Hearn had a store on the west side of the main street which was also across from Mr. Bird's. Mr. Cap's store carried mostly hardware and other items that were needed, such as farm equipment. He carried some shoes and overalls and a small inventory of groceries.

Mr. Tom Wood's store was on the south side of the railroad and on the west side of the main road. Mr. Tom Wood was more in the grocery business. Back in those days Bellville was a fairly good place to shop during the week, as people didn't have automobiles. In Mr. Wood's store you found not only groceries but there were certain meat products that he carried. As you know they did not have the refrigeration as we do today. He carried a much larger line of shoes and clothing such as overalls, men's shirts, and ladies items such as aprons and some dresses. You could get most of the basics you wanted at Mr. Wood's store, and it was a great gathering place. Turpentine workers as well as some farm workers and salesmen would be in and out most of the time. There was a checker game going most everyday. There was a large sized porch on the front of the store with benches on each side of the door where the people had a place to sit and eat or talk. There was a gas pump on the north corner of the porch.

Between Mr. Wood's store and Mr. Kennedy's house, there was a large open space. As a matter of fact, you could look up toward the schoolhouse and see it and the church. The brick schoolhouse faced east and the old wooden church faced north. Probably within three hundred yards, and in line with the church, was an old house that some black people lived in. Between that house and the school, but some distance north and closer to the branch, was where Mr. Tom Wood's turpentine still was located. The still was operated by Mr. Gene Ambrose and his brother. Gene's brother was a

---

[2]During the interview, Amiel indicated Main Street was not called by that name during the time he lived in Bellville.

barrel maker by trade, and he could wake up the whole town early in the morning when he started making barrels for the first cooking of tar. He had a good rhythm with his hammer as he put the metal bands around the barrel staves. The area between Mr. Kennedy's house and U.S. Highway 280 was vacant. You could look from the old Hearn home and see the church.

Q: Do you remember much about the train depot?

A: Let's walk over to the depot. As we stand here on the north side which faces Cap Hearn's store, you could see a large door where incoming freight and express items were kept until the people came and picked up the items. The long platform which ran along the side track and was on the south side of the station can still be seen. Part of the platform was covered, and this is where they had the tomato packing operation. In the mid-30s farmers began growing large crops of tomatoes. The tomatoes were picked just before they ripened, and while still green, they were brought to the platform for processing. This procedure required packing in wood boxes and loading into refrigerator cars. There was never any ice in the cars but the cars had doors on top of them that were left open, and the ventilation would ripen the tomatoes by the time they reached their destination. On the platform was other freight, such as machinery, rosin, turpentine, and cotton to be picked up by the local train that ran every day. Mr. Paul LeGrand was the station agent for the Seaboard Railroad. Mr. LeGrand had his office next to the enclosed part of the depot where incoming express and small freight items were kept until picked up. His many duties included selling passenger tickets, receiving and sending messages by telegraph, posting passenger train schedules and keeping tabs on freight, both incoming and outgoing.

Back then there were two waiting rooms where people purchased tickets, and would wait for the train to arrive. One room was for the black and one for the white people. There was always something going on and you can understand that the depot was an active place. There were messages to be handed up to the engineers about certain changes taking place in schedules. These included information such as roads under repair or the need to pass other trains operating on the same track. This was done by means of passing the message up to the engineer with a bamboo loop as the train passed the station. There were more freight trains in operation during those days than now, as the truck lines had not yet come into the picture.

Mr. LeGrand would let me help him from time to time by putting the labels on the outgoing freight. In return for this he was going to teach me how to send and receive the Morse code on the telegraph. That was the way stations communicated at that time. Sometimes he would give me a nickel for helping him. I remember Mr. LeGrand was addicted to Coca-Colas. I mean he loved them. When I would stop by he would say, "Kid, run down to the store and get me a Coke." He was referring to Tom Wood's store because it was closest to the station. Between Mr. LeGrand and me, we wore a path across the railroad track down to the store. In those days Cokes cost a nickel.

As a kid back then we always created some form of entertainment or contest. We would walk the rail to see how far we could stay on before we fell off. Lots of times we would walk to U.S. Highway 280 [there was no Highway 292 then], which seemed to be a long way at the time. Today, with the new highway, it seems much shorter.

Freight trains were not the only trains that ran in those days. We had passenger trains that operated on diesel fuel back then. Because of their shape they were nicknamed "Butthead." They had only one man, the engineer, to operate the engine. One of the men who was a regular was Uncle Billy Bodel. He would blow his air horn and wave at the kids who ran to see the train pass. When he stopped at the station, he climbed down and let some of the kids get up in the engine just to look around the cab and act as if they were the engineer.

Bellville had four passenger trains that came through each day. The early morning train ran at 8 a.m. from west to east and was popular because people could go to Savannah for the day and return on the evening train. The 10 a.m. train running from east to west usually brought the *Savannah Morning News*, and any other railway express items. In those days the Railway Express was a popular way of shipping merchandise in that it would arrive in the small towns the next day after it was ordered. The evening trains were also very popular as there were local people returning from Savannah or perhaps other places. The other attraction was that many people came to the depot to get their evening newspaper. This was the only way people had to receive the news. In the evening many of the people, young and old alike, would walk down to the station to meet the trains. Many would arrive before the train was due, and a good time was had by all as they visited and enjoyed the camaraderie.

The depot served the community in many ways. During the winter months it was the gathering place for the younger and older boys. Because of the pot-bellied stove in the waiting room in which we could build a fire, the room was comfortable for the older boys to play pitch-pennies. Whoever got their coin closest to the wall, won all the pennies. Then they'd start the game over again. Those of us who were younger became the cheering section for our favorite player. The older boys were Walter Emmett Daniel, Chick Daniel, Buck Daniel, and Cecil Daniel. Occasionally Roger Wood and Wallace Parker would join them. It was nice and warm there by the stove, and we all had a great time.

Q: Could you tell me more about any trips you took on the train?

A: Well, I took the train to Savannah several times, and it was an adventure. I also took it to Cordele. The train went all the way to Montgomery, Alabama. Back in those days the trains were comfortable. It was cheap transportation. You don't have that kind of transportation anymore.

Q: Please tell me about the products shipped out of Bellville.

A: During the watermelon season, they would load about five or six freight cars a day. We had the tomato harvest when the farmers would gather the tomatoes and bring them to the packing shed at the depot. The tomatoes were wrapped by experienced packers and put in wooden crates and then loaded into refrigerator cars for delivery to their destination. Of course, there always was cotton to be loaded as well as turpentine and rosin.

Q: What were some of Bellville's other buildings?

A: As you know, the cotton gin was one of the busiest businesses of all during the summer months. People brought their cotton to gin and since there was only one gin in Bellville there was usually a waiting period. Once the cotton was ginned, the seed was transported to the seed house by way of the auger which ran from the gin to the seed house across the street. People would pay their ginning bill with the seed. The seed was later loaded into freight cars and shipped to Savannah for processing. In the '30s Main Street, which ran north from Highway 280, was dirt. Highway 280 was also dirt during late 1920s and early '30s. The old Highway 280 ran close to your grandfather's [Mac Johnson's] house in east Bellville. When they paved Highway 280 they straightened it out. When they moved the highway, your grandfather's place then sat way back from the highway as it does now.

There was one other thing that was a real novelty to us kids. At that time the Army had troops stationed at Ft. Screven, on Tybee Island. Every summer they would leave Ft. Screven marching to Ft. Benning at Columbus, Georgia. They were infantry, and they would march across the state on Highway 280. They always camped at Bellville in an area between the brick school house and Mr. Nollie Parker's home. Seeing the soldiers was a big deal for us boys. Little did we know that in a few short years many of us would be soldiers ourselves. You could bet that we would be out there in the evening watching the soldiers go about their work feeding the horses and preparing the evening meal. The horses were used to pull the caissons and, of course, all this was just fascinating.

There are a lot of things that make this town such a fine place in which to live. I felt that I got my foundation and basics for life here in Bellville. We had schoolteachers that were concerned about our education. We lost a lot when they began consolidating the schools. We've torn down the foundations of the local type of school where the people came together, thus creating a family-oriented town. In my time there were only two hundred, more or less, living in Bellville proper. Every one of them were family-oriented, church people who had a lot to give. Everyone could be trusted, and people took care of each other. We traded Bellville High School for Pinewood Christian Academy, which speaks well for the community of Bellville. When I moved here in 1928 the old wood school building was still here. They had built the new brick building, and it was a little farther from Highway 280 and facing east. The wood building faced the highway. Mr. Nollie Parker bought the old building, and he and his family lived in it for a period of time. He was gradually tearing it down and using the materials to build another house farther west on Highway 280.

Q: Did you know any of the blacks in Bellville?

A: Yes, there was Uncle Will Black and Aunt Mary. They were real elderly. They lived close to where the House of Prayer is today. He liked to go 'possum hunting, and he would take all us boys--both black and white. Then there was Bubba and Georgia Smith. He helped out with the farming that Daddy was doing, and Georgia would help mother around the house with the laundry and cleaning. There were some younger boys that were always around. There was Walter and J.L. who would come by the Bickley place just to tease the little dog that my brother and I had. There was Willie and Meldren Cook. These and many more assisted in gathering tobacco and picking cotton.

Q: Do you remember early telephones in Bellville?

A: To my recollection there was only one telephone in Bellville when we were here, and it was in the train depot. If anybody got sick at night and they wanted to call Dr. Wallace Daniel or Dr. Rogers, they had to come wake Mr. LeGrand up and go down to the depot to use the telephone.

Speaking of Mr. LeGrand, he had some kind of alarm rigged up so that if something happened at the depot it would trigger an alarm in his house. So one night he heard something. He woke up and came over to our house. This was around midnight. He said, "David, there's something going on down at the station." So my daddy got his shotgun. Mr. LeGrand already had his. They proceeded to the depot to find out someone had broken into the station. The burglar jumped out the station building and took off on the run [laughter].

Q: As we walk down Main Street, can you tell me about some of the buildings present when you lived in Bellville?

A: As you leave Highway 280 on the south end of town you will be traveling north. The first house on the east [right] side of Main Street will be the Hearn home. The next small house belonged to the Styles. Now you come to Mrs. Benton's and next to her house was the house that we lived in before moving to the Bickley place. Just north of the house where we lived was a small house that set farther back from the road and this was Mr. Riggs' house. Now we are down to the branch that ran between Mr. Riggs' and the railroad. This completes all of the houses on the east of Main Street from Highway 280 and to the railroad. On the west side of Main Street going north from Highway 280 to the railroad you will find there were only two buildings. One was Mr. Kennedy's house which at that time was some higher than the street. Then you would come to Mr. Tom Wood's store which was very close to the railroad.

As we continue north on Main Street beyond the railroad on the east side you will see two small warehouses used for storing farm equipment, etc. Just behind these warehouses was Mr. Adam Bird's store and just beyond the store was Mr. Bird's home. Next you came to Mr. Lee Daniel's home. Continuing on up the east side of Main Street you came to Mr. Sheppard's house. After Mr. Sheppard's house there was nothing except wide open spaces and some sour orange trees, until you reached Mr. Ross Daniel's home, which is located on the southeast corner of the crossroads [current Highway 169 and Brewton Street]. On the northeast corner of the crossroads was Mr. Olin Daniel's home. Beyond Mr. Daniel's house there was only empty space. Just across from Mr. Olin Daniel was Mr. Jim Daniel's home. It was located on the northwest corner.

Now as we go south on Main Street you come to the home of Misses Sallie and Maude Brewton, which is located on the southwest corner of the crossroads. Between the Brewton place and Mr. Cleburn Daniel's home there was a large field. Mr. Daniel's house was on the west side of Main Street. Next to Mr. Cleburn's was a pecan orchard and next to that was the Bickley place. This is where my family lived from 1930 until 1932, when my father completed our new home and we moved. Mr. Cap Hearn had his garden next to the Bickley place, and next to his garden was Mr. Cap's home. The next home on the west side of Main Street was that of Mr. B.G. Tippins. There was an empty lot between Mr. Tippins' home and Cap Hearn's store. Now as we go back to the crossroads and travel a short way west we come to Mr. John M. Wood's home and farm. You can still see some of the old outbuildings.

Mr. Theodore Brewton lived up the railroad east of the center of Bellville. He was at one time the principal of Bellville High School. He was known by most of the boys at school as "Squire Bill." He kind of walked with his shoulders back and it was said that he walked out of his coat on one occasion. He was a good old fellow and sincere about teaching school. His actions were sometimes comical, to say the least. He had an old Ford four-door touring car that he drove to school. The right front door was stuck and anyone getting in the passenger side had to climb through the window. Just south across Highway 280 from Mr. Brewton's home was Mr. Mac Johnson's home and farm.

Mr. Nollie Parker's house was west of the schoolhouse facing Highway 280 and was considered a part of the Bellville community.

This covers all the people who were in the so-called limits of Bellville town. There were many farmers living south of Bellville who helped form the economic and social nucleus of the town. Along with that they were part of the moral fabric of the community. They had children who attended Bellville High School, and their families attended the local church. Some of the men sat on the board of trustees for the school. Although they were not a part of the immediate town they were the ones who helped make the overall community and town of Bellville complete.

Q: Do you have any final thoughts on growing up in Bellville?

A: It was just a way of life that people have lost. Many don't know anything about how country people grew up. Today everyone seems to have some type ego that they want to put forth. Back then, everyone believed in "live and let live." They enjoyed life, you see. Today you don't find that way of existence anymore. People are in a hurry to get somewhere else, and are too interested in material things.

You figure with the war and everything, a lot of people had to leave to find a job. Walter Emmett is one of the few that was able to stay around. He was in a business where he could remain here. Many of the other young men who grew up here had to leave to find employment. Many went into the service. Some went to the railroad. A lot of them left the community for other pursuits. Normally when this happens a community goes down. But this hasn't happened to Bellville. It is still a nice town. All the new homes out on Highway 280 and around the immediate area are an indication that people still want to live in Bellville. Of course, Bellville has changed some in the overall picture, but it hasn't changed in a negative way. That's the good thing about this community.

As I said before, growing up in Bellville gave me my foundation in life. This strength served me well during hardships as a soldier in World War II, and for my endeavors throughout my adult life. I am thankful that I passed Bellville's way.

I don't know if I've been any help, but I've tried. It is hard to put into words all the kind feelings I have about Bellville. It was 60 years ago when I left. However, because of my fond memories, it seems like only yesterday.

Interview with Judge Harry DeLoach
Claxton, Georgia - September 2, 1994

Question [Q]: What are your earliest recollections of Bellville?

A: I went to the town of Bellville as a child all through my early years. Back then, Tom Wood sold 25 pieces of candy for a nickel. Stopping by his store was a good way to get a piece of candy with the change I might have had at the time.

Bay Branch School and the Smith School consolidated into Bellville in 1921. I was in the second grade at that time. I went to the first grade at Bay Branch School, which was a one-teacher school. The Smith school was also a one-teacher school. As I recall, that's when they still had the model T school busses. At that time Mr. William Callaway was the principal at Bellville. Bellville was a four-teacher school then. The next year Mr. Turner came in as principal. Groover C. Turner, I believe, was his full name. He was from Ringgold, Georgia. He was principal for the next four years, 1922-1926.

The old cotton gin was where the bank sits now. I carried many a bale of cotton to that gin. Back then, we would usually grow 10 to 15 bales a year. Our farm was just a few miles south from Bellville. I was a little bit slower than my bothers in picking cotton, so my daddy would make me haul the cotton to the gin while my brothers were picking. I never did pick over about 130 pounds a day, but my brother Richard could pick over 200 every day. My sister Ruth was also a good cotton picker. I carried cotton to the Bellville gin until I went off to college.

Q: Did you drive a mule and wagon?

A: Well, it was a two-horse wagon to the gin.

Q: How was it growing up in the Bellville area?

A: It was wonderful. Of all the places my parents would let me go when I was a little boy, one was the home of Mr. George Brewton and Mrs. Lizzie. They were fine people. Also, I could go to spend the night with Benny Johnson and Wallace Parker. We always had a 410-gauge shotgun at our house, and I got my first one when I was ten years old. I learned to shoot it, too. I could shoot a cat squirrel or rabbit most any time. When I'd go to Wallace Parker's, they'd have a 12-gauge double barrel. We'd go hunting, and I'd do about as well with the 410 as he did with the 12-gauge. We'd have a grand time.

Q: The railroad came through in what year?

A: 1890 to 1892.

Q: Who were some of the early landowners?

A: Berry Brewton and Pulaski Smith. Berry Brewton owned the land just north of the branch, and also north of the railroad. John Wood was also a land owner.

Q: There was a terrible Bellville fire in 1901. Do you ever remember any stories about the fire?

A: Yes, my mother told me about it. She didn't describe it completely, but did say it burned down practically everything in Bellville at the time. The fire was disastrous to the town. Prior to the fire, there was a store there about where Bernie's store is now.

Over there where the brick store is [opposite Bernie's] was a huge building, kind of a complex that housed several different businesses. Around the turn of the century Bellville was the biggest town in this area. They had two doctors, an automobile dealership, and a cotton gin. They had a right smart of doings. They also had stores all the way to Highway 280.

Q: Did your father go to school in Bellville?

A: Yes, he did. His name was Glenn E. DeLoach.

Q: Where was the school located?

A: It was located up on the hill [west of Main Street (Highway 169), between Highways 280 and 292], where it remained until it was torn down. You don't remember the old Methodist Church, do you? The church was across the road from the schoolhouse. Where Mr. Waters lives now is about where the school was. There is a hill there, and it's a pretty area. That was the first school. I think the second was at the same location. The second school was also wooden. Then the brick building was built in 1922. I went to school in the old wooden building in 1921. Then the next year the school moved temporarily over next to the road [Highway 280]. Then the new brick school was built in the same place as the old building. When the brick building was torn down, the bricks were used to build the Luther Waters' home. He bought the land where the school stood and built him a home a little further west and south of where the brick building stood.

I started at Bellville School in 1921 and went there until I graduated in 1930, along with Benny Johnson, Carolus Daniel, and Wallace Parker. We were the four boys. Laverna Saturday, Helen Sheppard, Willie Mulligan, and Mildred Bunton were the four girls. Eight graduated from Bellville in the year 1930. Then we all went to Claxton High School.

When we opened up the school, we had to go to the Hearns each day to get water, which is a good 300 yards from the school. The school well would get caved in and such, and we couldn't use it.

Many of the teachers boarded at the Hearn's. The others boarded at the Adam Bird house.

Q: Can you tell me about the turpentine still?

A: One of the early turpentine stills belonged to my father. It was about here on the map [points to location on the Bellville map south of the railroad and west of Main Street]. My father built the still in 1928. The first cotton gin was there too. The reason I know this so well is the first two or three years I went to school, the Hearns would keep peanuts in the old cotton gin building. Some of the school boys would sorta help themselves, you know.

The new gin was built over there where the bank is now. The first gin was run by C.W. Hearn, Cap Hearn's father. The new gin burned also. This was a huge building, it must have been 40x60 feet.

Q: Can you tell me about Tom Wood's turpentine still?

A: Yes, I suppose it shipped 700 barrels a year. What happened was my daddy was in debt to Tom Wood. My father first gave him half the turpentine business to settle up. The value was $300--of all things. Later my father sold the rest of it to Tom for another $300. They moved the still from its original site to over here [points to map] where you can still see the remnants today [east of Main Street, just south of the railroad]. This was the only still in Bellville at the time.

Q: In addition to the Hearn grist mill, do you know of others?

A: Uncle Lee Kennedy had one. He set him up a grist mill on his farm. I remember going there as a child to carry corn to be ground. The farm was just next to Bay Branch Church. Three of the Kennedys lived out there. Raford was Uncle Lee's father, and Martin was his younger brother, and then Alfred Kennedy. Alfred raised and raced horses out there for years. He was killed in 1891.

Q. Can you tell me about some of the older houses in Bellville?

A: Well, there's the Pulaski Smith house. It's one of the oldest, if not the oldest in the Bellville section. Pulaski married into the Daniel family. Pulaski Smith was one of the school trustees, one of the church trustees, and one of the prominent leaders in the area. James B. Smith was clerk of the Superior Court of Tattnall County for some years. His son Daniel married Benjamin Brewton's daughter.

Q: I have a copy of a 1898 *Georgia Gazetteer* here. I know you were not born until 1914, but could you tell me if you recognize any of the names listed for the Bellville area?

A: The Bacons were black. I remember the Bazemores, Brazells, Brewtons, Callaways, DeLoaches, Hammocks, Kennedys, and Mattoxes. Old man Mattox was called "Parch." Then I remember the Moores, Riggs, Rogers,...yes, I remember all those families. Most of these homes extended south from Bellville.

Q: Can you tell me about the mail carriers?

A: Well, my daddy was a mail carrier about the turn of the century. He carried the mail in a horse and buggy. He would always eat dinner down there just north of Mendes, where he would get to about dinner time. Then he would circle around and come back into Bellville in the afternoon. His route would take him south of Bellville across the creek and go by the area of Bay Branch Church, then out in the flat woods to what was known as the Tootle place [Mr. J.M. Tootle]. Next, he would go by the Martin Kennedy place. Martin had a son that was a doctor. Then on down toward Mendes.

Q: Do you know about Bellville postmasters?

A: Well, the first one I knew about was Mr. Cap Hearn himself. The post office was in his store building. About 1912 to 1915, the mail route changed to start out of Hagan. Jim Elders was the postmaster at Hagan. Jonathan Collins was the mail carrier, and he carried the mail essentially the same route as my father did previously.

Q: Do you remember where the old Sallie Brewton house was?

A: Yes, you know the road coming by George Brewton's? The road forks off of Highway 280 to the right east of your place. Her house was where Highway 169 crosses that road north of Bellville.

Q: Did you ever work in your daddy's still?

A: Yes, I was one of his main haulers at one time. Daddy said he could send me across the river for a load of tar and set his watch by me getting back. He knew how long it took me and knew I didn't tarry along the road.

We had two different kinds of stills, a smaller and a larger one. The larger one was an eight barrel still. You poured eight barrels of crude turpentine gum into the still. Then you built a fire under the boiler and the heat would evaporate the turpentine. Then it would come out the still as steam and flow through the pipes running through a huge water container. The tub, as we called it, had two or three thousand gallons of water. The water cooled the turpentine as it went through the pipes, and then it came down into the barrels. We would usually get about a barrel and a half of turpentine out of eight barrels of crude tar.

The whole process would take roughly three and one-half to four hours. We'd usually settle for two stillings a day. But if we got behind, we sometimes did three stillings a day. This was hot, tiring, hard work. Sometimes the barrels would weigh five to six hundred pounds a piece, and they had to be rolled up the platform. Then they had to put the barrels up to the mouth of the still itself, and then pour them into the still.

The finished barrels would be put on the train to Savannah. We'd ship the turpentine and the rosin. Eight barrels of crude turpentine would produce a barrel and a half of spirits and about five barrels of rosin. The balance would be chips you would skim off the tar as it was boiling. The tar would go off as trash.

During the gathering of the tar, the barrels would be scattered in the woods about the distance it would take to fill a barrel. They used about an eight gallon bucket to put the tar in after they dipped it out of the cup. That is about as much as a man can carry--80 to 100 pounds when you got it full. You would end up with the full bucket close to the barrel. You sorta did a moon shaped pattern, so you'd always end up at the barrel when it came time to empty the bucket. They used this system to make collecting the tar easier. Before tin cups were used to catch the tar, pockets were cut into the trunk of the pine trees to catch the crude gum after trees were chipped weekly to produce the gum.

Working at the still could be dangerous. Sometimes the still would catch fire and burn up. With that huge tank of water the spirits flowed through, however, at least you always had water to fight a fire. You could control it pretty well.

It was a hard way to make a living. But in some ways it was better than farming because you could always sell your turpentine and rosin whereas sometimes you couldn't sell things you grew on the farm. It was interesting work. I never did learn to still, but I think I could have without any trouble. You could usually listen to the sound of the pipes in the big barrel the turpentine came into, and tell from the sound how well it was boiling in the boiler itself.

Q: Do you know how long Tom Wood operated the Bellville still?

A: Yes, Tom Wood received my daddy's part in 1932. The still was operated in the old location for several years before he moved it across the road. The new still was built somewhere around 1944 or 1945 and was operated until approximately 1960. Then people stopped chipping boxes [gathering tar]. The pine trees were worth more to leave them and use for lumber. When the war came on, everything changed. Before the war they shipped a lot of the turpentine and rosin overseas. After the war, the bottom fell out the market.

Q: Were there any other businesses in Bellville?

A: Of course, the Daniels have always had a sawmill. Even today they sell sawmill products. Then there was the cotton gin. There was the depot for railroad business. Your granddaddy Mac Johnson grew a lot of oats where the Pinewood School is now. There was a 20 acre field there. He would grow oats there at least every other year.

Around the turn of the century there were two country doctors there. Dr. Nichols was my uncle, and he married Aunt Mattie Daniel. I don't remember the other doctor, but there were two doctors there.

Also, about that time there was an automobile business in Bellville. That business was where Tom Wood's store later moved. This was the Adam Bird building, at the corner of Highways 169 and 292. When Tom Wood moved his store from south of the railroad, he moved it over to the Adam Bird building after Adam died.

The Hearn store was in operation many years and was where Bernie's is now.

Q: Are there any humorous incidents you remember?

A: Well, there were many tales about your great-uncle Theodore Brewton. They used to call him "Squire Bill," but not to his face. He was my teacher in the ninth and tenth grades, 1928, '29, and '30. In 1927 he lost the election for school superintendent. After he lost the election, he went up there and took over as principal of Bellville School and did both jobs. Mr. Theodore was a good teacher and was interested in the welfare of the community. He wrote a nice recommendation for my sister to go to nursing training. He did a lot such as that. Mr. Theodore was a good man.

One year during Mr. Turner's time, on April Fools' Day, I was the only boy above the fifth grade who didn't run away from school. Most of the girls did too. They deserted the school on April Fools' Day. They got in trouble later on. The principal, Mr. Turner, had them digging ditches in front of the school. They would build the dirt up in the center to build a walkway. In front of the Bellville School, it was roughly 100 yards to where that little road ran from Highway 280 to the Tom Wood store down the hill. Mr. Turner built a ramp about ten feet wide from the school all the way out to that road to form a walkway.

Mrs. Grace Hearn was a teacher, and a good one at that. Now, she would have some wonderful tales to tell. Herschel Hearn was born in 1902, and was 91 years old when he died.

The basketball court was right out there by the Bellville School. Herschel Hearn was 12 years older than I am and quite a basketball player. When Herschel got out of school in Claxton, he would come up to Bellville and practice basketball. When our bell rang at school one day, I turned and ran to get in line to go to the classroom. I ran right square into him. He said, "Son, can't you see where you're going? You're trying to run right over a grown man" [laughter].

At one time, the Bellville school was the largest west of Savannah and Hinesville. At the time my daddy went there, there were as many as two hundred students. Those students came from Savannah, Statesboro, and all around.

Q: Do you recognize any of these names [names in 1898 *Gazetteer*]?

A: S. Bird was probably Scott, Adam Bird's brother. The Birds were right well-to-do people back then. Adam Bird never married. He had a store in Bellville when I was a child. He owned the store that later became Tom Wood's store. Tom Wood had a frame building store south of the railroad, just north of the run of the branch. At one time, he did more business than Adam Bird and Cap Hearn put together. When Adam Bird died, Tom Wood evidently bought the store building as well as buying Adam Bird's former residence. He must have bought both from the Adam Bird estate.

I've heard the Stubbs name mentioned quite a few times, but I have no direct information. There were some Stubbs in Hagan later on.

Paul LeGrand was the depot agent all the time that I went to school in Bellville. His daughter Pauline was four grades ahead of me in school.

Uncle Jackie Brewton was the one who kept the courts straight during his lifetime. They'd ask if someone was qualified on a jury because of kinship. They'd call Uncle Jackie for the answer. They'd say, "Who was his granddaddy?" Mr. Jackie would reply, "Yes, he's qualified, he's not kin," or "No, he's not qualified." Jackie Brewton lived east of Bellville on what is now Highway 280.

There was an Overstreet. His turpentine still was about five miles south of Bellville. This was at "Tar City," approximately one-half mile on the old Reidsville Road off Highway 169. This was toward Reidsville, then south about a quarter of a mile. That's where his turpentine still operation was. He ran a store there also. There was a black one-teacher school there as well. He brought his products into Bellville to be shipped on the railroad.

Q: Can you tell me about the railroad?

A: There were four passenger trains a day, two going east and two going west. The first one in the morning was the passenger train going east to Savannah from Montgomery, Alabama. Then there was one about 9 or 9:30 going west from Savannah to Montgomery. It was the Seaboard Airline Railroad. Then in the afternoon, the "down" train would come through about 6 p.m. for Savannah. I believe the "up" train going west was a little earlier.

Q: Was the depot very busy?

A: Well, not that busy because Bellville was a small town. There would maybe be just one passenger to get on and one to get off. Now, it was a busy station during certain parts of the year. During watermelon time they would ship out 50 to 100 watermelon car loads a year from Bellville. They also shipped turpentine and cotton. They would load the cars on a side track, and most of the merchandise would be loaded off the trucks or wagons onto the depot shed platform and then from the depot platform into the cars. The train would leave empty cars next to the shed to be loaded out. There would be as many as ten cars to be loaded. There would always be one to three cars next to the cotton seed house by the railroad ready to be loaded out. There was an auger box that went over the road from the Hearn gin to the seed house. The seed would be transported in this manner.

Q: What's your opinion of Bellville?

A: It's a fine town, and that is because of the quality of people who live there now and lived there in the past. Historically, in Bellville, if you didn't walk the straight and narrow, you were told that you weren't needed around there. You've never heard of much crime around Bellville. The people look out for each other. That's as true today as it was in the past.

Bellville has always been one of the cleanest towns in this area. The residents take great pride in the way the town is kept up.

I always did well in the Bellville area in the elections for state judge. I've always considered it my home area, and the people supported me. I appreciated it too. People often come to me for help or advice, and I try to return their kindness to me by helping them. I ran eight times, and I never lost the Bellville district. I tried to be fair to everybody, and they seemed to appreciate it.

I left home in January in 1932, and I've been on my own ever since. I had just turned 17 when I went to the Berry School. The people of Bellville have been an inspiration for my entire life.

Bellville stands out in my mind as one of the choice places the world over for anybody to live. I hope that some of the information we've talked about will be useful in compiling its history.

Interview with Delma and Mary Daniel
Bellville, Georgia - July 7, 1995

Question [Q]: Mary, who were your parents and grandparents?

A: My mother was Helen Smith, and my maternal grandmother was Mary Eliza Tippins Smith. My mother's father was Pulaski Sikes Smith. My father was O.H. Daniel and his father was Enoch B. Daniel. My paternal grandmother was Margaret Elvina Laing.

My grandfather [Pulaski Sikes] Smith was the Bellville postmaster at one time. He died at the post office when my mother was just four years old. She said that that they went down to see about him, and she carried his hat back home. After his death, Grandmother Smith raised all those children herself. When Bellville was growing she kept some boarders to sort of help out. At the time she broke up housekeeping, all her boys worked for the railroad. Then she moved around among them.

Q: Can you tell us how your family came to Bellville?

A: Mary: Well, my Smith ancestors have been in this area since the 1800s. However, there were not too many people here before the railroad. My grandfather Daniel came here from Liberty County just before the railroad did. You see, they knew the railroad was coming through several years before the tracks were actually laid. He lived up here where the Mallards used to live [not far from the northwest intersection of Highway 169 and Brewton Street]. That's where they built their house when they came here. He was in the sawmill business. Back in those days, they had to move the sawmills to wherever the timber was. That's why he came here.

Delma: During the late 1800s there was plenty of timber around Bellville. It could be harvested nearby and sawed right here. Down in Liberty County you had to load the logs on a boat and run them down the canal. So you could say Enoch came to take advantage of the more plentiful timber here, and to gain the ability to transport the lumber by rail.

Q: Do you recall any stories about your grandfather Daniel?

A: Mary: When Enoch came here, he generally had company visiting all the time. A lot of the kin would come and live with him. That's the way it was done back then--kin would come for a visit and stay several months, or maybe even years [laughter].

Enoch was married twice. He had one daughter from his first wife. Enoch had six boys from his second marriage: Jim, Walford Lee, Enoch A., Olin, Ross, and Rufus.

Enoch died when we were real little [1919]. They said he got up and ate his breakfast and then laid down afterward. He died just after that from an apparent heart attack.

Q: Where did your family live?

A: Mary: When my daddy and mother were first married they lived out at the Shiloh community [out from Reidsville]. Then after I was born they built the house in Bellville. It was located next door to where we live now.

Miss Sallie and Aunt Maude lived in the house across the street [southwest corner of Highway 169 and Brewton Street] for years. They lived there ever since I was a little child. I believe the Tillmans lived in the house at one time. And then the Hendrys lived there. They later dismantled the house and moved it away down to Baxley.

Q: What year did you build this house you live in?

A: Delma: I came here in 1929, and we built it in 1930. Prior to that I lived at my mother and father's house in Bay Branch. We lived with Mary's parents about two years before we built this house. Our daughter, Helen, was born in that house, and our second, Ann, was born in this house.

Q: Who are your children?

A: Mary: Helen Wilkinson, Ann Ward, John Darwin, Nancy Clodfelter, and our youngest, Mary Alice Rumph.

Q: Where did you go to school?

A: Mary: I finished here in Bellville in 1928, and went to Claxton to finish the eleventh grade in 1929. Delma and I were in the same class. Some of my other classmates were Loulie Daniel Perkins, Grady Rogers, Wilease Barnard, Wilma Saturday, Mattie Lou, and Evelyn Daniel Mallard. We didn't have a school bus to ride to Claxton, and had to ride to school in a Model T. The students from Bay Branch would ride to Bellville on the bus and then ride with us in the automobile. We actually weren't treated that great down there [laughter]. We were definitely not in the "in-crowd." We were sort of thought of as being from the country.

I guess you could say Delma and I first started courting when he bought me a cup of hot chocolate at a Bellville School Halloween festival. We would have the festivals outside the school building. We celebrated Halloween back in those days. They would have dunking the apple games, etc. I remember that cup of chocolate was very hot. It's funny how you remember small details like that.

Delma: One thing they would do is put up a screen and the young ladies would walk behind it. There would be a light in the back so you could just see the faint silhouette on the screen. Well, the girls would go behind the screen one by one. You would bid on having dinner with the girl of your choice. You see, the girls had brought a basket lunch. It was called a box supper by some. You see, you had to identify your girl by her shape on the screen and hope you didn't bid on the wrong girl [laughter]! There would be cake walks also. They were quite popular.

I started to school in Reidsville. It was just over nine miles to Reidsville from our home in Bay Branch, and it took more than an hour to make the trip by wagon in the old days.

I came to Bellville School when Evans County was cut from Tattnall County. Besides going to school, my job was to drive the bus from Bay Branch. There were older students on the bus, but I was more mechanically inclined and they asked me to drive the bus.

The Bay Branch and Smithtown schools both consolidated with Bellville School. Smithtown was half way between Bay Branch and Bellville. Sapptown School consolidated over here too. We had finished at Bellville before Sapptown came over here. They had Model T buses to take the students to Bellville. They just had canvas for windows. It could get right cold in that "bus." Back in those days, the busses were built in blacksmith shops.

Mary: Of course, those of us in living in Bellville had to walk to school.

Q: Mary, you've lived in Bellville all your life?

A: Yes, I have. We'll be celebrating our 66th wedding anniversary on November 7th. We have been right here all those years.

Q: Can you tell me about the airplane crash in Bellville in 1919?

A: Mary: Yes. When the airplanes landed, we all went down to see them. That was great excitement. Most of us had never seen an airplane up close. When the plane crashed we all scattered in a hurry. It was frightening.

Delma: The day of the crash, I came to town in a wagon from our home in Bay Branch. I was sitting on top of a bale of cotton that was in the back of the wagon. They told us there was an airplane that had force-landed and was going to try to take off. My brother, Wright, was on one wagon, and I was on the other. So we walked up there to where the planes were.

The airplane had these big chocks ahead of the wheels. They asked somebody to volunteer to pull out the chocks. The pilot revved up the engine, someone pulled the chocks, and he took off. His front wheels hit the top of the wire fence at the end of the field. I don't remember about anybody being injured. The pilot apparently had some mechanical problems, and also miscalculated the distance. The soft dirt in the field could have slowed them down some. He only needed two more feet to clear the fence. I think the field belonged to Uncle Cleburn Daniel at the time. There was a second plane there also. After the first plane hit the fence, the second pilot did not try to take off. After the accident, they dismantled the planes, loaded them on railroad flat cars, and shipped them away.

Q: I've heard the community activity centered on the railroad. Is this correct?

A: Mary: Yes, we knew it was time to go to school by hearing the train come by in the morning. All of us Bellville children would walk to school together. We would stop at one another's house. The students were from Uncle Cleburn's family, Uncle Jim's family, and the Sheppard family. When we'd hear the train, we would start walking. We would turn right about where the City Hall is located and head up the hill. A little road went up to the school.

Q: Where did you go for entertainment?

A: Mary: We would go to Cedar Creek to picnic. They said don't ever go to the far side of the creek, because there was a sink hole there. Now, there is not enough water enough to wet your feet. We would go out there and go in bathing. We would normally walk there.

The Sunday School class would go once a year to Tybee. We thought that was a great adventure to go on the Savannah Beach pavilion. We would go down there and back on the train in the same day. We also had a picnic a time or two at Parker's Springs.

I've gone to Bellville Church all my life. We always had big Christmas programs. They would go to the river and get a big holly tree. They would haul the tree back on a wagon. The festivities would create great excitement among us children. We would tie the presents on the tree, and they would attach bells also. Stokes Bickley was the best Santa Claus. He would come in through the window. The church would be so full, it wouldn't hold all the people. They would have the program on Christmas Eve. Another tradition was to ring the church bell.

The cane grindings and peanut boilings used to be a big time. You know the John Wood place up here? There used to be a two-story house there. As I recall, they had a water well with a sweep. The first Wood house burned. In later years, the second house was moved across the street from us here and is where Emily Wood lives now. The Woods had cane grindings every year, and that was a big event. They had benches around, and you would sit, visit, and eat. They would boil the peanuts in a big washpot. There was, of course, some courting taking place also.

The Bird house was on the way to John Wood's. It was about half way between here and the Wood house. We thought it was haunted. We'd hurry by that house if we were walking at night.

Q: Please tell me a little about the street [George Brewton Street] here in front of your house?

A: Mary: We didn't even know this was named Brewton Street until lately. We just never knew it by that name. We generally referred to the street as the "cut off." In the old days, there weren't many people using the Brewton Street cut off then. It was just a little dirt road. The livestock and chickens used to roam around in the road all the time.

Q: Delma, tell us some more about yourself.

A: I was born in 1909. My father Harley Daniel boarded with Mary's grandmother when he went to school in Bellville. We had a log school out there at Bay Branch next to the church where I went my first few years. Then I came to Bellville. I later worked for Mary's father at the sawmill.

Mary: He came to Bellville to go to school and that's where we met. I didn't know him before he came. The five miles to Bay Branch was a long way. After Bellville School, then we went to Claxton High School.

Q: Delma, tell us more about the line of work you were in?

A: Delma: I was in charge of the upkeep of the Daniel sawmill machinery. The mill was manufactured by Frick. My father was in the sawmill business, cotton gin business, and blacksmith shop, etc. So I was trained in this type work. When I was going to school, I had an understanding with the teachers that when I had cash paying work that I would not come to school on those days.

Mary: You know my father's first sawmill was originally south of the railroad and Ennis Branch. Then it was moved behind the Sheppard house. Later, he moved the mill to Scott, near Swainsboro, and then on to Mendes. At one time he had a mill up next to the Cedar Creek Bridge. Next, the mill was located over behind Walter Emmett's house. Then they moved it up to where the Daniel's building is now.

Q: Can you tell me about the lumber you processed at the mill?

A: Delma: The largest dimensions we handled was 6 by 14 inches. Any bigger, we would take to Savannah. Your father, Charlie Johnson, could dress the larger timber, 12 by 12 etc., down at his mill in Savannah. I planed a lot of lumber in my day. For example, I dressed all the lumber that went in this house.

Q: How many people worked at the sawmill?

A: When the mill started off there were 12 to 15 hands. This number increased to about 35 to 40 at the height of the business. A lot of the lumber in the houses of this area was sawed and dressed over there at the Daniel sawmill. We mostly cut old patches of timber people were holding on to or stands of timber that were in the creek branches. Some of the hard to get to timber was the kind he bought.

We would normally buy what we called "round" timber, which was timber that never had been bled for turpentine. This timber was preferable because the turpentined timber was often "chipped" high up the side of the tree. The older turpentiners also chipped out boxes actually in the tree. We sawed what you call merchanable timber. If the specification called for 12 by 12, then you needed a streak of heart on all sides. Some orders called for all heart. I used to tote a little handbook, put out by the Southern Pines Association, in my pocket all the time. There were descriptions in the book of the various grades and sizes. The lumber brokers were in Savannah, and they took orders from all over. Some was shipped through New York, and much of it was shipped overseas. A lot of this timber was used for ship decking. It was about two and one-half inches thick, and was tongue and groove. We used to load five and six car loads at the time. We would make a special day of loading the lumber on the railroad cars. We would place some lumber in flat cars, and some in box cars. If we had timbers a certain extended length, then you might have to order special sized cars to fit the lumber. On some occasions we actually used two cars to haul the exceptionally long lumber.

Putting the lumber on the cars was a big job. We'd use long skids. One end of the skid was put on the flatcar and one end on the ground. The men would push the lumber up the skid on to the flatcar. Then the men on the car would stack it. There would be a couple of our best men on the flat car and eight or so on the ground pushing the lumber up the skids.

The sawmill was powered with steam. The fire was made with scrap wood and sawdust. We eventually went to electrical power.

Q: Do you remember when you first got lights in the homes of Bellville?

A: Delma: Yes. It was about 1934. Georgia Power wired this house for $15. Several girls from around here married the Georgia Power men that came to put up the wires. Electricity changed a lot of things around here. See that lamp? [Points to a beautiful antique kerosene lamp.] It's the one we used to court by. The kerosene lamps were smoky and didn't give off much light. However, you don't need much light to court by [laughter].

Q: Delma, what year did you retire?

A: I worked about 50 years at the sawmill and retired in 1977. For years after I retired, they asked me to come and work on the mill when they had particular problems. Sometimes I was the only one who knew how to fix it.

Q: When did running water come to Bellville?

A: Delma: We tied on to the water line from Mary's father's place in the mid- to late 1930s. He had a well bored and people began to join on. That was the first running water up this way. There was an electric pump at the Hearn house and the cotton gin, too. Then there was no town council to furnish water for the houses. Mr. Bascom Tippins had a deep well and a Delco light plant to run it.

Q: What was a Delco light plant?

A: General Motors made it. It generated electric power. There was a little one horse power engine that ran it.

Q: Did they have carbide lights?

A: Delma: I think some did. We had them in Reidsville. The apparatus would look like an air compressor tank sitting upright. You bought this rock that would be full of gas, or carbide fuel. You would buy it by the can. You pulled the lid off and poured it in the retort. You would fill it up half way with the fuel and halfway with water. There was a float in there like the float on a carburetor. The chemical reaction would take place and a gas would boil off. When the carbide reservoir needed recharging, it would be plum white inside. The residue is what people would use to paint their fences white. It would take an hour or two to generate enough gas to operate the lights. These memories are from before I was seven years old.

Q: I have been doing some research on the black churches in the area. Can you tell me about Bishop Grace and the House of Prayer?

A: Mary: He had quite a few followers in this area. They picked cotton in the summertime and earned money to give to him. They'd give a lot of what they made to the church. They would go to Savannah, and get baptized every year. They put out the red carpet for Bishop Grace when he came to town. After he died, you didn't hear much about the church.

Q: Do you remember when a black church stood up close to where the Daniel's building material facility is located?

Delma: There used to be Monk's Chapel up across the street from the electric motor company building. Fletcher Mills' father, Monk Mills, was the elder. He fired the sawmill boiler for Mary's daddy. Monk married Coot.

Q: What is the nicest part of living in Bellville?

A: Mary: This is just a good place to live. We never thought Bellville would be like this, as built up as it is. Now that the school is here, the people are from everywhere. Bellville is a quiet place with good people. Many new houses have been built, and it's a very desirable place to live.

In the old days, didn't anybody have a whole lot. We sort of made do with what we had. However, everybody had a good time. We now have a long lifetime of memories to remind us of the fine qualities of the place we call home.

Interview with Winton Bell
Bellville, Georgia - September 2, 1995

Question [Q]: Winton, how long have you lived in Bellville?

A: I was born here in 1918 and have lived here all my life, except when I was in the service.

Q: What were your parents' names?

A: My father went by the initials "D.O.," but his name was Dan. My mother was Agnes Valerie Burkhalter Bell.

Q: I have seen an old 1909 Tattnall County map, and there is a Bell place indicated just south of your home here on Highway 169. Was that your home?

A: Yes, that was our home place. About a mile from here.

Q: Who were your sisters and brothers?

A: There were 15 of us children, and our parents raised 12. Three died as infants. The ones that died were before I came along, and I didn't know them. I've got the history of the family in a book compiled by George Durrence.

My oldest brother was John Olen Bell. The oldest girl was Bertie Lee Bell, and she's still living. The next brother was Alton Bell, and he's passed away. He was one of the rambling ones of the bunch. Whenever people around here got about 15 or 16 years old, back in the old days, there wasn't anything much for them to do on the farm. If they didn't get married, then many of them caught a freight train. So, I don't know which was worse [laughter]. My brother Alton caught a train and ended up in the state of Oklahoma. He got a job there and worked in a copper mine. He married an only daughter, Aloysius Odessa Edwards. We always thought that all the people in Oklahoma had oil wells. Since he married an only daughter, we thought he would come back a millionaire. But, it didn't work out that way.

Alton stayed around Oklahoma a while, then wound up working in Arizona as an electrician. He and his wife had three children, and he was away from Georgia for 17 years. He lived in Arizona for a while and started up a business. He sold his business out there, and then came back to Georgia. He then moved to Arkansas and worked as an electrician there until his death.

The next child was Mae. Eula Mae had 16 children, 8 boys and 8 girls. They are all still living except one girl. Both Eula Mae and her husband have passed away. Most of the children live down around the community of Mendes, some in Atlanta, Jacksonville, and one up around Augusta.

The next one is my brother Cecil. He married a local girl and did all types of jobs like selling insurance, and wound up in Dothan, Alabama. He lived there about 30 years and passed away in Dothan and is buried there.

The next youngest brother is Woodrow. It's odd how things happen. Woodrow's story gets back to the brother that went to Arizona with his family. As I mentioned, Alton was working in the copper mines. He sent money for Olen to come out there to work. Olen wanted Cecil to go with him. This was along in 1929, I believe, just before the big crash came. My oldest brother Olen had a Model T Ford. Now I was old enough to remember this Model T Ford, a touring model, with a canvas top. He bought another old junk vehicle to get parts. The car had the old long running board on the side, and he and my Daddy took some wide boards and put them on the outside of that running board to store boxes on. There weren't any suitcases or anything like that. They used boxes and sacks to put their clothes in. Olen and his wife had three children, and Cecil was not married. So, this whole group took out in 1929 to drive to Ruby, Arizona in a Model T Ford. There were very few paved roads. However, they made it all the way and had only one flat tire. That's all the trouble they had. They slept by the road when night caught them. Cecil sent Woodrow money to go to Ruby, Arizona. They stayed out there until after the stock market crashed, and my oldest brother, Olen, came back home. The brother that went with them, Cecil, didn't come back home, and he got to rambling. He wound up in Michigan driving a truck on a big hydroelectric dam project. There was a good bit of work in that area. So, there was Woodrow and Alton left in Arizona. After the market crashed, Alton kept his job since he had been out there a while.

Cecil, who was in Michigan, sent Woodrow money to Arizona to come to Michigan where he could get a job driving a truck. Woodrow then left Arizona to go to Michigan. He was known to take a drink on occasion. He bought an old car, and took off for Michigan. Well, he got to drinking, and somewhere around Denver he had a wreck. There wasn't anything else to do--so, he joined the Army of all things [laughter]. He stayed in the Army for three years. He wrote mother that he was coming home. The brother in Michigan had already come home. Woodrow got his mustering out pay and wasted it, so he re-enlisted again. Then he came home, and later he died in Savannah.

The next child was Bonnie. She's just two years older than I am. She lives in Savannah.

I'm the only one who stayed here in the county and took up farming.

Q: Where was your father born?

A: Just this side of Glennville.

Q: Can you tell me about your grandfather Bell?

A: Yes, he had two brothers. They came from the Aiken, S. C. area. My daddy said his father settled in Glennville, just about three miles this side on Highway 301. One of the other brothers went to Louisville, Georgia, and the other one to Thomasville. Daddy said none of the three ever communicated with each other. My father moved to the Bellville area around 1914 or 1915.

Bellville was founded when the railroad came through. I've heard my daddy talk about when he hauled fertilizer in 200 pound bags in a one-horse cart. On the cart, you had a back band to hold the shaves up and belly band to keep it from tilting up. He said they would leave their farm three miles this side of Glennville, and make the 12 mile trip hauling fertilizer from the Bellville depot to the farm. It would take all day to make the round trip.

Q: Where was your family's original house in the Bellville section?

A: The house burned in the 1930s, around 1933. They owned this place [where Winton currently lives], and we moved over here. He had this place before the other house burned. There were about 75 or 80 acres here. They had bought this land, and the house was started in the 1920s. The house wasn't completed when they moved in, and all the flooring wasn't in, etc. Much of this land around here used to belong to the Durrences. Mrs. Hearn was a Durrence. That's the way the Hearns came by a lot of their land. My grandmother was a Durrence. That's how my folks got the place over where we lived [D.O. Bell place]. My mama's daddy, my granddaddy, died in 1916. They had about 300 acres over there divided three ways. One wound up with 88 acres and the other one 90, and maybe Mama had a little over 100. I don't know whether they drew numbers for it or grandmother just said, "This is your part." Grandmother Durrence was Lavenia Jane Durrence, and she married John M. Burkhalter.

Q: In the 1930s what crops did the area farmers grow?

A: They still planted cotton. What they called a two-horse farm then was about 50 to 60 acres of land with two mules. My father would plant about half of it in cotton, and the other in corn, peanuts, and velvet beans for the cows and hogs. We had to have the corn to feed the mules. My daddy started planting tobacco in 1926 or 1927. Pharris, your granddaddy, Mr. Mac, was already planting tobacco at that time. He was one of the first in the area.

This was a two-horse farm here of 56 acres. A sharecropper lived here in this house originally. My father also bought his home place in Glennville. He got half of the income from this one and half of the one at Glennville and all that we made on the two-horse farm here. All of it together didn't gross $1,000. But, we got by. We produced most everything we ate. The only thing we had to buy was flour, rice, and sugar. The corn was taken to be ground at the Hearn gristmill located at the gin in Bellville. The cotton was taken to the Hearn gin also.

When my daddy was farming that 50 acres he'd have about 25 acres of cotton. He farmed cotton religiously from the time I was big enough to know anything. All the other brothers had gone. When we came along we were the last six children, the sister above me on down. We kind of grew up like a family because the rest of the kids left as soon as they got to be 16 or 17 years old. When the cotton would get to opening it would be only three or four bolls to the stalk. Daddy started us to picking that cotton, and he didn't hire any help cause we picked all 25 acres. We started on one side, and it might take two weeks to get cross the field. By the time we got to the last four or five acres, just about all the bolls were open. While the rest of it was opening, we'd go out and pick cotton for our neighbors. We would try to get money to buy clothes to wear to school. Pharris, we often stayed out of school a month to pick cotton. Sometimes they would postpone school two weeks because people were not through picking cotton. I went to school when I could. We'd go to school the first day to get a room assignment. My sister Bonnie helped me get by. She was smart, and our two grades were in the same room. You know, third and fourth, etc. She would get my lessons from the teacher. She would help me with the lessons, and I'd send the homework paper back in by her. I would try to go in and stand the tests. If it hadn't been for her there isn't any way in the world I could have made it.

I could pick about 275 pounds of cotton a day. In about a bale an acre cotton, I'd pick around 30 pounds an hour. That was a croaker sack full. Thurmon Smith could pick over 300 pounds, and there aren't a lot of people who could do that.

I also worked at the Hearn gin some. I worked there one or two years before I went into the service. I made 90 cents a day! The day started at six in the morning, and it ended at 10 at night. If you worked from 10 until 12 you got paid extra for those two hours. You got an hour off for dinner and an hour off for supper. That was a long day [laughter]. If you divide 14 into 90 cents, I'm not sure just how many cents an hour that was [laughter].

Q: When you worked at the gin, what were your duties?

A: Well, most of the time another fellow and I ran the press. We put the strapping and bagging around the cotton. Of course, we did whatever came up. I wasn't a ginner, cause I was just a young boy. Along then they had a full-time ginner. You had to keep constant watch. It could also be dangerous. After the war, they had put in a black-seed gin. The one with regular saws was a green-seed gin. The black-seed cotton had a seed that was smooth like a pea. However, the lint stuck to the green seeds. The saws pulled that lint off. The way you ginned the black-seed was you had two rollers that were about five foot long. It ran like an old clothes wringer. It had some kind of leather fiber. If you ginned four bales a day with that, you did a good job. They also ran the gin at night. Several days I worked all day and night too. I would work at the press tying out the bales, and at night I'd feed the black-seed gin. I could feed it in my sleep [laughter]. Our government figured there was going to be a war back in 1938 and 1939, and they encouraged the farmers to plant long-staple cotton. They needed long-staple cotton for some of the materials that went into the war effort.

Q: When did you all get electric lights?

A: It would have been sometime either in 1938 or 1939. Up until that time we used kerosene lamps. That's how we got our lessons.

Q: How about telephone service?

A: Well, we had telephones before then. We had what you call a community phone. The phone went up to Mr. Hearn's store. He had one of those big wall mounted phones. Mr. Hearn was on Southern Bell, which went into Claxton. We couldn't call directly to Claxton from our house. My daddy would have to call Mr. Hearn, and he would relate the message by making another call. I asked my daddy about the system. He said the first fellow out of Bellville that wanted a telephone would pay to have the phone line built to his house. The next one that wanted it would pay to have it extended to their house, etc. My daddy had to build the lines from Mr. Riggs' to the Tippins' place and on down to where our old house used to be. He had to keep that line up. The lines were strung on poles. We had big, round batteries to power the phone. It was a pretty good system, and it worked well. This was probably in the mid-1920s. The system went all the way out to Bay Branch. I don't think it branched off too much. It went mainly down the main roads. This wasn't originally the main road. When my daddy moved up here, the road actually turned up there and went by where he lived, and then it came out by the Riggs'. The road looped around to the houses. As far as I know, the phone line didn't go on the north side of Bellville.

Q: When did they pave Highway 169?

A: It was paved in 1954. They had the paving project planned in 1938 or 1939. The Works Progress Administration [WPA] built the road, and they were going to pave it. The WPA had some people building roads, some repairing court houses, and some repairing schools. Anything to give work to folks. They built this road from Bellville to the county line, a distance of four miles. They had a dump truck or two, but most of the work, and all the stumps were dug out by manual labor. This way, many workers could be employed and this, of course, was the purpose of the WPA. The workers were paid a dollar a day. They would stake and pull a string to lay out the road. The ditches were dug with long-handle shovels. The fellow that did the fine tuning of the ditch had a shovel with a handle on it about 10 to 12 feet long. You have to understand these were mostly old folks. He would get the shovel full, turn around and pull the shovel full of dirt up the ditch bank. Instead of backing up, he would turn around to see where he was going. He wasn't going to a fire either [laughter]. They got it ready to be paved and even had the base on the road. They laid it down with a road plow. However, politics got into it, and it didn't get paved. My daddy told me they took the money needed to pave this road and built Liberty Street in Claxton as a truck by-pass. Highway 169 stayed unpaved from 1938 until 1954. In 1959 they started another project that widened the right of way and paved the road in accordance with state standards.

The project to pave Highway 169 north from Bellville was started about 1949. Mr. Tom Wood was a county commissioner then, and he was instrumental in getting the road paved. The road was repaved in 1959 at the same time as the rest of Highway 169 south from Bellville.

Q: Can you tell me about the origin of Highway 292?

A: That road was built in the early 1950s. I was elected to the board of county commissioners in 1955, and it was built before then. The reason that Highway 292 was built was the chairman of the highway department, Mr. Jim Gillis, lived in Soperton, and he was trying to get a shortcut to Savannah. I know they were having some right of way problems. The highway goes all the way to Mt. Vernon. Tom Wood worked on the project some before he left the county commissioners in 1950, and Wright Daniel, his successor, was commissioner when the road was finished.

Q: When was Highway 280 paved?

A: Well, let's see. I remember when I started school at Bellville, it was a dirt road. That was in 1924 or 1925. Highway 280 was built in the early 1930s. The old road used to go south of its present course by your grandfather's and then up behind Mr. Jackie Brewton's. Mr. Jackie didn't want to move his house and didn't want to turn it around, so they gave him enough money to build a new front porch on the back of the house.

Q: You have been members of the Bellville Methodist Church for a long time?

A: I joined in the 1930s. Lucy joined in 1946 or 1947, shortly after we were married.

Q: What is your earliest recollection of Bellville?

A: I recall the old wooden store of Cap Hearn. I remember when I started school in 1925. I was six years old. The new brick school was in operation by then. It hadn't been open too long. The Schoolboard consolidated Bay Branch and Smithtown Schools into Bellville School. Mr. Leonard Brewton had donated the land for the Smithtown School. I remember going to the Sunday School there. Later they consolidated with Sapptown School, north of Bellville. The old Sapptown building is still standing over at Wilton Threatt's.

I graduated in 1936. We had eleven grades in Claxton then. However, when I started, students just went through ten grades at Bellville. My brother Cecil was a good basketball player on the Bellville team. Herschel Hearn, Bobby Benton, and some of the Smiths were great players too. When I came along they had cut Bellville back to the ninth grade. Students went to Claxton for the tenth and eleventh grades. This is what Bonnie, my sister, and I did.

Q: Do you have any stories relating to the Bellville School?

A: Theodore Brewton was at Bellville when I was there. Years later, Mrs. Grace would tell funny stories that happened at the school. It seems that Mr. Theodore always wanted all the teachers to go home with him and eat dinner the last day of school. She said that when they got in his car to make the trip you could look down at the floorboard anywhere in the vehicle and see the ground through the many holes in the car's floorboards.

Mr. Theodore was school superintendent for a number of years. After he was superintendent, he taught a while at Bellville. When he was a teacher, they didn't have screens in the windows. As you know, he was baldheaded. One day he was showing us a problem on the blackboard. He used an old thick yardstick as a pointer for the board. Well, a fly lit on his head. He got bothered by the fly and tried to shoe him away with the pointer. He cracked himself across the head, and it brought blood. We didn't know whether to laugh or cry [laughter].

Q: What did you do after high school?

A: I started farming then. However, I wanted to go to college. The teacher's college, which is now Georgia Southern University, was in Statesboro. This was, however, during the Depression and nobody had any money. My daddy gave me ten acres of corn the year I graduated from high school. I had to pay for the fertilizer, etc., so it was like sharecropping. I wound up with profits from half of ten acres of corn. Well, corn at that time would make about 20 bushels per acre, and it would bring $1 a bushel. Anyway, I ended up with $75. I took the money and went over to the teacher's college. You had to pay $5 down to register and get a room. This was in 1937, and it was $75 a quarter to go to school. I went to see the dean and tried to lay a good story on him about my being a farm boy with no money, but with a desire to go to college. I was on my own. He told me that all the jobs were already taken. He said he wasn't sure but if I'd come and get started, maybe a quarter or two down the road, he might be able to help me. I came back and talked it over with mama and daddy. They tried all kinds of ways to find some money to help me, but we just couldn't scrape it up. So, we decided it was too big a risk to spend what little money I had to start school and then not be able to finish. After I didn't go, people who went over there told me that if I had made good grades they would have eventually found me a job. However, it was a big risk at the time. That was the extent of me going to college. Maybe I missed a lot by not going. But I've enjoyed life, and I have taken a lot of college courses over the years.

I continued to farm up until the war. I worked with my father until 1941. This was the days of the CC camps. Nolan Evans, Paul Riggs and his brother, Joe, and others went off in the CC camp. There were some CC boys camped up here at Reidsville, and they built roads all through the Hearn property. These roads served as fire breaks.

Q: When did you get called into service?

A: Well, the draft came along. Everybody went to sign up, and you were drafted by your birth date. They had a fishbowl in Washington, D.C., and they drew numbers out at random for individual birthdays. I was born September 27, 1918. Everybody that was born on that day nation-wide had that certain number. Those numbers were sent out to the draft board. They had a sequence to tell when they were going to call you. I was still farming with my daddy and working at the gin. I wasn't married, and I knew I was probably going to be drafted in 1941. I told my folks there was no use for me to do much farming. So, I told my daddy I would just work with him until I got called. I thought this would be about July or August. Along in April or May the draft board sent us a letter indicating the first ten men that were going to go, and I was one of them. They asked if we wanted to go a little early and be assigned to an all-Georgia outfit. Nolan Evans, who was raised here in the county, was also on the list. We were talking about it, and I suggested we go right away. We stood a good chance of being stationed nearby at Ft. Stewart. That's when they had that country western song, "We'll Be Back in a Year, Little Darling." We thought we'd be back in a year or so, but our Uncle Sam had other plans [laughter]. We went to the draft board and told them that we wanted to go. Nobody else had signed up at that time. Cecil Daniel was also in the first group. When the orders came out they were to take the first ten. But when they figured the specific number, Evans County only had to furnish two--myself and Nolan. Cecil Daniel came and said he would give me $5 for my position. Now, that was a big sum--a week's work. Well, I said fate maybe wanted this to be the way it should be played, and I'd just go ahead.

We went to Atlanta for induction. They had mobilized the National Guard. The National Guard during peacetime only had about 50 or 60 people in each anti-aircraft battery. In wartime, the strength was about 165 or 170. So, they needed about 100 additional men for each battery. We ended up in Ft. Stewart in June of 1941. We went on Carolina Maneuvers, which included about 250,000 soldiers training all across North and South Carolina. We stayed up there 12 weeks. We hadn't been back to Ft. Stewart long, 30 days or so, when Pearl Harbor was bombed. Then we were notified to ship out. We were some of the first troops to depart for overseas. We left in February 1942 and went by train to Ft. Dix, N.J. My goodness, it was cold there in February. The ground was frozen. We like to froze to death with very little heat in the tents. We had the 0-3 rifle, of WW I vintage, to practice with. Then they came out with the automatic Girand rifle. They were all packed in cosmoline preservative. We had a mess trying to get it off the rifles. We loaded our equipment on the *Normandy*, a French luxury liner, in New York harbor. We loaded everything we had on the ship, and we waited while they finished overhauling it. They were converting it to a troop ship. The ship caught fire, and turned over in the harbor with our stuff on it. Well, we were assigned to go with or without equipment. We had one anti-aircraft gun, a 40mm, to the battery, and we were supposed to have had four.

We stayed at Ft. Dix about two more weeks and then they sent us to Boston. We sailed out of there the 18th of February on the *Queen Mary*. We stayed on that ship 40 days and nights. We sailed from Boston and came down the coast and went just around Key West, Florida. We didn't have any escorts. We'd see a ship or airplane every now and then. They claimed we ran into a pack of submarines down in the Caribbean. It must have been true because one night we were on guard duty, and we were headed south. The next morning we were headed north as fast as we could. We had to get back to Key West to the cover of our airplanes.

From Key West we went on to Rio de Janeiro, Brazil. We stayed on the ship there. The harbor had a narrow inlet and they could use the submarine nets to keep the enemy subs out. There were supposed to be some subs off the coast. Our ship slipped out one night and hadn't gone too far when we saw a fire on the horizon where they had torpedoed a merchant ship in front of us. The *Queen Mary* was faster than any of the Navy escort ships. Therefore, it would go out without escort and go on a zigzag course. We left Rio and went around Cape Town, South Africa. We crossed the Indian Ocean to Fremantle, Australia. This port is on the west coast of Australia. They wouldn't let us off there, but they refueled and took on supplies. Then we sailed all the way around to Sidney on the east coast of Australia, and we unloaded there in April. We went by train up to Brisbane, and then on about three or four miles to the airport. We set up and stayed there a month. Later we learned that this was known as the Brisbane Line. The Australians had already evacuated the northern part of Australia. There were not a lot of folks up there.

After about a month in Australia, we left there and got on an old Dutch steamer that was loaded with gasoline, bombs, and everything in the world you wouldn't want to be close to. The deck was covered with 55 gallon drums of aviation gasoline and 500 pound bombs. We sailed across the Coral Sea to New Guinea. We landed there on May 3, 1942, and the Coral Sea battle took place the next day or two. We whipped the Japanese Navy, and this proved to be the turning point of the war. We were sent up there as sacrifice troops as a delaying operation to try to save Australia. We stayed there in New Guinea almost three years. We went through three big battles. Our unit went in behind the paratroopers, and we were positioned around the air base.

Editor's note: Winton Bell sent the following letter from Australia to his folks at home in Bellville.

Somewhere in Australia
Tuesday, April 7, 1942

Dearest Mother, Dad and All,

I hope by now that you have received word that we arrived in Australia o.k. We landed here about ten days ago. The trip coming over was a little tiresome, although we saw a good many interesting things. But I can't tell you where we went as it is a military secret. But maybe they'll let us write anything we want to before long.

We haven't seen any action yet, and I don't think we will for some time. We are all feeling fine and the people here seem glad to see us come. It sure is a pretty country, but I wouldn't trade Georgia for any part I've seen of it yet.

I sure hope everyone at home is getting along fine. And I sure hope that you can make a good crop this year and get a good price for it. I still haven't received any mail from home. But I hope we get some in the next few days. Tell all of the rest of them that I'll try to write them just as soon as I can get more time. Tell them all "Hello" for me.

Our time here is 14 hours ahead of your time. For instance, when it is 12:00 noon there it's 2:00 the next morning here.

So answer real soon, and I'll try to write more next time. But there isn't much they'll let us tell. Nothing much except that we are getting along fine. But as long as they will let me write, I certainly will.

Give my love to all. Your loving son and brother,

Winton

Tell all the boys "Hello."

Guess what, it's autumn over here now. For the seasons are opposite those in the U.S.

P.S.: Well, we just received our first mail since we left the U.S.A. You don't know how good it made me feel. I got three letters from you. One mailed the 13th, 16th, and 21st. I also received the box of candy. Haven't opened it yet but know it's good. Thanks for everything and give all my love.

As ever,
Winton

Q: How long did you stay overseas?

A: I came back October of 1944, and I was glad to be home! You know, the mail was censored, and we couldn't write home and tell anybody the details of what was going on. You never did know who was reading it, and it's best that it was handled that way for security reasons.

Q: When you came back from overseas, what did you do?

A: When we came back we came from the West Coast by train on two Pullman coaches. They reassigned us and sent us to Miami. The government took over the hotels there. We took two weeks to go through physicals. I came back with about ten of the people out of my original outfit. Everybody was sent a different way. I was sent to an artillery outfit at Ft. Sill, Oklahoma in November of 1944. I stayed there until I was discharged in July of 1945. I then came back to Bellville as quickly as I could [laughter].

Q: Who were some of the other Evans County boys in the war?

A: As I mentioned, Nolan Evans, was in my same unit. We went together and stayed together until we left New Guinea. Some in the unit went on to the Philippines and seems like some of them might have gone on to Okinawa. There was another one, Palmer Iler, from Daisy, that got killed. He was originally in a medical detachment. He and I both took a flying school test. He was going for an aircraft ride while they were perfecting skip bombing in Port Moresby harbor. They had the ten second delayed fuse on the bomb, and this gave the plane ten seconds to leave the target. There was an old ship in the harbor that had been grounded before the war, and they used it for practice. They were low-level bombing, and his plane never did come back up. I wrote him a letter, and he didn't answer. The letter was finally returned and had "deceased" marked on it. I wrote a letter to the lieutenant in charge of his unit and asked him what happened. The lieutenant wrote me back and told me the details. When I came back from overseas, I went to see the family and told them the story.

Nolan Evan's brother, Thurmon Evans, served in the European Theater. I often heard him ask, "What do the French drink?" He always answered "Coonyac" [laughter]. There were two Cooper boys from Bellville, Charles and Herschel Cooper in Europe. They lived down below us here on the Tippins farm.

Another one serving was Lawton Howard Rogers, who lives on the north side of Bellville. I had two brothers in the conflict. Dan served in the European Campaign, and Wallace was in North Africa. Wallace went first as Rommel was running across the sand over there out of control. When the war calmed down in North Africa, they sent him to Europe. My brothers went to see each other while they were there. They were in some of the roughest fighting in Europe. The brother next to me in age, Dan, was sent to Okinawa. When the war died down, he was sent home. He didn't have to go on to the occupation of Japan.

Look on the counter at Bellville Church for a list of local boys in World War II service. Their names are on a plaque in the first drawer or in that area.

Q: Could you describe your thoughts about World War II?

A: You know we've seen a lot of changes in the world. I didn't give my life, but there are those who did. I did a little bit of everything from manning my anti-aircraft gun to washing dishes and digging graves. You have those things that you did because everybody had to do their share. There were a lot of people dying. I gave what little time I did in service to make our country a good place to live. Today, you see people go out and burn the flag. To me, these people don't have values and don't know what sacrifice means.

Q: Have you been farming since you came back after the war?

A: Yes, I've been farming ever since. I got back from overseas in 1944, and Lucy and I married in '46. Lucy is from around Collins. We started dating when I came home on leave in 1945. Prior to that, we were both dating other folks. You might say our finding each other is proof things always work out for the best.

Q: What crops were you growing in the late '40s when you got back?

A: We were still growing cotton, tobacco, and peanuts. Peanuts were the main money crop. There wasn't much allotment before war, and during the war your could plant whatever you wanted. Then after the war they didn't need cotton seeds for oil as much, and they established allotments. All farms in the county that had been growing these crops got allotments.

Q: Can you tell me about growing watermelons?

A: My daddy grew them every year. They loaded them at Bellville. He'd haul them up there with a two-horse wagon.

This was along in '28 or '29. I don't think there was much going on with the watermelon business in the 1930s. They had a differential in the freight rate. Of course, the northern people owned the railroad. They could take a carload of freight shipped to Bellville and there was one charge, say $100. You turn around and load the car with cotton or watermelons and the freight going back north was about three or four times what it cost to come down here. That's the reason the South was still fighting the Civil War 100 years after the event. The fellow that finally got that situation straightened out was Carl Sanders. He wasn't able to when he was governor, but his law firm finally got a fair freight rate.

Q: Do you remember a group called the Piney Woods Rooters?

A: Yes. Hearn Lumpkin played and was the manager of the group. The Cooper boys, Charles and Herschel, were in the group. Their Uncle, Samps Cooper, played the fiddle for them. Gordon Baggs played the steel guitar. H.M. Tippins played lead guitar and the mouth organ. He wore a bow tie and could jiggle his Adam's apple to make it look like the tie was fluttering like a butterfly. It was a sight [laughter]. There were four or five members at different times. They played on the radio and around for school dances. Ashton Lanier played at times. He was a piano player. I also played a time or two with them. I never did play with them on the radio, but I played the guitar with the group at square dances around here. My brother, Dan, played a guitar and mouth organ. We all just had a good time. Sometimes you'd go play for a square dance, and take in the big sum of a dollar a night [laughter].

Q: What were some of the songs you all played?

A: Well, they were some "doozies." Songs like "Alabama Jubilee," "Turkey in the Straw," "Wreck of the Old '97," "Boil Them Cabbage Down," "Down Yonder," "Just Because," "Here Rattler, Here," "Orange Blossom Special," "Danced by the Light of the Moon," "Oh, Susannah," and "Danced All Night with the Bottle in Your Hand" [laughter].

Q: What kind of dancing did they do?

A: Mostly square dancing. Although anyway you could hold on to your partner would pass [laughter].

Q: You started as a County Commissioner in 1955?

A: Yes, 1955 to 1970, 16 years. Then I was fortunate enough to be re-elected from 1987 to 1991, and I started my current term in 1995.

After I came back out of service, I served on the draft board for 20 years as chairman. You know, they wanted veterans to serve on the board. I never had but one problem, and there was no cause for that other than some folks thought they were entitled to some favors. To be fair, however, there weren't any favors as far as I was concerned.

Q: In your earlier days on the County Commissioners, were there any accomplishments you were particularly proud of?

A: When I went on board in 1955, there were not many paved roads in Evans County. About the only roads paved in Evans County, was this one [Highway 169], which was just paved, and Highways 280, 292, 129, and 301. During the first 16 years I was on the board, and I didn't do it by myself, we paved over 100 miles of road and replaced 41 wooden bridges with concrete or either big pipe. We did away with a maintenance headache as far as the wooden bridges were concerned.

Also, the courthouse was in a bad state of repairs. The termites had eaten the framing, door facing, baseboards, and even some of the vital records. Nearly all *The Claxton Enterprise* newspapers were destroyed. We repaired the damage, cleaned out the building, and rebuilt it at the tune of $20,000. The County Commissioners asked if I would see the project through because I kept harping that something needed to been done [laughter]. We took help off the farm and went down to help refurbish the building. We used our trucks and hauled off debris with no charge to the county. Nobody would take on the repair contract, except by the hour because they were concerned what they would run into. We finally found somebody to do the carpentry, plumbing, and painting. I told them that I wasn't going to bother them while they were doing the work. However, they were to see that the project was done right. If it wasn't done right, I told them I was going to raise sand with them. They did good job and came in a few hundred dollars under budget!

I've enjoyed serving my community. Folks have been real kind to me and my family, and I hope I've helped someone along the way. This county and its people are very important to me.

Q: How do you feel about the Bellville area?

A: People always say that it's the cleanest little town they've ever seen. It speaks real well of the community. I know Hines [Daniel], Walter Emmett, and them used to clean up the town every Friday when they ran the sawmill. They had those mill hands to work the town from one end to the other. They cut the grass and even washed people's cars.

After I got on the Board of Commissioners, I had some of the roads paved in Bellville. There were not any curbs, gutters, or sidewalks. Mr. Tom Wood was a County Commissioner four years before I got on the board. He got the highway people to run some sidewalks and curbs by his house. Mr. Cap Hearn told us he saw the road foreman and asked him, "Are you going to put the sidewalk on the other side also." The foreman said, "No, when we do this we'll be gone." Well, Mr. Cap got hold of some folks and the next thing we knew, sidewalks were on the other side too [laughter]. After I got in office we got the road rebuilt to Federal specifications with curbs, gutters, and underground drains. This work helped set the little town off, and it's real pretty. You've been here at Christmas time, and you've seen the sacks "on fire" along the streets [laughter]. The folks go all out to make the place attractive.

We've been blessed in many ways. I am very proud of Lucy and our sons, Erney, Danny, and Gary, and their families. She's a wonderful lady, and she still hasn't run me off yet [laughter]. We will celebrate our 50th wedding anniversary in May, and it's definitely been great to be married to such a fine lady. I wouldn't trade her for anyone. It's been a good life.

Well, I still say Bellville is the best place in the world. It's the best community in the county, and I'm mighty proud to call it home.

Interview with Jimmie Styles
Bellville, Georgia - November 11, 1994

Question [Q]: Jimmie, can you tell me a little about yourself?

A: I was born and grew up in Bellville. I went to school here. I moved to Texas, and I've been there for 29 years. We started Tarrant County Jr. College in Ft. Worth in 1965. When we began we had no students, and when I retired last year we had about 30,000 credit students and close to 50,000 noncredit students on five campuses.

I was born in a house on our property here in Bellville before the current house was built. My mother, Hellon Benton Styles, was born in 1910 in a previous house on the same site where the house now stands. The house she was born in was probably one of the original houses of Bellville. It was torn down, and the lumber was used to build a barn that later burned. Unfortunately, a lot of our historical material was destroyed in that fire.

James Street is the eastern boundary of our property. Our house is located just north of the present-day Anderson House. In the early days I understand some of the houses faced James Street.

My father, Roy Thelmer Styles, had a real love of Georgia history. Over at Georgia Southern, he won the James Allen Bunce Award for writings on the seven wonders of Georgia. We still have the cup he was awarded and the original essay.

Q: Do you know if he did any writing about Bellville?

A: No, the only writing about Bellville he did that I know about is concerning the Boy Scout troop. The reason I brought the subject of troop #57 up today, at the Bellville School reunion, is that many of the people attending today are the fathers and mothers or other relatives of the original members of the troop. I thought they would find information about the troop interesting. I was too young to be a member of the troop during the war, but I joined it later. Winton Bell was the scoutmaster after Dad gave it up. In the early 1940s, the troop won a presidential citation. Back in those days, a citation of this importance was quite an accomplishment for a small town troop. I have a troop picture. On the left back row is Roy Styles, Scout Master. Members from left to right are Charles Johnson, Charles Hearn, B.G. Tippins, "C" Hearn, Bobby Styles, and front row center is Jimmy Collins. Please note this photo was taken in the southeast corner of the Bellville School yard, with the Old Bellville Methodist Church in the background.

Q: What brought your family here?

A: Dad was a Bellville schoolteacher from 1924 through 1926. Mother was one of his students. Mother and Dad were married in 1925. He was the principal in Bellville for seven years, from 1939 through 1945. Dad and Mother loved the people in Bellville, Claxton, and Evans County. He was the pastor of Rehobeth, Hagan, Antioch, and Bull Creek Baptist churches during the 1940s and 1950s. I met Jimmie Strickland, my wife, on the steps of Antioch Baptist Church the second Sunday of September in 1946.

Interviews 145

Q: Can you tell me about some of the sites in Bellville?

A: There used to be a turpentine still close to where the old Bellville School was located [south of Highway 292, north of Highway 280, and west of Main Street]. There was a cotton gin in that area also. This was north of the Bellville Church and School and south of the railroad.

The remnants of the gin and turpentine still were very visible in 1940. The turpentine still was west of the old gin. The site of the gin has tin and other metal debris there to this day.

In back of Luther Waters' house, there is a tin building still standing that was the first school bus barn and later was an Industrial Arts building for the school. This was in the late 1930s and early 1940s.

I have pictures of Bellville's ninth grade class. In it are Leon Griffin, Mac Lynn, who lives right up the street, Tim Aikens, who lived out by C.B. Smith, Ina Warren, Ora Lee Barrow, Jimmie Styles, Barbara Holland, and Patsy Smith. There weren't but eight of us. The photo was taken the day we finished school at Bellville. We were then going to attend school in the big city of Claxton [laughter]. I also have some photos of Mother about 1912 with Martha and Mae Hearn, who lived next door. I believe there is even a photo of your Johnson aunts and uncles.

The Bellville Methodist Church was in front of the southeast part of the schoolyard. The church faced north, and the school faced east toward Main Street. The school and church were about half way between the Parker place on Highway 280 and Main Street. The school had two clay basketball courts, a clay tennis court, and two large ten-hole outdoor toilets.

Q: Can you tell me more about the gin and still?

A: All the children of Bellville played in the old gin. We also used the dross from the still to start fires in the fireplace. The dross was just like gasoline in terms of flammability. There was an old well next to the turpentine still from which to draw water to run off a charge of turpentine and rosin. Remnants of the old well remain.

The Hearns moved their gin to the spot about where the bank is now. The gin burned, and they built another, more modern one. The turpentine still was moved east of Main Street, next to Buddy Benton's house. That must have been in the 1950s, because I was in the Navy then.

Q: What were some of the other points of interest?

A: There was Tom Wood's store, and Mr. Bascom Tippins had a store. Tom's store was just south of the railroad and right by the branch. The water from the branch would occasionally get almost up to it. Cap Hearn also had a store and ran the post office. There was a commissary of sorts for the hands that worked on some of the farms. The commissary was before my time. Bellville Town Hall is sitting about where the commissary was located.

Tom Wood moved his store to where Adam Bird had previously had his store. Mr. Bascom Tippins also had a store on that corner [northeast corner of Highway 292 and Main St. intersection].

Ennis Branch, which runs through Bellville, was the center of entertainment for all the boys and girls who grew up in this town [laughter]. We'd occasionally run up on a snake, which always created a lot of excitement. On Main Street, there used to be a concrete bridge on the branch where a big sewer pipe went through. We used to play a lot around the pipe. Bobby Styles, Johnny Clark, and other Bellville boys caught a three foot gator in the pipe. That was an exciting day!

The road grade of Main Street was built up when it was paved. You used to go up a slight incline to go up over the railroad tracks. Of course, the roads were dirt back then. During the dry summer months I would roller skate on the clay road in front of our house. I bought the skates from Charles Nelson for about 50 cents.

Mr. Wesley Parker had a huge cabinet shop back of Tom Wood's store. This must have been in the early 1940s.

Q: Are there any stories you would like to relate about Bellville?

A: There is a very interesting thing about the little road crossing the railroad tracks just on the west side of the depot. In 1937 or 1938, Bellville was plagued with robberies. So they decided to put an alarm on Tom Wood's store. It was understood that the men of Bellville would all respond if the alarm went off. It went off one night, and they saw the burglars coming out the store. The culprits jumped in their car and sped away. They went west on the dirt road that was just north of the depot. This was before Highway 292 was built. Several of the men ran down the track in a direct route to where the dirt road crossed the railroad track. Just as the car came around the little bend there they shot the car up. The robbers were not hurt, but their car was shot to pieces. There must have been a hundred or more bullet holes in the car. The vehicle was left there on the side of the road for years as a message "Don't fool with Bellville" [laughter]. As a kid I'd see the old car, near the Flowers' house, with all those shotgun pellet holes, and the impact was tremendous. It really would impress anyone. It sure got your attention.

Q: Tell me more about the depot and the trains.

A: If you look across the railroad tracks from the depot you can still see the old depot outhouse [laughter]. The depot itself still looks to be in pretty good shape.

Of course, another source of entertainment for kids was walking the railroad tracks. We'd make scissors out of straight pins or flatten two pennies together on the tracks. Once you put the pennies on the railroad track, the train would smash them together when it rolled over them. You could make all kinds of interesting things with this little technique. A young boy would only be limited by his imagination when it came to the fascination of the railroad.

On a hot summer Sunday afternoon the boys of Bellville were looking for something to do. There were always railcars on the siding. The boys began to push on one of the cars. It moved! One of the boys climbed on top of the car and applied the brakes. The car stopped! For a while the boys of Bellville pushed the car from one end of the siding to the other. Then it happened. The car derailed. To this day, some of the boys of Bellville have difficulty remembering all that happened on that summer afternoon [laughter].

Q: What do you remember most about the town?

A: Bellville has an interesting history. People from Bellville have made a mark on the world. If we could go back and learn the accomplishments of all those who went to school and lived here, it would be impressive. Coming from a small town country school, the achievements of the graduates are remarkable. It really is impressive. Take Jack Hearn for example. He is one of the leading biologists in the South. He developed any number of innovative things to help control unwanted plant growth in ponds, etc. His dad used to come down all the time, and we'd talk for hours about Bellville and some of the people who grew up here or went to school here.

The town has stayed pretty much the same over the years. When the land boom came for Bellville it seemed just to move right up Highway 280, then spread. Bellville has some beautiful homes, both old and new. It has always been a nice town to live in.

Q: Jimmy, I sure do appreciate your time in giving me this interview.

A: Pharris, believe me I've enjoyed it. Bellville will always be an important part of my life. I always enjoy coming back.

Interview with Darin McCoy
Bellville, Georgia - May 8, 1995

Question [Q]: Darin, I'd like to talk to you about your experience of growing up in Bellville. I first want to ask you the names of your parents and grandparents.

A: My father is Bobby McCoy. He was born and raised in Bulloch County near the Bryan County line. My mother is Janara Blalock. She was born in Bulloch County and lived there a few years in her early life. My grandfather decided he wanted to return to Evans County. They moved back here in 1954. My grandfather is Alvin Blalock and my grandmother is Melrose Anderson. She was born and raised just across the Bulloch County line, near Ephesus Church on Highway 301. They have lived here in Bellville since 1954. My grandfather bought the house he lives in now from Tom Flanigan. Tom, Grace Hearn's brother, lived there in the house behind the cotton gin and operated a garage downtown. He moved to Claxton and opened a shop there that his son and son-in-law now operate. My grandfather bought Tom's house and took over the business. My grandfather remained there until 1981 when he retired. My father then took over the business.

Q: Where did you go to school?

A: I went to school here in Bellville at Pinewood. Pinewood opened in 1970, I believe. I was four years old then and went to kindergarten in Claxton. Pinewood did not have a kindergarten at that time. I started at Pinewood in first grade and went all the way through high school there. I graduated in 1984. I was in the second class that went all the way through Pinewood.

Q: As a youngster, what are your recollections of Bellville?

A: I guess you could say I didn't know what the real world was because Bellville was so different. Everybody is family here. They look out for each other, and if you felt you needed anything, the community would help you. The world is not like that any more. Bellville is unique. We are all one big, happy family. When somebody is in need, we all come together and help that person.

Q: Do you remember the Hearn store at all?

A: Yes, I do remember it vaguely. I was very young when they moved it. I do remember very well when Bernie Anderson's store was located across the street from where he is now. He was where Tom Wood once had a grocery store. As a young child, I remember that most. Mrs. Grace Hearn was operating the post office from as far back as I remember. She retired from that position, and Ona Coleman took over as postmaster. She remained there for several years, and then Mildred Rogers took over. She is our present postmaster. She is the wife of Lawton Rogers.

Q: Darin, who are some of the people that influenced your life?

A: The person that has influenced me the most is my grandfather, Alvin Blalock. My mother was an only child, so my grandfather had no sons. When I came along instead of a grandfather-grandson relationship, it became more like a father-son situation. I've always thought that my grandfather had no enemies and that everybody liked him. I felt that I wanted to be liked and respected like my grandfather. You could say he has been my role model.

My grandfather was one of the original councilmen when Bellville was chartered as a city. I believe that was in 1959. He still remains a city councilman, and has never had opposition to that office. I always felt I couldn't wait until I could become a city councilman. However, I had to be 21 to do that. As soon as I turned 21, luckily there was a seat being vacated. I qualified for it, and ran for that office unopposed. I served two, two-year terms. I was told that we were one of the very few grandfather-grandson councilmen in the state. After my second term I did not seek re-election because I was planning to run for probate judge. Luckily, I qualified for that office, and I was elected.

Running for probate judge was quite an experience. There were about eight of us running. I ended up having to run in the primary, run-off, and general election. Fortunately I was elected, and I am currently the youngest probate judge in the state.

I was interested in making a change. I was employed with my father running his auto parts and hardware store. I had decided to make a career change. However, I was not sure what I wanted to do. It was as if this light came on and said running for probate judge was what I was supposed to do. I was encouraged by a lot of people in the county. They felt a young person needed to be in that position. Someone was needed who could learn the job and be there a while. I sat down and talked to a few people and made my decision when my grandfather told me that he thought that's what I needed to do. He said he'd do everything he could do to help me. I'm really proud to be in the office and hope the people of Evans County are glad to have me there. My grandfather helped me campaign. I don't think there was a corner of Evans County or a family that he didn't know. He was a great campaign manager. We made it and will hopefully stay in there for a while.

Q: How was going to school at Pinewood?

A: Well, I was raised in a Christian home. I think Pinewood was a very good influence on me. Religion is taught there as well as academics. They mix the right amount of religion in with the other courses. It was a good experience. Tab Smith was the founding headmaster at Pinewood. He remained there until my sophomore year. I think he is a great religious leader, and he has been a positive influence on the lives of many young people.

Q: What church do you attend?

A: I attend Bellville Methodist. At a young age my family transferred to Bellville, and we've been there ever since. The church has quite a history itself. A lot of the older people that I have looked up to here in Bellville are a vital part of that church. Many of our older citizens go there. They and their families are a big part of the fabric of Bellville. Mr. Walter Emmett Daniel and his family have attended that church every since it was built. His mother gave the land the church was built on. Among others, the Daniel and Hearn families have been a big part of that church.

Q: I understand your grandfather was at the famous 1974 Bellville bank robbery?

A: Yes, how could we forget that? The bank was built on the site of the old cotton gin. I remember the operation of the gin, although I couldn't have been but three or four years old. I can remember the loud, grinding sound from the cotton gin. Soon after it stopped operating, the Hearn's sold the land to the Claxton Bank and they built their branch there. I remember the grand opening of the bank. They got me to draw for the door prizes. Of course, I became close to the three ladies at the bank. June DeLoach was named manager when the bank was built and remains so today. I felt real close to the girls who worked there. One day at school during lunch I heard my teacher talking to another teacher about the bank robbery. I must tell you that I had a crush on one of the young ladies at the bank [laughter]. As a young boy, you always would look at these 18 or 19 year old girls and get these crushes. Knowing how fond of these ladies I was, it just tore me up that the bank had been robbed. I was so worried about those girls, that I couldn't wait to get home that day. Luckily, they were fine.

My grandmother witnessed the robbery. Their house is directly behind the bank, and she was on the back porch sweeping that morning. She could see through the drive-in window at the bank. She saw a guy with a mask on pointing a gun at the tellers. They had their hands in the air. That was during the early 1970s. In those days it was popular to have party line telephones. My mother and father were on a party line with my grandparents. My grandmother and my mother loved to talk on the telephone. Whenever you'd pick up the phone, one of the two of them was always on the line. Well, that morning my mother was on the phone, and Granny picked up and told Mother, "We need to call the police, the bank is being robbed." My mother just couldn't believe what she was hearing. She couldn't believe Bellville, Georgia was actually having a bank robbery. We have almost no crime and nobody ever bothers anyone. It was just hard to believe anybody was robbing the bank. Mother got off the first call, and she called down to the shop where my father and grandfather were working. She told them what Grandmother had said. Then Mother hung up and called the police. The police were aware of what was going on. One of the tellers had set off the silent alarm.

My grandfather also could not believe a bank robbery was taking place. I've heard him tell the story many times. It was misting rain at the time. He had taken a break from whatever job he was doing, and he was drinking a Coke. When he got the call from my mother about the robbery, he started walking to the bank with the Coke in his hand. When he got over there he found a white car still running and pulled up next to the bank. The windshield wipers were still going. He walked around the car and saw there was no tag. He said he almost reached in and switched the car off and took the keys out. He said something told him not to do that. So he continued to walk toward the bank's front door. As he opened the door and started in the two men were coming out. One of them pointed the gun at him and told him to go on into the bank and lie on the floor. He said he didn't argue with the instructions [laughter]. He went on in the bank, and he didn't see anybody. He called out and as he called out the girls got up from the floor. He made sure they were all right. He said it wasn't but a minute or two before the sheriff and other law enforcement officials arrived.

They caught the robbers not too long after the incident. I heard they had planned to rob the bank in Cobbtown that morning. However, something happened and messed up their plans, and they robbed the Bellville Bank instead.

Q: What happened to the girl at the bank you had the crush on?

A: Well, it wasn't long after that before I found out she had a boyfriend, and she was going to get married. Of course, I didn't like it too well [laughter].

Thinking of this girl reminds me of another story. The bank would close at 3 p.m., and I didn't get home from school until 5. So when I got home from school the bank was closed. Therefore, I only got to see the girls on Friday afternoons. We worked out a little way we could communicate. I would write her a note and put it in the night deposit. She would respond and leave the message outside under the mat at the bank. When I got home everyday I would take off for the bank to get my note [laughter].

Q: Any other Bellville incidents you recall?

A: Well, unfortunately we've had a number of automobile accidents at our two intersections. We also had a serious train derailment on the west side of town. The accident involved 12 to 15 cars. This was in the mid-1970s. I don't remember too many details about it. It was in front of where Harry Hollingsworth lives.

Q: Do you remember any other special problems the town has faced?

A: I remember that not too long after the town was incorporated, we got word the U.S. Postal Service was going to discontinue our post office here. We got very upset. Every since I can remember our mail was up by 8 a.m. and still today it's the same. Hines Daniel and "C" Hearn, Miss Grace's son, played an important part in talking to the right people to keep Bellville's post office open. This is just another example of Bellville sticking together for the common good of the residents.

Q: Can you give us more of your thoughts on Bellville as a place to live?

A: If you are talking to someone that is not from here, and you mention you are from Bellville, if they know anything about the town, the first thing they always say is that it is one of the cleanest towns they've ever been through.

We have progressed as time has passed. But yet I think the core of what Bellville is all about has never changed. Everybody loves their neighbors here. There is always someone to provide a helping hand in times of need. Bellville comes together and helps their fellow man. The residents take pride in their homes and their property. We care about each other. That has never changed, and I don't think it ever will.

I think Bellville excels because of the nature of the people. I've been here almost 30 years. As I said earlier, I was born and raised here. I don't know what opportunity could come knocking at my door that could get me to leave. I am real happy with my job. I enjoy seeing other parts of this country. I was out of the state this past week and enjoyed some of the history in the New England states. But at the end of the week, I was ready to come home. There is just such a positive influence in this town. There are so many people who mean so much to me. For example, Mr. Walter Emmett Daniel and his wife, Nita, are two of the most wonderful people we have here. His brother, Hines, was the original mayor. He remained mayor here as long as his health permitted him to serve. I think he was one of the reasons Bellville is the way that it is. He took pride in this town and did everything he could do to keep things up. I think Mr. Hines helped make it the fine place it is today.

Miss Grace Hearn also played an important part in Bellville's history. Her husband, Mr. Cap, and she were in an accident in the mid-70s. They were real concerned about Mrs. Grace as to whether she would survive. They originally thought Mr. Cap was going to make it fine. Well, as it turned out Miss Grace fully recovered and Mr. Cap died. The memories I have of him are in the hardware store where my father now has his business. After he sold the old store building and post office where Bernie's is now, he built a small brick building across the street and operated a hardware store with his son, Charles. I have a few memories of Mr. Cap. He and his family had a strong influence on Bellville. I grew up knowing Miss Grace. I have the highest respect for her and think she is one of the grandest ladies Bellville has ever seen. She's in her 90s now, but still hasn't lost her sense of humor. She was a member of Bellville Methodist Church and also the choir director for years and years. I've heard her tell many fascinating and humorous stories about being a schoolteacher in Bellville.

I have a lot of respect for my next door neighbor, Emily Wood. She came here to teach and met her husband, Roger. She's remained here ever since. The Wood family has been influential here also. Mr. Tom Wood died in the early 1970s. I have a few memories of him. He was quite a businessman. I had a good relationship with his wife, Ella Lee. I have a long friendship with their daughter Elizabeth.

Q: Any closing comments?

A: I am proud to say I am from Bellville. I do anticipate Bellville progressing as time goes on. I hope Bellville never loses what it was founded on. The closeness and pride that the residents have is unique. It seems to be something that is passed on from generation to generation.

Interview with David Groover
Bellville, Georgia - July 8, 1995

Question [Q]: Could you tell me about some of the old-time farm products shipped from Bellville?

A: Mr. Hearn used to tell me about how they grew watermelons. They were self-sufficient and would save the seeds. They would take a select looking melon and have some of the farm hands tear the meat up and get the seeds. They would get a barrel and put some water in it and put the seeds in the water. The faulty seed would float, and the good seed would sink. They would skim off the faulty seed and pulp, and keep repeating the process. Then they would pour the water off and strain the seeds from the bottom. They scattered the seeds out on newspapers on boards or a table and left them out in the sun a few days until they dried. Then they'd put them in some sort of metal container so the rats wouldn't get them and save them for planting the following year. So you see, they grew their own watermelon seeds.

I've heard a lot of the old-timers talking about the watermelon crop's demise. The produce broker would be on the other end and you never saw him. You would send him a carload of watermelons, and he would write back for $50 freight. The melons didn't bring enough to pay the freight, and being skeptical and from South Georgia with no money, the farmers didn't send the money because they felt like they were being taken advantage of. The broker had sold your melons and was looking for some extra money to boot.

They used to grow a round watermelon around here called a "Stone Mountain." They didn't grow them for the market because a round melon is hard to pack. You need a long melon for ease in packing, and they would use straw to pack them in the carbox. They don't have to be as careful now loading them on these 18-wheeler trucks because they are handled more carefully than back in the days of railroad. The railroad would "hump" the cars and they took a lot of jolting.

Q: Did you ever hear any Bellville stories relating to mules or other animals?

A: Well, this is a *true* story [laughter]. This occurred sometime in the 1920s or 30s. Mr. Inman [Hearn] said they had a mule with a good memory. This is the background. Mr. Inman's father, C.W. Hearn, had a pretty good turnover of inventory at the store, and the new merchandise came in on the train. You see, then the train ran four times a day. The merchandise would come in a big box two or three feet square that they called a dry goods box. Mr. Inman's family lived in the house across from where the Bellville Methodist Church is today. They would use one of the mules to haul the dry goods boxes from the train depot to the store. The box would be nailed up tight. The mules would be out there grazing under the cedar trees where the Bellville Church is now. After eating breakfast, one of the boys would go over there, gear up the mule, hook him to the wagon and go to the Bellville depot. When the train came by it would drop off a bunch of merchandise, and they'd use the wagon to haul it across the street to the store. Then they just unhooked the mule and took him over by the shade tree and left him tied after the delivery. Maybe at dinner time they'd go out and give him some water, feed him, and hook him back to the wagon. That afternoon there would be another two trains, one up and one back, that they'd have to off-load again. I would imagine most of the goods came out of Savannah. Mr. Inman said this mule would remember wherever you worked the mule the day before. If you were at a different location the next day, and if you didn't hitch the mule and he could get loose, he'd go back to that area where he had worked the day before. If you didn't tie him, you'd look around and he'd be gone. You might as well get in the road and walk to wherever the mule had been the day before, because that's where you'd find him.

I've heard a lot of the old-timers say that around dinner time they would be plowing and wonder what time it was. Since they didn't have the money for a watch, they never had that luxury. But, they would always have a farm bell back at the house, usually right outside the kitchen door. Of course, the wife did have a clock at the house. She would try to have dinner ready at 12 o'clock sharp. At noon, she'd step out there and give that dinner bell a few yanks. They said that when the old mule heard the bell, he would throw his head back, bray several times, and head for the house. You couldn't pull him on a new crop row. He knew it was time to go get some water and something to eat [laughter]. They said after you got halfway down the road to home, the mule would start picking up speed and walk faster. It didn't matter how tired he was. Of course, those boys were tired too. They would be working several hundred yards from the house, so there wasn't any need to drag the plow to the house. They'd cut the plow loose from the mule, and tie the lines up. The trace chain had a metal loop, and they would hang that up on the hame. Some of them would walk beside the mules, but most of the boys would jump up on him and ride. Now you could bet the mule was sweaty, but if you'd been walking since daylight you'd be sweaty too [laughter].

Q: Can you tell me your memories about the Hearn store?

A: We moved to Bellville one week before Christmas in 1961. At that time I can remember that over in one corner or the store, they had what was called a kerosene tank. It was rectangular in shape. It was encased in wood and all you could see was the flank and the spout. There were a few people who didn't have electricity and they would come up to the store and get a gallon of kerosene to use in lanterns and lamps. There was usually no top on the spout of the kerosene cans. "Cap" [Caughey's nickname] would pump a gallon of kerosene in the can and then put an Irish potato on the spout of the can. On one side they sold shoes, socks, and yard goods. On the other was the groceries and canned goods. In the back was the hardware. They carried such varied things as nuts, screws, bolts, fence wire, horse collars, and posthole diggers.

People would bring syrup and chickens and trade for groceries. The Hearns had a chicken coop there at the store. They would take a chicken in on trade. Somebody else would come by and buy it. Mr. Hearn told me in the 1920s and 30s they would take in syrup on a trade, and then they'd put it in a wooden barrel. When the barrel got full they would ship it out to a buyer.

Q: What kind of farm equipment did the Hearns carry?

A: International. They were International dealers for years. Now Inman's father, C.W. Hearn, wasn't a dealer. It was Mr. Inman and Uncle Caughey that took a dealership on about the late 1920s or early 30s. A lot of people were still farming with mule implements then. Some of them were still pretty skittish about a tractor. To save freight they would order this equipment in a car box. Everything would come knocked down, and you'd have to put it together. Riding cultivators, hay rakes, mowing machines, walking plows, etc., would require assembly. You'd get an instruction book in the box on how to put the piece of equipment together. So, on winter days when it was cold and rainy they would get over on the depot landing and put this stuff together.

The small warehouse [across from the Bellville Branch of the Claxton Bank] that belongs to Aunt Grace is where they would put the smaller tractors until they were sold. They would haul the tractor on a ton-and-a-half truck from the depot to the warehouse. Now, those old tractors with the metal wheels had to be cranked by hand. There was no battery, but there was a magneto. You didn't need a battery because they didn't have a starter, and there were no lights on it. In addition to tractors, they also sold International trucks.

I think Mr. Inman got to go to the International factory a couple of times. They would show him how the stuff was made. The International people encouraged the dealers to stock and sell genuine parts. Mr. Hearn believed in that. If the tractor had an original Champion spark plug, you could bet he'd put a Champion back in there when that spark plug burned out. Another plug might have worked just as well, but he'd want to go back to the original equipment. Of course, it helped the International company too because they could sell more of their parts.

Q: Will you tell me how the Hearns got into the tomato business?

A: This would have been in the late 1920s and early 30s when they planted tomatoes for shipment. A lot of people planted tomatoes. They would pick them green and let them ripen on the way to market. However, they didn't start with the tomato plant business until about 1935, and were the only ones in Bellville who grew them. They grew the tomato plants, pulled them, and shipped them north. Later on, W.D. Sands, Ernest Strickland, and Kelly Durrence started growing the plants. The Hearns were the first ones other than the Sims who grew them in Evans County.

The reason Mr. Inman said they got started with the plant business was that items such as corn, hogs, and cattle were so cheap that they were not making any money. When you were just general farming in those days, you weren't making enough profit to hardly survive. They were looking for a cash crop--and tomato plants proved to be a good choice. Sometimes the railroad would promote these diversification efforts to increase revenues from shipments on the railroad.

This was how the story went. The Sims brothers from down around Lanier in Bryan County owned some farmland between Claxton and Daisy. That is where they grew their tomato plants. They would ship the plants north for transplanting. They also had a plant barn, which has now been torn down. They used a fertilizer drill when they were planting and when they were going to side dress these tomato plants. However, the Sims didn't clean up the grain drill thoroughly, so every year in January they would call the Hearns up and say they needed another grain drill and to bring them one. So, Mr. Inman and one of the hired hands would get a new grain drill ready, load it on a ton-and-a-half truck, and take it to the Sims' plant farm. They would be in the process of planting the tomato plants there. Mr. Inman said he didn't tell anybody, but he would watch and closely observe what was taking place. He didn't try to get all his knowledge in one year either. He would maybe look one year to see how deep to plant the seeds, and another time he would find out how many seeds to put to 12 inches of row space, etc. Nobody else in this area was planting them except the Sims. Mr. Inman said it took him about three or four years to get the information he thought necessary to grow these plants. Then he went and talked to his brother Caughey about the deal. Inman and Caughey owned the farm, the general store, and the cotton gin fifty-fifty. The name of the business was H.C. Hearn and Company, and Mr. Inman used to always joke that he was the "and company" part of the operation [laughter]. He had to convince his brother Cap that they needed to try this tomato plant experiment. Cap asked Mr. Inman what he knew about growing the plants. Mr. Inman said, "Well, I been watching this deal for three or four years, and I think I have obtained enough knowledge that we can do it successfully." So, the Bellville tomato plant business was born.

Q: How did "Cap" Hearn get his nickname?

A: I asked him one time. He didn't remember where the nickname came from. He said he reckoned at some point as a kid he may have been wearing a cap and the name stuck.

Q: Can you describe some of the details of the tomato plant operation?

A: The workers would "pull" 50 tomato plants and put them in a bundle. These bundles would be held together with a rubber band. They paid the workers so much per bundle to pull the plants. They would have someone called a field walker to kind of keep things policed up, keep order, make sure the plants pulled were the correct size, and stop people from swapping rows, etc. The plants would leave the field by pickup truck and be hauled to Bellville where the Hearns owned a big building called the seed house. They would often store cotton seed in there and wait on the prices to go up. They also used the house as a packing shed for the plants. They would pack the tomato plant bundles in the wooden shipping baskets. The baskets were maybe 15 or 18 inches in diameter, and about 14 inches tall. Some referred to them as a "pony." There were people working at tables. They had a type of peat moss or sphagnum moss that they would buy from an individual who got it out of the Okefeenokee Swamp. They would buy it three or four months ahead of time and lay it out in the weather to dry out. They had a water spigot and a person would stand on the outside of the packing shed and keep this moss wet as they were packing the plants. The workers would bring the moss inside and put it on tables. They would mostly use women to pack the plants. They would put a handful or two of the moss around the roots of the plants and roll a pre-cut piece of paper around the roots. Then they would take the same rubber band and put it around the rolled piece of paper to hold the bundle together. The plants were then placed in the baskets for shipment.

The plants would be in transit two or three days, and the packers took these precautions because they didn't want the plants to dry out. Reduced transit time was important, and the truckers had to allow time to cross river ferries on their trip north and also avoid arriving on Sunday. They shipped the plants up to Virginia and Maryland, where they were transplanted in the field with a regular mechanical transplanter. Up in that part of the country at one time there were a lot of canning plants. They canned both tomatoes and relish.

Q: Was the tomato plant operation a good business for the Hearns?

A: I asked Mr. Inman if he made a profit on the tomato plants. He said he broke even the first year, and made a little something each year on the plants after that. He realized he needed a specialty crop to bring in more money than he was making on the type crops they were growing at that time. They grew tomato plants from 1935 to 1961. It was not uncommon on any given day to have as many as 200 workers out there pulling tomato plants. So, even though the wages were modest, they provided spending money for a lot of seasonal workers.

Q: Were there any particular varieties of tomatoes planted here?

Interviews 157

A: When they started off in 1935, the varieties had names like Rutger and Marglobe. This thing got to be big business and later on they changed the names to numbers. They would usually have four-digit numbers for different varieties.

I was talking with Cleve Freeman not long ago. Cleve was a plant inspector that worked for the state. These plants were certified, and this required an inspection. The plants required a lot of spraying and this sometimes caused problems. The plants had to be certified free of disease and insects. If the plants were not up to snuff, then Cleve would turn them down. Of course, if the plants were rejected by the inspector then nobody wanted them. Sherman T. Griffith from Maryland was the Hearn's broker. Sometimes a truck load of plants would have to be thrown away because the weather would make a quick change up north and would be too cold for the plants to survive. This was the Hearn's loss, not the brokers, if they had not already been paid for the plants.

What really put the plant operation out of business was the Japanese competition. The Japanese started growing or buying tomatoes overseas and exporting them by the boatloads to the United States. It put these small canning plants on the East Coast out of business.

Q: I'd like to turn to the subject of cotton. Do you recall any information about why most folks stopped growing cotton?

A: This happened in the early 1960s. At that time cotton was around 30 to 32 cents a pound. A lot of people just got tired of cotton. The foreign countries were producing it cheaper. Local farmers as a group kind of gave it up when it dropped down to about 28 cents a pound. People said they couldn't grow it for that price.

The old-time cotton plants could get about six or seven feet tall. A cotton plant has two crops, a top and bottom crop. At one time, a place in Claxton, Kaiser Agricultural Chemical Company, had a highboy that they used in spraying fields for the public. They would put what they called a drop on the highboy. It was a rubber hose about two feet long with a nozzle on the end of it. It would hang down in-between the cotton rows. They would put a special chemical in there to partially defoliate the plant. This would take off the bottom half of the plant's leaves. Then the farmer would get a cotton picker to go through and just pick off the bottom half of the cotton plant. A few weeks later you'd get the same highboy, defoliate the top, and then pick the top half. It wasn't unusual for Mr. Inman to make a bale and a half of cotton per acre using this method.

Mr. Inman had a profound love for cotton. Cotton seemed to be in his blood. He had always been around it and so had his father before him. Mr. Inman was a master farmer and everything was real neat and clean. He would go to great lengths to grow high quality cotton. Many people would only spray three or four times a season, but he would spray his cotton six or seven times to make sure the worms and boll weevils stayed out. Mr. Inman grew cotton into the mid-1970s. However, even he finally gave it up. He died in 1981, just 60 days short of his 80th birthday. To that day he loved the cotton business. The Hearns and cotton just seemed to always go together.

Q: Can you tell me about the Hearn cotton gin?

A: The gin burned in the early 40s. It was a two-story building. The black-seed gin was on the second floor, and the short-staple gin was on the ground floor. They had a rice mill and a grist mill in the gin building also. In the late 1920s just about every farmstead that had a wet spot on it grew a little rice. The Hearns grew some. This rice was brown and had a thick husk. The rice mill ground the husk off. The rice mill had played out by the 1940s, but the gristmill was still in demand. A lot of time the miller would take out a toll to pay for the milling. The Hearns were trying to render a service, because they really weren't making a profit on the grist and rice mill operations. They wanted to get out but didn't know how. However, the grist mill brought customers into the store.

Q: Could the cotton business be risky?

A: You bet! The cotton business could be high risk. When Inman and Cap's father, C. W. Hearn, passed away in the 1920s, he had six or seven hundred bales he was holding in storage. He would often mortgage the farm to obtain money to buy cotton for speculation. When the cotton went up he would sell it to a broker in Savannah or Augusta and make a profit. Sometimes you could make a small fortune doing this. After selling the cotton, he would then pay the loan off. He repeated this cycle very successfully several times over the years. When he was sick on his deathbed, he advised Cap to hold the cotton because he thought that cotton would go back up. Mr. Hearn had bought the cotton at 65 cents a pound and the price had declined to just a few cents per pound. Unfortunately, this is when the bottom dropped out and it took another 20 years to recover.

Q: Were they operating the turpentine still when you came to Bellville in 1961?

A: Tom Wood was not operating it as a still per se. They had a steel platform out there with some nozzles sticking up. They would take these used barrels and turn them over and pour the rosin out, and there would be a lot of thick rosin that would remain. They would then take the barrel and turn it over one of the steam pipes. They could steam about 10 or 12 barrels at a time on the platform. Underneath there was kind of a valley-like trough to catch the spirits and rosin. From there it would go into a storage tank. They had quit stilling in the traditional way, and were, more or less, recycling the product residue out of the barrels.

Q: Turning to some more lighthearted subjects, I've heard that some of Bellville's folks had some special sayings. What were some of them?

A: Mr. Tom Wood would take his four fingers and slap the inside of his hand and say, "I'll tell you what's so." Mr. Walter Emmett is famous for declaring, "I say." Mr. Inman would say, "Heck-a-mile." Sometimes Mr. Inman said, "black as Egypt" when describing a dark night. Now how did he know how black Egypt was [laughter]?

Q: Did Mr. Inman tell you any comical stories that occurred around Bellville?

A: Yes, he said the teen-aged boys would snitch one or two eggs a day and hide them in preparation for egg boiling parties. They would have a certain way to whistle toward each other's house that would signal all the boys to meet. There were three or four places they would gather around Bellville. If they whistled one way it meant one location and a different whistle would mean a second place, and so on. At the meeting place in the woods, they would have an old iron pot or a syrup can or something to boil water in. Four or five of the boys would build a fire and put the pot on the fire and start boiling the eggs. Then the card games would start. They were not gambling, but they played cards, told jokes, and just had a great time. They played Rook, Set-back, and I don't know what all else. When the eggs got done they would take the bucket and pour off the water. You didn't worry about finding the eggs you originally put in there, you just took the first two eggs you found. Well, Inman's mother had an old hen that was setting. They had gotten four eggs from the hen and didn't realize the condition of the eggs. When they turned the can over they all grabbed two eggs and some of the neighborhood boys cracked theirs first. To their surprise there was about a half a biddy in there. The boys said in amazement, "Looky here what we got, guess we got the prize." Mr. Inman said they couldn't laugh, but they knew where the "prize" came from. Of course, after that those boys lost their appetite for boiled eggs for a while [laughter].

Another episode concerned an embarrassing situation the boys got themselves in. The boys rode the mule and wagon out to Cedar Creek to go swimming. Now remember, boys in the country didn't have any swimsuits in those days. They usually picked themselves up a watermelon on the way, threw it in the back of the wagon, and drove out to the creek. This old mule was real gentle, and they didn't worry about tying her. So, they put their clothes on the side of the wagon and went skinny dipping. They had been out there playing and swimming and having a great time for a couple of hours. Well, they looked around, and the mule was gone [laughter]. Of course, not being as many houses then as there are now they could leave Cedar Creek and sneak back through the woods to their house. Cecil Daniel was one of them, and he hightailed it back through the woods to his house. He went in naked and got a changing of clothes. He then went around and found the mule and wagon and took it back up to Cedar Creek to pick up the rest of the boys. Now, Mr. Inman said they were some shook up young men till they got their clothes back!

There were many funny stories relating to a black gentleman named Andrew Richardson. He worked for Mr. Overstreet out in "Tar City," just south of Bay Branch. At Mr. Oversteet's commissary all he had was fat back, dry peas, dry butter beans, overalls, brogans, and shirts. The workers got tired of that and wanted to go to Claxton to get them a little piece of beef for Sunday dinner.

Anyway, on the days Mr. Overstreet "paid off" his workers, Andrew would sort of run a taxi service to carry the workhands to Claxton for 50 cents a head, round trip. During the weekends that he didn't pay off, Andrew would take his wife to town. On the way home he would stop at Bellville at Tom Wood's store to buy gas. Mr. Tom always pulled pranks on Andrew.

So, one day Andrew and his wife pulled up to buy some gas. Tom walked out and looked in the car, and made the comment in a loud voice, "Andrew, this lady doesn't look like the same one you were driving around last week." Andrew's wife heard what Tom said and got hot about that. Andrew followed Tom in the store and begged him to please go back out there and tell his wife the truth. Tom went back out and approached the car and said, "Ma'am, I wasn't joking a bit, you sure do look different today." He then just walked back in the store. Of course, Tom eventually told her he was only kidding and got Andrew off the hook.

One time this man who was a sharecropper for the Hearns came to the store about dark. He normally walked the mile or two to the store. In those days, these old country stores would stay open late at night, especially on Saturday. The only lights they had at the store were kerosene lamps. In the early 1930s the Hearns bought two Delco plants to power the lights. They put one up at the house and one at the store. During ginning season they also ran two lights over at the gin. One was at the scales and one where the operator was running the gin. The gin would run 14 to 18 hours a day. Anyway, this man who was a sharecropper came into town to get him a little piece of smoked sausage. He sat around and talked a while and then left and walked home. Well, he forgot the sausage and left it on the counter. When he got home he realized he forgot it so he walked back to the store. They hadn't closed yet, so he asked them if they had seen that little piece of meat. They had found it where he left it, but said in jest they hadn't seen it. He said, "Well, you know, if you'll let me see the sausage pan, I can pick it out and verify I left it because I remember exactly how that sausage looked." They gave it back to him after a good laugh.

Walter Emmett's family owned the sawmill and were a little more prosperous than the farmers. Mrs. Helen, his mother, had him dressed up in this nice little white linen outfit with short pants. Walter Emmett is very even-tempered, he's not one to get aggravated or mad. One of the men who lived in town and worked for the railroad loved to pick at the little boys. The story goes that Walter Emmett was walking to church by himself one morning. This man stopped Walter Emmett and pulled Walter's pants off and hung them on a sign. Well, most youngsters would have cried. Well, this didn't even phase Walter Emmett, and he just kept walking toward the church. The joke turned out to be on the man because he had to chase Walter Emmett down and put the pants back on him.

Q: I've heard a lot about your brother-in-law, Jack Hearn, and his work in citrus research. Can you provide some information on his career? [David provided the editor the following information via an article in the December 1995 edition of *Citrus and Vegetable* Magazine].

A: Another of Bellville's successful former residents is Jack Hearn, son of Inman and Elma Hearn. Jack Hearn is a world renowned geneticist who specialized in citrus variety improvement research. Employed almost 32 years as a researcher with the U.S. Department of Agriculture, Hearn was manager of the Orlando Horticulture and Breeding Research Unit. Hearn's experiments led to development of seven varieties of citrus fruits including tangerines, oranges, and grapefruit. As outlined in a December 1995 issue of *Citrus and Vegetable* magazine, "When the name C. Jack Hearn is mentioned, citrus growers stand in awe. Through innovative personal and cooperative research leadership, Hearn is recognized as the major factor in the scientific and technological advancement of citrus variety improvement research, both in the United States and worldwide."

Jack Hearn attended Bellville School and graduated from Claxton High School in 1953. He graduated from Abraham Baldwin Agricultural College, obtained his B.S. and M.S. degrees at the University of Georgia and his Ph.D at Texas A&M University. In 1996, U.S. Department of Agriculture inducted Dr. Hearn in their Science Hall of Fame in Washington, D.C.

Q: How do you feel about living in Bellville?

A: In my mind, there's no other place that compares. I enjoy Bellville's people, and have every since I moved here. My wife, Emily, is a wonderful woman, and we are proud of our family. We've got fine friends that make a difference. We're happy to be a part of a great community.

Interview with Bernie and Hilda Anderson
Bellville, Georgia - October 6, 1995

Question [Q]: Your store is located on the site of the former Hearn country store. When did you buy the property?

A: Bernie: We bought the Hearn store in 1970. I had a store out in the country for seven years. Then I bought Mr. Tom Wood out in 1963 and stayed over there seven years. I leased the Tom Wood store building. I then bought Mr. Cap's corner property and built the new store there. We've been in the store business 38 years now.

Miss Grace Hearn wanted Mr. Cap to retire. So I went to Mr. Cap and said, "I don't know what you are going to do with this store building, but I would like to buy it when you retire." He said, "Well, I don't know right now." I asked him to think about it. I went to the post office one morning later on, and he asked me if I wanted to talk about that little "business deal." He told me to meet him and Mr. Inman that afternoon at a certain location on the road to their farm. I went out there and Mr. Inman was already there before Mr. Cap pulled up. They had the figures on the store and presented them to me. He and Mr. Cap owned the business together, but I think Mr. Cap owned the building by himself. The price they quoted was fair, and we agreed to the sale. Then we got Harry DeLoach to do the legal paperwork. Mr. Cap said he would call Harry and have him meet us over at the old Claxton softball field to sign the papers. So, we went over to the baseball field and finished the transaction. They were *very* private about their business dealings.

I kept the Hearn store open six or eight months and sold the inventory down. Then we moved the building and built the new store. The old store was moved to Herbert Daniel's in 1970. There were actually two sections of the building. My brother tore down the part that was the post office, and he built a barn with the lumber. Herbert Daniel moved the other side where the store was as a whole building. He moved it to his farm. They moved the store by way of Manassas because the Bull Creek Bridge wasn't big enough to hold it.

Mr. Cap and Mr. Inman were hard workers. Mr. Cap didn't believe in taking a day off. After he sold the store to me, he would come by every day and sit on the porch. He had been there for 40 years, and it was hard for him to give up his association with the store.

Q: Please tell me about some of the residents of Bellville.

Hilda: There is an interesting story about Mamie Tippins. It relates to the first time our burglar alarm went off at the store. They had to come wake us up to tell us our alarm had gone off [laughter].

Bernie: Our store was over there in Mr. Tom's building. Somebody set off the burglar alarm. I jumped up and put my clothes on and went running over there to switch off the alarm. I went inside and turned the alarm off, and when I came back out the door Mamie Tippins came down the street with a shotgun. Mr. Cap Hearn and Alvin Blalock were close behind with their shotguns, and Tom Wood brought up the rear with his pistol. I just said, "Lord have mercy." All those guns scared me to death. They were all still in nightclothes. That taught us a lot about this town. The residents look out for each other.

Bernie: Back in the old days the depot was a big deal in the town. They told a story on Tom Wood concerning a break-in at his store. He said the nearest they ever came to catching anybody was when he was chasing a burglar from the store that night. He said, "I had to slow down, or I might have caught him" [laugher].

Hilda: The first year we were in Bellville we had gotten our presents for the children at Christmas. We left the gifts in the back of the store. That night when the children finally went to bed, Bernie, in his bathrobe, ran across the road and got the presents to put under the Christmas tree. The next day, our neighbor, Miss Mamie said, "Well I heard about Santa Claus all my life, but I finally got to see him in his bathrobe last night" [laughter].

Q: What were some of the "sayings" of your Bellville neighbors?

A: Bernie: Tom Wood always said, "Tell you what's so." Walter Emmett says, "I Say." Colquitt Sykes often remarked, "By gums."[1]

Q: I understand that you purchased your home from the Colquitt Sykes' estate. He seems to have been one of the more colorful members of the Bellville community. Can you tell me about Mr. Sykes?

A: Hilda: He left Bellville as a hobo on the train and wound up in Oklahoma. He said he left because the times were too hard around Bellville and there were too few opportunities. He must have left in the 1920s and moved back here in the 1940s.

Well, he struck it rich. He was one of the first millionaires in the county. He and his son had investments all over the world, including gold mines in Dahlonega, Georgia.

Bernie: Mr. Sykes' farm is out in the Kennedy Bridge area. The family still owns 1,500 acres out there. There is some fine hunting on that property.

Q: Can you tell me about Colquitt Sykes' wife?

A: Hilda: He met his wife, Valerie, out west, and her family was very wealthy. Some said they had oil money.

His wife was a nice person. She used to say she didn't know what in the world she would do after he died. My mother asked her how she knew she'd be here when he died. She replied that she had been sick all her life and people had taken care of her. She said, "He's never been sick and those are the ones that go first." It happened just that way.

Mr. Sykes looked after Mrs. Sykes real well. He took the back seat out of the Cadillac and put a bed there so she could be comfortable when they were traveling. He also had a chauffeur.

Bernie: He was short with me only once. He was waiting on her outside the house. I was inside talking to her. I came out and spoke to him. He said, "I'll say, by gums, you might get more done if you do your talking out here" [laughter]. "By gums" was his favorite expression.

---

[1] When Mr. Sykes left to go out West, he changed spelling of his name from Sikes to Sykes.

Q: What was the background on the Sykes' house you bought?

A: Bernie: We bought the house from a niece. Mr. Sykes wanted a one-story house because his wife couldn't climb stairs. There used to be a two-story house on the lot, and Mr. Sykes was raised in that house. I believe it burned down.

We must have bought the house in 1964. Mr. Sykes died just a little after I bought Tom Wood's store.

There are some unique features in the house. The fireplace is 84 inches long and the opening is 72 inches.

There were a lot of Mr. Sykes' papers left in the house. We gave them to his grandsons, and they were tickled to death to get them.

Q: How did you negotiate the purchase of the LeGrand house?

A: Bernie: We traded for the LeGrand house, including the furniture. During the negotiations with Mrs. LeGrand's son, Earl Wheems, I saw a double-barrel shotgun in the house that Mr. LeGrand used to shoot birds with. I sure did want that double-barrel shotgun since I was a bird hunter and all. After we traded on the house, I asked him about the shotgun. He also told me there was one thing he wanted in the house and that was an antique lamp. I said he could have it, and they took it and put it in their car. I told him that the shotgun didn't mean a thing to him, and he ought to let me have it. He said, "No, I got a use for it." I had the store in Mr. Tom Wood's building. He started to drive off and passed by the store where I was. He asked, "How much will you give me for the shotgun?" Then I said, "I think it's a fair trade for the lamp" [laughter]. After reconsidering, I told him, "Well, I'll give you $10 for it." He took the money and left. Well, we went over to take a closer look at the house we had just bought. As I was going through the house, I looked in the bedroom furniture drawers and the first one I pulled out had a $10 bill in it [laughter]. That paid for my shotgun! About a month later I got a letter from him, and he said we had done a lot of good trading. When he got home he said he had a guilty conscience about the shotgun. So, he sent me another $10 bill. I was going to tell him the story one day and return the money, but he died before I got a chance to do it.

Q: What is the small building behind your house?

A: Bernie: Paulene LeGrand, Paul's daughter, had a kindergarten in the little house. The house below us belonged to Paul LeGrand. It was the cook's house for Mr. Paul LeGrand. He ran the depot and lived here all his life. The little house even has its own fireplace. There was also a cook's house behind our house. Hilda's brother moved it to the river as a hunting cabin.

Q: I've heard a lot about Mr. Sykes' automobiles. Please tell me about them.

A: Hilda: He ordered the Rolls while he was overseas, and they shipped it to Jacksonville. Mr. Colquitt came to get my daddy, Felton Eason, to go with him to pick it up. They were good friends. He was very tall, and my daddy was short. They were a pair [laughter]. My daddy dressed up for the trip. After all, they were going to Florida [laughter]. Mr. Sykes just wore his everyday clothes to make the trip. When they got there the car salesman came around to where my daddy was and asked, "You think that man can pay for the car?" Felton told him, "Well, if he can't, I will" [laughter]. Felton said later he thought he had a total of three dollars in his pocket that day.

He first bought a Cadillac when he came back to Bellville. Then he bought the Rolls-Royce. He used to park his Rolls under that old barn behind our house. It was grayish blue. It was a sight to see that Rolls sitting in that broken down old barn [laughter]. He's probably one of the few people in history that has ever went out catching his cows in a Rolls-Royce.

Q: Do you recall any other stories about Mr. Sykes?

A: Hilda: Mr. Sykes had a mind of his own. Sometimes he stayed in a cabin out on their farm. While he was out there one year, Reverend Huggins was preaching homecoming at Eason's Chapel. Mr. Sykes had given a baby grand piano to the church. The preacher just insisted that Mr. Sykes be there for homecoming services. So, he went to church. However, he didn't hear too well. In the middle of the sermon he said, "Babe, that preacher ain't said nothing yet." They then just got up and left in the middle of the service. I was there, and I know that happened [laughter].

Q: Tell me about when Pinewood Academy came to Bellville.

A: Bernie: It was 25 years ago when the school was built. The first organizational meeting included Jimmy Rogers, Harold Kemp, myself, and others. There were 10 or 12 of us. We first met at the old Manassas School. The plan was for the school to be there in that building. I think Mr. Cap and Mr. Inman got together and decided they would like to see the school in Bellville. Mr. Cap owned the land where they wanted to site the school. Hines, Walter Emmett, Inman, me and others paid him a certain amount of money to get the school in Bellville. Mr. Albert Parker was a big contributor to the school over the years. Now, the school means more to my business than ever. We have student customers lined up every morning and every evening here. The students have been coming here since the school started. Now the children of former students are coming.

The supporters did a good job of paying off the debt. They would have entertainers come for fund raisers. We had Tom T. Hall, Dolly Parton, Barbara Mandrell, Jerry Lee Lewis, Hank Williams, Jr., Terry Gibbs, Jerry Clower, Bill Anderson, and Mel Tellis. The school made good money on the shows as the entertainers did not charge full price.

Q: Are there any more Bellville incidents you can think of?

A: Hilda: There was a train derailment one evening. Rommie and Gloria Thompson were eating dinner with us that night. We were sitting in the living room, and we heard the train coming. All of a sudden, the sound stopped. We talked about how quiet it got. I commented it sounded like that all the time. We didn't realize what happened until the next day [laughter].

Q: In your opinion, what makes Bellville such a fine town in which to live?

A: Hilda: It's one place that nobody ever bothers you till you need them. The residents are just as willing to help you as if you were kin.

Bernie: People try to do better around here. Everybody looks out for each other. The folks keep the town clean.

Hilda: People ask where you're from and you tell them Bellville. They ask, "Is that the little town we go through where it looks like they cut their grass every day?" Then they say, "Where in town do you live?" I say when you go through you'll notice there is one yard in a mess. I tell them, "That one is mine" [laughter].

Q: How did the Anderson House Restaurant get its start?

A: Hilda: We started the restaurant in 1992. My daughter, Harriet, and I bought the house from Emily Groover. I had wanted a place like the Hearn house. The inspector said I couldn't cater out of my home anymore. I just happened to have a chance to get the house. We were very fortunate. I enjoy the people that come here very much. All I've ever been used to doing was cooking. If you do what you like to do, you do a better job. I like this line of work, and I hope the folks enjoy coming here.

Bernie: The customers are the finest people you'd ever meet. We have choice people around this area. That's for sure.

Interview with Wallace Parker
Bellville, Georgia - July 6, 1995

Question [Q]: Wallace, your family has been associated with this area for some time. Your grandfather and Grandmother Parker had quite a large family. Do you remember your grandfather, John C. Parker?

A: My brother, Chadburn, says I saw him. But, I don't remember it. He said I was only about 3 years old at the time. They called my grandfather "Shad" for a nickname. Grandpa was Charlie Hearn's step-father.

Q: Do you have any details about your grandfather Parker's house.

A: It was up the road [Highway 280]. The home place was at the Evans/Tattnall County line. Part of the house was torn down some time ago and part was torn down in the early 1990s.

Q: Your father, Walter Nollie Parker, was a builder with a fine reputation. How was he trained to be a carpenter?

A: I know that he was an expert builder, but I don't know exactly how he learned the carpenter trade. I don't think he ever had any formal training. I guess it was just God's gift.

Papa was one of the best builders that ever was. The Tattnall County Campground tabernacle is his masterpiece. That thing has been shown and talked about everywhere. There are 6 x 6s and 8 x 8s there all boxed in. It all fits together perfectly.

Q: What other structures did he build?

A: He built the one-story John M. Wood house that was constructed after the two-story house burned down. This would have been sometime in the early 1900s. He also built Walter Emmett Daniel's house around 1938. There were two homes he built out close to the campground. There were numerous others that he made additions to as well.

Q: As you are no doubt very familiar with the Tattnall County Campgound, can you tell me more about the tabernacle?

A: When we went to the campground, we used to go on the road through Eldred Tippins' farm. We got on the road just the other side of Jessie Tippins' house. There was a dirt road that went on right out yonder to the campground.

As I said earlier, Papa built the tabernacle at the campground. I think he made the grand sum of a dollar a day or so. He drew the plans for it in the sand. It was all in his head. There were never any architectural drawings or designs. Of course, the building has changed some from its original configuration. On the south side of the tabernacle roof is where Pa made 'em take the shingles off. They were put on crooked, so he made them redo it. That was a lot of work to have to do twice. However, that's how he was--everything had to be done right.

The tabernacle pulpit used to be over on the north side. My brother Chadburn carved out the pews. They were cut with a foot adz and drawing knife. I still have those foot adz. Papa made a building template for the pews, and Chadburn followed it to build them. All of the lumber was hand-sawn. The tabernacle was built in the 1920s. You can see some nail heads on a roof beam made into the letters "C.A.P." Those are the initials of my brother, Chadburn Adolphus Parker. He helped Papa build the tabernacle, and when it was finished he put his initials up there. You can look at the braces and see every one of them is cut into the lumber. It was all done by hand with a crosscut saw. You couldn't find someone today that could do it to save your soul. All those braces are not just stuck up there and nailed. They are sunk into the posts and also into the plates. They are embedded in there with great care and precision.

Q: What are some of the traditions at the campground?

A: There is a dirt path all the way around the tabernacle. There was a Sunday ritual that you came to church and ate your dinner afterwards. Then the folks came out here and walked around the path as they visited. They stopped and talked to everybody. There was some courting done also. The spring of water down the hill used to be on the other side of the road. When they paved the road, they moved the road over a little east of where it used to be. It was a ritual to go to the spring. The boys and girls would go down there to shoot the bull.

Q: Any other information about the campground?

A: There was originally pinestraw on the dirt floor. Sometime before the beginning of campmeeting they would take the mule and wagon out and gather up the pinestraw. Most of the tents originally had dirt floors too.

We would come out here in the mule and wagon and spend the day. Mama would fix us lunch that we most often transported in a pan. She'd fix peas and rice, butterbeans, tomatoes, biscuit, and cornbread. She was the best cook in the world. There wasn't any meal served at our house without biscuit and cornbread. Everybody that ever sat at her table would say the same thing. Tommy Watson Newton, who married my sister, came to our house one day and asked mother if he could eat dinner with us. She said, "Sure." She went out there and killed two chickens and prepared a feast. The table was loaded with food. That man sat there and ate and ate. After he finished, he asked Mama if she would let him have two biscuits. He told Mama if she would wrap them up for him, he'd take them with him. She looked at him and said, "What's the matter with my biscuits?" He said, "There isn't anything wrong with these biscuits, I just wanted to take them home and show my wife what somebody can do in the kitchen!" [laughter]

Q: Can you tell me any other stories about the town?

A: Every Friday they would bring mullet on the train. The whole area around Cap Hearn's store and the depot at that time was just a big sand bed. The train would stop and unload the mullet on the railroad cart. Everyone would be standing around waiting on the fish. The fish would be gone within an hour. It was five cents a pound.

Q: Wallace, can you tell me more about yourself?

A: I was born in 1914. My mother was Emma Johnson, and she was the daughter of Virgil and Mary Ann Johnson. I was born in a house just across the road [south of Highway 292] and west from the depot. A house trailer is where the house used to be. There were nine of us children in the family. I went to Bellville School, and left Bellville to go into the Marines from 1933 to 1937. I went to Camp Wheeler, which was south of Macon, in 1939. Then I went to Robins Field where I worked in crating and shipping.

I was a carpenter by trade. I built Eloise Hodges' house in Bellville as well as several others in the area.

Q: When did your father buy the old Bellville School building?

A: It was in 1928 or 29. We lived in the schoolhouse for a period of time. Then we moved out and moved to the Bickley house. Then Papa tore down the schoolhouse and with the lumber built our house on Highway 280. We dismantled the school and put the timber in the old Hearn gin building until we could build ours. There is an old smokehouse there on the former house site today. The water well was just east of the smokehouse. I'm the one who dug the well. Chadburn and Coy Brewton wired the old house about 1930. The old wooden school faced south. The new brick school faced east and the church faced north. We lived in the wooden school building until about 1931. I could come out the back door of our house and go right to the schoolhouse.

Q: Please tell me about growing up in Bellville.

A: Nobody seemed to have much money, but we had plenty to eat and clothes to wear. Everyone was in charge of making their own happiness back then. You had to depend on yourself a lot. For entertainment in Bellville, we played kick the can down there at night. We'd go to the big culvert in front of Tom Wood's store and hunt bullfrogs, rake for crawfish to go fishing with, and just have a great time. We'd go up to the store and shoot the bull. We'd gather up on the front porch. There was some serious tale telling that went on. I've got some boards at the house that are 16 inches wide. These were shelves at Tom Wood's store. All the goods were on shelves on the wall. You didn't wait on yourself; they waited on you when you went in to buy something. You told Tom Wood what you wanted and he reached over or up and got it and put it on the counter. Most of his business was credit. Overextended credit became several people's downfall. There was nothing in the store that needed refrigeration.

Q: Who were some of your teachers and classmates at Bellville School?

A: Some of my classmates were Benny Johnson, Helen Sheppard, Buck Daniel, Chick Daniel, Walter Emmett Daniel, Richard DeLoach, Matha Riggs, and Lamar Riggs. All of us were in there together. They taught you reading, writing and arithmetic. There was no foolishness, either. Principal Grover Turner, who married my sister, used to whip some of those boys even after they got to high school.

Mr. Theodore was also one of my teachers. He could really spout Latin like no one you've ever heard. He could speak it fluently without looking at the book. He told me one time that he hadn't ever heard anyone pronounce Latin words quite like me. He made me get up in front of the class and recite it so everyone could have the benefit of my pronunciation. I don't think he meant this as a compliment [laughter].

Q: Are there any other stories about the school?

A: In 1928 or so, they called my mother and told her to put my brother Harold on the train and send him to Savannah. They needed another player on the basketball team there playing in a tournament. Harold went down there and got in the game. Just at the end of the game, he stopped about mid-court and threw the ball underhand. It went in the hoop, and they won the game. Other team members were Herschel Hearn, Bobby Benton, Buck Shannon, and Coy Brewton.

Q: I appreciate your time very much. It's been great to talk to you.

A: I've enjoyed it too. Times have changed a lot around this place. I have not thought about some of these things in a long time. I'm glad to know you're writing it down.

APPENDIX C

Bellville Methodist Church

Bellville's first Methodist Church was a wooden structure and was the center of the town's religious and social activities. (Photo from *The Claxton Enterprise*)

The Bellville Methodist Church has been an important part of the town since its beginning in 1890. The church members built this brick structure in 1947.

Bellville Methodist Church Sunday School Picnic - 1927. (Photo courtesy Emily Hearn Groover)

Bellville Methodist Church

This appendix includes material relating to the Bellville Methodist Church. First is a history of the church written by Rev. Kirk Loyless, a former pastor at Bellville. Next is a history of the Bellville Church United Methodist Women from a 1991 church publication, *Bellville United Methodist Church, 100th Anniversary.* Last, is a compilation of *Special Reminisces* by church historian Eloise Hodges.

History of Bellville Methodist Church

The Bellville Methodist Church has a long and interesting history. The church is approaching 100 years of service to the Bellville community and surrounding area. Sometime in the year 1890, a Sunday School was organized in the old Bellville Schoolhouse with Mr. E. B. Daniel serving as superintendent and Jesse Brewton as secretary. There were 17 members of this first Sunday School. The next year, 1891, the church itself was organized with twelve members. The first pastor was Rev. E.A. Sanders. The first services were held in the schoolhouse. Mr. Pulaski Sikes Smith donated some land near the schoolhouse for a church building which was erected in 1892 during the pastorate of Mr. R.M. Wesley. Total cost for this building was $1,000. The building was built by Mr. George Bird and Mr. O.H. Daniel.[1]

Plans for the present church building were begun in 1943 and work began in the latter part of 1945, completed in 1946 and dedicated on November 2, 1947.[2] Many improvements have been made to this original brick building since. Sometime in 1948-49, an annex was built featuring a fireplace, a small kitchen and two bathrooms. The steeple was added in 1961 along with other remodeling work including an enclosed entryway. The bell which hung in the old wooden church was found and purchased by Mr. Charlie Johnson and donated to the church. It now hangs in the steeple. Pews were placed in the sanctuary in 1963 as a memorial to Mr. Olin Hines Daniel, Sr. In 1966 a new annex was built which includes a kitchen, two rooms and a porch. This large room has since served as a gathering place for the members, for church dinners, and also other community groups. The old annex was converted into Sunday School rooms and a hallway. Much work was done to the church in 1974 including stained glass windows, new paint, new carpet, and the pews were refinished. Another stained glass window was installed behind the pulpit in 1980.

The history of the church is never just the listing of dates, buildings, and improvement to those buildings. Churches are not built with lumber, brick, or stained glass; but with lives which are our own. The history of the Bellville Church is written clearly in the lives of those who have been members and pastors here. The Sunday School started in 1890 continues to this day. The first choir, organized in 1954 by Mrs. Grace Hearn under the direction of Rev. Frank and Louise McCook, is still active now under the direction of Mrs. Kitty Plyler. Through almost 100 years there have been faithful musicians, Sunday School teachers, communion stewards, trustees, youth leaders, committee chairmen and members. The United Methodist Women's organization today is a part of a tradition of very active missionary work done by the women of the Bellville Church since its early history.

As we approach our second century as a church in Bellville our prayer is that we will continue to be faithful disciples of our Lord Jesus Christ.

Rev. Kirk Loyless
June 1990

> You are cordially invited to attend the
> Dedication Services at the
> Bellville Methodist Church
> on Sunday, November 2, 1947
> at eleven-thirty a. m.
> Bellville, Georgia
> Dinner will be served
>
> Mrs. H. C. Hearn   Mrs. J. C. Hearn   Mrs. H. W. Sheppard
> Committee

Invitation to 1947 Bellville Church dedication.

Methodist Women

The Bellville Methodist Church was organized in 1891 with twelve members. As the church grew in membership, the ladies organized the Ladies' Aid Guild. The purpose of the Guild was to aid the Parsonage family with food and other things that were needed. They also reached out into the community to do good for others. No foreign missions were involved.

The first president was Mrs. Mary Glisson Sconyers. Other members were Mrs. Mary Smith, Mrs. Jim (Jeanette) Daniel, Mrs. Bascom (Maggie) Tippins, and Mrs. Fannie Daniel. Mrs. Fannie Daniel was probably the second president. Mrs. Maggie Tippins was the church organist, and was very helpful with other programs of the church.

Church services were held once a month. Revival services were held once annually. The visiting preacher always stayed in the home of Mrs. John M (Evelani) Wood.

In approximately 1927, the Ladies' Aid was changed to the Woman's Missionary Society. Mrs. Jim (Jeanette) Daniel was elected its first president and served in this capacity for twenty-one consecutive years. Those present at this charter meeting were: Mrs. Jim (Jeanette) Daniel, Mrs. Olin (Helen) Daniel, Mrs. Cleburn (Carrie) Daniel, Mrs. Ross (Thiselle) Daniel, Mrs. Lee (Mary) Daniel, Mrs. H.C. (Grace) Hearn, Mrs. Nollie (Emma) Parker, Mrs. Theodore (Sadie) Brewton, Mrs. Maude Brewton, and Miss Nina Wood (Mrs. Felton Jordon).

This organization operated in the name of Woman's Missionary Society for several years.

In 1939 the Methodist Episcopal Church united with the Methodist Episcopal Church, South. The Woman's organization became known as the Woman's Society of Christian Service (W.S.C.S.).

In 1972 the Methodist Episcopal Church united with the Evangelical United Brethren Church forming the United Methodist Church. The women of the evangelical church were known as the Woman's Society of World Service. After uniting, the women of the two churches became known as the United Methodist Women.

The Bellville United Methodist Women continue today (1987) as a vital part of the Church with an active membership of twenty-seven. Along with the commitments of pledges to the Conference, the U.M.W. gives support to the many needs and projects that help to maintain and improve church property and facilities. They are truly a community of women whose purpose is to know God and to experience freedom as whole persons through Jesus Christ.

Special Reminiscences

Compiled by Eloise Hodges

Older recollections: Grace Hearn remembers when stewards and lay people (members) would collect money from other members for the purpose of paying the preacher and other expenses of the church. Aunt Sallie Brewton and John M. Wood were the most affluent payees, John Wood giving $20.00 per year. Grace Hearn and Mamie Tippins are two of the past pianists of the church.

1930: Mr. Beecher Smith was Sunday School superintendent. The minister was O.C. Cooper.

1939: Herman K. Nease began his 22 year tenure as Sunday School Superintendent. His wife, Lena, was pianist.

1941: Funeral - Martha Brewton Johnson, August 1, 1941. Martha Johnson died from a train accident just east of Bellville.

1942: Funeral - Walford Lee Daniel, March 20.

1943: Helen Smith Daniel gave land for a new church building. This is the present lot located at the intersection of Highways 280 and 169. The building committee composed of O.H. Daniel, H. Ross Daniel, Harry Smith, and T. J. Wood was named to construct a brick church building with Sunday School rooms.

1945: Work began on building the church during the latter part of the year.

1946: Present church building completed. The Stokes Bickley family gave pulpit furniture in memory of Mattie Wood Bickley. Pulpit bible was a gift from Elbert Miller family of Charleston, S.C. given in memory of Mr. and Mrs. Enoch Daniel. Lighted cross given in memory of Mr. and Mrs. Beecher Smith by their family. The cost of the new building was approximately $11,000. Membership was less than 150.

Funeral - First funeral in the new church was that of Cleburn Laing Daniel on June 27.

1947: Wedding , July 3 - First wedding in church Carolyn Daniel to Edwin Lawrence Head, Jr.

November 2, 1947 marked the dedication of the church building. Bishop Arthur J. Moore gave an impressive sermon and dedication.

1948: Funeral - James "Jim" H. Daniel, July 7.

1948-49: The social hall annex was added to the church building. The annex featured a fireplace, a small kitchen, and two bathrooms. Herman Nease and O.H. Daniel, Jr. were in charge of construction. Wilmer Nease and O.H. Daniel, Jr. built the cabinets.

1953: Funeral - John M. Wood, September 30.

1954: Grace Hearn organized the first choir at the new church under the direction of the pastor, Frank McCook and his wife, Louise. Grace Hearn directed the choir for 25 years, and also taught a Sunday School class that still bears her name.

Mae, Martha, Herschel, and Mildred Hearn (Shelor) gave the church its first electric organ.

1956: Funeral - Laverne Smith Sims, January 2.

Members broke ground for the parsonage. The foundation was laid in December.

1957: The Bellville, Sikes Chapel, and Union parsonage was completed March 1957, after four months of construction. The parsonage trustees at the time of building were: H.C. Hearn, Sr., and T.J. Wood, Bellville; Clyde Tucker, Union; and Bernice G. Tippins, Sikes Chapel. Helen Daniel Wilkerson and Anne Daniel Ward gave money for shrubbery around the parsonage. First parsonage family was Rev. C. H. Donaldson, Cora, Fran, Jack and two grandchildren, Herman and Erline.

October 27- Homecoming celebrated - 250 persons attended.

1958: Bellville, Union, and Sikes Chapel charge formed.

Wedding - Emily Elizabeth Hearn and John David Groover, September 21.

Wedding- Doris Nease and John Henry Rogers, May.

First air conditioner installed.

1959: A brass cross and candle holders were presented in memory of Mrs. Bennie Witcher Sheppard and Mr. Hiram Wallace Sheppard by their children, Charles, John, Elizabeth, Helen, and Virginia.

Wedding - Sallie Holland and H. Kenneth Nease, April 19.

1960: Funeral - Henry Ross Daniel, August 23. Uncle Ross was attending Sunday School when he was stricken.

Dedication services of Bellville Charge Parsonage, May 15.

On September 4, members gathered at the parsonage and presented a 1960 Plymouth automobile to the pastor, Rev. C.H. Donaldson.

1961: June 22. The building committee, O.H. Daniel, Herman Nease, and others, adopted architectural plans for remodeling the church. These plans included a steeple and an enclosed entryway with two Sunday School rooms that opened up into the sanctuary. Charlie Johnson gave the bell for the steeple. It is the original bell that hung in the first Bellville church, and had been sold to someone in Pembroke. Charlie bought it back, and gave it to the church.

Wedding - Carolyn Hendrix and Donald D. King, May 19.

1962: Funeral - Olin Hines Daniel, Sr., August 2.

Funeral - Jeanette Folson Daniel, December 11.

A Young Adult Sunday School class was organized, and J.G. (Jay) Hamner was the first teacher.

1963: Funeral - Carolus Wood Daniel, Sr., January 25.

Funeral - Curtis D. Smith, October 4.

The church pews were installed in memory of Olin Hines Daniel, Sr., by W.E. Daniel, Mary D. Daniel, Stella D. Daniel, and O.H. Daniel, Jr.

1964: Pearl Darsey Smith, wife of Curtis D. Smith, gave a pulpit bible in his memory.

1965: Wedding - Madeline Whalfant and Luther Gary Waters, November 28.

Funeral - Mary Lizzie Rogers died February 3. She taught a Sunday School class for many years and the class still is in her name. She was very active in Women's Society.

1966: Wedding - Paula Faye Riggs and Lewis Woodrow Bush, August 14.

Members converted the old social hall into two Sunday School rooms with an adjoining hall used for connecting the church with new annex. The present annex was built, including a kitchen, two rooms and a porch. O.H. Daniel, Jr., Chairman, and others participated in construction of the annex.

1967: Funeral - Elsie Jane Daniel Beasley, August 8.

1968: Wedding - Eloise Mercer Daniel and Roy T. Hodges, July 3.

1969: Wedding - Cheryl Waters and Capt. Jerome Mugerditchian, Feb. 15. First reception held in the new social hall.

Wedding - Nancy Elizabeth Daniel and Gregory K. Clodfelter, December 21.

The Inman Hearn family, long time members of the church, were named Evans County Farm Bureau Family of the Year.

1970: Wedding - Cathy Coley and Jim Nease, January 3.

Funeral - Mae Hearn, March 3.

Funeral - Thisselle Williams Daniel, May 22.

Wedding - Martha Louise Daniel and Carolus Wood Daniel, Jr., June 7.

Bellville Methodist Church 179

1971: Wedding - Kay Sims and Dennis Elton DeLoach, April 1.

Funeral - Thomas J. Wood, August 21.

1972: Funeral - Carrie Wood Daniel, September 8.

Funeral - Henry Caughey Hearn, September 17.

1973: Wedding - Mary Alice Daniel and William Edwin Rumph III, April 14.

1974: Stained glass window installed in sanctuary by individuals and family members in memory of and in honor of loved ones. Inside wall and woodwork painted. Original walls were stark white with dark stained woodwork. Recessed lighting and new overhead chandeliers were installed. Pews restained and refinished. Carpet given in memory of Henry Caughey Hearn by H.C. Hearn, Jr. Piano for the annex given by the family of Carrie Wood Daniel. Two brass vases given in memory of Miss Hattie Tapley by the family. The pastor, Heyward W. Stephens, worked diligently to have the church become a station charge.

1976: Funeral - Lena Hale Nease, May 3. The ministers for the funeral were William Peed and Eugene Scott. Mrs. Nease was pianist and Sunday School teacher for many years. She was also the first organist for the church and served in that capacity until Emily Hearn Groover became organist. Emily Groover was pianist when Mrs. Nease became the organist. The stained glass window behind the organ was given by the Nease family.

1977: Funeral - Helen Smith Daniel, May 28.

Funeral - Mary Holder Daniel, November 14. She was a Sunday School teacher. Collection plates later given in her memory.

Church member, Nancy Groover, crowned "Miss Pinewood Christian Academy."

1978: Bellville and Sikes Chapel became the Bellville charge, with Union Church going to a full time station.

Wedding - Judy Elaine Smith and William Eugene Scott, April 8,

Death - Sarah M. Baurer, December 13.

1979: Funeral - Olin Hines Daniel, Jr., August 15. A stained glass "Rose window" placed behind pulpit in memory of O.H. Daniel Jr., by his family and friends.

Bibles for pews given by Inman C. and Elma Hearn.

Church member, Nancy Groover, named "Miss Evans County" and represented the county in Miss Georgia pageant.

1981: Wedding - Nancy Elizabeth Groover and David Holland Womack, August 23.

Funeral - Inman C. Hearn, October 3.

Choir robes given by Eloise Grant in memory of Ethel LeGrand.

1982: The family of Inman C. Hearn replaced the church organ in his memory.

Paraments presented by Mr. and Mrs. Leonard Blalock.

1983: Communion set given in honor of Mr. and Mrs. Walter Emmett Daniel by their children, Emmett Olin and Peggy Daniel, Lenora, and Emmett, Jr.

Choir robes presented by Kathryn and Paul Riggs.

Funeral - Ella Lee Rogers Wood, July 11.

1984: The first church paid choir director was Kitty Plyler who began with the choir in March. Since that time the choir has presented an Easter and Christmas cantata each year.

1985: Funeral - Roy T. Hodges, July 4.

Funeral - Roger Wood, December 26.

Wedding - Debra Lynn Benton and Edward Scott Wilson, November 30.

Church member Emily Groover named "Evans County Woman of Achievement" by Business and Professional Women 1985-86.

1987: Wedding - Barbara Ruth Barton and Jerry Asbury Kicklighter, May 24.

Funeral - Martha Hearn, January 24.

1988: Funeral - Margaret E. Daniel, June 30.

Picture in annex, "Road to Gethsemane," given by Grace Hearn in memory of Woodrow Powell.

Pictures of pastors since 1968 given by Eloise Hodges in memory of her husband, Roy T. Hodges.

Church member, Elma Hearn, named "Quiet Disciple of the Year" Statesboro District.

Funeral - John William "J.W." Powell, November 9.

1989: New Methodist hymnals purchased by members of the church.

Funeral - William "Bill" Wilkerson, February 22.

1990: The Sunday School marked its 100th anniversary on June 6 with a homecoming celebration with dinner in the annex.

Bellville Methodist Church

Wedding - Michelle Motes and Michael Shane Bush, March 3.

Funeral - Mamie Matthews Tippins. She was church pianist for many years and often played the violin for services. She was also a Sunday School teacher. "Miss Mamie" often boarded teachers in her home, and she also taught music lessons for many years.

Funeral - Woodrow W. Branch, March 13.

1991: 100th Anniversary Celebration: 1891-1991, February 10. History and programs presented in booklet form. Bishop Richard C. Looney delivered the morning message and dedicated the service to all members past and present. Over 225 people enjoyed a bountiful dinner.

Anniversary - Paul and Kathryn Riggs celebrated their 50th wedding anniversary, May 11.

Anniversary - Dorothy and Luther Waters celebrated their 50th wedding anniversary, December 29.

1992: Wedding - Edra Rogers Smith to Marvin Matha Riggs, March 7.

Church member, Mandy Bell, crowned "Miss Rattlesnake Roundup."

The Bellville Lions Club meets twice a month in the church annex. Many of the members also attend the Bellville Church. The club was formed in May 1994 by people of the community including Rev. Bob Norwood, pastor at Bellville at the time. The Lions Club donates $600 per year to use the church annex as a meeting room.

At the South Georgia Conference held in June in Macon, Eloise Hodges, Church Historian, received a special certificate of merit at the Awards Night Historical Banquet.

1993: Funeral - William Ralph Mallard, February 13.

1994: Funeral - Rufus A. Hendrix, January 7.

Editor's note: Church member, Eloise Hodges, was presented Winton Bell Humanitarian Award, November 17. Hodges has been an advocate for people with mental retardation throughout her personal and professional life, serving extensively with the Association for Retarded Citizens at the local, state, and national levels.

1995: Bellville and Sikes Chapel charge dissolved. Members of Bellville Church paid Sikes Chapel for their interest in the parsonage. Bellville Church became a one-station charge.

Register of Members
Bellville Methodist Church
First Membership Roster, 1891 - 1901

Year after name indicates when the member joined the church.[3]

Daniel, E.B., 1891
Daniel, James H., 1891
Daniel, W. L., 1891
Daniel, Olin H., 1891
Bird, C.P., 1891
Fulcher, Joseph A., 1894[4]
Tippins, G.W., 1894
Tippins, Bascom, 1894
Tippins, Olle, 1894[5]
Worley, G.W., 1894[6]
Smith, C.C., 1894[7]
Smith, Clinton, 1894[8]
McInage, D.W., 1894[9]
Johnson, Wm.H., 1895[10]
Baggs, Berton, 1896[11]
Baggs, Olin, 1896[12]
Grice, Joseph T., 1896[13]
Baggs, Columbus A., 1896[14]
Smith, Lovick P., 1896
Smith, C. Beecher, 1896
Smith, Steward, 1896[15]
Smith, E.G, 1896
Williams, Daniel H., 1897[16]

McCord, John Dewitt, 1897[17]
Davis, John, 1898
Smith, R.T., 1899[18]
Hammock, S.C., 1899
Darsey, E.B., 1899[19]
McInage, Pasco, 1899
McInage, Rosco, 1899
Jackson, Frank C., 1899[20]
Jackson, Ethredge, 1899[21]
Jackson, Paul, 1899[22]
Jackson, W.R., 1899[23]
Cox, Walter R., 1899
LeGrand, W.L., 1899[24]
Olmstead, S.A., 1899
Daniel, C.C., 1900[25]
Daniel, Cleburne L., 1900
Daniel, Robert O., 1900[26]
Hendry, Dr. A.I., 1901[27]
Hendry, Fred, 1901
Mincy, Alex F., 1901
Brewton, Berry B., 1901

Register of Membership, 1912[28]

Brewton, Mr. B.B
   Mrs. B.B.[29]
   Miss Sarah M.[30]
   Miss Maud
   Wade H.
   Alice
   Annie
   Mrs. Mamie
Benton, James B.
   Ruby
   Willie

Bird, Miss Berta[31]
Bunton, O.F.
   Mrs. O.F.
Cox, Walter R.
   Mrs. Walter R.
Daniel, E.B.[32]
   Mrs. E.B.[33]
   J.H.
   Mrs. J.H.
   W.L.
   O.H.

    Mrs. O.H.
    C.L.
    Mrs. C.L.
    R.L.
    Miss Annie E.
    Mrs. Fannie
    Bayard
    Homer
    Thomas
    Susan[34]
    C.C.
Durrence, Mrs. T.H.
Glisson, Mrs. J.E.
    Hazzle
Hammock, S.C.
    Mrs. S.C.
    C.C.
    Ruth
Johnson, Mrs. M. C.
Myers, Mrs. A.M.
    Orie
    Odessie
    Dwight
Mattox, H.P
    Mrs H.P.
Osborne, J.H.
    Birdie[35]
    Ida
    Carrie
    Clydie
    Luther
Parker, W.N.
    Mrs. W.N.
    Chadborn
    Olive
Rowell, R.R.
    Mrs. R.R.
    Othis
    Julia
Shannon, Bertha
Shearouse, Mr. Alford
    Mrs. Alford
Smith, Mrs. M.E.
    J. Colin
    C.B.
    Mrs. C.B.
    Fannie
Tippins, B.G.
    Mrs. B.G.[36]
    Clyde
    Glenn M.
Tippins, L.H.[37]
Vaughn, Mrs. B.C.
Wood, J.M.
    Maggie[38]
    Nina
    Mattie[39]
    Jessie
    Johnnie
    Roger
Waters, J. Henry
    Mrs. J. Henry
    Ruth[40]

Names added in 1913

Brewton, Theodore
Bickley, Rev C.T.
    Mrs. C.T.
    Morgan
    Stokes
Cox, Eunice
    Edleen
Daniel, R.S.
Hammock, J.T.
    Mrs. J.T.
Johnson, Alma
Nippers, Mrs. Mary C.
Martin, John H.
    Mrs. Clara
    Mrs. Maxie Martin
Rewis, Fred
Smith, Rosco
    Mrs. Pearl
    Conrad
    Thurmand
    Hoke
Sconyers, Martha

Ministers of the Bellville United Methodist Church

1. E.A. Sanders, 1891
2. R.M Wesley, 1892
3. R.R. Norman, 1894
4. G. Fisher, 1895
5. J. Carr, 1896
6. G.W. Thoma, 1897
7. J.L. Rast, 1898
8. O.P. Simmons, 1899
9. R.M. Booth, 1899
10. S.J. Davis, 1900
11. C.S.G. Strickland, 1901
12. I.C. Jenkins, 1902
13. V.P. Scovil, 1903
14. C.H. McCord, 1904
15. J.T. Mims, 1905
16. C.H. McCord, 1906
17. P.H. Crumpler, 1907
18. George F. Austin, 1908
19. C.T. Bickley, 1909
20. Embree Sutton, 1911
21. J.A. Sconyers, 1911
22. C.T. Clark, 1912
23. Hamp Stevens, 1914
24. R.M. Allison, 1916
25. J.T. Budd, 1917
26. J.E. Channell, 1919
27. I.K. Chambers, 1923
28. H.C. Taylor, 1925
29. H.E. Wells, 1927
30. Roy Sampley, 1928
31. C.A. Morrison, 1929
32. O.C. Cooper, 1930.
33. F.J. Gordon, 1932
34. L.C. Howard, 1933
35. S.P. Clary, 1936
36. George R. Partain, 1938
37. Ernest W. Seckinger, 1942
38. C.C. Long, 1944
39. C.F. Starnes, 1946
40. R.G. Freeman, 1949
41. A.R. Crumpler, 1953
42. Charles Frank McCook, 1954
43. C.H. Donaldson, 1956
44. Curtis Cribbs, 1962
45. W. Eugene Scott, 1964
46. Leland Collins, 1966
47. W.A. Wilson, 1971
48. Jerry Lott, 1973
49. Heyward Stephens, 1974
50. William Peed, 1976
51. Troy Holloway, 1977
52. Tom Davis, 1982
53. Bob Norwood, 1983
54. Kirk Loyless, 1987
55. Hyatt Smith, 1992
56. James Duvall, 1995

Notes

[1] According to the program at the dedication of the church in 1947, the church continued to operate in the second story of the school building for six years after its organization. The new building was not constructed until 1897. Tattnall County deed records bear this fact out as found on page 452 of deed book Q. Mary E. Smith, guardian of P.S. Smith's children, donated the land to the trustees of the church, G.W. Tippins, E.B. Daniel, B.G. Tippins, J.A. Fulcher, and D.W. McQuaig. The date of the deed is October 27, 1897.

[2] In May 1946, the Bellville Church Trustees sold the old church building to F.L. Miller of Pembroke. He demolished the building and used the lumber to build an apartment house and office building in Pembroke. *The Claxton Enterprise*, "50 Years Ago," May 2, 1996.

[3] These records on file in Bellville Methodist Church.

[4] Roll indicates membership "dropped," no date indicated.

[5] Roll indicates left church in August 25, 1899.

[6] Transferred to Manassas.

[7] Transferred to New Prospect, March 18, 1899.

[8] Transferred 1903.

[9] Roll indicates "dropped," no date indicated.

[10] Transferred to Manassas.

[11] Transferred by letter, 1905.

[12] Transferred by letter, 1905.

[13] Transferred to Claxton

[14] Transferred by letter, 1905.

[15] Transferred to New Prospect, March 18, 1899.

[16] Roll indicates "dropped," no date indicated.

[17] Transferred to New Prospect, March 18, 1899.

[18] Transferred to New Prospect, March 18, 1899.

[19] Transferred October 11, 1899.

[20] Roll indicates "transferred."

[21] Roll indicates "transferred."

[22] Roll indicates "transferred."

[23] Transferred by letter.

[24] Transferred August 25, 1899.

[25] Transferred in 1900.

[26] Transferred by letter, no date indicated.

[27] Transferred by letter, 1905.

[28] These records on file in Bellville Methodist Church

[29] Death: 6-1-1912

[30] Death: 8-24-1914

[31] Married Collins

[32] Death: 12-5-1918

[33] Death: 7-27-1921

[34] Married McCall

[35] Married Lynn

[36] Death: 2-24-20

[37] Death: 7-1914

[38] Married Shuptrine

[39] Married Bickley

[40] Married Baggett

APPENDIX D

Old Bellville School

History of Bellville School

Simon Hearn and Wiley Rowe built the first school in Bellville in 1890. Bellville's founding fathers took the lead by establishing the first high school in what would later become Evans County. The building was torn down and replaced with a wooden single-story structure and later replaced with a brick building in 1922.[1]

Some of the early supporters of Bellville School were Pulaski Sikes Smith, George W. Tippins, B.B. "Berry" Brewton, John M. Wood, Enoch B. Daniel, and Charles W. Hearn. Much of the early financial support came from local residents, since the state and county failed to defray all the costs of teachers' salaries and other expenses. In about 1912 or 1913, local officials levied an additional tax for the support of the school. The Bellville School district was known as "Hogwallow" during these early years.[2]

During the first eight or nine years of the facility's existence, Bellville School was the largest school in Tattnall County. At one time the school had over 200 students. There were normally three teachers and 100 or more pupils at the school. Many students came to Bellville and boarded while attending school. These students were from Bulloch, Bryan, and Chatham counties.

Bellville's first teachers and principals were: W.L. Perdue,[3] from 1890 to 1893, originally from North Carolina; J.S. Davis and a Mr. Floyd, 1894. Davis was from Bulloch County and later from Wilkinson county, where he located and taught last. Mr. Floyd was from North Carolina originally, but moved to Tyson, Georgia; a Mr. Buxton, in 1895, from Burke County; E.B. Manning in 1896, from Carolina; Mr. L. Williams, in 1897, from Collins, Georgia; G.F. Ingram, in 1898, who taught at Hagan for several years; E.A. Rogers, in 1899; J. Arte Usher and wife, before he went to Savannah and became a doctor; Mr. Prevatt, assisted by Miss Minnie Long, in 1901; and I.S. Smith. Other early teachers were Rev. J.A. Pingston, W.W. Godbee, Eason Rogers, Genie and Frances Daniel, and Lyda Hughey.

The trustees abandoned the old Bellville School as consolidation began around 1921. The county built a new brick school at the cost of $12,000. In that year, Bay Branch and Smith schools combined with the newer Bellville School, and in 1931 Sapptown School joined with Bellville. Further consolidation occurred in 1938 when Claxton School took in Bellville's eighth and ninth grades. In 1954, all Bellville classes consolidated with Claxton.

In 1960 the trustees sold the school building to the City of Bellville. After unsuccessfully trying to sell the building to businesses, the town council sold the structure and three acres of land to Luther Waters. Waters dismantled the brick structure in 1962 and used the bricks to construct his home located on the site of the old schools.[4]

Over the years, hundreds of students passed through the doors of Bellville School. Dozens of teachers taught there, with many of them marrying local people.

The following *Claxton Enterprise* newspaper article gives the reader a look at the Bellville School in the early 1920s.

Bellville High School 1923 Graduation Exercise

Last Monday night April 30, the Spring term of the Bellville High School closed for the term.

This year's work has not been in vain. It sends forth three young women and four young men into the world of real life. With a vast amount of knowledge which they gathered working unfailingly under the tender care of the faculty.

The entertainment of the evening was given by the graduating class in the following order:
1. The welcome address by second honored student, C.C. Daniel.
2. Reading the best history paper of the year, "Self Government," by Miss Nina Lee Osborne.
3. Reading the class history by Coy Brewton.
4. The "Class Grumbler" by Roger Wood.
6. Valedictory by the first honored pupil, Miss Mildred Hearn.

After the close of the exercises the speakers of the evening, Hon. R. Lee Moore, was introduced by Col. Wade Brewton.

Col. Moore delivered his literary address from the great words, "Industry, Sobriety, and Economy." His speech was very interesting and had a great influence over all that heard it, and especially to the graduating class and the ones taking their place next year.

After Col. Moore's address came the presentation of the diplomas by the county superintendent of schools, Theodore Brewton.

The acceptance of the diplomas in behalf of the class was delivered by the class president, Carl Smith.

Then came the first address to those that would not be with the school during the future by Professor Turner.

His address caused many to break down in tears, especially the graduating class and every member of the faculty. This went to show that he not only loved the school but he is loved by all the school.

The scenery was very beautiful. The stage was decorated with pink and green crepe paper and pink roses, the class colors and flower. Each girl carried a large bouquet of roses and fern tied with ribbon. Both the boys and girls wore a bow of ribbon over their hearts, all in the class colors.

The program was carried out perfectly, without an error. Each one's part filling in like parts of a great machine.

We are very glad indeed to know that Professor Turner and Miss Flanigan[5] will be with the school again next year. This assures us that the school is going to accomplish much.[6]

Editor's note: In November 1993 the compiler of this book attended a reunion of the old Bellville School. The following account documents the occasion and provides a glimpse of life as a Bellville School student.

Proceedings of the Bellville School Reunion
November 13, 1993

Introduction

When invited to the Bellville School reunion by my friend David Groover, I was not sure what to expect at the event. I knew there would be a good meal at the Anderson House, and I also thought the reunion would be a good opportunity to meet people. However, I must admit I was not prepared for the wonderful experience that took place. I have never enjoyed fellowship with a friendlier, funnier, or more loving bunch of folks.

The festivities got underway at noon, on Saturday, November 13, 1993, when the group of former students, their families and friends gathered at the Bellville Methodist Church for a hour-long "social." This period was packed with many fun-filled stories told by the former Bellville School students. I have never heard such humorous tales told with so much gusto. As soon as one story concluded, someone would start another one. The group spent most of this time roaring with laughter. One would have thought the escapades took place yesterday. However, some of the stories originated seventy-five or more years ago. What fun!!

After the social, the group proceeded across the street to the Anderson House for some of Hilda Anderson's fine home cooking. The fellowship continued during dinner. Good friends, enjoying great food and fellowship, made it a great day. After lunch, the storytelling resumed as people stood in small groups in the front yard of the church. As the afternoon progressed, members of the crowd slowly left to make their way home. Many people commented that some of the past reunions had more attendees, but they could not remember one that had been more enjoyable.

Since I am interested in both history and people, the reunion was a real treat. I enjoyed the day so much that I decided to preserve it as best I can. This booklet is the result of that effort. A transcription of the proceedings begins at page one. There may be a few errors; however, I tried my best to accurately record the words of the speakers. Also included are photographs and other information relating to the event.

I have thought about this day several times since. What made the experience so memorable? It was a special time that only occurs when old friends get together to recall fond memories. The laughter that day echoed laughter from another time. A time when these students sat side-by-side at their desks, ate their lunches together, and played in the school yard among those who would become life-long friends.

Pharris DeLoach Johnson

Old Bellville School Reunion Social

Paul Riggs: I would like to welcome you today. I believe today is our fourth reunion. I know some of you have come a long distance, and some have come from across the street [laughter]. We are glad to have all of you here. I know there are some in here who don't know who everybody is. I think it would be nice if we go around the room and introduce ourselves. Tell us who you are, and a little about yourself. We'll start over here with Walter Emmett. Now, Walter Emmett doesn't talk that loud--like I do.

Walter Emmett Daniel: I'm Walter Emmett Daniel. This is my wife, Nita.

Winton Bell: I'm not really sure who I am [laughter]. You know, the other day I called someone and the phone rang and rang. Then an answering machine picked up, and I've never heard this one--a young lady said, "I'm lost" [laughter]. "I really am lost, and when I find myself I'll return your call" [laughter]. I actually know who I am, I'm Winton Bell. I'm married to the lovely lady, Lucy, at the end of the table. She will probably admit that fact when we get to her turn. I'm glad to see all of you. I'm looking forward to having a good time here, and a better time across the street [laughter]. Y'all stay with us.

Thurmon Smith: I'm Thurmon Smith, and I live three miles south of here.

Perry Lee DeLoach: Thurmon, you got a brother named Commodore?

C.B. Smith: He's afraid he has [laughter].

Perry Lee DeLoach: Mr. Thurmon joined the 90's club this year too.

Reedy Akins: I'm Reedy Akins, and I live in Claxton.

Paul Riggs: Now, Reedy was a Yankee for a while, but then he came back south.

Sammy Crumpton: I'm Sammy Crumpton, and I live in Savannah. This is my wife, Jackie. We have four children, and nine grandchildren. You know you were talking about the answering machine...my little granddaughter made an answering machine message, "At the sound of the tone leave your name and credit card number" [laughter].

Chick Daniel: I'm Chick Daniel. This is my wife, Mary, and daughter, Janette. You all know about the rest of it [laughter].

Joe Riggs: I'm Joe Riggs...kin to Paul. If I knew he was going to wear that shirt, I wouldn't have worn this one [laughter--they both had on identical shirts]. My wife wasn't feeling well, so she wasn't able to come.

Herschel Hearn: Joe, you remember when you cut off the pig's tale?

Joe Riggs: That wasn't me. It was Matha [laughter].

Bobby Styles: My name is Bobby Styles. I used to live right across the road, and now I live down in Richmond Hill, Ga.

Paul Riggs: Glad to have you, Bobby.

Sue Smith: I'm Sue Smith. I have my son, Stewart, and his wife, Heather, from Richmond Hill visiting here today. I live here.

Amiel Fountain: My name is Amiel Fountain and I grew up in Bellville. I left here in 1936 and it's good to come back and meet people. But you know it's hard to recognize them all...because they've changed, but I sure haven't [laughter]. This is my wife, Emily. She's from Savannah. We have two children, both living in California and we have five grandsons, ...but no granddaughters.

Nell Smith Hunt: I'm Nell Smith Hunt and I grew up in Smithtown. I'm Thurman Smith's sister. I lived in Baxley fifty some-odd years. Now I live at Magnolia Manor in Richmond Hill. I have two children and seven grandchildren.

Matha Riggs: I'm Matha Riggs. This is my wife, Edra. She has two grandchildren. We live in the first house down the road.

Pharris Johnson: I'm Pharris Johnson. I'm a Colonel in the Air Force, stationed at Warner Robins, Georgia. I have a farm, "Johnson Hill," just up the road. My father, Charlie Johnson, was raised here in Bellville.

C.B. Smith: I'm a network. I'm C-B-S [laughter]. Other than that I'm a trial to Perry Lee [laughter].

Paul Riggs: Miss Grace, I won't make you stand up since you're right here. You are Grace Hearn?

Grace Hearn: I was [laughter]. I still am. I'm Grace Hearn, although I was Grace Flanigan for a long time.

Voice: Tell 'em how old you are.

Grace Hearn: How old am I? I look and feel a lot younger than some of these others [laugher]. I'm 91. If I live to another February, I'll be 92.

Herschel Hearn: Well, I'll be 91 this February.

Voice: But, Miss Grace, you taught Herschel?

Paul Riggs: Yes, Miss Grace taught a lot of us. She straightened me out two or three times. She was a real good teacher, and some of her students were older than she was.

Charles Hearn: I'm Charles Hearn and I went to school in Bellville from 1931 to about 1940. This is my wife, Winselle. We have four children and three grand boys. We don't have any girls ...yet [laughter].

Rona Jane Blalock Wilkes: I'm Rona Jane Wilkes. I lost my husband October 15 after 52 years. We have four children and nine grandchildren.

Melba Blalock Rose: I'm Melba Rose. I live in Savannah and have two children and two grandchildren.

Carolyn Rogers: I'm Carolyn Blalock Rogers. I've lived in Savannah about 40 years. I have four granddaughters, one grandson, and one... *great*-granddaughter [laughter].

Loulie Perkins: I'm Loulie Perkins. I have one daughter, two granddaughters, and four great-grandchildren. I've been here a long time, and all my families live around here.

Ada Creech: I'm Ada Creech and I've been around here a long while [laughter]. I've been in the hairdressing business 53 years. I'm still working at it.

Paul Riggs: I don't know what happened to my hair dresser, but something sure happened [points to his bald head--laughter].

Jack Hearn: I'm Jack Hearn. Looking around here I must have been one of the last to go to Bellville school. I've moved around a little bit. I moved to Texas for a while. Then down to Orlando, Florida. I've been there for 31 years. I'm married and I have three children, a daughter and two sons. None of them married. Guess they haven't gotten it figured out yet [laughter]. I'm the younger brother of someone standing behind me. The only way to tell us apart is from the top [points to his hair--laughter]. I'm glad to be back.

Bill Hearn: I have the same hairdresser Paul does [laughter]. I'm Bill Hearn, Jack's older brother. My wife is Priscilla Smith Hearn. We live in Daisy. We've been living there since 1963.

Herschel Hearn: I'm Herschel Hearn, and I'm not going to tell you how long I've been around... but believe me it's been a right good while [laughter]. Almost as long as Grace, but not quite. I went to school in Bellville. I went to school in three separate schoolhouses in Bellville. They built that many while I was going to school. I was a slow learner... you see it took me a long time to get out [laughter]. I live in Kinston, N.C. I have four children, two boys and two girls. I've got one of them, Sarah, here with me.

Paul Riggs: Delma, you want to tell about your going to Bellville School?

Delma Daniel: They already know that story [laughter].

Paul Riggs: It's good to have you, Mary, and Stella here.

Perry Lee DeLoach: I'm sure that you all haven't known me as long as you have known Mrs. Ada [laughter]. The shocking point to me was to know that Ada has been a hairdresser for fifty what?

Ada Creech: 53 years.

Perry Lee DeLoach: You see, I'm so amazed because she told me she was just 47 years old [laughter]. This could be a day of confession [laughter]. If so, we've got a lot to learn today from this crowd. Cause I'll tell you...Herschel will soon be 91, and I imagine he could tell a lot on every one of us. I'm sorry that my wife couldn't come. But she had a headache and went to the doctor, and he gave her some medicine yesterday. The headache wasn't anything compared to the medicine [laughter]. Then I had to take over and do the doctoring myself. I gave her some ice cream and Coca-Cola and she got better, but didn't want to take a chance on getting worse. In any case, I got sick recently and had to go to Savannah. I had to stay three weeks and make a contribution to the United Way in Chatham County. I donated my big toe to them. Every time the doctor would see me he'd tell me that I had to quit doctoring myself and see a real doctor. Previously I would always refer to myself as Doctor DeLoach. But after making a mess out of my affair, I have given up the practice of medicine [laughter].

Nannie Kate Denton: All of you know Wallace I'm sure. I'm Nannie Kate DeLoach Massey Denton. Wallace and I have been married for a little over two years. Johnny and I have one daughter and three grandsons, and one great-granddaughter. Wallace has step-children living in Florida. We live in Hagan. We're very happy to see all of you here today.

Martha Odum: I'm Martha Eason Odum, and I live just a little piece down the road [laughter]. I have three children, two sons and a daughter. I have four grandchildren and one on the way.

Emily Groover: I'm Emily Hearn Groover. This is my husband, David. We live here in Bellville. We have two children and two grandchildren. I have two older brothers who're sitting over there. I think I must be about the youngest one here today [laughter].

Voice: She seems plum happy about it too [laughter].

Elma Hearn: I'm Elma Hearn. My children are Emily, Bill, and Jack. That's three children, seven grandchildren, and four great-grandchildren.

Evelyn Mallard: I'm Evelyn Mallard. I live at Magnolia Manor. I am very happy there. I have two daughters, three granddaughters, and one great-granddaughter. And, also one sweet little grandson [laugher]. I'm enjoying seeing all of you. I've looked forward to today for quite a while.

Phyllis Holland: I'm Phyllis Hodges Holland. I'm Ray Hodges youngest sister. I'm married to Gordon Holland. We have four children, three girls and a boy. We have four grandchildren, four step-grandchildren, and two great step-grandchildren.

Stewart Smith: I'm Stewart Smith and this is my wife, Heather. My mother introduced us earlier. We're glad to see a good contingency from Richmond Hill, 'cause that's where we live [laughter].

Helen Wilkinson: I'm Helen Wilkinson. B.J. and I have two children and seven grandchildren. We live in Savannah and Claxton (laughter).

Paul Riggs: B.J., did you ever come to Bellville School?

B.J. Wilkinson: No, but I came here for other reasons [laughter].

Paul Riggs: Well, as most of you know I'm Paul Riggs. That's my wife Kathryn down there. We have three children, six grandchildren, and two great-grandchildren. We have one more on the way that will be here for Christmas [laughter].

Voice: Is that a child or grandchild on the way?

Paul Riggs: That's a great-grandchild. Thank you for the compliment... [laughter].

Of course, we've all got stories to tell. So I think I'll tell mine and sit down and let the rest of you tell yours.

Most of you remember the old schoolhouse. That is the second one, not the two-story. Mr. and Mrs. Parker lived near there. James Harper ought to be here today. I'm not sure where he is. Anyway, way back when, he and I found a hen's nest over there under Mrs. Parker's house. So we robbed the eggs. We got us a can and went down to the branch to boil those eggs. While they were boiling, smoke was coming up from down there. Some of the boys went down to see what was going on. We wouldn't give them any of the eggs so they went and told on us. I forgot just who the principal was then, but he told us to bring some eggs back the next morning. He instructed us to go over there and give them to Mrs. Parker and tell her that we stole her eggs. I hated to do that, but we had to do it. I don't think James ever did. But I did. I went over there and told her we stole the eggs, cooked them, and enjoyed them. And, here they are right here [points to his stomach--laughter]. I had to tell daddy and mama about it, too. I will never forget that as long as I live. Of course, there were lots of other incidents that happened while I was in Bellville School. I want to give someone else a chance to tell their tales now.

C.B. Smith: I've got a tale all right, but it didn't have anything to do with the school. It was when Miss Grace here was my Sunday School teacher. She gave the class a picnic over at Cedar Creek. Well, I jumped in the water with my glasses on. I don't know why I didn't feel them come off, but I didn't. I came up without them, and they all asked me where my glasses were. I thought they were just ribbing me. They said I had 'em on when I jumped in, but I didn't believe them. One of the boys saw the glasses come off as I hit the water. He went over and dived down and found my glasses on the bottom and brought them back. So you talk about being lost and blind, that's as close as I've ever been [laughter].

Perry Lee DeLoach: Paul, I heard a real cute one this week. It didn't necessarily have anything to do with the Bellville School, but it does have to do with bankers. As you know, we've had some bankers come out of the Bellville School. Well, you see this fellow lived on a farm on the outskirts of town. He was a pretty big farmer. However, due the recession and draught, he got in a financial bind. So he went to the local bank and told the banker he was on hard times and needed $5,000. He really needed it quick to pay some bills. Well, the banker said, "I'm sorry but I can't lend you a dime, you know the times are hard. You've already got your limit in this bank, and besides the bank examiners are due here next week. I just can't help you." The farmer said, "Don't give me that...you know I need the money bad. I wouldn't be here if I wasn't desperate." The banker told him he just couldn't help him. The farmer continued to tell the banker he *had* to have the money. The banker finally said, "Well, I have a glass eye. If you will look in my eyes and correctly tell me which one is the glass eye, I'll write you a check on my personal account and make you the loan." The farmer agreed and got to staring at the banker's eyes. After a while the farmer said, "It's your left eye." The banker said, "That's right. I bet you there's a hundred people that's looked in my eyes and you're the first person that's got it right. How did you know that one was my glass eye?" recanted the banker. The farmer replied, "That's the one I thought I saw a hint of compassion in" [laughter].

Amiel Fountain: Now this didn't have much to do with compassion, but here goes. Mr. Miller was superintendent of schools. I was in the ninth grade. Spiro Mulligan and myself were down at the edge of the branch smoking some...ugh [laughter]. Rabbit tobacco, that's right. It was burning our tongues, but we thought we were having great fun. You know, Mr. Miller caught us and brought us back to the school office. He said, "Young men, you're just too old to whip. I could stand you up there and whip you, and you would just walk out and get a big laugh. I have a little trick that was taught me when I was going through school that will help you remember this situation and may keep you from smoking." So we said, "What's that?" Mr. Miller related, "I want you to learn the Declaration of Independence... all of it! Don't miss a word, because I know it and I'll catch you if you don't get it right. There is a good reason I know it. I was caught smoking, and I want you to learn it just like I did."

So this incident kept me from smoking, and it also helped me remember the Declaration of Independence. Of course, you remember up to a point, because it's written in typical legal language. It's the strangest thing but every now and then I lapse into it, "When in the course of human events, it becomes necessary for one people to dissolve the political bonds that have connected them with one another, and to assume...." [these words were recited very fast--laughter]. So I have never smoked again in my life, believe it or not.

Herschel Hearn: Now I got caught smoking in school, too. I don't know how many of you remember Bobby Bennett. Bobby and I were down around the branch down the hill there. Sam Jack Lester was our teacher. So he walked up on us, and asks if we are enjoying our smokes. We told him, "Yes," we were enjoying it very much [laughter]. So he put us to walking the campus. I was supposed to walk to my house and back to the school; Bobby was to walk toward his house and back. Now I didn't want to do that because my mama would see me walking out there, and she'd want to know what this was all about. So I told Bobby to walk the route toward my house, and I'd take the route toward his house. So he went that way, and I went this way. About the second time around the course as I passed Bobby he said, "I ain't walking another damn step" [laugher]. He told me when he got to the other end of the course he was going to take off. Well, the last time I saw him was his rear-end running over the hill over yonder. The teacher finally came out and asked where Bobby was. I told him I didn't know. The teacher wasn't dumb, and apparently had seen Bobby run off. So he took his coat off and went to try to catch Bobby. He ran all the way over that freshly plowed 40 acre field over there. He almost caught Bobby at the far fence, but Bobby dodged him just at the last minute. Well, this foot race got the teacher's dander up, so he looked for Bobby all afternoon. He even went to town looking for him. He finally caught him in Claxton. He shook him, and told Bobby that he was going to whip him good the next day at school. Then Bobby told him "so what" because he wasn't going back to the stinking school anymore. The next morning Bobby was supposed to go to school, and he told his mama he was sick and didn't feel like going that morning. She said, "Oh yes you are boy, and they're going to whip you, too. And you know what else? I'm going to whip you again when you get home." So Bobby got two whippings and learned his lesson the hard way [laughter].

Jack Hearn: Since Aunt Grace is here, I'll tell a story that happened to me. She was my teacher at the time. Of course, you know, when her students were nephews or nieces, that situation made it hard on her as a teacher. I'm sure it was more awkward for Aunt Grace than it was for us. I had this friend named Wylen Holland. Wylen and I were almost like brothers. We came to school one morning and it was freezing cold. There was ice in a big mud puddle in the school yard where the buses splashed and wore out a hole. It was about one inch thick all over the mud puddle. We had never seen ice like

Old Bellville School 197

that. Well, before school started in the morning we had spied all this. At recess, Holland decided he just had to have a big piece of this ice. So he leaned over and reached out as far as he could into the mud puddle to get a big piece that wasn't broken. Well, I pushed him right in [laughter]. I mean it was cold. Poor old Holland was about to freeze to death. Aunt Grace ran everybody out the schoolroom and told Holland to take his clothes off and get warmed up around the heater. She sent me home to get him a change of clothes. I lived close by and was about the same size. He needed to put something on so the rest of the class could come back in as they were now getting cold, too. So I brought the clothes back. Then Aunt Grace paddled me, and I mean a good one [laughter].

Voice: You better be good or she might do it again [laughter].

Another voice: Well, I can tell you from personal experience if she ever promised you one, you sure got it [laughter].

Perry Lee DeLoach: You know, one of the biggest problems we had coming to Bellville School was the older boys. You know, the ones just a little older that were always getting us younger ones in trouble. I'll take Alvin Blalock as an example. Alvin was one of the best knife throwers there ever was. You could draw a circle the size of a half-inch, and Alvin could throw a knife in the circle nine times out of ten. He bet me a quarter one day that he could stick the knife between my toes [laugher]. I happened to have a quarter, and I felt like I could use fifty cents, so I bet him. He stuck that knife in the middle of my foot, handed me a quarter, and turned around and walked off [laughter].

Sammy Crumpton: Perry Lee was talking about these older boys. I remember when I first came to Bellville I was in the third grade. There was one boy in our class, Perry Lee, that stood out about a foot taller than the rest of us. Well, if I remember correctly, he was the only boy in that class that was already driving a school bus [laughter].

Voice: And he was only in the fourth grade then [laughter].

Perry Lee DeLoach: You know, I've already told them... I figured when I got old enough to date the teachers, it was all down hill from there [laughter]. We had several students date teachers and that wound up their little ball of yarn. Even Miss Grace got a Bellville boy.

Herschel Hearn: Yep, there are a right good many. Girls and boys came to Bellville to teach, and went home hooked up.

Mary Crouse Daniel: Well, that was that sad mistake I made [laughter].

Perry Lee DeLoach: J.W. Powell prepared himself to be a teacher. I think the first year he taught was at Sapptown School. After one year at Sapptown School, he said he'd rather pick cotton [laughter]. J.W. could pick 500 pounds of cotton a day. That's the story they tell. Picking cotton at 500 pounds a day... it probably paid more than teaching, too [laughter].

Amiel Fountain: At fifty cents a hundred... that wasn't too bad.

Herschel Hearn: We got a fellow over there, Thurmon, who could pick 400. I could pick 200 pounds a day, and it made me mad because he could always pick 400.

Perry Lee DeLoach: I picked a hundred pounds of cotton one day, but had to pour five gallons of water on it to get it to weigh that much.

Martha Eason Odum: We would like to know how many teachers we have here today.

Paul Riggs: How many former teachers do we have here today? Miss Grace, Mary, Nita, Nannie Kate, and Stella.

Perry Lee DeLoach: Paul, Nannie Kate's teaching history was a total disaster. She went to Canoochee School and it closed, she came to Bellville and they closed it. That's quite a record [laughter].

Phyllis Hodges: If there are any pictures of us when we were in school, let's bring them next year. I would love to see some of those pictures if anyone has any.

Paul Riggs: Any of you that might have pictures, please bring them in next time.

Amiel Fountain: Why, they didn't even have cameras invented when most of these folks went to school [laughter].

Paul Riggs: Miss Grace, would you like to say something?

Grace Hearn: Yes, I'd just like to tell them about my "trouble." I'll stand up so everyone can hear me. One year, Mr. Turner, the principal, asked me to take his room for two classes, the tenth and eleventh grades. He wanted to trade for my room, the sixth and seventh, as I recall. Now I never had any trouble with my class for misbehavior. But when I went to teaching these eleventh grade boys I was only twenty or twenty-one. They were only about a year younger than I was, so they thought they could get around me. One year I was teaching one of the classes, I can't remember whether it was the tenth or eleventh. They kept talking after I asked them to be quiet. They just kept on. When the bell rang for dinner, I told them I wanted to see them before they went to dinner. I explained that I wanted them to find Mr. Turner before he left for dinner at Tom Wood's house. As I said, Mr. Turner was the principal and they were scared of him. They didn't want to go. They said, "No, don't send us to him. We will do anything you say to do. We don't want to go to him." I told them that they had waited too late. If they didn't go to him, they need not come back to me anymore because I didn't want them in my room. Well, after some time they did go find him as he was walking across the school yard. I was eating my lunch in the school room watching the boys through the window. They talked to him and then they came along on back. They were talking to themselves as they walked back, and I wondered what they were saying. By the time they got back I had finished my lunch. I said, "Did you see Mr. Turner?" They mumbled, "Yes Ma'am." I asked them what he said. The boys related, "He said if we didn't do right by you we could take our books and go home." That scared the life out of those poor boys. I can tell you I never had another lick of trouble out of those boys the rest of the year [laughter].

C.B. Smith: Wonderful, that's just wonderful [laughter]. Was I one of those?

Miss Grace: You just might have been [laughter].

Paul Riggs: We need to decide if we would like to continue this next year. What's everyone's feelings as to whether we should continue our reunions?

We have a motion and a second. Yes, we should continue to have the reunion the second weekend in November. Looks like the best idea is to have it at noon time, so everyone can get home in the daytime. That seems to suit everyone.

Hilda asked us to come in the front door whenever we get ready to eat. There will be someone there to take up the money.

Well, it's about one o'clock. Let's proceed over to the Anderson House for some good food and to continue our fellowship. Please don't forget to sign the book. Let's all stand and have grace here.

C.B. Smith: Our father, it has been so good that so many of us could get together who haven't seen each other in such a long time. We thank Thee for this opportunity for the happy occasion we are enjoying. Strengthen us by this meal and allow us to be better people. We ask in Thy name. Amen.

After a delicious meal at The Anderson House, the tale telling started again.

C.B. Smith: You know there were several stories about Theodore Brewton, our principal. We called him "Squire Bill." He was an eccentric person, and we had more fun out of him. He drove this old Model T. He would start in the school yard driving down the hill there where Tom Wood's old store was. He'd start down the lane, and a bunch of us would sneak behind Squire's Model T and grab the back bumper. Well, we'd stall out his car. We'd run away before he could catch us. We've seen him try to close the Model T door. Well, it wouldn't close right and it would bounce back. He'd try to shut it again, and it would sorta bounce back again. He kept getting hotter and hotter. He'd rare back and give it all he had, turn around, and start away. The door would have his coattail stuck, and there he was a'hanging [laughter]. He would try to get away with his coattail still in the door. He was a sport.

Chick Daniel: Mr. Theodore could smell cigarette smoke a mile away. He used to get after us for smoking all the time. He could smell it on us when he would referee our basketball games. It got so bad we had to stop smoking and go to chewing tobacco [laughter].

You know, the funniest thing I remember was one New Year's Eve. We didn't celebrate New Year's like the young folks do today. Some of us boys built a fire and stayed up till midnight. We decided to go to the school and ring the bell. You know, ring the old year out and the new year in. We went in the school and my buddy, Benny Johnson, bumped into Squire in the dark at the school house. Squire was, of course, a lot bigger than us boys. Well, Benny said, "Who in the hell is that?" We couldn't see anything, but Benny knew it couldn't be one of us. Squire says "hummm" in sort of a high pitched voice as only he could sound. You talking about moving... we cleared that school building and fast!! [laughter] We were scared to death of him, you know. He was quite a character.

One time the girls in the class asked Mr. Theodore if I could drive them to Claxton. He said, "OK." So I drove his old Model T to town. This was around 1931. I'll tell you that was the hardest car to drive. It was top heavy and steered all over the road. Man, what a time I had. I had visions of wrecking Squire's Model T, and that would have been some kind of serious trouble [laughter].

C.B. Smith: You know, I have just one more story. You heard about President Bush wanting to talk to Moses? It was before the President left office. Actually, this was before the Gulf War. Mr. Bush saw that they were going to fight over there. Since Moses was a great military strategist, the President thought it would be good to have a conference before hostilities started. He sent word to Moses that he wanted to see him. Then Moses sent word back to President Bush that he didn't want to talk to him. When asked why, Moses said, "The last time I talked to a "bush" I spent 40 years wandering around the desert" [laughter].

Herschel Hearn: Then there is the story about cutting off the pig's tail. Matha Riggs cut off a pig's tail next to the school yard, and the poor pig bled to death.

Chick Daniel: The only reason I didn't do it was because I went to cut the tail and missed it and cut my finger instead [laughter]. I still have the scar on my finger. The hog tried to run, and we were determined to catch that hog. I can't remember why we decided to cut the old hog's tail off, but it was sure a mistake. Matha's daddy had to pay for the hog. It cost him $25, and that was a lot of money then. What a story!!

(That's all, until next reunion)

Notes

[1] Most of the information for this account is based on an article in *The Claxton Enterprise*, August 3, 1989, "Bellville Once a Major Business Center," by Theodore Brewton, pp. 35-37.

[2] The district school trustees during this period were H.H. Daniel, H.L. Brewton, and Paul LeGrand. Evans County Deed Book 11, p. 150.

[3] Professor L.W. [Lonnie] Perdue moved to Montgomery County after teaching at Bellville. He was lynched there in 1895. The local paper carried the following story: "Charged with a crime the highest known to the law for which no bail was allowable, Prof. L.W. Perdue, an old man, long past the meridian of life, whose head was as white as the snow bank with the frosts of many winters, a man of superior intellect and unusual cultivation, a graduate of one of the finest colleges in America, an educator of eminence and ripe experience, was arrested and placed in jail at this place in the early days of October. No action was taken in his case at the regular October session of the grand jury, the matter going over to the adjourned term to be held the second week in December. Impatient, perhaps, at even this delay, he has been violently wrestled from the custody of the law and put to death by the friends, as is supposed, of the family of his victim...." November 28, 1895, Thad Evans, *Montgomery County, Georgia, Newspaper Clippings*, Vol. 1, 1886-1905, p. 197.

[4] Luther Waters, interview with editor, April 9, 1995. Waters gave the following account of how he came by the property. "I was living in Bellville and working down at Ft. Stewart. I had determined to move from Bellville, but Mr. Tom Wood came to see me to offer the school building if I would stay. He was part of the former trustees of the school which included Cap Hearn and Curtis Smith. They had first tried to sell the building to a garment factory, but the rooms were too small to accommodate that type business.

It took me a year or so to tear down the old building. I had to eat a lot of dust [laughter]. However, the wood and bricks were in fine shape. The auditorium had some 36 foot long 4 x 8s and 4 x 10s without a knot in them. They are under this house now, and I'll tell you I'm not worried about termites.

The school had been empty for several years and had been vandalized. The blackboards had been defaced, etc. However, later on Tom Wood put up a security fence around the facility. The school desks were left in the building, and I let anybody who wanted some have them.

My cousin, Harlan Waters, built the house with my help. We hired out the cleaning of the bricks. I worked on the house on my days off from Ft. Stewart. We finished it in 1964, and we've been here since."; Also see Evans County Deed Book 3, p. 200.

[5] Later Miss Flanigan became Grace Hearn

[6] *The Claxton Enterprise*, May 5, 1923.

Bellville Academy in the 1890s. (Photo courtesy of John Rabun, Jr.)

Simon Hearn and Wiley Rowe constructed the Bellville Academy about 1890. The first trustees were G.W. Tippins, E.B. Daniel, B.B. Brewton, L.M. Nichols, and J.T. Grice. The second-story of the building was used as a Sunday School. (Late 1890s photo courtesy of *The Claxton Enterprise*)

Old Bellville School

Students had to pump their own water at Bellville School. (1920 Photo courtesy of Jim Hearn)

Bellville Schoolteachers, 1923. *Left to right:* Betty Fowler, Gertrude Eaves, Mae Hearn, and Gladys Corey. (Photo courtesy of Jim Hearn)

Bellville School 5th Grade Class of 1937-38. *Left to right:* first row, Ted DeLoach, Franklin Griffin, Reedy Akins, Odis Rogers, Ray Hodges, Louise Moore, Eula Lee Colson (Rogers), n-known, unknown, Nell Sikes (Surrency). Second row, Charles Johnson, Wilbern Rogers, Hollis Sapp, Neal Daniel, Aaron Blalock, Annie Mae Rogers (Crapo), Sybil Griffin (Tucker), Eloise Hodges, Lida Holland (Rich), Ernest Warren, Erie Sapp, Mattie Kate Colson (Boatright), Martha Eason (Odum), unknown. (Photo courtesy of Eloise Hodges)

Bellville School 1922-23 Girls Basketball Team. *Left to right:* Avis DeLoach, Cora Bell Brewton, Mildred Hearn, Nellie Smith, Loree Brewton, Alva Daniel, and Winnie Daniel. (Photo courtesy of Loulie Perkins)

Herschel Hearn, *left*, and Bobby Benton were stars of the 1922-23 Bellville basketball team. (Photo courtesy of Jim Hearn)

Herschel Hearn could do all kinds of tricks with a basketball. (1923 photo courtesy of Jim Hearn)

Bellville basketball team, 1922-23. *Left to right:* Herschel Hearn, Bobby Benton, Buck Shannon, Wallace Smith, and Hogan Brewton. (Photo courtesy Lois Parker Lewis)

Bellville basketball team, 1932. First on left is Amiel "Cornbread" Fountain. (Photo courtesy of Amiel Fountain)

Bellville School bus in 1923. This bus was made from a cut down Model T frame. Canvas tarps served as window covers. (Photo courtesy of Loulie Perkins)

Professor Turner, *left*, principal at Bellville School, on a class field trip to Midway. Photo from 1920s. (Photo courtesy of Jim Hearn)

Bellville School, circa 1928. The small Sycamore trees in the photo are now very large and today mark the former location of the school. After the school was closed, Luther Waters used bricks from the structure to construct his home on the site in 1964. (Photo courtesy of Eloise Hodges)

Old Bellville School 207

Bellville School Class, c. 1923. *Left to right:* first row, Eula Mae Brewton, Alva Daniel, Clarence Lee Smith, Winnie Daniel, Mildred Hearn, C.C. Daniel, Nina Lee Osborne, and Grover Turner, principal. Second row, Bobby Benton, Wallace Smith, Roger Wood, Carl Smith, Cora Bell Brewton, Herschel Hearn, Avis DeLoach, Coy Brewton. (Photos on this page courtesy Loulie Perkins)

Tenth Grade Class, 1928. *Left to right:* first row, Mattie Lou Daniel, Clyde Riggs, Evelyn Daniel, J.P. Brazell, Dora Bunton, and Martha Hearn. Second row, Margaret Daniel, John Shepard, Wilma Riggs, Cecil Daniel, Loulie Daniel, Edgar Lewis, Elma Riggs, Otelia Newton, Charles Shepard, Mary Daniel, Wilma Saturday.

Theodore Brewton and his wife Sada in 1927. Brewton was County Superintendent of Schools and a former teacher and principal at Bellville. (Photo courtesy of Jim Hearn)

Three Bellville schoolteachers stroll to work in 1939. *Left to right:* Ariminta Green, Eugena Paxton, and Eloise Mercer Hodges. (Photo courtesy of Eloise Hodges)

Mrs. Clanton's Class, circa 1923, dressed for a school play. Wallace Parker is third from left on back row. (Photo courtesy of Wallace Parker)

Cover of 1949 Bellville School annual. (Photo courtesy Mary Tippins Conner)

Old Bellville School

Bellville School 4th and 5th grade class, 1946. *Left to right*: first row, Jimmy Sapp, Ernest Sapp, Tony Weathers, Edward Eason, Jack Hearn, Waldo Bunton, Bobby Daniel, Earl Clark, Carrie Brewton, Wylen Holland. Second row, Versie Sapp, Lorene Griffin, Vernon Rushing, Marcus Griffin Brown, Jean Moore, Lousie Nelson, Marian Lynn, Ann Martin, Mary Tippins, Betty Clark, Betty Tucker, Lillie Mae Brown. Third row, Bertha Williamson, Lloyd Williams, Edwin Akins, Clifford Tucker, Beatrice Kirkland, Lutrelle Colson, teacher Grace Hearn, Ruby Rushing, Johnny Waters, Shirley Cameron, Rita Rushing, Edward Colson, and Bobby Richey. (Photo courtesy Emily Hearn Groover)

Bellville 9th Grade Class, 1945/6. *Left to right:* first row, Madison Short (principal), Ina Warren, Ora Lee Barrow, Jimmie Styles, Barbara Holland, Patsy Smith. Second row, Leon Griffin, Mack Lynn, and Tim Aikens. (Photo courtesy Jimmy Styles)

Three Bellville School teachers at 1994 Bellville School reunion. *Left to right:* Mary Crouse Daniel, Grace Hearn, Nannie Kate DeLoach Denton.

Bellville School students, families, and friends attending reunion. *Left to right,* standing, ground level: David Groover, Gordon Holland, Emily Fountain, Jackie Crumpton, Janette Daniel, Matha Riggs, Nita Daniel, Chick Daniel, Walter Emmett Daniel, Helen Wilkinson, Stella Powell, Delma Daniel, Ann Daniel Ward, Evelyn Mallard. Top row, standing: Amiel Fountain, Melba Rose, Sammy Crumpton, Wallace Denton, Nannie Kate Denton, Carolyn Blalock Rogers, Bonnie Bell Hendrix, Phyllis Hodges Holland, Martha Odum, Sue Smith, Kathryn Riggs, Paul Riggs, Rona Jane Blalock, Jack Hearn, Perry Lee DeLoach, B.J. Wilkinson. Standing, right side, ground level: Winton Bell, Lucy Bell, Priscilla Hearn, Edra Smith. Sitting, second row: Emily Hearn Groover, C.B. Smith, Charles Hearn, Winselle Hearn, Nell Smith Hunt, Ada Creech. First row, sitting: Mary Daniel, Elma Hearn, Grace Hearn, Herschel Hearn, Sarah Hearn von-Foerster, Loulie Perkins, Bill Hearn.

APPENDIX E

Pinewood Academy

Editor's note: The following article by O.H. "Tab" Smith, Jr. highlights the remarkable story of Pinewood Academy. Tab Smith, Pinewood's first headmaster, rightfully holds the title of "Father of Pinewood Academy."

The Beginning: Pinewood Concept
Credited to Dr. Charles H. Drake

By O.H. Tab Smith

Pinewood Christian Academy can be traced to a concept in the mind of Dr. Charles H. Drake. The late 1960s was a time of turmoil and doubt among American youth and the Glennville physician dreamed of a school where, along with the teaching of American political values and of the morals and ethics of American heritage, the Gospel of Jesus Christ could be presented in a consistent, direct manner.

Dr. Drake took his ideas to the Rev. Sterling Bargeron of Reidsville since the pastor was known to have organizational abilities and a strong influence. The two men, realizing that it would require the involvement of more than one community to establish a school of any size, decided to attempt to get concerned people from Tattnall, Evans, and Toombs counties to meet for discussion. They decided to propose a Tri-County Christian Academy and called for a series of rallies to promote the idea. Several meetings were held and rather large numbers of persons attended, some of whom had the vision of Christian education and some who came simply from a negative frame of mind.

On January 16, 1970, Rev. Bargeron and James H. Rogers, a prominent young farmer who lived in the edge of Tattnall County at that time, came to see O.H. "Tab" Smith of Claxton. Smith had been employed for a number of years in a local industry, but had returned to graduate school at Georgia Southern with an eye to returning to education, the profession he had first chosen upon graduating from college. The visitors felt that Smith with his background in teaching, in broadcasting, and in public relations, would be a logical choice for head of the proposed academy since he was completing his graduate studies and would be qualified. During the visit, Smith indicated a tentative interest and asked for time to consider.

A meeting of certain individuals who had been chosen for their positive attitudes and common-sense approaches was held at the C&J Restaurant in Claxton on February 10, 1970. The men present formed a steering committee for the proposed school and began committing their intentions to record. This was followed by a February 17 meeting in

Glennville where additional plans were formed. A cost-study committee headed by Gary Smith of Claxton was commissioned to report on projected financial requirements. Tab Smith attended this meeting accompanied by Charles Tanner of Claxton and accepted the position of headmaster for the new school with the understanding that evangelical Christianity was to be the order of the institution with no denominational restrictions.

Faye Kemp, Loretta Scott, Delores Blalock, and Shirley Hearn met with Betty Smith at her home on February 23 to begin work on a mailing list for survey purposes. The task was monumental in view of the fact that several communities were involved. A survey letter was sent out, after several work meetings, and the return indicated a healthy interest in the school proposal.

Thus encouraged, the steering committee continued to meet regularly with the Reidsville Bank meeting rooms used for the purpose. The steering committee had begun considering the possibility of securing the old Manassas school building which had been abandoned by the public schools some years prior. The building offered an ample auditorium, but only had five rooms suitable for class purposes. The men felt, however, that this might be their best opportunity for a beginning. The property was held by a group of citizens in the Manassas community and an option to purchase was taken. On February 26 a work day was held and the structure was emptied of trash and clean-up was begun.

A series of rallies were held in Claxton, Reidsville, Glennville, and Pembroke with Tab Smith acing as spokesman for the academy. The basic concepts were outlined for all who attended and the dream of excellence was described. The result of these meetings was an enrollment commitment from sufficient families to insure the opening of the school. By this time it was apparent that involvement from Toombs County would be marginal at best. Tab Smith suggested a change in the proposed name to Pinewood Christian Academy, observing that the property in Manassas was shaded by round pines and the name would be typical of South Georgia. The idea was accepted and the legal process was begun.

In April of that year, a group of men from Evans County came forward with an offer to effect the location of Pinewood Christian Academy in Evans County. H.C. Hearn, Sr., owned just over ten acres in Bellville which he was willing to see used for location purposes. Mr. Hearn was interested in donation of the property and other citizens in Bellville were willing to share in the donation. Bernie Anderson, Inman Hearn, Hines Daniel, Alvin Blalock, and Walter E. Daniel organized the proposition and the result was the gift of ten acres plus for the building site. Albert Parker, Ralph Dixon, C.E. DeLoach, Jr., and H.C. Hearn, Jr. offered to add to the gift of land their support in terms of securing loans to pay for building costs. The offer was accepted on April 14 during a meeting in Reidsville. On April 17 a building committee meeting was scheduled, and Albert Parker of Claxton was asked to serve as chairman.

From the nucleus offered by the original steering committee, Pinewood Christian Academy enjoyed now its first official Board of Governors. With Bill Hearn as its first chairman, the board was comprised of a twelve-man Board of Directors (voting members) and a twelve-man Board of Advisors (non-voting members). The original members were: Calvin Brewton, Thomas Scott, Charles Strickland, Bill Hearn, Jimmy Rogers, Dr. Charles Drake, Jimmy Kennedy, Harold Kemp, Tab Smith, Don Cobb, and Grady Rogers on the Board of Directors and Hugh Cooper, Ralph Dixon, Rev. Sterling Bargeron, Hines Daniel, Albert Parker, H.C. Hearn, Jr., C.E. DeLoach, Jr., Jack Kennedy, Gene Patterson, and E.B. Register on the Advisory Council. The entire body met jointly on a weekly basis and eventually on a monthly basis. Bill Hearn, Tab Smith, Albert Parker, Ralph Dixon, Jimmy Rogers, Hines Daniel, and Harold Kemp visited many schools across the state in order to gather ideas for construction. On May 8, construction was begun on the original building which was designed to offer twelve classrooms, two offices, and an academic center for a library and auditorium purposes. The board had decided after much deliberation to limit the academy to eight grades for the first term and the building plans were made with this in mind.

The official ground-breaking ceremonies were held on May 25, 1970, with a good crowd of interested persons and dignitaries in attendance. Chairman Bill Hearn and Headmaster Tab Smith took turns with the spade.

On August 1 the Pinewood Christian League held its first meeting with Charles Tanner elected as president of the association of parents and teachers. The League planned its first fund-raiser for Saturday, August 8. Twelve pigs were used for the barbecue which netted $2600 for the organization. In that and subsequent years the League addressed itself to the raising of funds for school support. Pinewood's first Fall Festival was held in October, various programs followed in frequent succession, more barbecues, and then in November of 1971 the first country music show at Pinewood with Jerry Lee Lewis the main attraction. With fund-raising efforts in regular patterns and with generous donations, the school managed to keep its promise to operate without receiving funding from any outside source.

Headmaster Smith wrote to many well-established private schools in order to gain ideas for academic set-up. A textbook list was established and orders were placed for books, furniture, and various supplies. The procedure of securing a faculty was initiated by the headmaster and a faculty was formed. The first faculty meeting was held in Smith's home on Saturday, September 5, 1970.

Both the new faculty and the Board of Governors reflected the make-up of Pinewood's constituency in that the various communities were represented. (Involvement from Pembroke and Bryan County grew as time passed and eventually the board took this into consideration. Early, however, support was primarily from Claxton, Glennville, and Reidsville.) The first faculty was comprised of Ada Lou Waters, Henrietta Rogers, Betty Durrence, Annette Hamner, Thomasine Bargeron, Reba Kennedy, Paula Bush, Lothair Smith, Mable

Adams, Jane Parker, Ruth Anderson, Elizabeth Herritage, and Effie Smith. Betty Smith served as secretary for the first term and J.L. Benton assumed the position of custodian.

Books for the new academy had been received and stored at the home of Headmaster Smith. On September 7, Harold Kemp and Bill Hearn brought a truck and moved the supplies into the new building. Painting and furniture construction continued on into that night before the opening of the institution for classes.

Tuesday, September 8 was the first day of school at Pinewood Christina Academy. As students and parents packed the academic center, Headmaster Smith initiated education at Pinewood with these words form Psalms 34:

> I will bless the Lord at all times; His praise shall continually be in my mouth.
> O Magnify the Lord with me, and let us exalt His name together. Come, ye children, hearken unto me: I will teach you the fear of the Lord.

Enrollment that first term was 252 students in grades one through eight. The major emphases were established that term in the minds of children enrolled. The new faculty responded to the philosophy presented by the headmaster and a general feeling of accomplishment against formidable odds was experienced! As is true in almost all cases wherein something new is attempted, there was misunderstanding and criticism from people who did not choose to participate. This however, quickly began to change as Pinewood became a reality. The spiritual emphasis, the emphasis upon basic education and the upholding of American values became evident and resulted in many persons joining the enterprise as things progressed.

During the first five weeks of classes, interest in some type of athletic program surfaced. From the beginning, the officials of the academy agreed that priorities must be kept in the proper order, but this interest in sports required consideration. Intramural football was organized with Bernie Anderson and Lamar Hendrix taking the lead in coaching. The first game ended in a tied score of 8-8, appropriately enough. Overtures now were made to Robert Toombs Academy in Lyons and the first competition was established. Pinewood played its first football game against another school on November 12, defeating Robert Toombs 18-14.

Other activities which were to become traditional began during the first term at Pinewood. The first Christmas program was held on December 8, involving grades 6, 7, and 8. Effie Smith directed the event. Then on Sunday, April 4, 1971, the first Palm Sunday program was given. Various programs were produced involving all the students.

Construction on the Upper School Building was begun during the spring of 1971. With Hines Daniel as building chairman, the construction was completed in advance of the second term of classes. The structure offered classrooms for grades eight through twelve, a gymnasium in its center, a lunchroom, laboratory, library, and offices.

The second term at Pinewood saw 452 enrolled in grades one through eleven. With Ruth Anderson having replaced Jane Parker during the first term the faculty members returned for the second year with the addition of the following teachers: Louisa Todd, Leigh Threlkeld, Dana Beasley, Jan Rogers, Elaine Dreggors, Joe Eason, Barbara Howard, Wayne Buffington, L.W. Bush, and Ralph Walton. Bush was employed at that time not only as a member of the high school faculty, but to serve as Athletic Director for the developing athletics program. In similar fashion, Ralph Walton served as Curriculum Director. Ruby Cooper and Geraldine Williamson joined the office staff and Martha Benton began a long tenure as director of the lunchroom.

In following years, Pinewood Christian Academy continued to develop and, in many instances to innovate in academic matters. Enrollment eventually soared well over six-hundred and a kindergarten program was added. A college credits program was begun in 1976-77 and for several terms offered first-year college courses though joint enrollment with Brewton-Parker College. Headmaster Smith was active in assisting in the formation of several other private schools and eventually served as First Vice-president of S.E.A.I.S., the largest private school association in Georgia. The academy became recognized as a leader in traditional education, and eventually, as a power in sports competition. Information and advice was often requested by other private schools and, upon a few occasions, by public schools in the state.

The success of Pinewood Christian Academy came from the dream of excellence, independence, and commitment. Jesus Christ was presented as life's necessity and in return He blessed the efforts of common people who were willing to work for what they believed.

O.H. "Tab" Smith was the first headmaster at Pinewood Christian Academy, and he became known as the "Father of Pinewood." (1970 photo courtesy of O.H. "Tab" Smith)

Pinewood Academy's groundbreaking took place May 25, 1970. O.H. "Tab" Smith looks on as Bill Hearn lifts the first spade full of dirt. (1970 photos on this page courtesy of O.H. "Tab" Smith)

Original Pinewood Christian Academy Board of Governors. *Left to right:* Calvin Brewton, Thomas Scott, Hugh Cooper, Charles Strickland, Ralph Dixon, Bill Hearn, Dan Eden, Sterling Bargeron, Jimmy Rogers, Hines Daniel, Dr. Charles Drake, Albert Parker, Jimmy Kennedy, Harold Kemp, H.C. ("C") Hearn, Jr., Tab Smith, and Don Cobb.

Pinewood's Directors burn their note of indebtedness in the mid-1970s. Due to the tremendous success of the school, the directors retired the note early. *Foreground, Left to right:* Albert Parker, Bill Hearn, and Lewis Smith. (Photos courtesy of O.H. "Tab" Smith)

A series of fund raising concerts helped Pinewood pay off its debt early. Here we see a young Dolly Parton and Porter Wagner on Pinewood's stage.

Pinewood Academy 219

Pinewood played its first football game with Robert Toombs Academy in November of 1970. Pinewood defeated Robert Toombs 18-14. (1970 photos on this page courtesy of O.H. "Tab" Smith)

Pinewood's first football team in 1970. Bernie Anderson *(center, last row)* was the head coach.

Pinewood School in 1995.

PINEWOOD CHRISTIAN ACADEMY
UPPER SCHOOL BUILDING

DEDICATED IN HONOR OF
ALBERT PARKER

FOR HIS FAITHFUL BENEVOLENCE AND LOVING
SUPPORT OF PINEWOOD CHRISTIAN ACADEMY.

HIS DEDICATED EFFORTS AND INFLUENCE HAVE
HELPED MAKE PINEWOOD CHRISTIAN ACADEMY
A UNIQUE REALITY, OFFERING A QUALITY
EDUCATION IN A CHRISTIAN ENVIRONMENT.

ERECTED 1971
DEDICATED 1988

Albert Parker was one of the most generous benefactors of Pinewood.

Pinewood sign on 292.

Pinewood Football Stadium.

APPENDIX F

Bellville Businesses

Bellville's Businesses

One of the pioneer businesses of Bellville still in existence today, is the Daniel Lumber Company. E.B. (Knuck) Daniel began operating his sawmill in 1889, producing much of the lumber used to build the homes and businesses of the Bellville section. "Knuck" Daniel's son, O.H. Daniel, continued the tradition and, by 1939, operated one of the "most modern" sawmills in the area. The mill had the capacity to saw almost any size lumber, and also had a planing mill to turn out the finished product. According to an advertisement, the accuracy of the mill "makes their product highly satisfactory to the customer who is saved many extra labor dollars by having material that will fit and does not need to be reworked on the job."[1] Today, the Daniel family continues to operate their building materials business in Bellville.

During the 1950s, Peninsula Lumber Company operated a large sawmill on the eastern edge of Bellville at the present site of Gillman Paper Company woodyard. Bill Doster was the sawmill manager. Peninsula leased the property from Charlie Johnson. In 1955 the company sustained $50,000 in damages due to a diesel engine fire. Shortly thereafter the mill began operations again with electric power in place.[2] The mill closed in the early 1960s, and Gillman Paper Woodyard started operation on the site later in the decade.

Warren Wilbanks and his son, Reg, operate one of the state's largest apiary companies. The business, on the western edge of Bellville, is well known to beekeepers throughout the state and nation. Although the enterprise began solely with the production of honey, it expanded to production of packaged bees and raising queens for sale both nationally and internationally. The operation started out on Wilbanks' farm in a small building in 1951 and expanded to a 10,000 square foot Bellville facility in 1975. The Wilbanks family has a long association with beekeeping going back to Wilbanks' grandfather who kept bees for his personal honey use. The family moved from Commerce, Georgia to Evans County in 1948.[3]

Union Camp Corporation opened its world-class Bellville tree nursery in 1958. The Hearn family, including Mae Hearn and Mildred Hearn Shelor, sold the 174 acres, part of the family home place tract, for the tree operation.[4] Senator Herman Talmadge gave the dedication speech wearing his traditional red tie and suspenders. His theme was the importance of the forest industry's new developments in promoting tree farming as key to the expansion of Georgia agriculture. According to *The Claxton Enterprise* newspaper article, "The nursery completes a new link in the chain of developments that are making the pine tree Evans County's major source of revenue." In addition to the acreage used to grow the seedlings, the Bellville facility included a seed orchard for grafting trees and a cold storage plant for maintaining pine seeds. A Union Camp official summed up the nursery's objective with the statement, "We are most desirous of being good neighbors and part of the expanding business life of the area."[5]

The following account describes the first years of the Bellville tree nursery's operation:

> In March 1958, Union Bag-Camp Paper Corporation's Bellville, Georgia nursery was planted for the first time. Enough seeds were sown to produce an anticipated yield of 22,000,000 pine seedlings for the 1958-59 planting season. When the last seedling was lifted, the nursery, which is ideally located and equipped with the latest in modern equipment and facilities, was found to have produced top-grade seedlings. The nursery is staffed by a permanent party of five and provides seasonal employment of thirty-five residents of the Evans County area.[6]

The Claxton Bank opened its Bellville branch, designed to resemble the main office in Claxton, in June of 1974. The Claxton Bank built the branch to better serve the residents of the area and also to provide banking for increased commerce expected from the new Georgia-Pacific plant one-half mile from the eastern limit of Bellville and the recently developed Evans County industrial park located between Bellville and Hagan.[7] A large crowd attended the bank's opening. Located on the site of the old Hearn cotton gin, the bank opened with a deposit by Inman Hearn. The historic significance of the deposit was great, since Hearn formerly worked at the gin on the same location as far back as 1917. Adding to the sentimental significance of the transaction, the check deposited by Inman was payment for his cotton crop. At that time, Inman was one of only two farmers planting cotton in Evans County. June DeLoach, the new branch manager, said of the first deposit, "In the old days people used to drive up to this site and deposit cotton--now they drive up here and deposit money." She then added, "It's all for progress."[8]

One of the most notorious events in Bellville's history occurred on October 16, 1974. The date marked the robbery of the Bellville branch bank. June DeLoach witnessed two armed men getting out of their car and proceeding toward the bank. One carried a pistol and the other a shotgun. She knew it must be a robbery and set off the bank's silent alarm, which also started the camera. The two men entered the bank and instructed DeLoach to open the vault. They then told DeLoach and the two tellers to lie down on the floor behind the teller's cages. In the midst of the robbery, nearby resident Alvin Blalock entered the bank. He and his wife sensed something amiss after seeing the get-away car outside the bank with the engine still running. The robbers instructed Blalock to join the tellers on the floor.

The men entered the vault, loaded approximately $21,000 cash in a black bag, exited the bank, and sped away in their car. Police later found the escape car about 10 miles from Bellville. The FBI and local law enforcement agencies apprehended several suspects in short order. Juries found two of the men guilty in subsequent trials, and the judge sentenced them to jail. A third prime suspect was found not guilty.[9]

Gold Kist Farm Supplies opened its doors in 1967. This business was originally incorporated as the Farmer's Mutual Exchange in Claxton in 1944. The company purchased the land for the store from H.C. Hearn, Sr. in 1965.[10]

Bobby McCoy operates a garage and auto parts store in Bellville. The garage was formerly owned by his father-in-law, Alvin Blalock, and before Blalock, operated by Tom Flanigan. Flanigan operated the shop from 1947 through 1954, when Blalock took over. Prior to Flanigan, the Hearn family managed an International tractor dealership at the site.[11]

One of Bellville's newest businesses is the Anderson House Restaurant. Located in the house formerly owned by the Hearn family, the restaurant provides family dining and catering. The proprietors, Hilda Anderson and Harriett Anderson, have an outstanding reputation for serving some of the finest food in the area.

Notes

[1] "O.H. Daniel, Lumber Manufacturer," *The Claxton Enterprise*, July 20, 1939.

[2] "$50,000 Loss By Fire At Peninsula Lumber," *The Claxton Enterprise*, February 3, 1955. The article went on to say, "At about 11:30 a.m., last Thursday, the lumber company near Bellville caught fire and before apparatus from nearby towns could get it under control over $50,000 worth of machinery and lumber went up in smoke. There was only about fifty percent insurance to cover the loss."

[3] "Local Family Operates One of State's Largest Apiaries," *The Claxton Enterprise*, June 19, 1975.

[4] This was the first of three sales from members of the Hearn family to Union Camp. Emily Hearn Groover, interview with editor, September 23, 1995.

[5] "Union Bag-Camp Opens Large New Tree Nursery at Bellville," *The Claxton Enterprise*, September 18, 1958; On September 2, 1995 the editor interviewed the current manager of the Bellville Tree Nursery, Bill Pryor, and the following is an excerpt. "Don Ryder was the first Bellville supervisor in 1958. John Hamner followed Don. Paul Riggs was next. I've been here since 1983, and really enjoy it. I was here about two years before Paul retired. We've got a good group of people to work with. We only have five full-time employees at this location, but we have our seed orchard just south of here at the Southern States tract. Four or five more people work there.

There has been a lot of pine tree genetics research done at our Bellville facilities. The hard part about genetics research is separating the genetics from the environmental factors. They decided to put in the greenhouses to speed up the process of getting the trees to flower. They did this by controlling the amount of heat, light, water, and fertilizer. The result is a superior pine seedling that is heartier and grows faster.

We have two full-time Ph.D.'s, and four full-time technicians. The nursery never has been a large employer like Claxton Poultry. However, over the years it has provided a lot of seasonal employment. More importantly, it provided winter employment. This was very important in the 1950s and 60s. Farmers then didn't have much work in November and on through the winter. As a result, most of our workers were local farmers. Now farming has become a year round business, so we're hiring people with less experience on the farm. A lot of them are young people who get their start here.

Union Camp looked at about five different sites before they chose Bellville for the nursery. They took into consideration the soil type, topography, and location. The original site was about 80 acres, and it was almost perfectly flat. This was important because in the pine tree operation, we keep the soil bare a good bit of the time. The location was also important by how it fit in geographically with the Union Camp Savannah mill's territory. This site is almost dead center in the Savannah mill's procurement area. The distance to get to the various company-owned forests is about the same. We can deliver the seedlings and be back within a day. Yes, Bellville and Union Camp pine trees have had a long and important association. It's been a mutually good relationship."

[6] Union Camp Press release, 1958, obtained from Bellville Nursery; Another news release of December 12, 1981 highlights the career of long-time nursery supervisor Paul Riggs. "Paul Riggs -- Mr. Green Thumb"

It is an understatement of some magnitude to say Paul Riggs has a "green thumb."

The supervisor for the Bellville, Georgia, tree nursery of Union Camp Corporation has been responsible for growing over 620 million seedlings over the last quarter of a century. Indeed, his thumb may be the greenest.

He has actually brought to life a forest of 850,000 acres, which could eventually result in the harvesting of an estimated 25 million cords of pine pulpwood. At the present rate of consumption, this amount would supply the Savannah pulp and paper mill, the world's largest, for 16 years.

Growing seedlings in the fertile soil of Evans County near Claxton came naturally to Paul Riggs. He spent most of his early years growing cotton, corn, and tobacco on the family farm near the predominantly agricultural community of Bellville.

Also included in this early work experience, appropriately enough, was the cutting and shipping of pulpwood for the Savannah mill.

When the company decided to build a nursery at Bellville, Riggs was an obvious choice to ramrod the operation from day one. He was employed as construction foreman and upon completion of the project in 1957, he was named nursery foreman. He was promoted to nursery supervisor in 1973 with overall responsibility for the Bellville operation.

Riggs, obviously, plays a key role in the management of Union Camp's woodlands. The quality and quantity of pine seedlings grown at Bellville have a significant effect on the growth and development of the hundreds of thousands of acres of pine plantations established from these seedlings.

Fred W. Haeussler, Savannah Woodland Region Land Manager for Union Camp, recognized Riggs' contribution to the company's forest regeneration efforts when he observed, "You would have to search long and hard to find a person who could maintain the degree of excellence that Paul Riggs has at Bellville through the years. He is an uncommon man dedicated to his job and this dedication is apparent in the quality of the products he grows. We depend on him in many ways."

Actually, Riggs' reputation as a nurseryman goes beyond Union Camp. In a select group of southern forest tree nurseryman, he is recognized as a leader -- "the best."

The man just knows how to grow pine trees!

[7] Georgia-Pacific purchased the property for their pine lumber and chip mill from the Charlie Johnson, Sr. estate in 1972. This land was originally part of the Jackie Brewton homestead. Editor.

[8] "Branch Bank's First Depositor--Once Ginned Cotton on Same Site," *The Claxton Enterprise*, June 6, 1974. The other farmer still growing cotton in Evans County was Winton Bell.

[9] Aubrey Strickland, *It Can Happen to Any Country Banker*, privately published, 1995, pp. 37-57.

[10] Letter from James Bruner, Gold Kist, to editor, October 12, 1995.

[11] Tommy Flanigan, interview with editor, February 19, 1996.

Making one of the first oil deliveries in the area that included Bellville are Jake Hollingsworth, *left*, and Roger Wood. (Circa 1909 photo courtesy of Georgia Department of Archives)

Modern-day view of the Bellville Depot. This train station was once the hub of business activity for Bellville. The City of Bellville plans to restore this building to its former appearance through a historic preservation project.

Remains of Tom Wood's turpentine still, a once thriving Bellville business.

This outhouse once served the Bellville depot. It still stands south of the railroad.

Remnants of Tom Wood's turpentine still. These metal cups were once used to collect the "gum" for the still.

Bellville Businesses

Inman Hearn standing on the dock of his Bellville gin. His father, C.W. Hearn, built the original gin south of the railroad and in 1917 moved it to the site where the bank now sits. (Photos on this page courtesy of Emily Hearn Groover)

Hearn Gin operation in 1960s. The Hearn gin provided employment for many Bellville residents over the years. The Murray gin pictured was one of the most modern in the area.

Inman Hearn shown with blue lupine demonstration plants. In 1940 blue lupine was first planted in the state and Bellville was one of three demonstration sites. The plant was a soil builder for tomato fields, but was discontinued because it proved toxic to livestock.

These building along the railroad in Bellville have been owned by the Hearn family for many years. The right portion of the building served as a cotton seed storage shed. The Hearns also used it as a location for packing and shipping tomato plants.

1950s photo of Peninsula Lumber Company. Located on the eastern edge of Bellville on Highway 280, this site is now occupied by Gillman Paper Company Woodyard.

Circa 1955 photo of Daniel sawmill in Bellville. (Photo courtesy of Walter Emmett Daniel)

Three generations of the Walter Emmett Daniel family. *Left to right:* Emmett, Walter Emmett, and Emmett, Jr.

Union Camp Pinetree Nursery is located just south of Bellville.

Above: Nursery workers "lift" seedlings for transshipment. (1984 photo courtesy of Union Camp)

Left and below: Senator Herman Talmadge at dedication of nursery in 1958. The senator wore his traditional red tie and suspenders. (Photos courtesy of Union Camp)

As Union Camp Nursery supervisor, Paul Riggs ("Mr. Greenthumb") oversaw the production of millions of pine seedlings. (1981 photo courtesy of Union Camp)

Don Ryder was the first Bellville Union Camp Nursery surpervisor. (1960 photo courtesy of Union Camp)

Workers at the Bellville Nursery in 1960. *Standing, left to right:* Lawson Lewis, Paul Riggs, Lowel Helmuth, Velma DeLoach, Rommie Thompson, Elma Hearn, Willie Roundtree, Myrtle Lee Roberts, Billy Anderson, Bessie Boyette, J.E. Boyette, Gertie Waters, Lindell Calloway, Emily Odum, Terry Branch, Ruth Berner, Maury Wasson. *Kneeling:* John Clark, Don Ryder (Nursery Superintendent), Ellie Hackle, Rupert Odum, Mark Odum, and Wilton Threatt. (Photo courtesy of Union Camp)

In 1974 the Claxton Bank constructed the Bellville Branch on the former site of the Hearn Gin. Inman Hearn observes progress on the building. (Photo courtesy of Emily Hearn Groover)

Above: June DeLoach, manager of the Bellville branch of the Claxton Bank.

Left: Bellville Branch of Claxton Bank as it looks today.

Bellville business Goldkist was once called Farmer's Mutual Exchange.

The Bellville branch of the Claxton Bank was the scene of a robbery in October 1974. The bank's surveilance camera provided these photos. Pictured is one of the two robbers *(right)* and C.B. Eddins, a Lance snack vendor who happened onto the scene. (Photos courtesy of Aubrey Strickland)

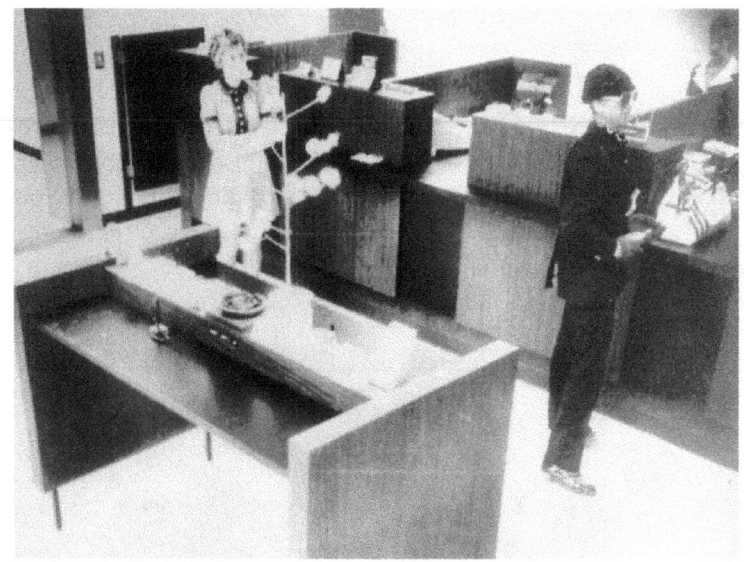

Branch manager, June DeLoach, *left,* watches as the second robber fills bag with cash. The FBI arrested suspects in the robbery a few weeks after the crime took place.

Bernie's Store

Bernie Anderson, local merchant, bought the land where the former Hearn store stood. He built a new store there in 1972. The Bellville post office is on the left.

Bernie Anderson

Bobby McCoy operates an auto repair business in Bellville. His father-in-law Alvin Blalock previously ran a similiar business at the same site.

McCoy's auto repair and hardware store.

Bobby McCoy

Wilbanks Apiaries is one of the largest such companies in the state. Warren Wilbanks, *below left*, and his son, Reg, ship packaged bees and honey to domestic and foreign customers.

The Wilbanks Apiaries produces honey for world-wide shipment.

Reg Wilbanks *(right)* inspects packaged bees prepared for shipment.

One of the area's finest restaurants, The Anderson House, is located in the historic former Hearn home constructed in the early 1890s. Proprietors are Hilda Anderson *(left)* and her daughter Harriett.

APPENDIX G

Historic Houses of the Bellville Area

Historic Homes of the Bellville Area

The homes of a community reflect its character. Bellville has many interesting, beautiful, and well-maintained homes.[1] This appendix will highlight those houses of the immediate area that are at least 75 years old. Among the historically significant homes in the town of Bellville are two of the county's few remaining ante-bellum dwellings: the James B. Smith house and the Berry Brewton house. Located four miles northeast of Bellville is another ante-bellum home, the Jonathan Bacon Brewton house. There are others with documented histories dating to the 1870s. However, the majority of the older homes located in the town limits are from the period subsequent to the railroad's arrival in 1890. Among the architectural types found in the Bellville area are plantation plain, hall-and-parlor, shotgun, Georgian plan, and bungalow.

Many of these houses have charm, grace, and character. When they were built, however, they had squeaky floors, were cold in the winter, and had primitive kitchens by today's standards. Further, they were frequently out-of-plum and were not perfectly level or square. Nonetheless, their workmanship and character gives these houses qualities of both dignity and style. It took great craftsmanship and skill to build these structures. Builders constructed these homes with hand planes and saws, not the power tools available today.

Deed records indicate the sale of Bellville house lots beginning in 1890.[2] Soon thereafter, houses began to spring up in the new town. Early photographs reveal that owners did not always immediately remove the stumps from their house lots and that the roads were often muddy and rutted. However, by the mid-1890s Bellville assumed the aspects of a rustic town with its stores, residences, and a few streets.

Several advances in house construction were in place when residents built Bellville's early homes. More efficient steam power had replaced most of the older water powered sawmills. Hence, sawed lumber was available in quantities. Nails replaced the previously used wooden pegs. These early nails were square in shape and differed in appearance from the machined ones seen today. Nails allowed use of smaller dimensioned lumber which, in turn, provided more flexibility and economy in building.

There are several common traits of most of the architecture of Bellville and the surrounding area. The majority of the nineteenth-century homes are of the style architecture relating to a hall-and-parlor or modified "dogtrot" type in that the structures had a spacious hallway going down the center of the house with rooms on either side.[3] This vernacular house feature provided a breezeway to help deal with the dreadfully hot summers. High ceilings in the rooms also contributed to good ventilation. Large windows allowed maximum light to penetrate the rooms. Builders covered most interior walls with beaded tongue and groove pine boards.

Builders often separated the kitchen from the rest of the house. Sometimes a breezeway attached the kitchen and in other cases the kitchen was a contiguous part of the back end of the house. The purpose of this arrangement was to prevent possible kitchen fires from spreading, and to keep kitchen heat away from the living quarters. Fireplaces were normally on the outside walls of the house. Still another feature of these early houses was the raised flooring. Owners built the homes far above the ground to promote ventilation and also to lessen the threat of termites. For example, at one time Bellville's James B. Smith house was so far above the ground that cotton bales could be stored underneath.

Another early component of homes for families with a large number of children were the "boys' houses." Families built these smaller structures behind the main house to provide a "dorm" for the boys of the family. At least two of Bellville's older homes, the Berry Brewton and Hearn-Parker-Cox houses, had this arrangement.[4]

One of the main elements of landscaping of early Bellville was the swept yard. Residents typically kept yards free of grass, weeds, and ground cover. In some cases homeowners even swept their yards in ornamental patterns. They most often made the yard brooms from gallberry bushes because of the stiffness of the branches. Residents considered this dominant landscape feature a sign of good housekeeping, and it also served as a means to help keep rodents and snakes away from the yards.[5]

Judging from vintage photographs of Bellville's older homes, fences were a prevalent feature. These fences were often of the picket style for the town's lots and the rail type on the surrounding farms. The fences served several important functions. First, they separated the house from the livestock that had free range of the area. This measure allowed the enjoyment of flowers and other amenities out of the reach of hungry animals. Fences also served to keep the children in designated play areas and protect them from the livestock. A 200 pound sow could wreak havoc to an unsuspecting child if she thought her piglets were in danger. Some residents of the town today remember free roaming livestock as late as the 1930s.[6]

Another feature of all of Bellville's older homes is the presence of a prominent porch. In the long, hot summers the porch was a gathering place for people and, no doubt, their pets. Often situated to catch the prevailing summer breezes, the porches provided shade without confinement. Men enjoyed this part of the house for relaxing and visiting. Women often found porches an ideal place to do chores like mending or shelling peas and butter beans. Another important function was to serve as a location for "sparking" among the young folks. Many of Bellville's young men could trace their first kiss to a girl sitting in a swing on a front porch. Indeed, front porch swings contributed to many successful courtships in Bellville.

The early building material of choice was heart pine. Until it all but disappeared, Southern longleaf heart pine was the preferred wood in the South from Colonial times. Heart pine has deep roots in the history and architectural heritage of the United States. The first colonists discovered the longleaf pine growing in a relatively small area along the Southeastern seaboard. The 150 to 450 year old trees grew to 170 feet tall and were five feet in diameter. They produced close-grained heartwood that proved to be unexcelled as building material for the times. Heart pine is known for its strength, durability, and beauty. However, these qualities were to hasten the eventual downfall of this prized lumber's availability. Because of the great demand for heart pine, combined with improper turpentining and reforestation, this valuable resource almost disappeared. Found mostly in protected forests, today less than one percent of the virgin growth longleaf pine remains. The Bellville area was rich with this resource until the turn of the century when the supply began to dwindle. Many of the area's finest historic homes are of this material.

For those starting farms in the area, the trees that provided the lumber for the houses were normally cut from stands on the property. First, the house site had to be cleared of the virgin forests that covered it. After property owners cut the trees with two-man crosscut saws, mule teams dragged the timber off in carts to the sawmills. Farmers burned the stumps, dug them out by hand, and then pulled them away by mule teams. The builders sawed the logs into lumber at nearby mills in Bellville or the surrounding area.

There were several prominent builders from the Bellville area. A very early one in the section was Amos Hearn. He died in the Civil War, but before the war he built several notable residences including the A.D. Eason house in the Undine community. Simon Hearn and Wiley Rowe constructed the Bellville Academy in 1890. After the town began, Rowe was a leading builder in Bellville, and he constructed several of the town's original dwellings. Some years later, Nollie Parker's legendary skill as a quality carpenter was well known throughout the county.[7]

The following is a survey of the homes of the Bellville area that are at least 75 years old. Included are photos of both current and past houses. Photos without credits were taken by the editor in 1995/1996.

The Hearn House, circa 1917. Mae, Mildred, Martha, and Eulalia Hearn (on porch).

C.W. Hearn House

This house at the northeast corner of the Highway 280 and Highway169 intersection is one of the oldest in the town. Originally constructed for Tom Grice, the house was purchased by C.W. and Eulalia Hearn in 1899. C.W. Hearn was a store owner, gin operator and town postmaster. The Hearns had seven children, five of whom were born in the house. Two of Hearn's daughters, Mae and Martha, inherited the house and lived there until their deaths in 1970 and 1987, respectively. In 1987, their niece, Emily Hearn Groover, inherited the house, and her son, Alan, and his wife Dawn lived there until December 1991. The house now serves as a family dining restaurant called The Anderson House.

Since the house was only a short distance from the Bellville School, the Hearns graciously opened their doors to offer room and board to the educators who came to teach. Many of the schoolteachers, while staying with the Hearns, met local boys, married, and made Evans County their home. When you walk through the front door into the parlor, you almost expect to hear the laughter and soft whispers of young ladies and their beaux talking of future plans.[8]

The Hearn house is a one-story, hall-and-parlor with rear ell house with a pressed tin, gabled roof. The windows are one-over-one, and the wood panel door has sidelights. The wrap-around shed porch has tapered posts on brick piers. The foundation is brick pier and the house has exterior brick chimneys. There are numerous out-buildings.[9]

James B. Smith House

One of the oldest houses in the county is the James Bell Smith house located just south of the Highway 280 and Highway 169 intersection. James B. Smith purchased this land in 1851, and the house dates to 1854 or 1855.[10] Smith was the son of James and Frances "Fanny" Bell Smith, and the grandson of Simon and Mary Smith. Simon Smith was a Revolutionary War soldier from North Carolina. The Smith family owned thousands of acres of land from Bellville south to Bull Creek. James B. Smith's mother, Fanny Bell, is the person for whom residents named the town. The current owner of the house is Walter Emmett Daniel, a descendant of James B. Smith.

The house is of original hand-hewn log construction and weatherboards now cover the exterior. Wooden pegs hold the logs together. Dovetail notching, providing strength and durability, is evident in the joints. The house is an example of the plantation plain type and is one-and-a-half-story with a crimped tin gable roof. It has six-over-six (refers to the number of window panes in upper and lower sash) windows, wood panel doors, and a full-width shed porch with square posts. The foundation is brick pier and the exterior brick chimney is corbel capped. The home has solid shutters on the upstairs story and a detached kitchen or "boys' room." There are outbuildings including barns, crib, shed, and tobacco barn.

"Boys' room" at the rear of house.

Logs are full dovetail notched and show expert craftsmanship.

Historic Houses

Views of the James B. Smith House *Clockwise from top:* Cantilevered roof surrounds the chimney, porch railing connected by notching, doors include handmade latch, wooden door latch, upstairs view of top floor, hand-hewn timbers still bear the mark of broad axes, and wooden shutters add to the home's charm.

(Late 1890s photo courtesy Dorothy Durrence)

Bascom Tippins House

Located just northwest of the Highway 280 and Highway 292 intersection on Main Street is the Bascom Tippins house. Tippins (1875-1939) was one of Bellville's most famous sons. He was a state legislator for ten years beginning in the late 1920s and was also president of the First National Bank of Claxton. He operated a general store across the street from his home for many years. His second wife, Mamie Mathews Tippins, lived in the home until her death in 1990. Bascom Tippins' daughter, Mary Tippins Conner, currently owns the house.[11]

The house is one-story with a weatherboard exterior. It is an L-shaped house with crimped tin roofing and a multi-gabled roof. It has two-over-two windows, a wood panel door with sidelights, and a wrap-around shed porch with round posts. The house sits on a brick pier foundation and has an exterior end corbel capped brick chimney. The house had a white picket fence for many years. The date of construction is early 1900s.

(Circa 1900 photo courtesy of Emily Hearn Groover)

H.C. Hearn House

Caughey and Grace Hearn lived in this house for many years, and Miss Grace still owns it. Located just north of the Bascom Tippins house on Main Street, this two-story home dates to the 1890s. Wiley Rowe constructed this dwelling. Before the Hearns, Emily Parker and Alene Parker lived in the house.[12]

The two-story house has a weatherboard exterior with a crimped tin, hipped roof. The windows are two-over-two. The front door is wood paneled and the house features a wrap-around shed porch with square posts. It has a brick pier foundation with an interior brick chimney. The house originally had a second floor front porch. From the vintage photo above, several other alterations are evident.

Above: Circa 1905 photo courtesy Emily Hearn Groover

Bird-Wood House

Located west of Main Street and just north of the Highway 169 and 292 intersection, this house belonged to Bellville merchant Adam Bird at one time. Bird previously lived with his mother in this home. Later, State Senator Tom Wood bought the house and lived there until his death in 1971. His wife Ella Lee also lived in the home until her death. A daughter, Elizabeth, lives in the house today. Tom Wood was a Bellville businessman who owned a store, turpentine still, and trucking business.

The L-shaped, one-story house has an aluminum siding exterior, with an asphalt shingled, gabled roof. The windows are one over one and the front door is wood panel. The full-width shed porch has wrought iron posts. The siding and wrought iron railings are a later alteration. The house has a brick pier foundation and exterior brick chimney. The three-sided bay at front is a significant feature. Early photos indicate the bay once had windows.

Sheppard House

Located on Main Street, this house was occupied by Dr. Sheppard, a pharmacist. The house dates to approximately 1922. Other previous residents of the house include Edward and Onita Blalock and Willie Mable Ponder Bennett. Juanita Branch currently owns this house.[13]

The house is one-story bungalow style and has a weatherboard exterior. The windows are two-over-two, and the front door is wood paneled. The porch is full-width hipped with square posts. It has a crimped tin hipped roof with a shed dormer, brick pier foundation, and an interior corbel capped brick chimney.

Above: John Wood and his wife, Eveline Elizabeth Durrence Wood, and family pose in front of their home. (Photo courtesy of the late George Durrence)

Right: The second John M. Wood home was moved to Main Street in the 1960s.

John M. Wood House

John M. Wood was a farmer and large landowner in the Bellville area. He was the son of Roger Wood, from England, and Nancy Tippins Wood from Tattnall County. John Wood married Evelyn Durrence. Their prominent two-story house was on the northwest edge of town. It had a two-story front porch with gingerbread accents.

The house burned in the early 1900s, and a one-story house was built on the same location. Nollie Parker constructed this second structure. Some of the original out-buildings are still present at the house site.

In the early 1960s, John's son, Roger, had the one-story house moved to its present location on the west side of Main Street. The house lot previously belonged to the Bickley's. Stokes Bickley married Mattie Wood, Roger's sister. Roger's widow, Emily, currently lives in the house. According to her, the interior of the house is much like it was when occupied by the John Wood family.[14]

The house has a weatherboard exterior and asphalt shingles on a hipped roof. The windows are two-over-two, and the house has a wood panel door. The house has a shed porch with square posts. The structure is on a brick pier foundation and has an exterior end brick chimney. Wallace Parker renovated the house after Wood moved it to its current location. The house dates from the early 1920s.

(1960 photo courtesy of Emily Hearn Groover)

Sallie and Maude Brewton House

Sarah Martha "Sallie" Brewton and Maude Brewton lived in a home at the southwest corner of the intersection of Main Street and Brewton Street. Maude was Sallie's niece. Sallie's brother Wade also lived in this home at one time. Maude and Wade's parents were William and Dora Brewton. Sallie was the daughter of Simon J. and Matilda Brewton. The Hendry family lived in this home prior to the Brewtons. This home was moved to Appling County in the 1970s.[15]

O.H. Daniel Sr. House

O.H Daniel, Sr. was in the sawmill business all his life. Daniel's son, Hines, was the first mayor of Bellville, and was instrumental in the town's development. O.H. Daniel, Sr. was the son of Enoch B. Daniel, originally from Liberty County, and Leah Hodges Daniel. This house was one of the first in the town to have running water. After O.H. Daniel built the house at the northwest corner of Main Street and Brewton Street, his brother Jim Daniel and wife, Jeanette, lived there until they built their house across the street. O.H. Daniel and wife, Helen, moved back from Soperton and lived in the house for their remaining years. The children of Helen and O.H. Daniel, Sr. currently own the home.[16]

This one-story house is a Georgian plan type with weatherboard exterior and asphalt shingles on a gabled and hipped roof. The windows are two-over-two, and the front door is wood paneled with sidelights. The house has a wrap-around shed porch with tapered posts on brick piers. It has a brick pier foundation and interior end corbel capped brick chimney. There is a shed out-building on the north side of the home.

Ross Daniel House

Lee Daniel, brother of O.H. Daniel, Sr. built his home on Main Street just south of his brother's house. Lee and his wife, Mary Holder Daniel, lived in the home, then built and moved into a smaller home down the street. The house was rented by several families including the Sheppards and Will and Gladys Williams. Lee Daniel then sold the house to his brother, Ross Daniel and his wife, Thessille Williams Daniel. Ross Daniel operated sawmills in various locations before he moved back to Bellville. Willie Mable Ponder lived in the home after the Daniels. Bellville Mayor, Jerry Coleman, and his wife, Ona, currently own this home.[17]

This house is a one-story Georgian plan house with asphalt shingle roofing on a gabled and hipped roof. The windows are one-over-one and the front door is wood paneled with sidelights. The house has a wrap-around shed porch with square posts, and has an interior corbel capped brick chimney. The house also has shed out-buildings.

(1992 photo courtesy Altamaha Georgia Southern Regional Development Center)

Jim Daniel House

The Jim Daniel home was across the street and west of the O.H. Daniel, Sr. home. Jim Daniel was the son of Enoch B. Daniel and brother of O.H. Daniel, Sr. and Ross Daniel. Jim Daniel married Jeanette Folsom. The three Daniel brothers lived on three sides of the intersection of Main Street and Brewton Street (old Bellville to Manassas Road). Jim Daniel operated a sawmill with Herman Nease and also hauled lumber for a number of years. The Jim Daniel home was on the northwest corner of the intersection. This house was moved about four miles beyond Brewton Bridge off of Highway 169 in the late 1980s.[18]

It was a one-story, weatherboard exterior double-pen house. It had asphalt shingles and a gabled roof. The home had two-over-two windows and a wrap-around shed porch with square posts. It had a brick pier foundation and interior corbel capped brick chimney.

Looking east from the Enoch Daniel home after a severe storm about 1918. The Sallie Brewton home is in the center portion of the photo. (Photo courtesy Lois Parker Turner)

Enoch B. Daniel Home

Enoch Daniel, an early resident and sawmill operator, built his home on the northwest side of town near the site on which the Mallard home now stands. Enoch Daniel contributed greatly to the development of Bellville, supporting both the Bellville Academy and Methodist church. The above photograph was taken from the steps of Daniel's home. The picket fence was typical for older homes in town. The Daniel House no longer exists.

(Photo courtesy of Delma Daniel)

Dr. Loving Nichols House

Dr. Loving Nichols was one of the first doctors to arrive in the new town of Bellville. He moved his office to Bellville from Bay Branch in the 1890s, and his home also dates from this period. He practiced in Bellville and was prominent in the town's affairs until poor health forced him to move out west. His home was located in the eastern section of town.[19]

This home appears to have had a broken-gable type roof, and was different from many other Bellville homes in that the front porch roof was contiguous with the main house roof line. The picket fence was a prominent feature. Bellville photographer A.H. Prince made the above picture.

Tenant Cabin

Pictured above is a typical single-pen type cabin occupied by many of the railroad section hands. These cabins once dotted the landscape and typically had board-and-batten construction. Once located on Highway 292 west of town, this cabin no longer exists.

House of Paul LeGrand's Cook

This small house sits behind Bernie Anderson's home on Highway 292 just west of his store. It was a cook's house for the Paul LeGrand family, who previously lived next door. The house is complete with its own fireplace. Paul LeGrand's daughter, Paulene, taught kindergarten in this small house for a number of years.[20]

(1972 photo courtesy of Devane Parker Lewis)

Nollie Parker House

Nollie Parker built his home with lumber from the old Bellville schoolhouse which he purchased for $300 in the late 1920s. Parker was a master builder who constructed the Tattnall County Campground tabernacle and many other structures around the Bellville area.[21]

The smokehouse remains on the grounds today at the former house site on the north side of Highway 280 about one-third mile west of the Bellville Methodist Church. After Mrs. Parker's death in 1971, the family sold the home and land to Inman Hearn, Walter Emmett Daniel, O.H. Daniel, Jr., and Harold Kemp. Later Kemp bought Hearn's interest in the house.

(Photo from *History of our Locale*)

Hearn-Parker-Cox House

The land located along Highway 280 at the Evans/Tattnall County line was part of an original 400 acre state land grant to Jeremiah McDaniel in 1804. John Chadburn Parker bought the place from the Amos J. Hearn estate in 1866. Amos died in the Civil War. Hearn and his wife Nancy Emily Brewton built the original house. It was a log home, with a later-added kitchen. His son, Charlie (C.W.) Hearn, was born in this house April 11, 1864, just three days before Amos died in Savannah. Emily married John Chadburn Parker second. Lilah Cox, Emily's daughter, later occupied the house. Tommy Flanigan dismantled the structure about 1993.[22]

Noted architectural features of this home were a cantilevered roof over the chimney and a full-width front porch.

Johnson Tenant House

Located approximately 100 yards east of the C.W. Hearn house on Highway 280 was the Mac Johnson tenant house. This house, torn down in 1993, was the house in which families working on the Johnson farm lived. Sidney Johnson and later his son, Jim, owned this house.

The house was a one-story bungalow with weatherboard exterior. It had crimped tin roofing and a gabled roof. It had six-over-six windows and a wood panel door. The full-width gabled porch had square posts. The house had a brick pier foundation and an interior brick chimney. Of modest size and without paint, the house was typical of bungalows built in the area in the 1920s.

Mac Johnson House

Located on the eastern edge of town south of where the railroad track crosses Highway 280 is the Mac Johnson house. Mac married Martha P. (Dolly) Brewton, daughter of Berry Brewton, and this land was part of the property given to her father in 1860 by his father, Benjamin Brewton. With the help of local builder Wiley Rowe, Johnson constructed the house about 1901. The editor of this book is the current owner of the house and farm known as "Johnson Hill."[23]

The one-story house has a weatherboard exterior and was originally a central hall, L-shaped house. During a 1988 renovation of the house, the editor removed the kitchen from the rear of the house. The gabled roof is crimped tin. The house is on a brick pier foundation, and the structure is of heart pine construction throughout. The 8 by 10 inch sills are hand-hewn. The six-over-six windows are not original to the house. There are two exterior and one back-to-back interior brick chimneys. The full-width, hipped front porch has turned spindle posts. The site contains several original out-buildings.

Berry Brewton House

Another of Bellville's ante-bellum homes is the Berry Brewton house. Located on Warren Wilbanks' farm on the eastern edge of Bellville north of Highway 280, the house originally was on the site where the Wilbanks' house now sits. In the late 1950s, Wilbanks moved the Brewton house down a lane about 100 yards east of its original location. Constructed by William E. Tippins in 1856, the house was blown down in a storm and Tippins rebuilt it in 1857 or 1858. In 1860 Brewton paid Tippins $1400 for the home and 393 acres of land. Brewton's youngest son, Theodore, lived in this home for many years. Wilbanks' grandson now occupies the house.[24]

Builders constructed the one-and-a-half-story, plantation plain type house with extremely wide rough-sawed boards of heart pine. Brewton sawed the boards at his father's mill on Cedar Creek. The house has a gabled roof, while the porch has a shed roof.

Left: Part of an original rail fence at the Berry Brewton farm. Rail fences were once a familiar sight at the Bellville area old homesteads.

Jackie Brewton House

Located on the eastern edge of Bellville, the Jackie Brewton home was originally north of the old Dublin-Savannah road. However, when the state paved Highway 280 in the 1930s, the highway engineers changed the road's course to the north side of the home. Instead of turning the house around to face the new road, the state paid Brewton to build a front porch on what had been the back of his house. This wood frame house was moved from the site in the 1960s. The above photo, taken in the early 1950s, shows Brewton with four of his siblings, *left to right*, Jackie Brewton, Mary B. Collins, Bob Brewton, George Brewton, and Theodore Brewton. The house was on land given to Jackie Brewton by his father, Benjamin Berrian Brewton, in 1887. The southern portion of this farm is now the site of the Georgia Pacific plant.

Named for President Andrew Jackson, "Uncle" Jackie Brewton possessed a remarkable memory and was an expert on Evans County family history. According to Judge Harry DeLoach, Brewton was often called upon to appear at the courthouse to testify whether a prospective juror could serve based on kinship to the defendant in the case. Brewton, a life-long farmer and resident of the Bellville area, lived at his home until his death in 1957.

Built in the early 1890s, the house was constructed with the help of Joe Hendrix. The frame house replaced Brewton's log home located at the same site. The weatherboard exterior home had two-over-two windows and a tin roof. Two log out-buildings are still present on the site.[25]

Above: William H. Hodges House circa 1910. (Photo courtesy Tommy Flanigan)

Left: Hodges House demolition in 1993.

William H. Hodges House

The William (Bill) Hodges House was once located 1.7 miles southeast of Bellville on the Bill Hodges Road (county road 36). Tommy Flanigan dismantled the home in 1994. Hodges (1851-1939) constructed this home about 1906. The state originally granted the land to William Hodges' father, Irwin Jackson Hodges (1824-1897) in 1848.[26] The Ball family lived in this house for a number of years.

The home was two-story and had a weatherboard exterior. It was a Victorian-era house with a combination of wooden and later-added asphalt shingles on a multi-gabled roof. It had two-over-two windows and a three-sided projected bay. The front door was one-half glass and one-half wood with sidelights. The home had a wrap-around shed porch with square posts and a brick pier foundation. It had three interior corbel capped brick chimneys. Among the significant details of this house were gingerbread, shingled pediment decoration, and fretwork.

Left: George W. Tippins with one of his fine horses in the 1890s. Tippins was instrumental in development of Bellville. (Photo courtesy of Joy Tippins)

The Tippins House dates to the 1870s. An old water well and sugar cane grinder are still present on the grounds.

George W. Tippins House

Located approximately two miles south of the Highway 280 and Highway 169 intersection is the George W. and Helena (Smith) Tippins home. George Tippins played an important part in the development of Bellville. He died when his barn collapsed on him in 1908. His son, Bascom Tippins, Sr., inherited the house. Bascom Tippins, Jr. owned the home after his father, and his widow, Joy Tippins, is the current owner of the home. Wooden pegs join the timbers in this house built in the 1870s.[27] The house has a gabled roof and has exterior end brick chimneys. It has a full-width front porch with square posts.

Benjamin B. Brewton Cabin

One of the oldest existing photographs of a Bellville area home is that of the Benjamin Brewton homestead. The location of this log home was approximately two and one-half miles south of Bellville on the Bellville-to-Mendes Road that preceded Highway 169. It was in front (east) and just north of the Leonard Brewton home. Ben married Sallie Calhoun in 1875 and set up housekeeping at the farmstead. It was a log structure covered with weatherboards. There were several Ben Brewtons in nineteenth-century Tattnall County, and they are often confused with one another. This Ben Brewton was the son of Jonathan and Margaret Brewton and died in 1881 at 30 years of age. Ben Brewton's widow, Sallie, is pictured on the left, and two of their children, Addie Butts and Leonard Brewton are on the right. The wood shingle roof and stick-and-clay chimney are evident from the photo. A granddaughter of Ben Brewton, Edith Smith, recalls this log cabin still standing in the mid-1920s. The cabin was typical of the period in rural Tattnall County.[28]

Left: The Leonard Brewton home about 1907. *Left to right:* Sallie Brewton, Leonard Brewton, and Addie Butts. (Photo courtesy Edith Smith)

Leonard Brewton House

Leonard Brewton (1877-1958) was one of the first County Commissioners of newly created Evans County, Justice of the Peace for the Bellville District, and a charter member of Rehobeth Church. The son of Ben and Sallie Brewton, Leonard Brewton built his home just west of his father's original cabin on what is now Highway 169 about 1901. Leonard Brewton planted the beautiful pecan orchard that now surrounds the place about 1916. There were also three sharecropper houses on this property at one time. Leonard Brewton's grandfather, J.B. Brewton, bought this land in 1875 from James B. Smith. The parcel was part of two original land grants to George U. Tippins and James A. Tippins.[29]

The hall-and-parlor with rear ell home is one-story with weatherboard exterior. The home originally had significant gingerbread fretwork. Asphalt shingles cover a gabled roof, and the house has two-over-two windows and a wood paneled door with sidelights. It has a full-width shed porch with square posts and turned balustrade. The house has a brick pier foundation.

Commodore Beecher Smith House

Located about one-half mile south of the George W. Tippins home on the east side of Highway 169 is the C. Beecher Smith house. The son of Daniel H. and Nancy Brewton Smith, Beecher (1872-1939) built the house and rented it to others prior to his marriage to Bessie Nelson. Surrounded by pecan orchards (Smith had a pecan tree nursery and also cultivated grapes), the house dates from about 1900. Beecher's son, Hoke Smith owned the home for several years after his father's death. Beecher's son, Thurmon, and his wife Willa, bought the place in 1961 and currently live in the house.[30]

The one-story bungalow house has exterior weatherboard siding. It has crimped tin roofing on a gabled and hipped roof. The windows are diamond paned-over-one and the front door is wood paneled with a transom. The house has a full-width hipped porch with bungaloids, exterior end corbel capped chimneys, and a brick pier foundation.

Claude C. Smith House

Across Highway 169 (west) from Thurmon Smith's home is the Claude C. Smith House. Claude Smith (1865-1928) was a son of Daniel H. and Nancy Brewton Smith. Claude married Sheldonna Rogers first, and second, Mary Jane Jenkins. The house dates from about 1918. Gary and Leigh Bell currently occupy this home, which they have extensively renovated.[31]

The home has wrap-around front and side porches with round posts. The windows are six-over-six. The asphalt shingled roof is gabled and hipped.

Dan O. Bell House painting by Elveda Threatte. (Photo courtesy Winton and Lucy Bell)

Dan O. Bell House

Located 1.3 miles south of the Highway 280 and Highway 169 intersection on the west side of Highway 169 is the home of Winton and Lucy Bell. This home formerly belonged to Bell's father and mother, Dan O. and Agnes Valerie (Burkhalter) Bell. The home, constructed in the 1920s, originally had a high roof. The Bells had the roof lowered when they renovated the home in the early 1960s. Winton Bell is the founder of Bell Farms, a large farming operation in the Bellville area.[32]

The above painting by Elveda Threatte provides a glimpse of how the home looked prior to renovation.

H.H. Daniel House

The H.H. Daniel home, now owned by Loulie Perkins, is in the nearby Bay Branch community south of Bellville. Harley H. Daniel, father of Loulie, was Ordinary for Tattnall County from 1907 until 1915. Shortly after Evans County was formed, he moved here and built his house in 1916. The lumber came from his farm and the logs were sawed at his own sawmill. Daniel built all the mantels and did the finishing work on the home. At that time, labor was 75 cents to $1 a day. The men who built the home were John Easterling, a Mr. Meriman, and Henry Miller. Willie Bazemore did the brick work. Prior to the Daniel house, the Martin Rogers old home place was on this site. Harley and Mozelle Daniel had 13 children and gave each of them a place of their own. Perkins inherited this house in 1955.[33]

The two-story house has a weatherboard exterior. It has a gabled and hipped roof with asphalt shingles. The windows are two-over-two and the front door is one-half wood and one-half glass with sidelights. The home has a wrap-around shed porch with bungaloids. It has a brick pier foundation and interior end corbel capped brick chimneys. The house has several out-buildings.

W.W. Daniel Home

Bay Branch is the location of the W.W. Daniel home. A contractor named Dutton built the 11-room house for Daniel in 1895. W.W. Daniel cut the timber for the house from the farm. In 1917, Daniel's son, J.U. Daniel remodeled the house. J.U. Daniel was the father of Mattie Lou Daniel who lived in the house until her death in 1979. The Daniel family still owns this home.[34]

The two-story plantation plain house has a crimped tin, gabled roof. The windows are six-over-six and the front door is wood paneled with sidelights. The house has a full-width portico hipped porch with square posts. The house sits on brick piers and has exterior end brick chimneys. There are several out-buildings including a log crib. Other significant house details are a once-detached kitchen and a second floor balcony. The white picket fence is exquisite.

Clockwise from top: Log corn crib, picket fence with accents, second story balcony, detail of saddle-notched log corn crib.

(Photo courtesy of Loulie Perkins)

Old Daniel Home Place

This 1890 photo shows the original W.W. Daniel home place in the Bay Branch area. W.W. Daniel lived in this home prior to building his two-story house. Pictured *(left to right):* unknown, Bessie Nichols, Harley Daniel, Dr. Loving Nichols, Mattie Daniel, and Tom Girardeau. The group is pictured with croquet mallets, and, no doubt, was enjoying a sports day.

The house features a wooden shingle roof and wooden shutters. The structure appears to sit three feet or more above the ground.[35]

Jonathan Bacon Brewton House

Jonathan B. Brewton built his home on the Dublin to Savannah stage route (now Highway 129) prior to 1860. Brewton was a farmer, Clerk of Tattnall Court, and Tattnall state representative for two terms. For many years this home was known as the Jim Hendrix place. This house, 3.5 miles northeast of Bellville, is on the west side of Highway 129 just south of the Highway 169 and Highway 129 intersection. According to tradition, it was a stop on the old stage route. There was a store across from the house on the east side of the road. The house originally had two stairways rising side-by-side with a partition between them. This feature served to separate the family's boys and girls as well as stage travelers staying overnight. Jonathan's widow, Margaret, inherited the home and surrounding 426 acres in 1898 (Jonathan died in 1897 and these acres were set aside for her dower). Jonathan acquired the land in 1849 from his father, Benjamin Brewton, and Jonathan's uncle, Samuel Brewton. This land was part of an original land grant to Jonathan's grandfather, Nathan Brewton. The location was also the site of Hawpond post office. Local tradition holds that Amos Hearn constructed this home.[36]

The house is a two-story, weatherboard exterior plantation plain structure. It has asphalt shingles on a gabled roof, and also has lightning rods. The windows are six-over-six and the front doors are wood paneled. There is a full-width shed porch with square posts and square balustrade. The home has a brick pier foundation and exterior end brick chimney. The house originally had two front chimneys, one on each side of the front of the house. At one time the structure had wood paneled shutters instead of the present louvered ones. A small out-building that at one time served as the Hawpond Courthouse, sits a few yards south of the home. George and Susan Willcox currently own this historic house.

A.D. Eason House

Located in the nearby Undine section, the A.D. Eason House is an excellent example of an ante-bellum plantation plain structure. One hundred forty years after construction of the house, it remains in the Eason family today. The builder of this home was a local carpernter, Amos J. Hearn. Hearn began the house July 8, 1856, and the Eason family moved in exactly one year later. Hearn signed his name in chalk on a rafter, and the inscription is still visible.

A.D. Eason kept an account book for the costs of building the home. The total cost of the house, including labor, was $1,925. The entire paint job, inside and out, cost $85. The book further details the various items needed to complete the construction and provides a comprehensive historical account of building costs in the 1850s.[37]

The two-story home has a weatherboard exterior with a shingled, gabled roof. The home has eleven rooms and has a full-width, two-story monumental portico porch with square posts. The house has a brick pier foundation and an exterior end corbel capped brick chimney. The structure is substantially the same as when it was built except for a renovated kitchen. The present owner, Margaret C. Eason, widow of A.D. Eason III, restored the home in the early 1990s.

(Circa 1910 photo courtesy John Rabun, Jr.)

Joshua Collins Home

Located a few hundred yards south of the J.B. Brewton House on what is now Highway 129 was the Joshua Collins home. Collins (1840-1929) built the house on land conveyed to him in 1887 by his father-in-law, J.B. Brewton. The land was the east end of a tract granted to John Everett in 1790. According to the Everett deed in the Liberty County Grant Book, this land was originally in that county. Joshua Collins was the son of John and Mary Collins, and Joshua married Elizabeth Brewton, daughter of J.B. and Margaret Brewton. The Joshua Collins home burned in the early 1900s.[38]

As the above picture represents, this home was one of the finest in the Bellville section. Intricate gingerbread millwork accents the front porch. The roof line is somewhat unusual for the area. The home had interior, corbel capped chimneys.

Notes

[1] Darin McCoy, interview with editor, May 8, 1995.

[2] Tattnall County Deed Book N.

[3] *A Field Guide to American Houses*, by Virginia and Lee McAlester, characterizes these houses as hall-and-parlor or central hall. The 1982 Altamaha Georgia Southern Architectural and Historic Properties list this type house as "modified dogtrot." *The Georgia Living Places* by the Georgia Department of Natural Resources refers to this type as third generation dogtrot. This architecture was probably inspired by the dogtrot concept, but local examples of these houses were not originally built as a true dogtrot. These third generation dogtrot frame homes often had two, square front rooms with a central hallway. The hallway front door enclosure was frequently flanked by glass panels. Appendages to these houses were common, forming either an "L" or "T" shape.

The original dogtrot was a log cabin that had an open hallway connecting two rooms on either side. These open areas created a breezeway and spaces for animals and children to "trot" through.

[4] Lucile Hodges, *A History of Our Locale*, 1965, p. 99.

[5] Mary Daniel, interview with editor, April 23, 1996. Daniel commented, "We cut the gallberry bushes and beat the leaves off of them. Then the limbs were tied together with string. We used these brooms to sweep the whole yard. We even had to sweep under the house!"

[6] Delma Daniel, interview with the editor, July 7, 1995.

[7] Hodges, *Locale*, pp. 99-100. Amos Hearn constructed the A.D. Eason house in 1856 and 57. Tradition says Amos Hearn also constructed the Jonathan B. Brewton House (on Highway 129 northeast of Bellville) sometime prior to 1860. Nollie Parker was the chief architect and builder of the Tattnall County Campground tabernacle.

[8] According to an Anderson House brochure, "You'll find many things about The Anderson House that will remind you of 'a place right out of the past.' It could be their friendly wrap-around porch that beckons with its white-washed swings and cane rockers, or maybe the sprawling yards surrounding the house that are full of flowering plants and shrubs. Perhaps as you stroll the grounds, unique features like the cement goldfish pond or any of the many out-buildings will stir memories and bring back a smile! One of the most interesting buildings here, the old-time boiler shelter, may remind you of long ago cane grindings that perhaps you were a part of with your parents or grandparents. A place where for years, inhabitants of this house enjoyed making sugar cane syrup in the fall and winter months.

'Fannie (Hilda's mother) just cooked and whoever wanted to, just stopped by and ate,' Hilda explained. 'I wanted to do something like she had.'

The Andersons are pleased that you have come and hope to see you again very soon! The door is always open--just like home!"; This information taken from a brochure on the Anderson House Restaurant.

[9] In this and subsequent house descriptions, the editor used the 1982 Altamaha Georgia Southern Architectural and Historic Properties Survey Forms. This survey, a copy of which is in the Evans County Public Library, is of great use in researching historic properties of the area.

[10] Tattnall County Deed Book DEF, pp. 234/235.

[11] Mary Tippins Conner, interview with editor, July 7, 1995.

[12] Charles Hearn, interview with editor, April 18, 1996.

[13] Emily Hearn Groover, interview with editor, February 24, 1996; Emily Wood, interview with editor, September 2, 1995.

[14] Wallace Parker, interview with editor, July 6, 1995.

[15] Delma Daniel, interview with editor, July 7, 1995.

[16] Ibid.

[17] Ibid.

[18] Ibid.

[19] Ibid.

[20] Bernie Anderson, interview with editor, October 6, 1995.

[21] Devane Parker Lewis, interview with editor, February 24, 1996.

[22] Evans County Deed Book 4, p. 484; Emily Groover, interview with editor, February 24, 1996.

[23] Theodore Brewton, interview with Charles P. Johnson, Jr., May 9, 1961; Tattnall County Deed Book DEF, p. 478.

[24] Theodore Brewton, interview with Charles P. Johnson, Jr., May 1962 and July 21, 1963; Tattnall County Deed Book DEF, p. 520.

[25] Theodore Brewton, interview with Charles P. Johnson, Jr., May 9, 1961; Harry DeLoach, interview with editor, September 22, 1994.

[26] Tattnall County Land Grant Book, 1837-1905, p. 183.

[27] Joy Tippins, interview with editor, February 24, 1996.

[28] See Appendix A for further information on this family; Edith Smith, interview with editor, May 6, 1996. Edith recalls that the structure was in a deteriorated condition when she was a little girl, and that she and her siblings played in the old cabin; Tattnall County Deed Book H, pp. 450-57.

[29] Ibid.

[30] An account of the family is available in a "Daniel Harrison Smith (1841-1892)" sketch, found in the Evans County courthouse; Thurmon Smith, interview with editor, February 19, 1996.

[31] Ibid.

[32] Winton Bell, interview with editor, September 2, 1995.

[33] "Many of Evans' Finest Homes on Drive-by Tour Next Week," *The Claxton Enterprise*, August 3, 1989; Loulie Perkins, interview with editor, July 10, 1996.

[34]Loulie Perkins, interview with editor, July 10,1996.

[35]Ibid.

[36]Tattnall County Land Grant Book 1837-1905, p. 183; Evans County Deed Book 5; Information also obtained from a Union Central Insurance Company title abstract for Henry J. Brewton, 1924; James A. Hendrix purchased the house in 1936; Hodges, *Locale*, p. 34; Further details provided by John Rabun, Jr., Atlanta, in his letter of 6 June 1996.

[37]Hodges, *Locale*, p. 99.

[38]John Rabun, Jr., letter, 6 June 1996; Cannie DeLoach, interview with editor, 22 June 1996; Liberty County Grant Record Book, p. 13.

APPENDIX H

*Tax Lists and
Cemetery Records*

This appendix contains several miscellaneous records of the Bellville District. First, is a voters list from 1898 when Bellville was still in Tattnall County. Second, is a listing of tax payers from the new Bellville District in 1915. Next is a record of burials in the Daniel-Smith-Tippins Cemetery in Bellville and the Simon Smith Cemetery on Highway 169.

1898 Voters' Book for 1376 District
Tattnall County, Georgia

Listed is name, age, and occupation

Alexander, C.J., 36, farmer
Bath, B.B.
Bazemore, W.H., 28, farmer
Bird, Adam, 23, clerk
Bird, G.P., 46, farmer
Bird, S., 26, merchant
Brady, J.E., 45, minister
Brazell, G., 38, farmer
Brewton, A.J., 33, farmer
Brewton, B.B., 64, farmer
Brewton, H.L., 22, school teacher
Brewton, J.B. Jr., 27, "nothing"
Brewton, W.H., 32, farmer
Guy, B., 66, cooper
Carter, D.O., 47, naval stores
Daniel, H.H., 28, farmer
DeLoach, J.M., 40, farmer
DeLoach, Jessie M., 22
Driggers, Bryant, 46, farmer
Driggers, Dan E., 22, farmer
Durrence, Troy, 23, farmer
Eason, G.A., 23, farmer
Eason, H.T., 28, woodsman
Easterling, J.S., 26, woodsman
Fulcher, J.A., 53, merchant
Grice, W., 21, postmaster
Guy, G.S., 21, cooper
Guy, J.B., 28, cooper
Hammock, A.E., 46, public works
Hearn, C.W., 34, merchant
Hodges, D.A., 38, farmer

Hodges, J.R., 26
Hodges, N.B., 38, farmer
Hyman, C.D., 26, railroad agent
Jackson, Samuel, 53, painter
Jenkins, John H., 52, farmer
Johnson, William H., 47, blacksmith
Kennedy, J.H., 30, M.D.
Kennedy, M.A., 29, farmer
Kennedy, W.A., 39, farmer
Lynn, R.A., 53, farmer
Martin, J.J., 69, farmer
Martin, J.N., 21, farmer
Mattox, E.P., 45, farmer
Mattox, H.L., 24, farmer
Mikell, Charles, 38, farmer
Miller, M.B., 22, farmer
Millen, James A., 50
Moore, M.E., 22, farmer
Moore, W.R., 23, farmer
Morris, E.A., 32, farmer
Nelson, W.B., 41, cooper
Newton, Jas. H., 24, naval stores
Nichols, L.M., 39, physician
Noble, George, 59, merchant
Oneal, S.E., 24, farmer
Overstreet, M.B., 37, farmer
Parker, J.C., 62, farmer
Parker, J.E., 24, teacher
Parker, W.N., 29, farmer
Riggs, A.B., 55, merchant
Rogers, A.C., 26, farmer

Rogers, J.H., 30, farmer
Rogers, M.E., 52, farmer
Rogers, M.W., 25, hotel
Rogers, U.A., 21, farmer
Rogers, W.E., 31, merchant
Rogers, W.N., 27, farmer
Rowe, W.I., 38, mechanic
Sikes, John R., 47, farmer
Smith, C.C., 33, farmer
Smith, J.E., 25, farmer
Smith, John W., 29, farmer
Smith, E.G., 21, farmer

Stephens, J.E., 23, farmer
Stubbs, J.L., 26, merchant
Tillman, G.V., 37, merchant
Tippins, B. Glen, 23, G & A railroad agt.
Tippins, G.W., 43
Todd, E.L., 31, farmer
Todd, J.M., 25, farmer
Todd, J.M., 65, farmer
Tootle, J.M., 46, woods rider
Tootle, Martin, 40, farmer
Windows, A., 53, farmer

The "colored" voters book listed the following individuals.

Bacon, Willis, 45, farmer
Brewton, Jonas, 48, farmer
Cade, Dan, 33, public works
Cade, West, 26, public works
Carr, Primus, 35, public works
Coleman, Ceazar, 42, farmer
Collins, George, 23, farmer
Collins, York, 44, farmer
Cook, Daniel, 40, farmer
Cornegia, George, 42, public works
Eason, Joe, 26, farmer
Eason, Willie, 25, farmer
Ganey, C.P., 31, farmer
Grant, S., 35, farmer
Hogan, Tom, 47, farmer
Johnson, Homer, 28, farmer
Lyde, Zack, 32, farming

Mathis, F.L., 42, public works
Moody, Willis, 24, farmer
Moore, Henry, 32, public works
Newton, Pat, 39, public works
Rivers, Issac, 36, public works
Shank, Charlie, 29, farmer
Shuman, J.S., 31, farmer
Smith, Andrew, 35, farmer
Smith, Bosom, 33, farmer
Smith, E.B., 30, farmer
Taylor, Frank, 46, farmer
Tillman, J.D., 39, farmer
West, Bill, 26, public works
West, John, 27, public works
Williams, Peter, 44, public works
Wooten, Anthony, 26, public works

Bellville G.M. District Residents

Presented below is a listing of tax payers in the new Bellville District, G.M. 1739th, in 1915. After name is the number of acres owned in the county. Names with asterisks indicate the ownership of a town lot.

Returns for White Tax Payers
    Brewton, William B., 280
    Bell, Mrs. Agnes V., 115
    Brewton, H.L., 237
    Brewton, Mrs. Frances E., 120[1]
    Brewton, Miss Sarah M.,* 315
    Brewton, R.B., 261
    Brewton, Henry J.,* 403
    Brewton, Theodore
    Brewton, George A., 386
    Brewton, Boyd B., 108
    Brewton, A.J., 26[2]
    Bazemore, William H., 300
    Bird, Scott and Adam, 270
    Bird, Adam*
    Bird, Mrs. Mollie*
    Butts, Mrs. W.A.*[3]
    Brady, William E.
    Bickley, C.T.*
    Boyett, James F.
    Benton, James B.*
    Bell, Daniel O.
    Cribbs, Jesse W., 205
    Cribbs, Hiram W.
    Cribbs, Horace A.
    Campbell, William J.
    Collins, Jimps E., 93
    Daniel, Mrs. Fannie
    Daniel, O.H. & Co.
    Daniel, W.L.
    Daniel, Rufus L.

Daniel, Cleburn, 49
Daniel, Enoch B., 128[4]
Daniel, Mrs. Sarah F., 323
Daniel, Harley H., 323
Daniel, James U., 234
Daniel, James H., 33
Daniel, Olin H., 35
DeLoach, Mrs. G.E., 100
DeLoach, Glenn E., 80
DeLoach, James E.
Elders, James M., 260
Evans, James
Evans, Jefferson E.
Gignilliat, Norman G.
Griffin, Mrs. Mattie
Hodges, William H., 350
Hodges, Irwin J.
Hammock, C.C.*[5]
Hammock, Clyde C.
Hammock, Barney A.
Hendricks, Remer
Hendricks, Mrs. Nancy, 809
Hearn, Nancy E., 130
Hearn, Charles W.,* 1308
Jenkins, Jonathan W.
Jones, D.E.,* 100[6]
Johnson, Martha P., 71
Johnson, M.C.
Jernigan, C.P.
Kennedy, M.M.[7]
Kennedy, Benjamin C., 130

---

[1] By A.J. Brewton
[2] For B.B. Brewton Estate
[3] By H.L. Brewton
[4] Agent for wife
[5] Admn. estate of S.C. Hammock
[6] Executor estate of Z.L. Lyde
[7] Agent for R.F. Kennedy

Kennedy, Martin M., 100
Kennedy, Henry A.
Lucas, Mahlon E.
LeGrande, Paul
Mangum, Arthur M.*
Mangum, William R.
Moore, Alfred H.
Myers, A.M.
Moseley, J.W.
Moseley, E.J.Z., 180
Miles, Noah W.
Mikell, Willie A.
Mattox, Miss Ida J.
Mattox, E.R.
Mattox, Henry L.
Mattox, Howell P.
Mattox, James P.
Nelson, Robert M.
Nunally, Mrs. Sallie M.*
NeSmith, Jonathan C., 237[8]
Osborne, James H.
Osborne, Luther
Parker, Nancy E., 325
Parker, Walter N., 28
Padgett, W.N.
Padgett, Mrs. O.R.
Riggs, Loran A.
Rewis, Freddie
Smith, Stuart P., 190
Smith, Ira, 156

Smith, Lovick P., 35[9]
Smith, C.B., 55
Smith, A.
Smith, Roscoe T., 177[10]
Smith, Joseph A., 34[11]
Smith, English, 40[12]
Smith, Mrs. Mary E., 77
Smith, Mrs. M.E., Admx., 125
Smith, C.C., S.P., C.B.*
Smith Claudius C., 323
Sikes, Daniel W.*
Sikes, Mrs. D.W.
Sconyers, Mary E.*
Sanders, Jonathan F.
Shannon, Mrs. Lela
Shannon, Oscar P.
Sikes, Charles V.
Threatt, Jesse S.
Threatt, Bedford A.
Tootle, James S., 90
Tippins, Bascom G.,* 202
Tippins, Glenn M.
Tippins, B.G. & Co.
Weathers, Marvin L.
Whitaker, James F.
Waters, William W., 78
Waters, Jonathan H., 90
Wood, Jonathan M., 655
Wood, Thomas J.

---

[8] Agent for wife
[9] Agent for wife
[10] Agent for wife
[11] Agent for wife
[12] Agent for wife

Returns for "colored" tax payers

- Akins, E.
- Bacon, Clifford
- Bennett, Cain A.
- Bennett, Jno.
- Black, William M.
- Butts, Mose
- Collins, Ellen
- Collins, George
- Collins, Joe
- Dunston, Charlie
- Ellis, Rias
- Gay, Conner
- Gay, Elliot
- Jones, Tom
- Kennedy, Pennie, 140
- Kennedy, Alex, 73
- Kennedy, Ben, 80
- Kennedy, Dan, 395
- Kennedy, Eli C.
- Kennedy, Walter H., 80
- Kimbals, Adam
- McCalip, Henry J.
- McFadden, Wash
- Mincy, Thomas
- Peterson, Warren
- Pierce, B.G.
- Poe, Edgar
- Porter, Gillie Ann, 50
- Roberts, Emma
- Sherman, Robert L.
- Smith, Robert
- Tillman, Ben
- Williams, Emma
- Williams, James L.
- Williams, Joe W.
- Williams, Pete W.
- Williams, Sandy
- Woodin, Autrey
- Woodney, Will
- Young, Jno. R.

The only known cemetery in the town limits of Bellville, the Daniel-Smith-Tippins burial ground is among the oldest in the county. Located at the southeast corner of the Highway 280 and Highway 169 intersection, the cemetery is the resting place for many of Bellville's prominent citizens.

Daniel-Smith-Tippins Cemetery

Daniel, Helen Smith
7/11/1889 - 5/26/1977

Daniel, Olin Hines, Sr.
11/21/1878 - 8/2/1962

Daniel, Olin Hines, Jr.
6/8/1924 - 8/13/1979

Mann, Mildred Estella (Wife of Samuel B.)
3/18/1873 - 8/20/1892

Parker, Queen A.M. (Wife of Lt. J.C.)
7/6/1846 - 8/10/1862

Powell, John William
2/19/1910 - 11/9/1988

Smith, Dewitt Clinton
12/21/1881 - 9/24/1955

Smith, Georgiana (Wife of James B.)
2/1/1823 - 9/26/1870

Smith, James B. (Mason)
2/1/1823 - 1/25/1891

Smith, Ladora Flowers
7/23/1894 - 10/1/1981

Smith, Little Carl Bliss (Son of P.S. & M.E.)
6/28/1886 - 5/9/1888

Smith, Mary Eliza Tippins
7/28/1859 - 12/8/1939

Smith, Pulaski Sikes
12/10/1856 - 6/19/1894

Smith, Rachael (Wife of James B.)
7/28/1834 - 8/12/1900

Tippins, Alline Edwards
4/3/1905 - 8/8/1968

Tippins, Bascom G. (Husband of Mamie A. Matthews)
1/4/1875 - 1/3/1939

Tippins, Bascom G., Jr.
11/17/1926 - 5/12/1992

Tippins, George W.
3/29/1855 - 5/29/1908

Tippins, Helena V. Smith (Wife of Geo. W.)
4/5/1852 - 5/20/1893

Tippins, Infant Daughter of G.W. & H.V.
4/17/1893 - 8/20/1893

Tipins, Inf. son of B.G. & M.M.
8/29/1916 - 8/29/1916

Tippins, Maggie May Bird (Wife of Bascom G.)
1/14/1880 - 2/23/1920

Tippins, Mamie Matthews (Wife of Bascom G.)
9/23/1901 - 3/23/1990

Tippins, W. Clyde
8/10/1902 - 4/24/1980

Vaughn, Jennie Tippins
1889 - 1932

Wilkes, P.E. (Wife of D.N.)
4/26/1850 - 6/2/1881

Wilkinson, B.J.
4/15/1923 - 1/18/1995

Wilkinson, William D.
6/19/1957 - 2/22/1989

Trinity Church of the Nazarene

Located on Highway 169 just north of Bull Creek and approximately three miles south of Bellville is the Trinity Church of the Nazarene. The historic Simon Smith Cemetery sits just east of the church. The Rev. Walter Hanson originally organized this church in Claxton in 1912. Records available at the church indicate charter members included the following: Mrs. C. Bagett, B. Eason, R.M. Nelson, N.K. Nelson, Mrs. S. Eason, J.J. Eason, Mrs. R.M. Nelson, Mrs. M.S. Riggs and Mrs. R. Slater. Members moved the church to Manassas in 1915, and then to its present location in 1965. The first pastor at the present site was E.L. Starkey. The original trustees were M. Brazel, Mrs. P.G. Jenkins, Sr., and Mrs. M.R. Riggs.

Simon Smith Cemetery
(Located behind Trinity Church of the Nazarene)

Bacon, Charles F.
6/22/1900 - 5/7/1971

Bacon, Mildred Smith
12/12/1909 - 5/16/1985

Bailey, Joseph
8/9/1881 - 6/1/1967

Bailey, Bertha S.
8/23/1881 - 4/17/1969

Boyett, William Asbury
4/20/1903 - 12/28/1982

Boyett, Eva Mae
10/27/1908 - 9/15/1993

Brazell, Margarette Leigh (Infant Dau. of Mr. & Mrs. Marcus J.), 4/23/1966

Fowlkes, Anna Mae
10/2/1894 - 10/18/1986

Hunt, Olen
11/28/1904 - 12/14/1985

Kelly, Lela Nelson (Wife of Stuart Smith [1] and Stuart Kelly [2])
2/13/1887 - 8/8/1964

McClendon, Henry F.
1916 - 1982

Lucas, Infant Son of M.E. & Laura
5/27/1912 - 6/26/1912

Morgan, M.D.
6/1/1828 - 6/1/1890

Moore, Infant Son of H.L.P & Laura
1/26/1892 - birth & death

Moser, Evelyn
4/19/1939 - 2/14/1980

Rucker, Cleve "Buddy"
5/27/1922 - 6/7/1976

Setzer, Dana S.
Mason, 1902 - 1933

Starkey, Elred Leroy
6/22/1907 - 2/27/1983

Smith, Alva L., Sr.
6/7/1892 - 3/8/1979

Smith, Bessie
12/1/1880 - 12/2/1946

Smith, C. Beecher
2/6/1872 - 1/16/1939

Smith, Colton Burgoine
12/7/1903 - 12/12/1921

Smith, Daniel A. (Son of Mr. & Mrs. S.P.)
4/29/1913 - 6/16/1913

Smith, Daniel (Son of Mr. & Mrs. C.B.)
12/23/1913 - 6/16/1913

Smith, Daniel H.
10/29/1841 - 10/29/1892

Smith, Hoke Brooks
12/6/1904 - 9/29/1988

Smith, Infant (Son of Mr. & Mrs. C.B.)
12/23/1916 - 12/23/1916

Smith, John C.
3/8/1812 - 10/26/1858

Smith, Labella Maud
12/15/1879 - 3/4/1886

Smith, Nancy
5/12/1843 - 7/1/1885

Smith, Queen A.
8/18/1867 - 5/22/1889

Smith, Ruby Stuart (Dau. of Mr. & Mrs. S. P.)
12/15/1914 - 3/8/1918

Smith, Robert Conrad
6/20/1901 - 12/31/1981

Smith, Simon (Revolutionary War Soldier)
1758 - 1827

Smith, Stuart Plunkett
2/15/1875 - 5/15/1915

Smith, Thelma A., (Dau. of Mr. & Mrs. R.T.)
8/17/1905 -8/22/1906

Smith, Shelldona Rogers (Wife of C.C.)
5/8/1868 - 6/7/1892

Ward, Lee Alfred
10/28/1895 - 2/2/1992

INDEX

Index

Entries in italics indicate a photograph. Page numbers with an "n" suffix refer to a footnote.

Adams, Mable, 215
Agricultural products,
 cotton, 27-29, 58n, 59;
 livestock, 32; soybeans,
 32; tobacco, 30;
 tomatoes, 60n;
 watermelons, 30, 124
Aikens, Tim, *209*
Akins, Edwin, *209, 286*
Akins, Reedy, 191, *203*
Alderman, Tootsie, 21
Alexander, Benjamin, 87
Alexander, C.J., 282
Alexander, James B., 9
Alexander, Joe, 87
Allen, Mona Lee, ix
Allison, R.M., 184
Ambrose, Eugene, 39, 112
Anderson House
 Restaurant, 244, 277n
Anderson, Bernie, viii, ix,
 44, 45, 77, 111, 161-
 165, 213, 215, *219, 237*
Anderson, Bill, 164
Anderson, Billy, *233*
Anderson, C.D., 13
Anderson, C.W., 22
Anderson, Harriett, 165,
 224, *238*
Anderson, Hilda, viii, ix,
 161-165, 224, *238,* 277n
Anderson, Ruth, 215
Anthony, Della, 85
Anthony, Stuart, 90n
Archer, Ann Jane, 87
Architecture. *See* Historic
 Homes
Arnold, Mr., 16
Aron, Elbert, 31
Austin, George F., 184
Bacon, Charles F., 289
Bacon, Clifford, 286
Bacon, Landis, 103

Bacon, M., 22
Bacon, Mildred Smith, 289
Bacon, Willis, 22, 283
Baggs, Berton, 182
Baggs, Columbus A., 182
Baggs, Gordon, 42, 142
Baggs, Olin, 182
Bailey, Bertha S., 289
Bailey, Joseph, 289
Ball, T. S., 22
Bargeron, Sterling, 45,
 212, 214, *217*
Bargeron, Thomasine, 214
Barnard, Daniel, 12
Barnard, Sarah L., 22
Barnard, Wilease, 126
Barrow, Ora Lee, 145, *209*
Barton, Barbara Ruth, 180
Bath, B.B., 282
Baurer, Sarah M., 179
Baxly, Aaron, 4
Bay Branch School, *76*
Bazemore, J.S., 22
Bazemore, William H., 13,
 22, 36, 282, 284
Bazemore, Willie, 271
Beal, Thomas, 36
Beasley, Carrie, ix
Beasley, Dana, 216
Beasley, Elsie Jane Daniel,
 178
Beasley, Janie, 37
Bell, Agnes Valerie
 Burkhalter, *97,* 132, 270,
 284
Bell, Alton, 132
Bell, Bertie Lee, 132
Bell, Bonnie, 133, 134
Bell, Cecil, 132, 133, 134,
 137
Bell, Dan O., *97,* 270, 284
Bell, Dan, 39, 42, 141
Bell, Danny, 143

Bell, Erney, 143
Bell, Ernie W., 39
Bell, Fannie, 87
Bell, Gary, 44, 143, 269
Bell, Jack W., 39
Bell, Joe, 138
Bell, John Olen, 132, 133
Bell, Leigh, 269
Bell, Lucy, ix, 141, 143,
 270
Bell, Mae, 132
Bell, Mandy, 181
Bell, Winton, viii, ix, 25,
 29, 38, 42, 102, 132-
 143, 191, *210,* 270
Bell, Woodrow, 133
Bellville Baptist Church,
 (Black), 55n
Bellville Baptist Church,
 20
Bellville Claxton Bank
 Branch, 223
Bellville United House of
 Prayer. *See* Grace,
 "Daddy"
Bellville: 1901 fire, 22-24;
 1919 airplane crash in,
 37; bank robbery, 223;
 basketball played in, 43;
 businesses in, 221-238;
 domestic life in, 42-43;
 early settlers, 4; early
 town history, 7-22;
 family histories, 83-91;
 highways in, 38; Lions
 Club, 44; mail delivery,
 43; Methodist Church,
 172-186; militia district,
 24-25; mule trade in, 37;
 nearby communities at
 founding, 12-13; school,
 187-210; town charter,
 47

Bennett, Bobby, 196
Bennett, Cain A., 286
Bennett, Jno., 286
Bennett, Mable Ponder, 247
Benton, Bob, 39
Benton, Bobby, 43, 108, 137, 169, *204, 205, 207*
Benton, Buddy, 145
Benton, Debra Lynn, 180
Benton, Frank, 47
Benton, J.L., 215
Benton, James, *24,* 84, 182, 284
Benton, Ruby, 182
Benton, Willie J., 84, 182
Berner, Ruth, 233
Bickley, C.T., Mrs., 183
Bickley, C.T., Rev., 25, 183, 184, 284
Bickley, Mattie Wood, 176, 250
Bickley, Morgan, 183
Bickley, Stokes, 24, 88, 128, 176, 183, 250
Bird, Adam, *24, 72, 74,* 112, 116, 119, 123, 248, 282, 284
Bird, Berta, 182
Bird, C.P., 182
Bird, G.P., 282
Bird, George, 19, 20, 173
Bird, Maggie May, 88
Bird, Mollie, 284
Bird, Scott, 21, 88, 123, 282, 284
Black, Mary, 115
Black, Will, 115
Black, Wm. M., 286
Blackstone, William, 88
Blalock, Aaron, *203*
Blalock, Alvin, ix, 45, 148, 150, 161, 213, 197, 223
Blalock, Delores, 213
Blalock, Janara, 148
Blalock, Leonard, 180
Blalock, Melrose

Anderson, 148, 150
Blalock, Onita, 249
Blalock, Rona Jane, *210*
Blocker, Grady, *81*
Blocker, J.J., 22
Bodel, Billy, 113
Boney, Pat, 62
Booth, R.M., 184
Bowers, Frank, 21
Boyett, Eva Mae, 289
Boyett, James F., 284
Boyett, William Asbury, 289
Boyette, Bessie, *233*
Boyette, J.E., *233*
Boyette, Jesse J., 36
Bradley, D.M., 21
Brady, J.E., 282
Brady, Manda, 22
Brady, William E., 284
Branch, Juanita, 249
Branch, Terry, *233*
Branch, Woodrow W., 181
Braswell, Charles, 19
Brazell, G., 22, 282
Brazell, J.P., *207*
Brazell, J.W., 13
Brazell, Margarette Leigh, 289
Brazell, Rachel, 87, 88
Brazell, W.M., 22
Brewton Mill, 51n
Brewton, A.J. "Jackie," 84, *98,* 123, 136, *263,* 282, 284
Brewton, Alice, 182
Brewton, Allen Jackson, 84
Brewton, Annie, 182
Brewton, B.B., "Berry," 5-8, 13, 17, 18, 20, 21, 22, 50n, 51n, 84, *93,* 118, 182, 188, *202, 262,* 263, 282
Brewton, Ben B., (son of Jonathan B. Brewton) 85, 266, 267
Brewton, Benjamin Lester,

84
Brewton, Benjamin, (son of Nathan Brewton) 5, 12, 50n, 51n, 84, *92, 120*
Brewton, Boyd B., 284
Brewton, Calvin, 45, 214
Brewton, Candacy Tippins, 7, 84, 87, *94,* 182, 262
Brewton, Carrie (Beasley), *209*
Brewton, Charley M., 84
Brewton, Charlotte, 84
Brewton, Clavin, *217*
Brewton, Cora Bell, 37, *204, 207*
Brewton, Coy, *97,* 168, 169, 189, *207*
Brewton, David Giles, 84
Brewton, David Jesse, 13, 17, 84
Brewton, Dora, 251
Brewton, E.R., 39
Brewton, Eleanor, 84
Brewton, Eliza, 50n
Brewton, Elizabeth, *99*
Brewton, Emma Kate, *97*
Brewton, Eula Mae, *207*
Brewton, Ezekiel, 50n
Brewton, Florence, 84
Brewton, Frances E., Mrs., 284
Brewton, George Asbury, 84, 118, 121, *263,* 284
Brewton, Henry C., 36
Brewton, Henry Jackson, *99,* 284
Brewton, Henry Leonard, 25, 85, *97,*137, *266, 267,* 282, 284
Brewton, Hogan, 43, *97,* 108, *205*
Brewton, Ida Clanton, *99*
Brewton, J., 22
Brewton, J.B. Jr., 22, *99,* 282
Brewton, J.C., Rev., *95, 99*
Brewton, J.S., 13

Brewton, James F., 50n
Brewton, Jane, 50n
Brewton, Jesse, 20, 173
Brewton, Jonas, 283
Brewton, Jonathan Bacon, 6, 12, 13, 25, 52n, 266, 267, *274*
Brewton, Lizzie, 118
Brewton, Lonnie, 37
Brewton, Loree, *204*
Brewton, M. Dan, 39
Brewton, Mamie, 182
Brewton, Margaret Addie, 85, 266, 274
Brewton, Margaret, *99*
Brewton, Martha E., 87
Brewton, Martin, 50n
Brewton, Mary, 50n
Brewton, Maude, 126, 175, 182, 251
Brewton, Maudie Durean, 84
Brewton, Minnie Neta, 84
Brewton, Mitilda U., 86
Brewton, Nancy C., 84
Brewton, Nancy Fontaine, 5, 49n, 84
Brewton, Nancy, 87
Brewton, Nannie K., *99*
Brewton, Nathan, 4, 49n, 51n, 84, 274
Brewton, Nathan, Jr., 50n
Brewton, Nettie Iola, 84
Brewton, Parthenia, 10
Brewton, R.B., 284
Brewton, Robert B., 84, *263*
Brewton, Rosa May, 84
Brewton, Sadie, 175
Brewton, Sallie Calhoun, 85, 266, *267*
Brewton, Sallie, *95, 99,* 121, 126, 176, 251
Brewton, Samuel, 50n, 274
Brewton, Sarah Jane, *99*
Brewton, Sarah M., 182, 284
Brewton, Simon J., 50n, 86, 87
Brewton, Simon W., 6
Brewton, Simon, 105
Brewton, Susan Katherine, 85
Brewton, Theodore, 17, *74*, 84, 106, 116, 122, 137, 168, 183, 199, *208*, 263, 284
Brewton, W. Ralph, 39
Brewton, W.B., 13, 22
Brewton, Wade H., 36, 182, 189, 251, 282
Brewton, Will, 50n
Brewton, William Henry, 24, 84
Brewton, William, 251
Brewton, Wm. B., 284
Brewton's Church, 5, 50n
Brown, Anthony A., x
Brown, Lillie Mae, *209*
Brown, Marcus, *209*
Brown, Ruby, ix
Budd, J.T., 184
Buffington, Wayne, 216
Bull Creek, Ga., 12
Bunton, Dora, *207*
Bunton, Mildred, 119
Bunton, O.F., 182
Bunton, O.F., Mrs., 182
Bunton, Waldo, *209*
Burch, John E., 21
Burch, Pearl, 41
Burkensteiner, Mr., 21
Bush, Lewis Woodrow, 44, 46, 178, 216
Bush, Michael Shane, 181
Bush, Paula, 214
Butts, Addie, *266, 267*
Butts, Mose, 286
Butts, W.A., Mrs., 284
Butts, William Arthur, 85
Cade, Dan, 283
Cade, West, 283
Callaway, E., 13
Callaway, J.A., 13, 22
Callaway, Nancy Elizabeth, 84
Callaway, William, 118
Calloway, Lindell, *233*
Cameron, Shirley, *209*
Campbell, William J., 284
Carr, J., 184
Carr, Primus, 283
Carter & Co., 21
Carter, D.O., 32, 282
Chambers, I.K., 184
Channell, J.E., 184
Cimbie, Martha Louise, 85
Civil War, 6-9; Tattnall Invicibles, 7; Tattnall Rangers, 7; Tattnall Volunteers, 7
Clark, Betty, *209*
Clark, C.T., 184
Clark, Earl, *209*
Clark, John, *233*
Clark, Johnny, 39, *78*, 88
Clark, Rebecca, 88
Clary, S.P., 184
Clodfelter, Gregory, 178
Clodfelter, Nancy, 126
Clower, Jerry, 164
Cobb, Don, 214, *217*
Cobb, Don, 45
Cohen, G.M., 21
Coleman, Ceazar, 283
Coleman, Jerry, ix, vii, 253
Coleman, Ona, ix, 25, 148, 253
Coley, Cathy, 178
Coley, Jr., Lee, 39
Collins, Ellen, 286
Collins, George, 283, 286
Collins, J.B. & Bro., 21
Collins, James D., *80, 98*
Collins, Jimps E., *24, 74,* 284
Collins, Joe, 286
Collins, John, 276
Collins, Jonathan B., 68, 84, *98*
Collins, Joshua B., *98*

Index 295

Collins, Joshua, 6, *98, 99,* 276
Collins, Leland, 184
Collins, Mary B., 84, *263,* 276
Collins, Mary, 276
Collins, Nancy Brewton, *99,* 276
Collins, Steve, *99*
Collins, York, 283
Colson, Edward, *209*
Colson, Harry D., 39
Colson, Lutrelle, *209*
Colson, M.N.C., 6
Colson, Mattie Kate (Boatwright), *203*
Conley, Fred, 85
Conner, Mary Tippins, ix, 246
Conner, Wilson, 87
Cook, Daniel, 283
Cook, Meldren, 115
Cook, Willie, 115
Cooper, Charles, 39, 42 141, 142
Cooper, Herschel, 39, 42, 141, 142
Cooper, Hugh, 214, *217*
Cooper, O.C., 102, 176, 184
Cooper, Ruby, 215
Cooper, Samps, 42, 142
Corey, Gladys, *203*
Cornegia, George, 283
Cox, Edleen, 183
Cox, Eunice, 183
Cox, Lilah Parker, *94,* 259
Cox, Walter R., 86, 182
Cox, Walter R., Mrs. 182
Creech, Ada, 193, *210*
Cribbs, Curtis, 184
Cribbs, Hiram W., 284
Cribbs, Jesse W., 284
Cribs, Horace A., 284
Crosby, J., 22
Crumpler, A.R., 184
Crumpler, P.H., 184

Crumpton, K. Pruit, 39
Crumpton, Samuel F., 39, 191, 197, *210*
Crumpton, Wamond A., 39
Crumpton, William D., 39
Cummings, M.E., Mrs., 22
Daniel Sawmill, 18, 73, 128-129, 222, *231*
Daniel, Aaron, 4
Daniel, Alva, *204, 207*
Daniel, Annalilza Bird, 85
Daniel, Annie E., 183
Daniel, Bayard, 183
Daniel, Bobby, *209*
Daniel, Buck, 114, 168
Daniel, C.C., 43, *70, 75* 106, 182, 183, 189, *207*
Daniel, C.L., Mrs., 183
Daniel, Carolus Wood Jr., *42, 80,* 119, 178
Daniel, Carolyn, 176
Daniel, Carrie Wood, 175, 179
Daniel, Cecil K., 39, 138
Daniel, Cecil, 41, 114, 159, *207*
Daniel, Chick, 114, 168, 191, 199, 200, *210*
Daniel, Cleburn, 36, 88, 116, 127, 176, 182, 183, 284
Daniel, Delma, viii, 41, 44, 85, 125-131, 193, *210*
Daniel, E.B., Mrs., 182
Daniel, Eloise Mercer, *42,* 178
Daniel, Emmett, *231*
Daniel, Emmett, Jr., 180, *231*
Daniel, Enoch B., "Knuch," 18, 20, 85, *93,* 102, 125, 155, 173, 176, 182, 185n, 188, *202, 222,* 284
Daniel, Enoch, 85
Daniel, Evelyn, *207*
Daniel, Fannie, 175, 183,

284
Daniel, Frances, 188
Daniel, Genie, 188
Daniel, Harley, 22, 25, 38, *96,* 106, 128, 271, *273,* 282, 284
Daniel, Helen Smith, 54n, 175, 176, 179, 254
Daniel, Henry Ross, 85, 177
Daniel, Herbert, 77, 106, 161
Daniel, Homer, 183
Daniel, Issac, 6
Daniel, J.H., Mrs., 182
Daniel, James Hardee, 85, 182, 284
Daniel, James U., 272, 284
Daniel, Jeanette Folson, 175, 178, 254
Daniel, Jim H., 116, 125, 127, 176, 252, 254
Daniel, Jim, *96*
Daniel, John, *40,* 44, 126
Daniel, Lanora, 180
Daniel, Leah Hodges, 254
Daniel, Lee, 36, 116, 253
Daniel, Margaret, 41, 180, *207*
Daniel, Martha Louise, 178
Daniel, Mary Alice, 179
Daniel, Mary Buxton, *43*
Daniel, Mary Crouse, *210*
Daniel, Mary D., 178
Daniel, Mary Holder, 179
Daniel, Mary Helen, viii, 85, 125-131, *207, 210*
Daniel, Mattie, 22, 272, *207, 273*
Daniel, Mozele, 271
Daniel, Nancy Elizabeth, 178
Daniel, Neal, *203*
Daniel, Nita, 151, 191
Daniel, O.H. & Co., 284
Daniel, O.H. Sr., 20, 44,

54n, 85, 116, 125, 173, 178, 182, 222, 252, 254, 284
Daniel, O.H., III, 47
Daniel, O.H., Jr., 39, 45, 85, 143, 151, 176, 178, 179, 213-214, *217,* 252, 258
Daniel, O.H., Mrs., 183
Daniel, Peggy, 180
Daniel, R.L., 183
Daniel, R.S., 183
Daniel, Robert O., 182
Daniel, Ross, 116, 125, 176, 253
Daniel, Rufus "Dick," *69*
Daniel, Rufus Lester, 85, 125, 284
Daniel, Sarah F., 284
Daniel, Sid, 39
Daniel, Stella D., 178
Daniel, Susan, 183
Daniel, Thisselle Williams, 178, 253
Daniel, Thomas, 183
Daniel, W.E., Mrs., 41
Daniel, W.I., 13
Daniel, W.L., 182, 284
Daniel, Walford Lee, 85, 125, 176
Daniel, Wallace, Dr., 115
Daniel, Walter Emmett, ix, 41, 45, 85, 114, 117, 143, 149, 151, 158, 160, 162, 168, 178, 180, 191, *210,* 213, *231, 258*
Daniel, William W., 6, 12, 13, 22, 63n, 272, 273
Daniel, Winnie, 75, *204, 207*
Daniel, Wright, 24, 38, 127
Daniel-Smith-Tippins Cemetery, 287-288
Danton, Ga., 12-13, 35n
Darsy, E.B., 182
Davis, Dan, 27, 58n

Davis, J.S., 188
Davis, John, 182
Davis, Mr., 104
Davis, S.J., 184
Davis, Tom, 184
Davis, William, 37
DeLaoch, Perry Lee, 191
DeLoach, Avis, *204, 207*
DeLoach, C.E., Jr., 45, 213
DeLoach, David, 44
DeLoach, Dennis Daniel Jr., 179
DeLoach, Eliza, 22
DeLoach, G.E., Mrs., 284
DeLoach, Glenn, 79, 119, 121, 284
DeLoach, Harry, vii, ix, 118-124, 161
DeLoach, J., 22
DeLoach, J.A., 13
DeLoach, J.M., 282
DeLoach, James E., 284
DeLoach, Jesse, 50n
DeLoach, Jessie M., 282
DeLoach, June, 150, 223, *234-235*
DeLoach, Perry Lee, 191, 193, 195, 197, *210*
DeLoach, Richard, 168
DeLoach, Ruth, 118
DeLoach, Sarah E., 22
DeLoach, Ted, *203*
DeLoach, Velma, *233*
DeLoach, W.H., 22, 25
Denton, Nannie Kate, 194, 198, *210*
Denton, Wallace, 39, *210*
Dixon, Ralph, 45, 213, 214, *217*
Donaldson, C.H. Rev., 177, 184
Donaldson, Cora, 177
Donaldson, Fran, 177
Doster, Bill, 222
Drake, Charles, 45, 212, 214, *217*

Dreggors, Elaine, 216
Driggers, Bryant, 282
Driggers, Dan E., 282
Duncan, Leonard, 39
Dunston, Charlie, 286
Durrence & Bazemore, 21
Durrence, Betty, 214
Durrence, Cleve, 88
Durrence, Elizabeth Grice, 88
Durrence, George, 132
Durrence, Herschel, 36
Durrence, Jane Elizabeth, 84
Durrence, John, 88
Durrence, Kelly, 155
Durrence, Lavenia Jane, 134
Durrence, Stephanie, ix
Durrence, T.H., Mrs., 183
Durrence, Thomas A., 88, 50n
Durrence, Troy, 282
Durrence, Wearing, 19
Duvall, James, 184
Eason, A.D., III, 275
Eason, Abraham D., 9, 10, 13, 50n, 88, 275
Eason, Edward, *209*
Eason, Elizabeth Julian, 87
Eason, Felton, 163
Eason, G.A., 282
Eason, H.T., 282
Eason, J.T., 13, 21
Eason, James T., 13
Eason, Joe, 216, 283
Eason, M.W., 13
Eason, Margaret C., 275
Eason, Mary, 87
Eason, Oka, 52n
Eason, Tim, ix
Eason, Willie, 283
Easterling, J.S., 282
Eaves, Gertrude, *203*
Eddins, C.B., *235*
Eden, Dan, *217*
Edwards, Aloysius Odessa,

Index 297

132
Edwards, Buckie, 10
Edwards, William, 50n
Elders, Edith, 106
Elders, James M., 284
Ellis, Rias, 286
Evans County, Ga.:
  background, 3; county;
  boundaries, 3; map,
  facing page 32
Evans, Beulah, 86
Evans, Clement A., Gen., *9*
Evans, James, 284
Evans, Jefferson E., 284
Evans, Nolan, 93, 138
Evans, Thurmond, 39, 141
Everett, John, 276
Eves, Gertrude, 102, *203*
Fisher, G., 184
Flanigan, Tom, 112, 148,
  259, 264
Folsom, Jeanette, 85
Foss, L.L., 58n
Fountain, Amiel, viii, 110-
  117, 192, 195, 198, *205,
  210*
Fountain, David T., 110
Fountain, Emily, 192
Fowler, Betty, 102, 106,
  107, *203*
Fowlkes, Anna Mae, 289
Foy, Manassas, 12, 22
Freeman, Cleve, 60n, 157
Freeman, R.G., 184
Fry, Date, 87
Fulcher, Joseph .A., 20,
  21, 23, 182, 185
Fulmer, Frank E., *79*
Ganey, C.P., 283
Gay, Conner, 286
Gay, Elliot, 286
Gibbs, Terry, 164
Gignilliant, Mr., 104
Gignilliant, Norman G.,
  284
Gillis, Jim, 136
Girardeau, Tom, 273

Glisson, Hazzle, 183
Glisson, J.E., Mrs., 183
Glisson, Se, 86
Glisson, Segal, *236*
Godbee, W.W., 188
Goff, Emily, 41
Goldkist Inc., 224
Gordon, F.J., 184
Gordon, John B., 8
Goss, Eva Gordon, 84
Grace, C.W. "Daddy, "
  Bishop, 37-38, 63n, *82*,
  104, 130,
Grant, Eloise, 180
Grant, S., 283
Graves, Clara, 87
Green, Ariminta, *208*
Grice, Agnes, Smith, J.P.,
  85
Grice, Edwin R., 85
Grice, Eveline Smart, 85
Grice, James B., 85
Grice, Joe, 5, 85
Grice, Joseph T., 20, 22,
  25, 85, *93,* 202, 243
Grice, Lillie, 85
Grice, William, 85, 282
Griffen, Lorene, *209*
Griffin, Franklin, *203*
Griffin, Leon, 145, *209*
Griffin, Mattie, 284
Griffin, Sybil, *203*
Griffith, Sherman T., 157
Grooms, J.J., 9
Groover, Alan, 44, *77,* 243
Groover, David, viii, ix,
  44, 47, 153-160, 177,
  190
Groover, Dawn, 243
Groover, Emily, viii, ix,
  44, 85, *92,* 102, 160,
  165, 177, 179, 180, 194,
  209, 210, 243
Groover, Nancy, *77,* 179,
  180
Guest, Emily, 88
Guy, B., 282

Guy, G.S., 282
Guy, J.B., 84, 282
Guy, Marinda Seran, 84
Hackle, Ellie, *233*
Hagans, T., 22
Hall, Tom T., 46, 48, 164
Hammoch, Barney A., 284
Hammoch, Clyde, *74,* 284
Hammoch, J.M., 22
Hammoch, S.C., 182
Hammoch, S.P., 22
Hammock, A.E., 282
Hammock, C.C., 183, 284
Hammock, J.A., 22
Hammock, J.T., 183
Hammock, J.T., Mrs., 183
Hammock, John, 10
Hammock, Ruth, 183
Hammock, S.C., 183
Hammock, S.C., Mrs. 183
Hammond, A.J., 13
Hammond, J.A., 13
Hammond, John, 88
Hamner, Annette, 214
Hamner, John, 44, 178
Hardee, Silas, 87
Harden, William, 9, 10
Harkins, Miss, *96*
Harper, James, 195
Harvey, Ophelia Parker,
  94
Harvey, W.T., 86
Hawpond, Ga., 12, 25
Head, Edwin Lawrence,
  176
Hearn, "C," 80, 144, 151
Hearn, Amos, 6, 57n, 85,
  89n, *92*, 105, 242, 259,
  274, 275, 277n
Hearn, Anthony, 57n, 107
Hearn, Bessie, *70, 97,* 105
Hearn, Bill, 45, 193, *210,*
  214, *217-218*
Hearn, C.W., 20, 21, 23,
  24, 27, 28, 37, 39, 58n,
  72, 77, 85, 86, *94, 97,*
  103, 105, 111-113, 120,

121, 137, 143, 153, 154, 158, 161, 167, 188, 229, 259, 282
Hearn, Charles, 77, *80*, 144, *210*, 214, 284
Hearn, Elma, 180, 194, *210, 233*
Hearn, Grace, 34, 62n, *77*, 86, 102, 123, 137, 148, 173, 175, 177, 180, 189, 192, 197, *209, 210*, 247
Hearn, H.C., Jr., 39, 214
Hearn, Henry Caughey, "Cap," *24*, 25, 28, 29, 36, 45, 47, 62n, *74, 77*, 86, *97,* 105, 108, 154, 177, 179, 213, 224
Hearn, Herschel, viii, 28, 43, *70, 72,* 102, 123, 137, 169, 177, 191, 192, 196, 197, *204, 205, 207, 210*
Hearn, Inman C., 41, 47, 45, 57n, 60n, *72*, 86, *97,* 180, 153, 155, 157, 158, 159, 161, 178, 213, *229, 230, 234,* 258
Hearn, Jack, viii, 147, 160, 193, 196, *209,* 210
Hearn, Jesse, 85
Hearn, Mae, 40, *70, 97,* 105, 145, 178, 203, 243
Hearn, Martha, 41, 105, 107, 145, 177, 180, *207,* 243
Hearn, Melvina, 85
Hearn, Mildred, 177, 189, *204, 207, 243*
Hearn, Nancy Eulalia Durrence, 41, 86, 94, *97, 243,* 284
Hearn, Shirley, 213
Hearn, Simon, 85, 173, 188, *202*
Helmuth, Lowel, *233*
Hendricks, J.H., 13
Hendricks, Nancy, 13, 19, 284
Hendricks, Remer, 284
Hendrix, Bonnie Bell, *210*
Hendrix, Carolyn, 177
Hendrix, Euzebia, 84
Hendrix, James, 8
Hendrix, Jim, 274
Hendrix, Lamar, 44, 215
Hendrix, W.R., 13
Hendry, A.I., Dr., 35, 182
Hendry, Fred, 182
Hennesy, David, 4, 17
Hennesy, Rebecca, 4
Herritage, Elizabeth, 215
Hester, Linda Johnson, ix
Historic Homes: Bell, Dan O., 270; Bird-Wood, 248; Brewton, Ben B., 266; Brewton, Berry, 240, 262; Brewton, Jackie, 263; Brewton, Jonathan B., 13, 240, 274, 279n; Brewton, Leonard, 267; Brewton, Sallie, 251; Collins, Joshua, 276; Daniel, Enoch B., 255; Daniel, H.H., 271; Daniel, Jim, 254; Daniel, O.H., Sr., 252; Daniel, Ross, 253; Daniel, W.W., 272; Eason, A.D., 275; Hearn, C.W., 243; Hearn, H.C., 247; Hearn-Parker-Cox, 241, 259; Hodges, William H., 264; Nichols, Loving, Dr., 256; Parker, Nollie, 258; Sheppard, 249; Smith, C. Beecher, 268; Smith, Claude C., 269; Smith, James B., 54, 240, 244; Tippins, Bascom, 246; Tippins, George W., 265; Wood, John M., 250
Hodges, D.A., 22, 282
Hodges, Eloise, ix, 168, 180-181, *203, 208*
Hodges, Irwin J., 13, 264, 284
Hodges, J.R., 282
Hodges, Lafayette, *99,* 104
Hodges, Leah, 85
Hodges, Lucile, vii, 10, 13, 17, 22
Hodges, N.B., 22, 282
Hodges, Ray, *203*
Hodges, Roy T., 178, 180
Hodges, S.L., 13
Hodges, Sheldona Matilda, 84
Hodges, T.J., 13
Hodges, William H., 264, 284
Hodges, William, 4, 49n
Hogan, Tom, 283
Hogan, Willie, 106
Hogwallow, Ga., 13, 188
Holder, Mary, 85
Holland, Barbara, 145, *209*
Holland, J., 13
Holland, Lida (Rich), *203*
Holland, Phylis, 194, *210*
Holland, Sallie, 177
Holland, Wylen, 196, *209*
Hollaway, Troy, 184
Hollingsworth Jake, 227
Hollingsworth, Harry, 151
Howard, Barbara, 216
Howard, J.S., 13
Howard, L.C., 184
Hughey, Lyda, 188
Hulsey, Dewey, 46
Hunt, Nell Smith, 192, *210*
Hunt, Olen, 289
Hyman, C.D., 20, 282
Iler, Palmer, 140
Ingram, G.F., 188
Jackson, Ethredge, 182
Jackson, Frank C., 182
Jackson, Paul, 182
Jackson, Samuel, 282

Index

Jackson, W.R., 182
James, Glenda DeLoach, ix
James, Tom, 286
Jenkins, Donnie, 86
Jenkins, I.C., 184
Jenkins, J.H. & wife, 22
Jenkins, John H., 13, 282
Jenkins, Jonathan W., 284
Jenkins, Laura Julia, 85
Jenkins, Walter, 39
Jernigan, C.P., 284
Jernigan, Jesse, 6, 8, 13, 51n
Johnson, Alma, 183
Johnson, Ann, x
Johnson, Benny, 118, 168, 199
Johnson, Charles, Jr., 39, *80*, 144, *203*
Johnson, Charlie, *80*, 81, 129, 173, 177, 222
Johnson, Emma, 86, 168
Johnson, Homer, 283
Johnson, Jim, 260
Johnson, Mac, 84, 111, 115-116, 122, 134, 260, 261, 284
Johnson, Martha P., 63n, 84, 138, 176, 261, 284
Johnson, Pharris D., *81,* 190, 192, 261, *291*
Johnson, Sidney, 39, 260
Johnson, Wm. H., 282
Jones, Alma, 86
Jones, D.E., 284
Jones, J.W., 13
Jordan, Felder, 88
Jordan, W.J., 9
Jordon, William J., 10
Kelly, Lela Nelson, 289
Kemp, Faye, 213
Kemp, Harold, 45, 164, 214, *217*, 258
Kennedy, Alex, 286
Kennedy, Alfred, 13, 120
Kennedy, B., 22
Kennedy, Ben, 286

Kennedy, Benjamin C., 284
Kennedy, Cecil, 108
Kennedy, Dan, 22, 286
Kennedy, Eli C., 286
Kennedy, H. 13
Kennedy, Henry A., 285
Kennedy, J.H., 22, 282
Kennedy, J.L., 22
Kennedy, Jack, 214
Kennedy, Jimmy, 45, 214, *217*
Kennedy, Lee, *74*, 120
Kennedy, Leena, 85
Kennedy, Martin, 13, 22, 120, 282, 284, 285
Kennedy, Raford, 120
Kennedy, Reba, 214
Kennedy, S., 22
Kennedy, W., 22
Kennedy, W.A., 22, 282
Kennedy, Water H., 286
Kicklighter, Jerry Asbury, 180
Kimbals, Adam, 286
King, Donald D., 177
King, Mrs., 111
King, Rosa, *69*
Kirkland, Beatrice, *209*
Laing, Margaret Elvina, 85
Lamar, James H., 8
Land Grants, 4, 49n
Lanes, J.A.J., 50n
Lanier, Ashton, 42, 142
Lanier, Ella, 87
Leak, P.W., 21
LeGrand and Son, 21
LeGrand, Ethel, 180
LeGrand, Homer, 16, LeGrand, Paul, 16, *24*, 36, *73*, 104, 111, 113, 123, 163, 285
LeGrand, S.W., 18
LeGrand, W.L., 182
Leibbett, Horace E., 25
Lester, Sam Jack, *24*
Lewis, Devane Parker, ix

Lewis, Edgar, *207*
Lewis, Herry Lee, 164
Lewis, Lawson, *233*
Long, Bert, 21
Long, C.C., 184
Long, H.C., 18
Long, Minnie, 188
Looney, Richard C., Bishop, 181
Lott, Jerry, 184
Loyless, Kirk, Rev., 173, 184
Lucas, Mahlon E., 285, 290
Lumpkin, Hearn, 42, 142
Lyde, Zack, 283
Lynn, Mack, *209*
Lynn, Maltida Yeomans, 86
Lynn, Marian, *209*
Lynn, R.A., 22, 86, *92*, 282
Maddox, C., 22
Magee, Henry, 87
Mallard, Carolyn Daniel, *210*
Mallard, Evelyn, 126, 194
Mallard, Mattie Lou, 126
Mallard, William Ralph, 181
Mandrell, Barbara, 164
Mangum, Arthur M., 285
Mangum, William R., 285
Mann, Mildred Estella, 287
Mann, Samuel, 287
Manning, E.B., 188
Marshall, Ron, 46
Martin, Ann, *209*
Martin, Clara Parker, *94,* 183
Martin, J.J., 22, 282
Martin, J.N., 282
Martin, John H., 183
Martin, Maxie, Mrs., 183
Mathis, F.L., 283
Mattox, E.P., 22, 282

Mattox, E.R., 285
Mattox, H.P., Mrs., 183
Mattox, Henry L., 282, 285
Mattox, Howell, 103, 183
Mattox, Ida J., 285
Mattox, J.A., 13
Mattox, James P., 285
McArthur, Minnie, 88
McBride, Sue, 86
McCalip, Henry J., 286
McCall, Sharon, x
McClendon, Henry F., 290
McCooey, Gail, x
McCook, Charles Frank, 173, 177, 184
McCook, Louise, 173, 177
McCord, C.H., 184
McCord, John Dewitt, 182
McCord, Rachel, 86
McCoy, Bobby, 44, 75, 224, *237*
McCoy, Darin, viii, ix, x, 47, 148-152
McCoy's Garage, 224
McDaniel, Jeremiah, 4
McFadden, Wash, 286
McInage, D.W., 182
McInage, Pasco, 182
McInage, Rosco, 182
McLeod, D., 22
McMillan, A.S., 21
McQuaig, D.F., 19
McQuaig, D.W., 20, 185
McQuinn, Frank, 23
McRae, A.P., 6
Mikell, Alex D., 36
Mikell, Charles, 22, 282
Mikell, Willie A., 285
Miles, Elden, 105
Miles, Noah W., 285
Miller, Elbert, 176
Miller, F.L., 185
Miller, Gabe S., 87
Miller, Henry, 271
Miller, M.B., 282
Milles, James A., 282

Mills, Coot, 130
Mills, Fletcher, 130
Mills, Monk, 130
Mims, J.T., 184
Mincy, Alex F., 182
Mincy, James, Lt., 51n
Mincy, Thos., 286
Moody, Willis, 283
Moore, A.C., 22
Moore, Alfred H., 285
Moore, Arthur J., 176
Moore, H.L.P., 290
Moore, Henry, 283
Moore, Jean, *209*
Moore, Louise, *203*
Moore, M.E., 282
Moore, M.R., 22
Moore, R. Lee, 189
Moore, W.R., 282
Moore, W.V., 25
Morgan, Dutchess, 86
Morgan, E.F., 13
Morgan, M.D., 290
Morgan, William, 12, 50n
Morris, E.A., 282
Morris, James H., 39
Morris, Paul, 39
Morris, Prather, 39
Morrison, C.A., 184
Moseley, E.J.Z., 285
Moseley, J.W., 285
Moser, Evelyn, 290
Motes, Michelle, 181
Mugerditchian, Jerome, Capt., 178
Mulford, Charles B., 4
Mulligan, Willie, 119
Murray, Joseph M., 46
Myers, A.M., 285
Myers, A.M., Mrs., 183
Myers, Dwight, 183
Myers, Odessie, 183
Myers, Oril, 183
Nail, Robin, ix
Nease, Doris, 177
Nease, H.K., 41, 47, 176, 177, 254

Nease, Jim, 178
Nease, Lena Hale, 176, 179
Nease, Wilmer, 176
Nelson, Louise, *209*
Nelson, Robert M., 285
Nelson, W.B., 282
NeSmith, Jonathan C., 285
Newman, E. Watson, 36
Newton, D.C., 18, 20, 22, 23
Newton, Jas. H., 282
Newton, Otelia, *207*
Newton, Pat, 283
Newton, Watson, 167
Nichols, L.M., *202,* 282
Nichols, Loving, Dr., 19, 22, 68, *96*, 122, 256
Nichols, Mattie Daniel, *96, 273*
Nippers, Mary C., 183
Noble, George, 282
Norman, R.R., 184
Norwood, Bob, Rev., 44, 181, 184
Nunnally, Alphus, "Alvis," 36, *74*
Nunnally, Rags, *24*
Nunnally, Sallie M., 285
Odum, Emily, *233*
Odum, Mark, *233*
Odum, Martha Eason, 194, 198, *203, 210*
Odum, Rupert, *233*
Olliff, Margaret Brewton, *99*
Olmstead, S.A., 182
Oneal, S.E., 282
Osborn, J.H., 25
Osborne, Birdie, 183
Osborne, Carrie, 183
Osborne, Clydie, 183
Osborne, Ida, 183
Osborne, J.H., 183, 285
Osborne, Luther, 183, 285
Osborne, Nina Lee, 36, 189, *207*

Overstreet, M.B., 282
Padgett, O.R., Mrs., 285
Padgett, W.N., 285
Parker, Alace, 86
Parker, Albert, 45, 164, 213, 214, *217, 218,* 220
Parker, Alene, *94,* 247
Parker, Chadburn, 167, 183
Parker, Clara E., 86
Parker, Clarence, *72,* 86, *94*
Parker, Emma, 22, 175
Parker, Georgia, 86
Parker, Harold, 37, 108
Parker, J.C., 282
Parker, J.E., 282
Parker, Jane, 214
Parker, Joe, 86, *94*
Parker, John Chadburn, 6, 10, 13, *24,* 86, 87, *94,* 105, 166, 259
Parker, Julian H., 86, *94*
Parker, Lavenia, 86
Parker, Lila, 86
Parker, Martha, 87
Parker, Mary, 86
Parker, Matilda Jane, 86
Parker, Nancy Emily Brewton, 57n, *94,* 247, 259, 285
Parker, Odessa, 86
Parker, Olive, 183
Parker, Ophelia, 86
Parker, Queen A.M., 287
Parker, W.N., Mrs., 183
Parker, Wallace, ix, viii, 114, 118-119, 166-169, *208,* 250
Parker, Walter Nollie, 10, 42, 71, 86, 104, 115, 116, 166, 173, 183, 258, 282, 285
Parker, Wesley, 146
Partin, George R., 184
Parton, Dolly, 164, *218*
Patterson, Gene, 214

Paxton, Eugena, *208*
Peed, William, 179, 184
Peeples, Bertha, 85
Peninsula Lumber Co., 222
Perdue, L.W., 201n
Perkins, Loulie Daniel, ix, 126, 193, *207, 210,* 271
Peterson, Warren, 286
Phillips, Laura B., 110
Pierce, B.G., 286
Pinewood School, 45-46, 211-220
Pingston, J.A., 188
Plyler, Kitty, 173, 180
Poe, Edgar, 286
Porter, Gillie Ann, 286
Powell, John William, 85, 180, 198
Powell, Louise, 41
Powell, Nita, 85
Powell, Stella, *210*
Powell, Woodrow, 180
Prince, Arthur H., 20, 21, 69, 256
Pryor, Bill, ix, 44, 225n
Rabun, John, Jr., ix, 279
Rackley, Eugene, 16
Railroads, 13-17, 35, 52n, 53n, 114; Savannah and Western, 14-15, Georgia and Alabama, 15; Savannah, Americus, and Montgomery, 14-15; Seaboard Air Line, 16
Rast, J.L., 184
Register, E.B., 214
Rewis, Fred, 183, 285
Richardson, Andrew, 159
Richey, Billy, 39
Richey, Bobby, *209*
Riggs, A.B., 282
Riggs, Clyde, *207*
Riggs, E.T., 22
Riggs, Edra Smith, ix, 54n, 181, 192
Riggs, Elliot, 86
Riggs, Elma, 86, *207*

Riggs, Hattie, 86
Riggs, Joe, 19, 39, 44
Riggs, John Paul, Jr., 44
Riggs, Kathryn, 180, 181
Riggs, Lalah, 86
Riggs, Lamar, 39, 168
Riggs, Lola, 86
Riggs, Loren, 86
Riggs, Lovan A., 285
Riggs, Marvin Matha, 39, 86, 168, 181, 192, 200, *210*
Riggs, Mode, 86
Riggs, Paul, 44, 138, 180, 181, 190, 191, 193, 194, 195, 225n, *233*
Riggs, Paula Faye, 178
Riggs, Sallie, 41
Riggs, Shelton, 86
Riggs, Tim, 86
Riggs, Walton Rogers, 86
Riggs, Willam Shepherd, 6, 22, 86
Riggs, Wilma, *207*
Rivers, Issac, 283
Robers, Jimmy, 45
Roberson, Joyce, 88
Roberts, Emma, 286
Roberts, Myrtle Lee, *233*
Rogers, A.C., 282
Rogers, Annie Mae (Craps), *203*
Rogers, Carolyn Blalock, 193, *210*
Rogers, Charlie, 86
Rogers, E.A., 188
Rogers, Edwin, 39
Rogers, Ella Lee, 88, 203
Rogers, Grady, 45, 126, 214
Rogers, Henrietta, 214
Rogers, J.H., 22, 283
Rogers, J.J., 13
Rogers, J.P., 25
Rogers, James H., 45, 212
Rogers, Jan, 216
Rogers, Jimmy, 44, 164,

214, *217*
Rogers, John "Duffy," 85, *94*
Rogers, John Henry, 177
Rogers, Julia C., 87
Rogers, Lawton H., 39, 141
Rogers, M.E., 13, 22, 283
Rogers, M.J., 22
Rogers, M.W., 283
Rogers, Martin, 271
Rogers, Mary Lizie, 178
Rogers, Mellie Hearn, *94,* 105
Rogers, Mildred, 24, 148
Rogers, Odis, *203*
Rogers, Ora, 85
Rogers, Sheldonna, 269
Rogers, Sue Nell, 39
Rogers, U.A., 283
Rogers, Uriah, 50n
Rogers, W.E., 283
Rogers, W.N., 283
Rogers, Wilbern, *203*
Rose, Melba Blalock, 192, *210*
Roundtree, Willie, *233*
Rowe, Wiley, 19, 188, *202*, 242, 247, 261, 283
Rowell, Julia, 183
Rowell, Othis, 183
Rowell, R.R., 183
Rowell, R.R., Mrs., 183
Rucker, Cleve, 290
Rumph, Mary Alice, 126
Rumph, William Edwin, III, 179
Rushing, Rita, *209*
Rushing, Ruby, *209*
Rushing, Vernon, *209*
Ryder, Don, *233*
Sampley, Roy, 184
Sanders, E.A., 184
Sanders, Jonathan F., 285
Sandiford, Ralph, 106
Sands, W.D., 155
Sapp, Erie, *203*

Sapp, Ernest, *209*
Sapp, Hollis, *203*
Sapp, James Duron, 44
Sapp, Jimmy, *209*
Sapp, Versie, *209*
Saturday, Laverna, 119
Saturday, Wilma, 126, *207*
Savage, W.A., 21
Scarbrough, Howard, 44
Schwabe, Ed, vi, ix
Sconyers, J.A., 86, 184
Sconyers, Martha, 183
Sconyers, Mary E., 285
Sconyers, Mary Glisson, 175
Sconyers, Mary Parker, *94*
Scott, Eugene, 179
Scott, Loretta, 213, 214
Scott, Thomas, 45, *217*
Scott, William Eugene, 179, 184
Scovil, V.P., 184
Seckinger, Ernest W., 184
Setzer, Dana S, 290
Shank, Charlie, 283
Shannon, Bertha, 183
Shannon, Buck, 108, 169, *205*
Shannon, Lela, 285
Shannon, Oscar P., 285
Shearous, Alford, 183
Shearous, Alford, Mrs., 183
Sheppard, Bennie, Mrs., 177
Sheppard, Charles, 39, 177, *207*
Sheppard, Dr., 105, 249
Sheppard, Elizabeth, 177
Sheppard, Helen, 119, 168, 177
Sheppard, Hiram Wallace, 177
Sheppard, John, 177, *207*
Sheppard, Virginia, 177
Sherman, Robert L., 286
Sherman, W.T., Gen., 8

Shuman, J.S., 283
Shuptrine, John, 88
Sikes, America, 103
Sikes, Charles V., 285
Sikes, D.W., Mrs., 21, 285
Sikes, Daisy, 16, *68*
Sikes, Daniel W., 285
Sikes, Daniel, Dr., 6, 87
Sikes, Georgia Ann, 87
Sikes, J., 13
Sikes, J.B., 13, 22
Sikes, John R., 283
Sikes, John, 50n
Sikes, Nell (Surrency), *203*
Sikes, Rosa, 103
Sim's Farm, 155
Simmons, Dorothy, ix
Simmons, O.P., 184
Simon Smith Cemetery, 289-290
Sims, Kay, 179
Sims, Laverne Smith, 177
Smith, A., 285
Smith, Alexander A., 87
Smith, Alva L., Sr., 290
Smith, Alvarader Beauregard, 87
Smith, Andrew, 283
Smith, Bessie, 290
Smith, Betty, 213, 215
Smith, Bosom, 283
Smith, Bubba, 115
Smith, Byrd, *24*
Smith, C. Beecher, *99,* 176, *182,* 268, 285, 290
Smith, C.B., Jr., 41, 145, 191, 192, 195, 198, 200, *210*
Smith, C.B., Mrs., 183, 268
Smith, Carl, 189, *207,* 287
Smith, Clarence L., 39, *207*
Smith, Claudius Clarence, 87, 182, 269, 283, 285
Smith, Clinton, 182
Smith, Colin, 16

Index

Smith, Colton Burgoine, 290
Smith, Conrad, 183
Smith, Curtis D., 178
Smith, Daniel A. 290
Smith, Daniel H., 9, 13, 87, 89n, *92,* 120, 269, 268, 290
Smith, Daniel, 290
Smith, Dewitt Clinton, 39, 87, 287
Smith, Dorsey, 39
Smith, E.B., 283
Smith, Edith, *97,* 266, 278n
Smith, Effie, 215
Smith, Elender, 87
Smith, Embree, *210*
Smith, English Gartrell, 44, 87, 54n, 86, 87, 89n, *99,* 283, 285
Smith, Euzeby, 87
Smith, Ezzie, 87
Smith, Frances Bell, 17, 87, 183, 244
Smith, Georgia Ann, 87, *92,* 287
Smith, Georgia, 115
Smith, Godiva, 87
Smith, Grace, 106
Smith, H.G., 22
Smith, Harry, 90n, 176
Smith, Helen, 87, 125
Smith, Helena, *69,* 85, 88
Smith, Henry Clay, 88
Smith, Hoke, 183, 268, 290
Smith, Hyatt, 184
Smith, I. S., 188
Smith, Ira, 285
Smith, J. Colin, 87, 183
Smith, J. Wallace, 39
Smith, J.E., 283
Smith, J.W., 22
Smith, James B. II, 87
Smith, James B., 6, 10, 18, 50n, 54n, 87, 88, 90n, 120, 244, 267, 287
Smith, James, 87, 244
Smith, Jim B., III, viii, 87, 90n-91, *95*
Smith, John C., 290
Smith, John W., 283
Smith, Joseph A., 285
Smith, Joseph W., 39
Smith, Judy Elaine, 179
Smith, Labella Maude, 87, 290
Smith, Lewis, *218*
Smith, Lothair, 214
Smith, Lovick P., 87, *99,* 182, 285
Smith, M.A., 13
Smith, M.E., Mrs., 183, 285
Smith, M.W., 13
Smith, Maire, 41
Smith, Mary Eliza Tippins, 85, 125, 185, 285, 287
Smith, Mary S., 22
Smith, Mary, 86, 87, 175
Smith, Michael, 87
Smith, Mildred, 87
Smith, Nancy, 290
Smith, Nellie, *204*
Smith, O.H. "Tab," Jr., ix, 45, 46, 149, 212, 214, *216, 217, 218*
Smith, O.H., "Tab," Sr., *95*
Smith, Oscar M., 87
Smith, Ostelle, 44
Smith, P.A., 13
Smith, Patsy, 145, *209*
Smith, Pearl Darsey, 178
Smith, Pearl, 183
Smith, Pulaski Sikes, 17, 18, 25, 26, 73, 85, 87, 88, *93, 118,* 120, 125, 188, 287
Smith, Pulaski Sikes, II, 87
Smith, Queen Ann Mozell, 87, 290
Smith, R.T., 182
Smith, Rachael, 287
Smith, Rebecca, 87
Smith, Robert Conrad, 290
Smith, Robert, 286
Smith, Roscoe, 87, *99,* 183, 285
Smith, Ruby Stuart, 290
Smith, S., 22
Smith, S.P., 285
Smith, Shelldona Rogers, 290
Smith, Shirley, ix
Smith, Sikes, 18
Smith, Simon, 4, 86, 290
Smith, Steward, 182
Smith, Stewart, 194
Smith, Stuart Plunkett, 87, 285, 290
Smith, Sue, 192, *210*
Smith, Thelma, 290
Smith, Thurmon, 59n, 135, 183, 191, 268
Smith, Tillie Parker, *94*
Smith, Ulala, 87
Smith, Ursula, 87
Smith, Wallace, 108, *205, 207*
Smith, Will, 86
Smith, Willa, 268
Southwell, William, 10
Spann, Charles O., 46
Stanley & Pughsley, Inc., 29
Starkey, Elred Leroy, 290
Starnes, R.G., 184
Stephens, Heyward W., 179, 184
Stephens, J.E., 283
Stevens, Hamp, 184
Stewart, Billy, 44
Strickland, Aaron B., 87
Strickland, Aubrey, ix
Strickland, C.S.G., 184
Strickland, C.T., 13
Strickland, Charles, 45, 214, *217*
Strickland, Ernest, 47, 155

Strickland, Henry, 6
Strickland, Jimmie, 144
Strickland, Lex W., 25
Strickland, Marcus, *31*
Strickland, W.A.P., 22
Stubbs, J.L., 283
Stubbs, M.J., 21
Styles, Bobby, 39, 80, 144, 146, 191
Styles, Hellon Benton, 84, 144
Styles, Jimmie, viii, ix, 144-147, *209*
Styles, Roy, 39, 40, 41, 80, 84, 144
Surrency, J.M., 13
Sutton, Embree, 184
Sutton, Stella, 85
Sykes, Colquitt, viii, 103, 162, 163, 164
Sykes, Valerie, 162
Talmadge, Herman, Senator, 222, *232*
Tanner, Charles, 213
Tapley, Hattie, 179
Tattnall Campground, 9-11, *71*
Taylor, Frank, 283
Taylor, H.C., 184
Tellis, Mel, 164
Thomas, G.W., 184
Thompson, Gloria, 164
Thompson, Louise, 41
Thompson, Mary, 87
Thompson, Rommie, x, 44, 164, *233*
Threatt, Bedford A., 285
Threatt, Jesse S., 285
Threatte, Elveda, 270
Threatte, Wilton, 137, *233*
Threlkeld, Leigh, 216
Thrift, Mary, 41
Tillman, Ben, 286
Tillman, G.V., 20, 21, 283
Tillman, J.D., 283
Tillman, Stephen M., 87
Tippins, Anna Cannady, 88
Tippins, Asbury, 12, 50n, 51n
Tippins, B.G. & Co., 285
Tippins, Bascom G., 16, 20, 22, 25, *35*, 44, *72, 74*, 88, 116, 130, 144, 145 182, 183, 246, 265, 283, 285, 288
Tippins, Bascom, Jr., 33, *68, 80,* 265
Tippins, Bernice G., 177
Tippins, Clyde, *24, 68, 72, 74*, 183
Tippins, Cornelia Ann, 87
Tippins, Eliza, 87
Tippins, G.W. & H.V., 288
Tippins, Genie, 88
Tippins, George Eason, 87
Tippins, George U., 4, 50n, 267
Tippins, George W., 13, 18, 20, 22, 25, 87, 88, *96,* 182, 185, 188, *203, 265, 283,* 288
Tippins, Glenn M., 183, 285
Tippins, Glenn, 6, *74*
Tippins, Grover, 88
Tippins, H.M., 42, 142
Tippins, H.W., 13
Tippins, Helena V. Smith, 288
Tippins, Henrietta Matilda, 88
Tippins, J., 22
Tippins, James A., 4, 50n
Tippins, James Otto, 88
Tippins, Jessie, ix, 166
Tippins, John Underwood, 87, 88
Tippins, Joy, 265
Tippins, L.A.H., 6, 9-10, 13, 87
Tippins, Lala, 88
Tippins, Maggie May Bird, 288
Tippins, Maggie, *68*, 175
Tippins, Mamie, *74*, 88, 161, 176, 181, 183, 246
Tippins, Mary Eason, 84
Tippins, Mary Elizabeth, 87, 88
Tippins, Mary, *209*
Tippins, Matilda U., 87
Tippins, Nancy Pinkin, 87
Tippins, Nancy, 88
Tippins, Olle, 182
Tippins, Parthenia Ann, 87
Tippins, Parthenia Emily, 88
Tippins, Phillip Glenn Jr., 88
Tippins, Phillip Glenn, 87, 88, *94*
Tippins, Phillip, 4, 50n, 87
Tippins, Rachel Brazell, 10, 87
Tippins, Sarah Miriam, 87
Tippins, Stella, 88
Tippins, William Eason, 9, 87, 262
Tippins, William W., 6, 50n, 84, 87, 88
Todd, E.L., 283
Todd, J.M., 22, 283
Todd, Louisa, 216
Todd, Willie, 37
Tootle, Durwood, 47
Tootle, J.M., 120, 283
Tootle, J.S., 22
Tootle, James , 6, 285
Tootle, Martin G., 9
Tootle, Martin, 283
Trinity Church of the Nazarene, *289*
Tucker, Betty, *209*
Tucker, Clifford, *209*
Tucker, Clyde, 177
Turner, Grover, 118, 123, 168, 189, 198, *202, 207*
Turpintine Industry, 32-33, 61n, *79*, 121, 122

Index

Union Camp Tree Nursery, 222-223, 225n
Usher, J. Arte, 188
Van Valkenburg, James, Lt. Col., 8
Vandiver, Ernest, Gov., 47
Vaughn, B.C., *74*
Vaughn, B.C., Mrs., 183
Vaughn, Jennie Tippins, 288
Walton, Ralph, 215, 216
Ward, Anne Daniel, 126, 177, *210*
Ward, Lee Alfred, 290
Ward, Pelam, 21
Warren, Ernest, *203*
Warren, Ina, 145, *209*
Wasson, Maury, *233*
Waters, Ada Lou, 214
Waters, Beecher, 43
Waters, Cheryl, 178
Waters, Dorothy, 181
Waters, Gertie, *233*
Waters, Harlan, 201n
Waters, J. Henry, 183
Waters, J. Henry, Mrs., 183
Waters, James W., 50n
Waters, Johnny, *209*
Waters, Jonathan H., 285
Waters, Luther, 145, 178, 181, 188, 210n
Waters, Nancy, 50n
Waters, Ruth, 183
Waters, William W., 285
Watkins & Co., 21
Way, Andrew, 4, 49n
Weathers, Marvin L., 285
Weathers, Tony, *209*
Wells, H.E., 184
Wells, J.H., 46
Wells, L.T., 22
Werkheiser, Bill, ix
Wesley, R.M., 173, 184
West, Bill, 283
West, John, 283
Whalfant, Madeline, 178
Wheems, Earl, 163
Whitaker, James F., 285
Whitten, Lucille, 85
Wilbanks Apiary, 222
Wilbanks, Reg, *236*
Wilbanks, Warren, 18, 222, *236*, 262
Wilcox, George, 274
Wilcox, Susan, 274
Wildes, P.E., 288
Wilkerson, Helen Daniel, 177
Wilkerson, William, 180
Wilkes, Duncan, 87
Wilkes, Rona Jan Blalock, 192
Wilkinson, B.J., 194
Wilkinson, Helen, 126
Wilkinson, Helen, 194, *210*
Williams, Daniel H., 182
Williams, Emma, 286
Williams, Evelyn, 43
Williams, Hank, Jr., 164
Williams, J.H., 22
Williams, James L., 286
Williams, Joe W., 286
Williams, L., 188
Williams, Lewis, 4
Williams, Lloyd, *209*
Williams, Peter, 283, 286
Williams, Sandy, 286
Williams, Thessille, 85
Williamson, Bertha, *209*
Williamson, Geraldine, 215
Wilson, Edward Scott, 180
Wilson, Flora, 85
Wilson, Homer, *79*
Wilson, Stella, 85
Wilson, W.A., 184
Womack, David Holland, 179, 180
Wood, Alice Parker, *94*
Wood, Carrie Ola, 88
Wood, Charlie, 88
Wood, Elizabeth, *79*, 248
Wood, Ella Lee, *79*, 152, 180, 248
Wood, Emily, 41, 128, 152
Wood, Evelyn, 88
Wood, George, 88
Wood, Jessie Mae, 88, 183
Wood, John Hartridge, 88
Wood, John M., 17, 18, 20, 42, 88, 116, 118, 128, 166, 176, 183, 188
Wood, Johnnie, *78*, 183
Wood, Jonathan M., 285
Wood, Maggie Elizabeth, 88, 183
Wood, Mattie Eulala, 88
Wood, Nina Nancy, 88, 175, 183
Wood, Roger, 25, 37, 41, 47, 50n, *78*, 87, 88, 114, 152, 180, 183, 189, *207, 227,* 250
Wood, Roger, Sr., 87, 88
Wood, Thomas J., 285
Wood, Tom, *24*, 36, 38, 61n, 70, *78, 79*, 88, *95*, 112, 118, 120, 122, 136, 143, 145, 146, 158, 161, 168, 176, 177, 179, 228, 248
Wood, W.H., 13, 22, 86
Wood, Willie, 88, *94*
Woodin, Autrey, 286
Woodney, Will, 286
Wooten, Anthony, 283
World War I, 36
World War II, 39-41; residents serving in, 39
Worley, G.W., 182
Wright, Wesley R., 21
Young, Jno. R., 286

About the Author

Colonel Pharris DeLoach Johnson is a career logistics officer in the United States Air Force whose previous assignments include base, headquarters, and air logistics center level jobs at locations both in the U.S. and overseas. During the time he compiled this book, he was assigned to the Warner Robins Air Logistics Center at Robins AFB, Georgia.

Colonel Johnson's roots go deep into Evans county history. He is a descendent of some of the area's oldest pioneer families, including the Brewton, Tippins, and DeLoach families, and his farm, "Johnson Hill" located on the eastern edge of Bellville, has been owned by members of his family since 1850. Johnson has one other book to his credit, *Evans County and the Creation of Ft. Stewart, Georgia*.

The railroad tracks of Bellville led to the town's establishment and today serve as a reminder of its rich heritage. Hopefully this book will help us remember the past and those who came before us.

Editor